AA004042

CLOUD COMPUTING 2025

The Sixteenth International Conference on Cloud Computing, GRIDs, and Virtualization

April 6 - 10, 2025

Valencia, Spain

CLOUD COMPUTING 2025 Editors

Andreas Aßmuth, Fachhochschule Kiel, Germany

Sebastian Fischer, Ostbayerische Technische Hochschule Regensburg, Germany

Christoph P. Neumann, Ostbayerische Technische Hochschule Amberg-Weiden, Germany

Printed from e-media with permission by:

Curran Associates, Inc.
57 Morehouse Lane
Red Hook, NY 12571

CURRAN ASSOCIATES INC.
proceedings
.com

Some format issues inherent in the e-media version may also appear in this print version.

International Academy, Research, and Industry Association (IARIA)
412 Derby Way
Wilmington, DE 19810

Phone: (408) 893-6407
Fax: (408) 527-6351

petre@iaria.org

Additional copies of this publication are available from:

Curran Associates, Inc.
57 Morehouse Lane
Red Hook, NY 12571 USA
Phone: 845-758-0400
Fax: 845-758-2633
Email: curran@proceedings.com
Web: www.proceedings.com

Table of Contents

Kosmosis: Crypto Rug Pull Detection and Prevention by Fusing On- and Off-Chain Data in a Knowledge Graph 1
Philipp Stangl and Christoph Peter Neumann

Practical Acoustic Eavesdropping On Typed Passphrases 9
Darren Furst and Andreas Assmuth

Graph of Effort: Quantifying Risk of AI Usage for Vulnerability Assessment 17
Anket Mehra, Andreas Assmuth, and Malte Priess

On the Necessity of Measuring Security in IoT 25
Tobias Eggendorfer and Katja Andresen

A Forensic Analysis of GNSS Spoofing Attacks on Autonomous Vehicles 32
Tobias Reichel, Mathias Gerstner, Leo Schiller, Andreas Attenberger, Rudolf Hackenberg, and Klara Dolos

GFDG: A Genetic Fuzzing Method for the Controller Area Network Protoco 40
Miguel Stey, Murad Hachani, Philipp Fuxen, Julian Graf, and Rudolf Hackenberg

Intrusion Detection using Peer-to-Peer Distributed Context-Information for Electric Vehicle Supply Equipment 46
Julian Graf, Christoph Moser, Philipp Fuxen, and Rudolf Hackenberg

A Transformer-Based Framework for Anomaly Detection in Multivariate Time Series 52
Fabian Folger, Murad Hachani, Philipp Fuxen, Julian Graf, Sebastian Fischer, and Rudolf Hackenberg

Theoretical Integration of Hyperledger Fabric in Gaia-X: Towards an Approach for Federated Data Access 58
Liron Ahmeti, Klara Dolos, Conrad Meyer, Andreas Attenberger, and Rudolf Hackenberg

PERTD - Cloud Application Threat Modeling 63
Aspen Olmsted

Trends for Pulling HPC Containers in Cloud 69
Vanessa Sochat

Consistent Access to Cloud Services across Regions for Large Enterprises 81
Prisha Goel, Pavvan Pradeep, Aditi Srinivas M, Dhruv Sanjaykumar Ratanpara, and Shilpa S Krishna

Combining Flows and Rules in a Low-Code Platform for Smart Water Management 88
Jens Nicolay, Bjarno Oeyen, Samuel Ngugi Ndung'u, Thierry Renaux, Maxime Demarest, Boud Verbeiren, and Wolfgang De Meuter

Latency-Aware Task Offloading Mechanism for Mobile Edge Computing 94
Abdulelah Alwabel

Running Kubernetes Workloads on Rootless HPC Systems using Slurm 100
Jonathan Decker, Soren Metje, and Julian Kunkel

Configuring Edge Devices That Are Not Accessible Via The Internet 108
Sebastien Andreo and Uwe Hohenstein

LLM-based Distributed Code Generation and Cost-Efficient Execution in the Cloud 114
Kunal Rao, Giuseppe Coviello, Gennaro Mellone, Ciro Giuseppe De Vita, and Srimat Chakradhar

Proactive Optimization of Virtual Machine Placement Using Predictive Models Based on Time Series 122
Naby Doumbouya and Mhand Hifi

CLOUD COMPUTING 2025

Forward

The Sixteenth International Conference on Cloud Computing, GRIDs, and Virtualization (CLOUD COMPUTING 2025), held on April 6 – 10, 2025, continued a series of events targeted to prospect the applications supported by the new paradigm and validate the techniques and the mechanisms. A complementary target was to identify the open issues and the challenges to fix them, especially on security, privacy, and inter- and intra-clouds protocols.

Cloud computing is a normal evolution of distributed computing combined with Service-oriented architecture, leveraging most of the GRID features and Virtualization merits. The technology foundations for cloud computing led to a new approach of reusing what was achieved in GRID computing with support from virtualization.

The conference had the following tracks:

- Cloud computing
- Computing in virtualization-based environments
- Platforms, infrastructures and applications
- Challenging features
- New Trends
- Grid networks, services and applications

Similar to the previous edition, this event attracted excellent contributions and active participation from all over the world. We were very pleased to receive top quality contributions.

We take here the opportunity to warmly thank all the members of the CLOUD COMPUTING 2025 technical program committee, as well as the numerous reviewers. The creation of such a high quality conference program would not have been possible without their involvement. We also kindly thank all the authors that dedicated much of their time and effort to contribute to CLOUD COMPUTING 2025. We truly believe that, thanks to all these efforts, the final conference program consisted of top quality contributions.

Also, this event could not have been a reality without the support of many individuals, organizations and sponsors. We also gratefully thank the members of the CLOUD COMPUTING 2025 organizing committee for their help in handling the logistics and for their work that made this professional meeting a success.

We hope that CLOUD COMPUTING 2025 was a successful international forum for the exchange of ideas and results between academia and industry and to promote further progress in the area of cloud computing, GRIDs and virtualization. We also hope that Valencia provided a pleasant environment during the conference and everyone saved some time to enjoy this beautiful city.

CLOUD COMPUTING 2025 Steering Committee

Carlos Becker Westphall, Federal University of Santa Catarina, Brazil
Alex Sim, Lawrence Berkeley National Laboratory, USA
Andreas Aßmuth, Fachhochschule Kiel, Germany
Uwe Hohenstein, Siemens AG, Germany
Aspen Olmsted, Wentworth Institute of Technology, Boston, USA
Christoph P. Neumann, Ostbayerische Technische Hochschule Amberg-Weiden, Germany

CLOUD COMPUTING 2025 Publicity Chair

Francisco Javier Díaz Blasco, Universitat Politècnica de València, Spain
Ali Ahmad, Universitat Politècnica de València, Spain
José Miguel Jiménez, Universitat Politècnica de València, Spain
Sandra Viciano Tudela, Universitat Politècnica de València, Spain

CLOUD COMPUTING 2025

Committee

CLOUD COMPUTING 2025 Steering Committee

Carlos Becker Westphall, Federal University of Santa Catarina, Brazil
Alex Sim, Lawrence Berkeley National Laboratory, USA
Andreas Aßmuth, Fachhochschule Kiel, Germany
Uwe Hohenstein, Siemens AG, Germany
Aspen Olmsted, Wentworth Institute of Technology, Boston, USA
Christoph P. Neumann, Ostbayerische Technische Hochschule Amberg-Weiden, Germany

CLOUD COMPUTING 2025 Publicity Chair

Francisco Javier Díaz Blasco, Universitat Politècnica de València, Spain
Ali Ahmad, Universitat Politècnica de València, Spain
José Miguel Jiménez, Universitat Politècnica de València, Spain
Sandra Viciano Tudela, Universitat Politècnica de València, Spain

CLOUD COMPUTING 2025 Technical Program Committee

Sherif Abdelwahed, Virginia Commonwealth University, USA
Vibhatha Abeykoon, Voltron Data Inc., USA
Nikunj Agarwal, Amazon, Inc., USA
Maruf Ahmed, The University of Technology, Sydney, Australia
Mays Al-Naday, University of Essex, UK
Reem Al-Saidi, University of Windsor, Canada
Mubashwir Alam, Marquette University, USA
Abdulelah Alwabel, Prince Sattam Bin Abdulaziz University, Kingdom of Saudi Arabia
Mário Antunes, Polytechnic of Leiria, Portugal
Filipe Araujo, University of Coimbra, Portugal
Mohammad S. Aslanpour, Monash University, Australia
Andreas Aßmuth, Fachhochschule Kiel, Germany
Odiljon Atabaev, Andijan Machine-Building Institute, Uzbekistan
Babak Badnava, University of Kansas, USA
Carlos Jaime Barrios Hernandez, Universidad Industrial de Santander, Colombia
Mohammadreza Barzegaran, University of California Irvine, USA
Luis-Eduardo Bautista-Villalpando, Autonomous University of Aguascalientes, Mexico
Carlos Becker Westphall, Federal University of Santa Catarina, Brazil
Laura Belli, University of Parma, Italy
Leila Ben Ayed, National School of Computer Science | University of Manouba, Tunisia
Nicola Bena, Università degli Studi di Milano, Italy
Salima Benbernou, Universite Paris Cite, France

Simona Bernardi, University of Zaragoza, Spain
Peter Bloodsworth, University of Oxford, UK
Larbi Boubchir, University of Paris 8, France
Jalil Boukhobza, University of Western Brittany, France
Antonio Brogi, University of Pisa, Italy
Roberta Calegari, Alma Mater Studiorum-Università di Bologna,Italy
Jon Calhoun, Clemson University, USA
Juan Vicente Capella Hernández, Universitat Politècnica de València, Spain
Arielle Carr, Lehigh University, USA
Roberto Casadei, Alma Mater Studiorum - Università di Bologna, Italy
Adithya Rajesh Chandrassery, National Institute of Technology Karnataka, Surathkal, India
Ruay-Shiung Chang, National Taipei University of Business, Taipei, Taiwan
Ryan Chard, Argonne National Laboratory, USA
Hao Che, University of Texas at Arlington, USA
Bo Chen, Michigan Technological University, USA
Dawei Chen, InfoTech Labs - Toyota Motor North America R&D, USA
Yitao Chen, Arizona State University, USA
Yue Cheng, George Mason University, USA
Dalila Cherifi, University of Boumerdes, Algeria
Claudio Cicconetti, National Research Council, Italy
Daniel Corujo, Universidade de Aveiro | Instituto de Telecomunicações, Portugal
Fábio M. Costa, Institute of Informatics (INF) | Federal University of Goiás (UFG), Brazil
Alexandre da Silva Veith, Nokia Bell Labs, Belgium
Sajal Dash, Oak Ridge National Laboratory, USA
Luca Davoli, University of Parma, Italy
Patrizio Dazzi, University of Pisa, Italy
Noel De Palma, University Grenoble Alpes, France
Mª del Carmen Carrión Espinosa, University of Castilla-La Mancha, Spain
Simon Pierre Dembele, University of Tartu, Estonia
Frederic Desprez, INRIA, France
Karim Djemame, University of Leeds, UK
Ramon dos Reis Fontes, Federal University of Rio Grande do Norte, Natal, Brazil
Steve Eager, University West of Scotland, UK
Nabil El Ioini, Free University of Bolzano, Italy
Rania Fahim El-Gazzar, Universty of South-Eastern Norway, Norway
Ibrahim El-Shekeil, Metropolitan State University, USA
Levent Ertaul, California State University, East Bay, USA
Javier Fabra, Universidad de Zaragoza, Spain
Fairouz Fakhfakh, University of Sfax, Tunisia
Yuping Fan, Illinois Institute of Technology, USA
Umar Farooq, University of California, Riverside, USA
Tadeu Ferreira Oliveira, Federal Institute of Science Education and Technology of Rio Grande do Norte, Brazil
Sebastian Fischer, University of Applied Sciences OTH Regensburg, Germany
Kaneez Fizza, Swinburne University of Technology, Australia
Stefano Forti, University of Pisa, Italy
Somchart Fugkeaw, Sirindhorn International Institute of Technology | Thammasat University, Thailand
Katja Gilly, Miguel Hernandez University, Spain

Jing Gong, KTH, Sweden
Chander Govindarajan, IBM Research, India
Poonam Goyal, Birla Institute of Technology & Science, Pilani, India
Jordi Guitart, Universitat Politècnica de Catalunya - Barcelona Supercomputing Center, Spain
Saurabh Gupta, Graphic Era Deemed to be University, Dehradun, India
Abdelhay Haqiq, Information Sciences School in Rabat, Morocco
Seif Haridi, KTH/SICS, Sweden
Herodotos Herodotou, Cyprus University of Technology, Cyprus
Uwe Hohenstein, Siemens AG Munich, Germany
Soamar Homsi, Air Force Research Laboratory (AFRL), USA
Md Rajib Hossen, The University of Texas at Arlington, USA
Li-Pang Huang, Tempus, USA
Yujie Hui, Ohio State University, USA
Anca Daniela Ionita, National University of Science and Technology POLITEHNICA Bucharest, Romania
Murat Isik, Stanford University, USA
Mohammad Atiqul Islam, The University of Texas at Arlington, USA
Saba Jamalian, Roosevelt University / Braze, USA
Fuad Jamour, Amazon Web Services (AWS), USA
Weiwei Jia, New Jersey Institute of Technology, USA
Carlos Juiz, University of the Balearic Islands, Spain
Sokratis Katsikas, Norwegian University of Science and Technology, Norway
Zaheer Khan, University of the West of England, Bristol, UK
Ioannis Konstantinou, CSLAB - NTUA, Greece
Sonal Kumari, Samsung R&D Institute, India
Venkatesh Kunchenapalli, Flexport, San Francisco, USA
Rohon Kundu, Lund University, Sweden
Julian Kunkel, Gesellschaft für wissenschaftliche Datenverarbeitung mbH Göttingen (GWDG), Germany
Giuliano Laccetti, University of Naples Federico II, Italy
Frédéric Le Mouël, INSA Lyon / University of Lyon, France
Kyungyong Lee, Kookmin University, South Korea
Sarah Lehman, Temple University, USA
João Leitão, Universidade Nova de Lisboa, Portugal
Mingchu Li, Jiangxi Normal University, China
Kunal Lillaney, Amazon Web Services, USA
Xue Lin, Northeastern University, USA
Enjie Liu, University of Bedfordshire, UK
Pinglan Liu, Iowa State University, USA
Xiaodong Liu, Edinburgh Napier University, UK
Jay Lofstead, Sandia National Laboratories, USA
Rafael Lopes Gomes, State University of Ceara (UECE), Brazil
Zainab Loukil, University of Gloucestershire, UK
Hui Lu, Binghamton University (State University of New York), USA
Weibin Ma, University of Delaware, USA
Chathura Madhusanka Sarathchandra Magurawalage, InterDigital Europe Ltd., UK
Hosein Mohammadi Makrani, University of California, Davis, USA
Andras Markus, University of Szeged, Hungary
Shaghayegh Mardani, University of California Los Angeles (UCLA), USA
Stefano Mariani, University of Modena and Reggio Emilia, Italy

Attila Csaba Marosi, Institute for Computer Science and Control - Hungarian Academy of Sciences, Hungary
Romolo Marotta, University of l'Aquila (UNIVAQ), Italy
Jean-Marc Menaud, IMT Atlantique, France
Philippe Merle, Inria, France
Nasro Min-Allah, Imam Abdulrahman Bin Faisal University (IAU), KSA
Preeti Mishra, Graphic Era Deemed to be University, Dehradun, India
Takashi Miyamura, NTT Network Service Systems Labs, Japan
Prateeti Mohapatra, IBM Research Lab, India
Francesc D. Muñoz-Escoí, Universitat Politècnica de València, Spain
Ioannis Mytilinis, National Technical University of Athens, Greece
Tamer Nadeem, Virginia Commonwealth University, USA
Hidemoto Nakada, National Institute of Advanced Industrial Science and Technology (AIST), Japan
Akash Nayak, IBM Research, India
Antonio Nehme, Birmingham City University, UK
Richard Neill, RN Technologies LLC, USA
Christoph P. Neumann, Ostbayerische Technische Hochschule Amberg-Weiden, Germany
Bogdan Nicolae, Argonne National Laboratory, USA
Jens Nicolay, Vrije Universiteit Brussel, Belgium
Ridwan Rashid Noel, Texas Lutheran University, USA
Alexander Norta, Tallinn Technology University, Estonia
Aspen Olmsted, Wentworth Institute of Technology, Boston, USA
Matthias Olzmann, noventum consulting GmbH - Münster, Germany
Brajendra Panda, University of Arkansas, USA
Christos Papadopoulos, University of Memphis, USA
Arnab K. Paul, BITS Pilani, India
Sibendu Paul, Amazon Prime Video, USA
Alessandro Pellegrini, National Research Council (CNR), Italy
Sathya Peri, Indian Institute of Technology Hyderabad, India
Nancy Perrot, Orange Innovation, France
Tamas Pflanzner, University of Szeged, Hungary
Paulo Pires, Fluminense Federal University (UFF), Brazil
Agostino Poggi, Università degli Studi di Parma, Italy
Saul E. Pomares Hernandez, Instituto Nacional de Astrofísica, Óptica y Electrónica Tonantzintla, Puebla, Mexico / SARA Group, LAAS-CNRS, Toulouse, France
Pavana Prakash, University of Houston, USA
Walter Priesnitz Filho, Federal University of Santa Maria, Rio Grande do Sul, Brazil
Abena Primo, Huston-Tillotson University, USA
Mohammed A Qadeer, Aligarh Muslim University, India
George Qiao, KLA, USA
Zhihao Qu, Hohai University, China
Francesco Quaglia, University of Rome Tor Vergata, Italy
M. Mustafa Rafique, Rochester Institute of Technology (RIT), USA
Kunal Rao, NEC Laboratories America, USA
Danda B. Rawat, Howard University, USA
Kaustabha Ray, IBM Research, India
Daniel A. Reed, University of Utah, USA
Christoph Reich, Hochschule Furtwangen University, Germany

Sashko Ristov, University of Innsbruck, Austria
Javier Rocher Morant, Universitat Politecnica de Valencia, Spain
Ivan Rodero, Rutgers University, USA
Mohamed Aymen Saied, Laval University, Canada
Benjamin Schwaller, Sandia National Laboratories, USA
Wael Sellami, Higher Institute of Computer Sciences of Mahdia - ReDCAD laboratory, Tunisia
Jayasree Sengupta, Birla Institute of Technology, Mesra, India
Jianchen Shan, Hofstra University, USA
Larisa Shwartz, T.J. Watson Research Center IBM, USA
Muhammad Abu Bakar Siddique, University of California, Riverside, USA
Altino Manuel Silva Sampaio, Escola Superior de Tecnologia e Gestão | Instituto Politécnico do Porto, Portugal
Alex Sim, Lawrence Berkeley National Laboratory, USA
Sima Sinaei, RISE Research Institutes of Sweden, Sweden
Akshit Singhal, University of Texas at Arlington, USA
Bowen Song, University of Southern California, USA
Hui Song, SINTEF, Norway
Polyzois Soumplis, National Technical University of Athens, Greece
Georgios L. Stavrinides, KIOS Research and Innovation Center of Excellence | University of Cyprus, Cyprus
Cesar A. Stuardo, ByteDance, USA
Grażyna Suchacka, University of Opole | Institute of Informatics, Poland
Jingwei Sun, Duke University, USA
Vidhya Suresh, Atlassian Inc , San Francisco, USA
Vasily Tarasov, IBM Research, USA
Zahir Tari, School of Computing Technologies | RMIT University, Australia
Bedir Tekinerdogan, Wageningen University, The Netherlands
Ajay Lotan Thakur, Intel, Canada
Parimala Thulasiraman, University of Manitoba, Canada
Orazio Tomarchio, University of Catania, Italy
Salman Toor, Uppsala University, Sweden
Homero Toral-Cruz, University of Quintana Roo, Mexico
Mert Toslali, IBM Research, USA
Reza Tourani, Saint Louis University, USA
Rajesh Vayyala, PRA Group, Inc., USA
Antonio Virdis, University of Pisa, Italy
Raul Valin Ferreiro, Fujitsu Laboratories of Europe, Spain
Massimo Villari, Università di Messina, Italy
Kewei Wang, Northwestern University, USA
Teng Wang, Oracle, USA
Hironori Washizaki, Waseda University, Japan
Mandy Weißbach, Martin Luther University of Halle-Wittenberg, Germany
Sebastian Werner, Information Systems Engineering (ISE) - TU Berlin, Germany
Michael Wilkins, Northwestern University, USA
Liuqing Yang, Columbia University in the City of New York, USA
Bo Yuan, University of Leicester, UK
Christos Zaroliagis, CTI & University of Patras, Greece
Bo Zhang, Scientific Computing and Imaging Institute | The University of Utah, USA

Zhiming Zhao, University of Amsterdam, Netherlands
Jiang Zhou, Institute of Information Engineering - Chinese Academy of Sciences, China
Yue Zhu, IBM Research, USA
Jan Henrik Ziegeldorf, RWTH Aachen University, Germany
Wolf Zimmermann, Martin Luther University Halle-Wittenberg, Germany

Copyright Information

Kosmosis: Crypto Rug Pull Detection and Prevention by Fusing On- and Off-Chain Data in a Knowledge Graph

Philipp Stangl* and Christoph P. Neumann†

*Department of Computer Science
Friedrich-Alexander-Universität Erlangen-Nürnberg, Erlangen, Germany
e-mail: philipp.stangl@fau.de
†Department of Electrical Engineering, Media and Computer Science
Ostbayerische Technische Hochschule Amberg-Weiden, Amberg, Germany
e-mail: c.neumann@oth-aw.de

Abstract—**Rug pulls have become a major threat to the integrity of blockchain ecosystems, with illicit activities surging and resulting in significant financial losses. Existing approaches to prevent rug pulls focus on transaction graph analysis within blockchain networks, but these methods are limited. We propose Kosmosis, an incremental knowledge graph construction approach that integrates semantically-enriched blockchain data with social media insights into a unified knowledge graph to identify and prevent rug pulls. We demonstrate how Kosmosis can extract semantic information from blockchain transactions using the application binary interface to decode smart contract interactions and tag addresses based on their extracted relationships. We provide a technical description of the knowledge graph construction process, highlighting key components, such as address relation extraction, tagging, and entity resolution. Our research aims to provide a more comprehensive understanding of blockchain ecosystems and contribute to the development of robust anti-fraud measures.**

Keywords-blockchain; knowledge graphs; cyber fraud; rug pull; security; smart contracts.

I. Introduction

Crypto assets use distributed ledger technology, like blockchain, as decentralized transaction ledger and for proof of ownership. Different types exist, each with unique roles: 1) Cryptocurrencies, like Bitcoin, function as digital currencies for storing or transferring value. 2) Fungible tokens are interchangeable tokens with various utilities in blockchain ecosystems, often crucial in Decentralized Finance (DeFi) protocols. 3) Non-Fungible Tokens (NFTs), in contrast, are unique digital assets proving ownership and authenticity, holding distinct values and cannot be exchanged on a one-to-one basis with other tokens.

In recent years, illicit activities in crypto have surged. Chainalysis reported a record $20.6 billion in illicit transactions in 2022 [1]. Since the rise of DeFi in 2020 and NFTs in 2021, rug pulls have become a major fraud scheme [2], threatening investors and integrity of the crypto asset sector.

The primary method for detecting fraudulent activity is transaction graph analysis within blockchain networks [34]. However, this approach has two key limitations. First, transacting parties are pseudonymous, with only their blockchain addresses publicly visible. Tracking an address is possible, but linking it to a real-world entity is challenging, as the analysis is restricted to observable blockchain data. Second, this method focuses only on asset type, quantity, and sender/receiver, ignoring transaction semantics, such as what happened in a transaction that caused the assets to get transferred, is not covered, thus, limiting the depth of analysis.

Knowledge Graphs (KGs) can integrate fragmented knowledge from diverse data sources, enabling semantic queryingand reasoning. They offer a holistic view for detecting fraud patterns in highly connected datasets [5]. A KG consists of uniquely identified entities and their semantical relations, structured ontologically. Their open-world assumption allows continuous data integration, enhancing crypto asset fraud analysis and fraud prediction.

The remainder of this paper provides a technical perspective on the Kosmosis approach to incremental KG construction, complementing its use case outlined in Section II in extension to [6]. The use case focuses on detecting and preventing rug pulls, a threat relevant across various blockchain platforms, with our prototype specifically targeting the Ethereum blockchain due to its widespread adoption. To support this objective, we first provide background information on the Ethereum blockchain and graph-based blockchain data mining methods in Section III. We then describe the Kosmosis approach to incremental KG construction in Section IV, emphasizing the pipeline that serves as the foundation for the detection phase of the use case. Finally, we outline future work in Section V and conclude the paper with a discussion of our findings.

II. Kosmosis Objectives & Use Case

To illustrate the vision of Kosmosis-enabled rug pull prevention methods, we described a hypothetical user story about homer_eth in [6]. The user story method of use case illustration was adopted from our previous work in [7]. Kosmosis aims to leverage a KG to enhance security in blockchain ecosystems by identifying and alerting users before they interact with fraudulent projects.

A. Over-Aching Objectives of Kosmosis

Objective 1: Identifying and Alerting Users of Rug Pulls. With rising crypto scams, Kosmosis seeks to integrate blockchain data, social media, and other KGs into a unified KG. This facilitates semantic querying and reasoning, enabling the development of alerting methods based on cross-domain semantic analysis—where knowledge about on-chain behaviors and social media interactions can be correlated—to detect anomalous patterns and assign addresses with a risk score.

Objective 2: Incremental Construction of the KG. To maintain high data freshness, Kosmosis requires a pipeline for integrating updates without full reconstruction. This ensures the integration of the latest available information while preserving existing data.

Objective 3: Extracting Blockchain Transaction Semantics. Transaction graphs typically show asset transfers but lack semantic insights. Kosmosis extracts transaction semantics by decoding smart contract interactions using their Application Binary Interface (ABI), which aids in detecting sophisticated fraudulent behavior. At present, our prototype specifically targets the account-based transaction model, as implemented in Ethereum. Expanding the framework to other blockchains employing different accounting models, such as UTXO-based systems, is a future objective.

B. Summary of the Kosmosis Use Case of Rug Pull Prevention

In our position paper [6], a hypothetical user, Bob, who is relatively new to the NFT market, illustrates Kosmosis' potential for rug pull prevention. A rug pull is a scam where victims authorize fraudulent transactions. According to [2], rug pulls occur in five stages: 1) project creation, 2) pre-mint hype, 3) token price setting, 4) accumulation of capital, and 5) exit scam. The use case is based on the true story of the threat actor Homer_eth, an NFT creator and 𝕏 user, who launched his first NFT collection, *Ether Bananas*, followed by the release of *Ether Monkeys* and *Zombie Monkeys*.

Of these three NFT collections, *Ether Monkeys* created the biggest medial buzz, because it promised additional utility through a casino to gamble and a decentralized autonomous organization to govern the NFTs, according to [8]. This buzz draws Bob into the fray. Bob bought his first NFT from Homer_eth and became an active participant in Homer_eth's growing community. Bob's involvement in the community deepened over time. He engaged in discussions, shared his excitement with fellow members, and earned himself a whitelist spot that allows Bob to mint the upcoming NFT project *Ether (ETH) Banana Chips* by Homer_eth. Convinced of its potential, Bob minted the NFT when the opportunity arose, unaware of the underlying risks associated with his investment.

Unbeknownst to Bob, the proceeds from the mint were not locked within the smart contract for future development, as initially promised. Instead, these funds were directly transferred to the deployer address associated with Homer_eth. Subsequently, Homer_eth either redirected these proceeds to a new deployer address—potentially to facilitate a future fraudulent scheme, or transferred them to an exchange to realize profits from previous deceptive activities. Following the launch of *ETH Banana Chips*, the community experienced a prolonged period of uncertainty, marked by an absence of updates or communication from Homer_eth. For several months, no new developments were reported, leaving stakeholders uncertain about the project's trajectory. It was not until March 2022 that Homer_eth resurfaced, announcing a final NFT project, titled *Froggy Frens*. However, due to backlash from the community, Homer_eth deleted his 𝕏 account and vanished [8].

C. Kosmosis Extension

Kosmosis identifies potential rug pulls by semantically analyzing transaction patterns encoded within smart contract interactions and cross-referencing blockchain addresses with real-world entity data from social media and other external sources. Our approach is grounded in the assumption that scammers publicly disclose or explicitly link blockchain addresses in their social media posts to promote their scams. This linkage is crucial for Kosmosis, as it provides the primary method of associating blockchain transactions with social identities, which enhances the semantic richness of the constructed KG.

The detection logic within the KG evaluates transactions that involve high-risk state changes, such as bulk asset transfers shortly after a token mint event, and assigns risk scores based on the presence of correlated indicators (e.g., rapid withdrawal to external accounts controlled by the deployer). These risk scores can trigger automated alerts before submitting a new transaction, providing timely warnings to users. Had Bob used Kosmosis, it would have analyzed the transaction history prior to submitting his mint transaction to Ethereum. The system would have issued a rug pull warning based on patterns of fund diversion to deployer addresses.

III. BACKGROUND

This section covers background on rug pulls and blockchain technology, with a particular focus on the Ethereum blockchain, as detailed in Section III-A. Following the blockchain aspects, we discuss related graph-based approaches for blockchain data mining in Section III-B. On the social media aspects of Kosmosis, our prior work includes correlating Reddit data with traditional stock market trends [9] and analyzing Twitter/𝕏 data using SPARQL [10].

A. The Ethereum Blockchain

Blockchain technology is founded on the principles of immutability, decentralization, transparency, and cryptographic security, and it has been applied across various domains in recent years. For example, it has been utilized in the financial sector (e.g., [11]), as well as in supply chain management, either through a single blockchain [12] or by leveraging multiple interoperable blockchains [13]. A significant subset of blockchain technology is smart contract platforms, which facilitate the development of decentralized applications through self-executing smart contracts. This section provides an overview of the key concepts of Ethereum as a representative smart contract platform. It covers fundamental aspects such as smart contracts, their execution environment, and the account-based transaction model, which are essential for the subsequent sections.

1) Blockchain Data Structure: A blockchain is a data structure whose elements called blocks are linked together to form a chain of blocks [14]. Each block comprises two parts: a body and a header. The body of the block contains a set of transactions. A transaction typically involves the transfer of assets between a sender and a receiver. These participants are represented by addresses, which are unique alphanumeric strings that clearly specify the origin and destination of each transaction. Further, the block body is used to generate a unique identifier called the block hash. The block header contains a reference to the unique identifier of its immediate predecessor, known as the parent block.

2) Smart Contracts: Through smart contacts, which are executable source codes that enforce the terms and conditions of particular agreements, a smart contract platform like Ethereum facilitates the development of decentralized applications [15]. Once deployed on the blockchain, the smart contract is assigned an address where the code resides and cannot be altered or tampered with. By writing custom smart contracts, developers can create and manage tokens that adhere to the standards ERC-20 for Fungible Token (FT) or ERC-721 for NFT. An ABI specifies the functions and data structures exposed by a smart contract, allowing external applications to understand the capabilities of the contract. Further, an ABI defines a format for encoding and decoding data that is passed between smart contracts and external applications. This ensures a consistent and standardized way to exchange information.

The Ethereum blockchain manages ETH as the native cryptocurrency of the platform. It operates with the Ethereum Virtual Machine (EVM) as a fundamental building block, serving as the execution environment for smart contract code. Smart contracts, primarily written in a high-level language such as Solidity, undergo compilation into EVM bytecode. This bytecode is the executable format used by the EVM to enact smart contract functions. To interact with this bytecode, a contract ABI is utilized, which acts as a bridge between the high-level language and the low-level bytecode. In this context, an EVM disassembler plays a crucial role; it reverses the bytecode back into a more readable format, aiding developers in understanding and analyzing the code deployed on the Ethereum blockchain. Figure 1 shows the processes involved in deploying smart contracts to the Ethereum blockchain and reading contract data from it, including compilation and deployment steps, and the interaction between a web application and the Ethereum blockchain. The left side shows the compilation and deployment of a smart contract, and the right side depicts an interaction with the contract (e.g., from a web application).

3) Externally Owned Account: Unlike smart contracts, Externally Owned Accounts (EOAs) are controlled by real-world entitys through private keys, enabling them to initiate transactions, such as transferring crypto assets or executing functions of a smart contract. When an EOA sends a transaction to a smart contract, it triggers the code of the contract to execute according to its predefined rules.

4) Account-based Accounting: For the record-keeping of transactions, blockchains utilize an accounting model. Compared to other blockchains, such as the equally well-known Bitcoin blockchain that uses the Unspent Transaction Output (UTXO) model, or its successor the extended UTXO [17] utilized by the Cardano blockchain, whereas Ethereum employs the account-based accounting model.

The account-based model can be best understood through the analogy of a bank account. This approach mirrors how a banking account operates. Like a bank account that tracks the inflow and outflow of funds, thereby reflecting the current balance, the account-based model in Ethereum maintains a state that records the balance of Ether. Thus, it is inherently stateful. Each transaction results in a direct adjustment to this balance, akin to a deposit or withdrawal in a bank account. This model's stateful nature ensures that at any given moment, the system can accurately reflect the total amount of Ether held in each account, offering an up-to-date view of account balances within Ethereum.

5) Token Minting: Token minting refers to the process of generating new tokens. Fungible tokens are typically minted by their creator either at the project's launch or gradually over time. This issuance is governed by predefined rules or algorithms embedded within the project's smart contracts.

The minting of NFTs involves participants other than the original token creator, commonly known as token minters. These individuals engage in the process by invoking a specific function within a smart contract, designated as `mint` in the ERC-721 token standard. Executing this function results in an increase in the total supply of NFTs while simultaneously assigning the newly minted tokens to the blockchain address of the minter.

The minting process for NFTs is frequently facilitated through a dedicated minting platform. Prospective minters or investors must contribute a predefined amount, as determined by the creator, to initiate the minting process. This contribution enables them to mint one or multiple NFTs, depending on the stipulations outlined in the smart contract. Beyond enabling the creation of new NFTs, this process also serves as a mechanism for directly transferring ownership from the NFT creator to the NFT minter.

B. Rug Pull Detection Methods

This section examines two main approaches used for rug pull detection: smart contract code analysis and graph-based methods. Smart contract code analysis entails a comprehensive examination of a contract's source code to extract and interpret the semantic behavior of transactions. For instance, [18] leverages this approach to uncover potential vulnerabilities and fraudulent patterns within smart contracts. Their proposed method, "Tokeer," systematically dissects the code to identify suspicious patterns and functions that may indicate a predisposition to rug pull schemes.

Graph-based techniques, on the other hand, leverage graph theory and data mining to analyze blockchain network graphs, as blockchain transactions naturally form graphs [19]. Elmougy and Liu [20] describe three graph types for blockchain networks: *money flow transaction graphs* (representing how asset flow over time), *address-transaction graphs* (showing asset flow across transactions and addresses), and *user entity graphs* (clustering addresses potentially controlled by the same user to deanonymize them). Graph-based rug pull detection often uses network embedding techniques, such as graph convolutional networks (e.g., [21]), to automatically extract features from the blockchain network.

IV. The Kosmosis Approach to Incremental Knowledge Graph Construction

To incrementally construct a KG that integrates data in a continuous and periodic way, we propose a multi-stage pipeline, as illustrated in Figure 2. It originated from a master's thesis [22] and consists of three stages: Data ingestion, data processing, and knowledge storage. We use italics to emphasize on conceptual aspects and typewriter text for technical operations.

The initial stage, data ingestion, captures the raw data from the primary data sources (blockchain and social media) as well as enrichment data sources (e.g., another knowledge base). This phase is characterized by its versatility in the frequency of data acquisition: it can be 1) *continuous*, to capture real-time updates from sources such as blockchain nodes, 2) *incremental* for new posts via the 𝕏 Streaming Application Programming Interface (API), 3) *periodic*, to capture new entries in structured data sources like relational databases at regular intervals, or 4) *event-based*, responding to events that are emitted upon new entity additions to the KG.

Following the ingestion stage, the data processing stage is initiated, which is partitioned into distinct workflows tailored to handle each type of ingested data. This segmentation allows for specialized processing depending on the structure of the raw data. For instance, for text data sources, natural language processing techniques, such as named entity recognition [23], can be used to ensure that the data is accurately interpreted, and contextual relationships are discerned.

In the third and final stage, the refined data is loaded into the knowledge storage, where it is systematically organized within a triplestore, a type of database optimized for storing and retrieving data in Resource Description Framework (RDF) format. The triplestore can then be used for semantic querying capabilities to extract actionable insights from the KG for downstream processes. For the KG, we use the EthOn [24] ontology that formalizes the concepts and relations within the domain of the Ethereum network and blockchain. EthOn is written in RDF and Web Ontology Language (OWL).

A. Blockchain Data Processing

The blockchain data processing workflow continuously ingests new transactions from the blockchain via websocket connections. Websockets enable open, interactive communication sessions between a client and a server, facilitating real-time data transfer without the need for repeated polling. Upon receiving these transactions, the workflow processes and integrates them into the KG by first extracting the address relationship, followed by tagging the addresses, and finally fusing the addresses with the entities of the KG.

1) Address Relation Extraction: In order to provide answers to "why" and "how" assets were transferred in a transaction, Kosmosis implements a pipeline module titled *Address Relation Extraction*. The responsibility of this module is to extract the semantic information in a blockchain transaction through decoding the input data of a transaction using the ABI of the smart contract a blockchain address is interacting with.

First, the ABI is requested from Etherscan [25] and Sourcify [26] via their respective REST APIs. If the ABI cannot be successfully fetched from one of the aforementioned sources, the module resorts to reconstructing the ABI from the smart contract byte code, which is available at any time since the bytecode is deployed on the blockchain. This operation enables

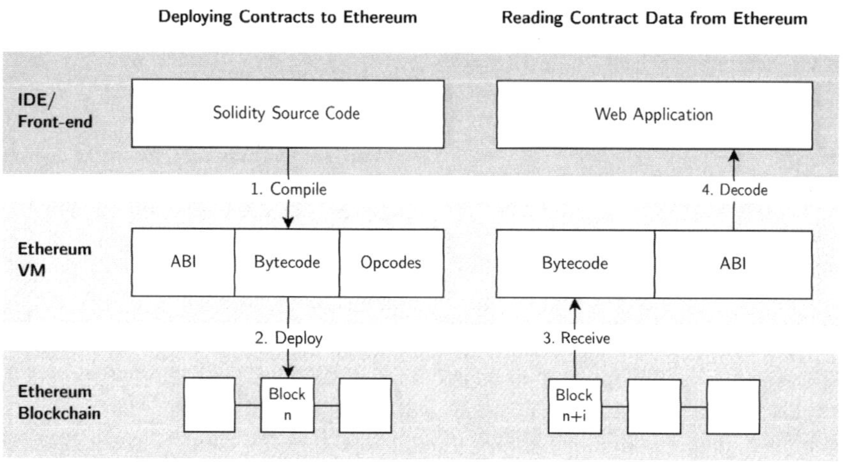

Figure 1. Schematic representation of deploying and reading from smart contracts. Adapted from Takeuchi [16].

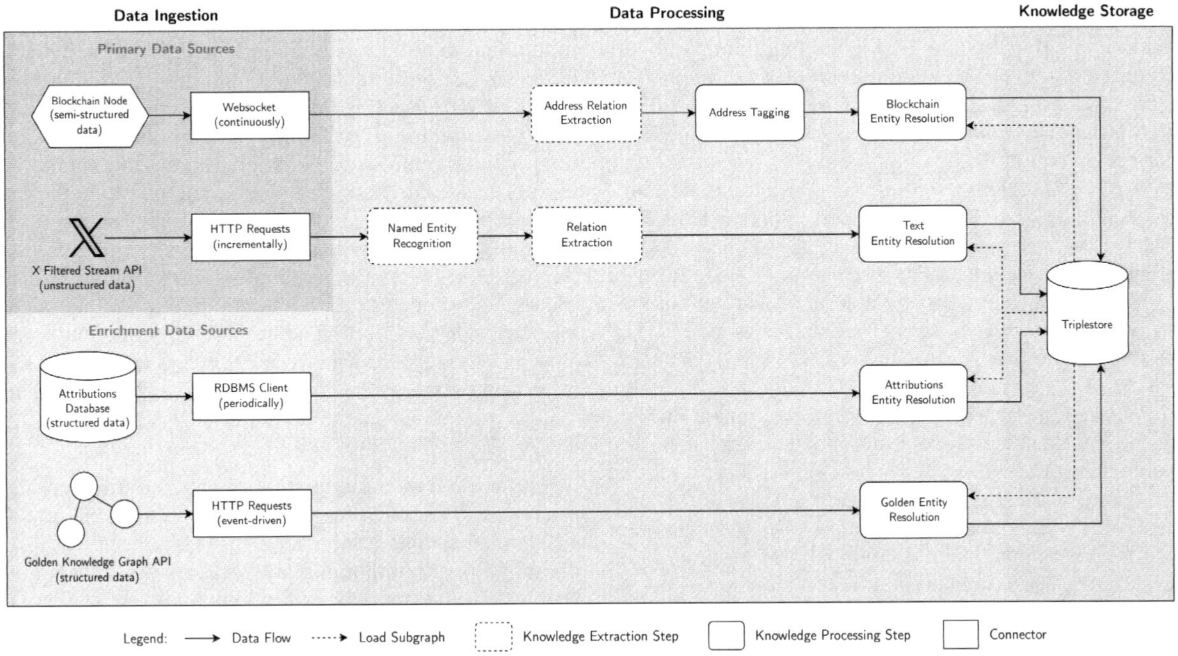

Figure 2. A high level overview of the Kosmosis pipeline.

the decoding of transactions and the interaction with smart contracts beyond their compiled state.

The initial step involves the disassembly of the bytecode of the smart contract. This operation, referred to as `DISASM`, decomposes the bytecode into a series of readable opcodes and associated data. Disassemblers (e.g., *pyevmasm* [27]) facilitate this step by translating the bytecode back into a form that represents the original instructions and operations defined within the smart contract.

Following disassembly, the algorithm initializes by creating an empty array intended to store the ABI and defining lists of opcodes that either change the state or read from the state of the blockchain. These opcodes include `SSTORE`, `CREATE`, `CREATE2` for state-changing operations, and `SLOAD` for state-reading operations, reflecting the fundamental actions a smart contract on the EVM can perform [11].

The core of the algorithm iterates over selector/offset pairs within the disassembled bytecode. Selectors serve as identifiers for functions in the EVM, facilitating the mapping to the corresponding functionality. If a given offset does not match any destination within the program's destinations, the iteration skips to the next pair, ensuring only valid functions are considered.

Upon finding a valid function destination, the algorithm retrieves the function definition and assigns tags based on its behavior. This tagging process involves analyzing the opcodes contained within the function and any related jump destinations. The purpose is to categorize functions according to how they alter the blockchain state, using a depth-first search algorithm to navigate through the function call graph.

An `AbiFunction` object is then created for each valid function, with its payable status determined inversely by the presence of a notPayable marker at the corresponding offset. The algorithm next assigns mutability attributes (nonpayable, payable, view, or pure) based on whether the function alters state, reads state, or neither. This classification is crucial for understanding how functions interact with the blockchain and their implications on transaction costs and permissions.

Finally, the algorithm decides on the inclusion of inputs and outputs in the function signature, informed by the presence of specific tags. For instance, tags indicating data retrieval or state mutation influence whether parameters are classified as inputs or outputs. This granular control ensures that the ABI accurately reflects the interface of the smart contract, allowing for effective transaction decoding.

Currently, the method for extracting semantic information from smart contract transactions relies partly on predefined heuristics, such as recognizing specific function names like "mint." However, we acknowledge that scammers could circumvent these simplistic heuristics by obfuscating or renaming functions. Future improvements will incorporate advanced transaction pattern analysis rather than function naming alone, enhancing resilience against simple obfuscation techniques.

2) Address Tagging: Since the exact identity of a real-world entity controlling a blockchain address is often unknown, it can still be categorized and tagged accordingly. The *address tagging module* tags the sender and receiver address based on their extracted relationship from the preceding address relation extraction module. For instance, an EOA deploying a smart contract is tagged as deployer in case of a contract creation transaction. Likewise, if an EOA is sending Ether to an NFT contract T via a contract function containing the word "mint," the EOA is tagged as is tagged as NFT minter of T. Tags are subclasses of EOAs and contract accounts, extending the address concept of the EthOn ontology.

3) Blockchain Entity Resolution: The blockchain entity resolution module is responsible for resolving blockchain addresses to either new entities or existing ones in the KG, by using the extracted information from preceding steps. It begins with mapping the result data from the preceding steps into the RDF format, adhering to the ontology defined by the KG. This ensures that the data is structured in a way that is compatible with the KG's existing schema.

Following the mapping to RDF, the next phase involves fusing this RDF data with the KG. This is accomplished through a two-step process. Initially, a subgraph that is relevant to the processed data is loaded into the system. This step, commonly referred to as "blocking," narrows down the scope of the resolution process to the most relevant segments of the KG, thereby enhancing the entity resolution process.

Subsequently, the system proceeds to match the newly processed data with the corresponding entities within the KG. This matching process is crucial for identifying where the new data fits within the existing structure and for ensuring that it is integrated in a meaningful way. In certain cases, the fusion process may also involve the clustering of entities. This is particularly relevant for blockchain data, where unique characteristics of the data can be leveraged to enhance the integration process.

For instance, when dealing with blockchains that utilize an account-based accounting model, address clustering heuristics can be employed to further refine the fusion process. One such heuristic is the deposit address reuse, as proposed by Victor [28]. Kosmosis uses deposit address reuse for blockchain data from Ethereum to resolve entities more effectively.

B. Text Processing

The workflow starts with the input of unstructured data from the 𝕏 Filtered Stream API [29], which is incrementally streamed and parsed via a long-lived HTTP request into the pipeline. The first step in processing this data is named entity recognition, where the system identifies and classifies named entities present in the text into predefined categories, such as the names of persons, organizations, and locations.

The next step is relation extraction. This process involves identifying and extracting relationships between the named entities that were previously recognized. For instance, it could determine that a person named "Alice" works for a company named "Acme."

The final step in the text processing workflow is the entity resolution, achieved through blocking and matching. For each new entity, the system identifies all other entities within the KG that need to be considered for matching. Considering the growing size of the KG, through the incremental updates, it is important to limit the matching process to as few candidates as possible [30]. The method of limiting candidates is known as blocking, which confines the matching process to entities of the same or most similar entity type.

Following the blocking that serves as a preliminary filtering step, the matching is performed. This involves a pairwise comparison of the new entities with those existing entities in the KG identified during the blocking phase. Its objective is to identify all entities that are sufficiently similar and, therefore, potential candidates for matching. This pairwise comparison relies on a nuanced assessment of similarity that encompasses both the properties of the entities and their relational connections within the KG. By evaluating both property values and the nature of relationships to other entities, the system determines the degree of similarity between entities.

C. Enrichment Data Processing

Enrichment data enhances the data obtained from primary data sources with supplementary context regarding real-world entitys. Attributions involve the mapping of blockchain addresses to their corresponding real-world entities. This task is largely dependent on data sourced from a network of experts, such as team members from blockchain projects. The input data for the attribution process is typically not consistent in its timing, as it depends on when the experts provide updates or when new information becomes available. As a result, the enrichment data processing workflow is designed to operate at regular intervals, ensuring that the KG is updated systematically and remains as up-to-date as possible.

To further enrich the KG, data from external knowledge bases is integrated. In our case, we use the *Golden Knowledge Graph* due to its concentrated information on tech startups and cryptocurrencies. This external graph offers a wealth of information about crypto projects, including details about their founders, team members, and project descriptions. Such depth of data provides a valuable context that can significantly improve the understanding of entities in the constructed KG.

The workflow for integrating knowledge from an external KG is event-driven, activated once the knowledge storage indicates the addition of new entities from the social media platform 𝕏. Then, the workflow triggers a process to pull in additional background information from the Golden Enrichment API [31]. It uses the 𝕏 username that has been newly included in the KG as unique identifier to fetch relevant data.

D. Quantity Structure of the Knowledge Graph Data

In our prototype implementation, data was ingested at rates averaging 10-15 transactions per second (each averaging 5KB) from Ethereum blockchain nodes and roughly 200 tweets per minute (each averaging 2KB) from the X filtered stream API. This combined ingestion rate corresponds approximately between 3.4 to 4.9 MB per minute of raw data. Our prototype runs on a standalone cloud server instance with 32 GiB RAM and 8 vCPUs (AWS EC2 m5.2xlarge) with a 512GB SSD, managing real-time data ingestion and processing workloads. The semantic enrichment introduces minimal latency (less than 5 seconds per transaction batch), thus allowing for near-real-time KG updates. The KG constructed by Kosmosis accumulates triples at an approximate rate of 2.5 to 6 million triples per day, depending on transaction activity and the level of detail extracted from social media.

While the described hardware configuration proved adequate for prototype-level or small- to medium-scale deployments, a production implementation aimed at analyzing multiple blockchain networks or higher data volumes would necessitate scaling to multiple compute nodes, each handling dedicated tasks such as blockchain data ingestion.

V. Conclusion and Future Work

In this paper, we demonstrated how to build a knowledge graph from blockchain and social media data using the Kosmosis approach to incremental knowledge graph construction. It complements our previous use case paper [6] that provided a real-world example of how Kosmosis can detect fraudulent activity, with a high-level technical discussion about the Kosmosis pipeline.

In the exemplary scenario, a threat actor known as Homer_eth executed five NFT project heists within two months, accumulating over $2.8 million in profits. We summarized our user story, in which Kosmosis provides a knowledge graph that improves the detection of such fraudulent schemes. Kosmosis fuses on- and off-chain data, thus, it becomes the basis for semantic querying and reasoning over a graph of entities and the relationships among them, facilitating analyses for cybercrime and fraud prevention, with the current focus on rug pulls as a major fraud scheme.

The initial findings of our research on Kosmosis have shown promising results, indicating the potential of our approach in identifying and preventing rug pulls. However, there are ample improvement opportunities for Kosmosis in future work.

It will be necessary to refine the filters used in the ingestion of data from the 𝕏 Filtered Stream API. The current process of data ingestion depends on the presence of direct links to blockchain addresses in social media posts. For instance, the ability to link the user Homer_eth with the *EtherReapers* smart contract was solely facilitated by the explicit mention of the smart contract address in Homer_eth's announcement post on 𝕏. This example underscores the limitations of the current approach, which may overlook relevant connections in the absence of direct references. Consequently, a more sophisticated approach is required to ensure a broader and still relevant dataset is captured to associate 𝕏 users with their respective blockchain addresses.

Additionally, the implementation of knowledge fusion, the process of identifying true subject-predicate-object triples [32], sourced from the blockchain and social media stands out as a critical next step. By fusing multiple records representing the same real-world entity into a single and consistent representation [33], knowledge fusion would allow for a more accurate representation of real-world entitys in the knowledge graph.

Currently, our prototype is limited to blockchains utilizing the account-based accounting model, like Ethereum. Recognizing the diversity in blockchain architectures and their unique features, we aim to allow for the integration of blockchains using a different accounting system, like Bitcoin. This expansion is essential for broadening the applicability and utility of Kosmosis across different blockchain platforms.

In conclusion, the Kosmosis pipeline supports the ingestion of unstructured, semi-structured, and structured data, as well as the ingestion of new data at different time intervals. It supports continuous ingestion in a stream-like fashion, incrementally, periodically, or event-based ingestion. During construction, the semantics of blockchain transactions are extracted to address "why" and "how" crypto assets were transferred.

References

[1] Chainalysis, "The 2023 crypto crime report," Chainalysis, Feb. 2023, [Online]. Available: https://go.chainalysis.com/2023-crypto-crime-report.html (visited on 01/31/2025).

[2] T. Sharma, R. Agarwal, and S. K. Shukla, "Understanding rug pulls: An in-depth behavioral analysis of fraudulent nft creators," *ACM Trans. Web*, vol. 18, no. 1, Oct. 2023, ISSN: 1559-1131. DOI: 10.1145/3623376.

[3] A. Khan, "Graph analysis of the ethereum blockchain data: A survey of datasets, methods, and future work," in *2022 IEEE International Conference on Blockchain (Blockchain)*, IEEE, Espoo, Finland: IEEE, 2022, pp. 250–257.

[4] F. Béres, I. A. Seres, A. A. Benczúr, and M. Quintyne-Collins, "Blockchain is watching you: Profiling and deanonymizing ethereum users," in *2021 IEEE International Conference on Decentralized Applications and Infrastructures (DAPPS)*, Online: IEEE, 2021, pp. 69–78. DOI: 10.1109/DAPPS52256.2021.00013.

[5] X. Zhu *et al.*, "Intelligent financial fraud detection practices in post-pandemic era," *The Innovation*, vol. 2, no. 4, 2021.

[6] P. Stangl and C. P. Neumann, "The Kosmosis Use Case of Crypto Rug Pull Prevention by an Incrementally Constructed Knowledge Graph," in *Proc of the 2nd Workshop on Data Engineering for Data Science (DE4DS) in conjunction with the 21st Conference on Database Systems for Business, Technology and Web (BTW'25)*, Bamberg, DE, Mar. 2025, forthcoming.

[7] C. P. Neumann and R. Lenz, "The alpha-Flow Use-Case of Breast Cancer Treatment – Modeling Inter-Institutional Healthcare Workflows by Active Documents," in *Proc of the 19th Int'l Workshops on Enabling Technologies: Infrastructures for Collaborative Enterprises (WETICE 2010)*, Larissa, GR, Jun. 2010, pp. 12–22. DOI: 10.1109/WETICE.2010.8.

[8] ZachXBT [@zachxbt], "Homer.eth (formerly @homer_eth) rug pull analysis," X, X Corp., May 26, 2022, [Online]. Available: https://x.com/zachxbt/status/1529973318563946496 (visited on 12/05/2023).

[9] T. Bauer *et al.*, "Reddiment: Eine SvelteKit- und ElasticSearch-basierte Reddit Sentiment-Analyse," German, Ostbayerische Technische Hochschule Amberg-Weiden, Technische Berichte CL-2022-06, Jul. 2022. DOI: 10.13140/RG.2.2.32244.12161.

[10] B. Hahn *et al.*, "Twitter-Dash: React- und .NET-basierte Trend- und Sentiment-Analysen," German, Ostbayerische Technische Hochschule Amberg-Weiden, Technische Berichte CL-2022-07, Jul. 2022. DOI: 10.13140/RG.2.2.15466.90564.

[11] G. Wood, "Ethereum: A Secure Decentralised Generalised Transaction Ledger," (Ethereum project yellow paper), Parity Technologies, 2024, [Online]. Available: https://ethereum.github.io/yellowpaper/paper.pdf (visited on 01/29/2024).

[12] S. Wang, D. Li, Y. Zhang, and J. Chen, "Smart contract-based product traceability system in the supply chain scenario," *IEEE Access*, vol. 7, pp. 115 122–115 133, 2019.

[13] P. Stangl and C. P. Neumann, "FoodFresh: Multi-Chain Design for an Inter-Institutional Food Supply Chain Network," in *Proc of the 14th International Conference on Cloud Computing, GRIDs, and Virtualization (Cloud Computing 2023)*, Nice, France, Jun. 2023, pp. 41–46. DOI: 10.48550/arXiv.2310.19461.

[14] Z. Zheng, S. Xie, H. Dai, X. Chen, and H. Wang, "An overview of blockchain technology: Architecture, consensus, and future trends," in *2017 IEEE International Congress on Big Data (BigData Congress)*, Boston, MA, USA: IEEE, 2017, pp. 557–564. DOI: 10.1109/BigDataCongress.2017.85.

[15] O. Marin, T. Cioara, L. Toderean, D. Mitrea, and I. Anghel, "Review of Blockchain Tokens Creation and Valuation," *Future Internet*, vol. 15, no. 12, p. 382, Nov. 27, 2023, ISSN: 1999-5903. DOI: 10.3390/fi15120382.

[16] E. Takeuchi, "Explaining ethereum contract abi & evm bytecode," Medium, Jul. 16, 2019, [Online]. Available: https://medium.com/@eiki1212/explaining-ethereum-contract-abi-evm-bytecode-6afa6e917c3b (visited on 12/07/2023).

[17] M. M. Chakravarty *et al.*, "The extended utxo model," in *Financial Cryptography and Data Security: FC 2020 International Workshops, AsiaUSEC, CoDeFi, VOTING, and WTSC, Kota Kinabalu, Malaysia, February 14, 2020, Revised Selected Papers 24*, Springer, 2020, pp. 525–539.

[18] Y. Zhou *et al.*, "Stop pulling my rug: Exposing rug pull risks in crypto token to investors," 2024.

[19] H. Huang, W. Kong, S. Zhou, Z. Zheng, and S. Guo, "A survey of state-of-the-art on blockchains: Theories, modelings, and tools," *ACM Computing Surveys (CSUR)*, vol. 54, no. 2, pp. 1–42, 2021.

[20] Y. Elmougy and L. Liu, "Demystifying fraudulent transactions and illicit nodes in the bitcoin network for financial forensics," in *Proceedings of the 29th ACM SIGKDD Conference on Knowledge Discovery and Data Mining*, ser. KDD '23, Long Beach, CA, USA: Association for Computing Machinery, 2023, pp. 3979–3990. DOI: 10.1145/3580305.3599803.

[21] L. Chen *et al.*, "Phishing scams detection in ethereum transaction network," *ACM Trans. Internet Technol.*, vol. 21, no. 1, Dec. 2020, ISSN: 1533-5399. DOI: 10.1145/3398071.

[22] P. Stangl, "Design and Implementation of an Incremental Knowledge Graph Construction Pipeline for Investigating Crypto Asset Fraud," Masterarbeit, Ostbayerische Technische Hochschule Amberg-Weiden, Apr. 2024. DOI: 10.5281/zenodo.14518573.

[23] J. Li, A. Sun, J. Han, and C. Li, "A survey on deep learning for named entity recognition," *IEEE Transactions on Knowledge and Data Engineering*, vol. 34, no. 1, pp. 50–70, 2020.

[24] J. Pfeffer, "Ethon: Ethereum ontology," ConsenSys Software Inc., Dec. 7, 2023, [Online]. Available: https://ethon.consensys.io/ (visited on 12/07/2023).

[25] Etherscan, "Etherscan: The ethereum blockchain explorer," Etherscan LLC, Dec. 7, 2023, [Online]. Available: https://etherscan.io/ (visited on 12/07/2023).

[26] Sourcify, "Sourcify: Source-verified smart contracts for transparency and better ux in web3," 2023, [Online]. Available: https://sourcify.dev/ (visited on 12/07/2023).

[27] F. A. Manzano and J. Little, "Pyevmasm: Ethereum virtual machine disassembler and assembler," Crytic, 2024, [Online]. Available: https://github.com/crytic/pyevmasm (visited on 01/25/2024).

[28] F. Victor, "Address Clustering Heuristics for Ethereum," in *Financial Cryptography and Data Security*, J. Bonneau and N. Heninger, Eds., vol. 12059, Cham: Springer International Publishing, 2020, pp. 617–633, ISBN: 978-3-030-51279-8. DOI: 10.1007/978-3-030-51280-4_33.

[29] X Corp., "Filtered stream introduction," X Corp., 2024, [Online]. Available: https://developer.twitter.com/en/docs/twitter-api/tweets/filtered-stream/introduction (visited on 01/25/2024).

[30] M. Hofer, D. Obraczka, A. Saeedi, H. Köpcke, and E. Rahm, "Construction of Knowledge Graphs: State and Challenges," 2023, eprint: 2302.11509 (cs.AI).

[31] Golden Recursion Inc., "Golden Enrichment API: Enrich research, sales, and marketing with fresh, canonical knowledge.," Golden Recursion Inc., 2024, [Online]. Available: https://golden.com/product/api (visited on 01/25/2024).

[32] X. L. Dong *et al.*, "From data fusion to knowledge fusion," *Proc. VLDB Endow.*, vol. 7, no. 10, pp. 881–892, Jun. 2014, ISSN: 2150-8097. DOI: 10.14778/2732951.2732962.

[33] J. Bleiholder and F. Naumann, "Data fusion," *ACM Computing Surveys*, vol. 41, no. 1, pp. 1–41, Jan. 15, 2009, ISSN: 0360-0300, 1557-7341. DOI: 10.1145/1456650.1456651.

Practical Acoustic Eavesdropping On Typed Passphrases

Darren Fürst
Department of Electrical Engineering,
Media and Computer Science
Ostbayerische Technische Hochschule
Amberg-Weiden, Amberg, Germany
e-mail: d.fuerst@oth-aw.de

Andreas Aßmuth
Faculty of Computer Science and
Electrical Engineering
Kiel University of Applied Sciences
Kiel, Germany
e-mail: andreas.assmuth@fh-kiel.de

***Abstract*—Cloud services have become an essential infrastructure for enterprises and individuals. Access to these cloud services is typically governed by Identity and Access Management systems, where user authentication often relies on passwords. While best practices dictate the implementation of multi-factor authentication, it's a reality that many such users remain solely protected by passwords. This reliance on passwords creates a significant vulnerability, as these credentials can be compromised through various means, including side-channel attacks. This paper exploits keyboard acoustic emanations to infer typed natural language passphrases via unsupervised learning, necessitating no previous training data. Whilst this work focuses on short passphrases, it is also applicable to longer messages, such as confidential emails, where the margin for error is much greater, than with passphrases, making the attack even more effective in such a setting. Unlike traditional attacks that require physical access to the target device, acoustic side-channel attacks can be executed within the vicinity, without the user's knowledge, offering a worthwhile avenue for malicious actors. Our findings replicate and extend previous work, confirming that cross-correlation audio preprocessing outperforms methods like mel-frequency-cepstral coefficients and fast-fourier transforms in keystroke clustering. Moreover, we show that partial passphrase recovery through clustering and a dictionary attack can enable faster than brute-force attacks, further emphasizing the risks posed by this attack vector.**

Keywords-Cloud Computing; Passphrases; Unsupervised Learning; Acoustic Side-Channel; Dictionary Attack.

I. INTRODUCTION

As a critical component of modern computing infrastructure, Cloud Services underpin everything from enterprise operations to personal data storage and application access. Securing access to these services is managed through Identity and Access Management (IAM) systems. A fundamental aspect of IAM is user authentication, which, despite the growing adoption of multi-factor authentication, still frequently relies solely on passwords and passphrases. This continued reliance on passwords presents a significant security challenge, as these credentials are vulnerable to a variety of attacks, such as side-channel information leakage. Side-channel attacks aim to infer sensitive information from a system by analyzing unintended emissions, such as power consumption, electromagnetic radiation, or, in the case we explore here, acoustic emanations.

The sounds produced by keyboard typing can reveal valuable information about the typed characters. While other attacks might require physical proximity to the target device, exploiting acoustic emanations, allow for eavesdropping without user awareness or evidence on the targeted device. This makes acoustic side-channel attacks a realistic and potentially devastating threat to password security. This paper investigates the feasibility of leveraging these keyboard acoustic emanations to infer typed passphrases. We are particularly interested in exploring unsupervised learning techniques, transfering the dictionary demodulation method used by Yang et. al for their WiFi attack [1], to the acoustic side-channel. Unsupervised methods offer a more practical approach for real-world attacks as they do not require labeled training data specific to each target user and keyboard. This paper aims to contribute to this understanding by exploring and evaluating methods for acoustic passphrase recovery.

Figure 1. Example of a login screen, where the target types their passphrase to login

The rest of the paper is organised as follows: Section II reviews previous works on side-channel attacks targeting physical user input via keyboards. Section III discusses typing mannerisms and highlights the challenges posed by various typing styles. Next, Section IV outlines the methodology behind common password generation, followed by an explanation of the algorithm for passphrase recovery in Section V. Section VI presents the results of hyperparameter tuning, model evaluation, attack performance, and the faster-than-brute-force augmentation technique. Finally, Section VII concludes the paper with a summary of the findings and potential future work.

II. Related Works

Side-channel attacks have been extensively studied across various modalities, demonstrating the feasibility of inferring sensitive information without directly accessing the target system. In this section, we distinguish between supervised and unsupervised approaches on user input on keyboards.

A. Supervised Approaches

Supervised methods rely on labeled training data to infer keystrokes or other sensitive information. Whilst demonstrating high accuracy, they are impractical for real-world attacks, as they necessitate collecting labeled data for each target, as well as keyboard.

Asonov and Agrawal [2] first demonstrated that keystrokes could be distinguished by analyzing frequency differences, using the Fast Fourier Transform (FFT), to discern between 30 keys on a keyboard with 79 % accuracy. Subsequent work explored additional features, such as Mel Frequency Cepstral Coefficients (MFCC) [3] [4] and cross-correlation [5] [6].

Building on these early studies, recent advances have leveraged deep learning. A deep learning-based approach achieved a classification accuracy of 95 % on phone-recorded laptop keystrokes and 93 % on Zoom-recorded audio [7]. Similarly, Slater et. al. built an end-to-end keystroke segmentation and classification system, achieving a character error rate of 7.41 % for known typists and 15.41 % for unknown typists [8].

Owusu et al. used phone accelerometers to estimate touched screen regions, recovering 59 out of 99 six-character passwords [9]. Murali et. al. combined acoustic data with motion data from gyrometers to achieve 86 % accuracy in key recovery using smartphone sensor fusion [10].

By detecting vibrations through accelerometers, Marquardt et al. recovered 80 % of typed content from a keyboard by placing a mobile device on the same surface [11]. Barisani and Bianco in turn used laser microphones to detect vibrations from laptop screens and utilised a dictionary attack to recover typed words [12].

Visual-based inference techniques have also been explored. Sabra et al. showed that even subtle upstream movements of the shoulders during typing could be used to recover typed words from video calls [13]. Moreover, studies have shown that electromagnetic emissions [14] and changes in Wi-Fi channel state information [15] can also reveal sensitive keystroke information.

While these supervised methods lay the important groundwork of exploring reliable feature engineering and preprocessing techniques, as well as establishing general feasibility, with many works achieving impressive accuracy in discerning keystrokes, their reliance on labeled data significantly limits their applicability in practical scenarios.

B. Unsupervised Approaches

Unsupervised approaches, which do not rely on labeled data, present a more promising approach for practical attacks, enabling an attacker to eavesdrop on targets, without prior knowledge and without altering the target's system.

Dictionary-based attacks have been used effectively in recovering typed words from keyboard acoustic emanations, making use of natural language properties. Berger et al. achieved a success rate of 73 % for 7 to 13 character words being in the top 50 guesses using cross-correlation and a dictionary attack [5]. Another method leveraging Time-Difference-of-Arrival (TDoA) measurements from smartphones achieved a 72.2 % key recognition rate [16].

Zhuang et. al. used Hidden Markov Models to iteratively generate labels from unlabeled audio recordings, increasing classification accuracy over time. This method recovered up to 96 % of typed characters from a 10-minute recording [17]. Yang et al. demonstrated an unsupervised Wi-Fi channel-state information attack achieving a 95 % word recovery ratio after 150 typed words [1].

Another attack based on TDoA measurements demonstrated 94 % keystroke recovery using millimeter-level audio ranging on a single phone [3].

Whilst some supervised works argue that training data can be recorded via video calls or infected devices, these substantially decrease attack surface and practicality. In constrast, unsupervised methods, such as employed in this work, provide a feasible manner of eavesdropping via these side-channel mediums, as they do not depend on prior knowledge of the target's typing style or environment, making them a real threat.

III. Typing Mannerisms

Typing ability can affect how a person types a message, with experienced typers typically displaying more consistent typing patterns. This consistency could increase vulnerability to audio-based attacks due to more consistent sounds from their keystrokes. However, their faster typing speed and reduced inter-keystroke pauses might make it harder to distinguish the start and end of keystrokes. In contrast, less experienced typers type more slowly but are likely to have less consistent motions, possibly causing greater variability in sound.

Dhakal et al. analyzed 136 million keystrokes from 168.000 volunteers, categorizing typers into eight groups based on metrics such as words per minute and error rates. They found that all groups exhibited at least a 19 % rollover ratio, where multiple keys are pressed consecutively before being released [18]. This rollover complicates keystroke segmentation, as it is difficult to determine which press and release belong together. Furthermore, a study of 30 typers revealed a significant variation in the number of fingers used, with only three using perfect touch typing [19]. This highlights the challenges in modeling typing patterns due to the diverse techniques used.

The key challenges are:

- Rollover technique complicates keystroke segmentation
- Typing error rates vary between typers
- Variability in typing styles and proficiency

To mitigate these issues, participants were instructed to avoid using rollover patterns for easier segmentation, while recording audio samples. In a real attack, this could be addressed by focusing on initial key presses or using likely press-release combinations. In Section VI, both press-only segmentation and press-release segmentation are evaluated for suitability.

A. Selected Features

Liu et al. used MFCC for K-Means clustering to reduce errors in Time Difference of Arrival measurements [3]. Asonov and Agrawal's neural network, trained with FFT, achieved 79 % accuracy for the top candidate and 88 % for the top 3 [2]. Berger et al. [5] and Halevi et. al. [6] found cross-correlation to outperform FFT and MFCC in keystroke classification, yielding better precision and recall scores. Zhuang et al. showed that using MFCC allowed for correctly classifying more keystrokes than using FFT, their analysis did not include cross-correlation [17].

While FFT seems less promising from existing literature than cross-correlation and MFCC, it is included in the evaluation, as it is easily computable. Thus, the following methods are used alone and in conjunction in the experiments: MFCC, FFT, Cross-Correlation.

IV. Generating Natural Language Passwords

This section explains the process of generating natural language passwords used for the attack evaluation.

The UK's National Cyber Security Centre (NCSC) recommends using three random words for constructing passphrases, as adding special characters complicates memorability. They consider passphrases made from three random words to be 'strong enough' [20]. Diceware [21] follows a similar approach, mapping each word to a five-digit number. A word can be looked up by its number, obtained by rolling a dice five times, removing human bias in word selection. The Electronic Frontier Foundation (EFF) has created two wordlists based on this concept, optimised for both memorability and password strength [22].

Despite the NCSC's recommendation, humans tend to create weak passwords from a limited set of words [23]. The Yahoo data breach [24] reveals that certain passwords appear far more frequently than others, indicating a strong pattern in human-generated choices. While this chart reflects password frequencies rather than passphrase word frequencies, it suggests that human-generated passphrases may also follow predictable patterns. In contrast, Diceware-generated passphrases benefit from the uniform randomness of the word selection process, making them potentially more secure.

We generate five passphrases each of differing length with 3 to 8 words for 30 passphrases in total from EFF's Long Wordlist to test passphrase recovery. These are shown in Appendix A.

V. Text Recovery

The text recovery process can be viewed as breaking a substitution cipher, where cluster indices replace the original alphabetic characters based on keystroke sounds. The final step involves a dictionary attack to map clusters to their correct alphabetic character, producing words. The described method of finding words and demodulating was used in [1] to recover longer typed messages via Wi-Fi channel-state information and is used in this work to recover passphrases formed of 3 to 8 words, which would not be possible with n-gram statistics or other statistical methods, due to the short message length, via the acoustic side-channel.

A. Finding Words

Words in natural language are separated by delimiters, typically spaces or hyphens. By leveraging natural language statistics, educated guesses about which cluster represents the delimiter can be made. If the initial guess does not result in a meaningful message, one can iteratively try the next largest cluster [1]. In a passphrase with n words, the delimiter appears $n-1$ times and is thus likely one of the larger clusters.

B. Inter-Element Relationship Matrix

To identify word candidates, we use features such as word length, letter frequencies, and same-letter positions. An inter-element relationship matrix [1] is constructed, where letters are compared and marked with 1 for identical letters and 0 for differing ones. This results in a symmetrical matrix, which describes each word or concatenation of words by length and frequencies and positions of same letters.

	l	e	v	e	l
l	1	0	0	0	1
e	0	1	0	1	0
v	0	0	1	0	0
e	0	1	0	1	0
l	1	0	0	0	1

	r	a	d	a	r
r	1	0	0	0	1
a	0	1	0	1	0
d	0	0	1	0	0
a	0	1	0	1	0
r	1	0	0	0	1

Figure 2. Example of two words, with the same inter-element relationship matrix, although their letters differ. The coloring is added to enable quick comparison of the symmetrical matrix.

C. Joint Demodulation

The candidate selection and dismissal process is based on the Joint Demodulation method from Yang et al. [1]. This involves concatenating candidate words from a dictionary and comparing their inter-element relationship matrix with the matrix of the audio cluster. Concatenations resulting in a different inter-element relationship matrix are discarded as potential passphrases. If no words are found for a concatenation, the last appended word is skipped and added to the undemodulated set [1], where it is later resubstituted with the letter-mappings found by demodulating the concatenation of the remaining words.

VI. Experiments

The experiments were conducted using the Diceware Long Wordlist [21] as a dictionary.

A. Hyperparameter Search

To identify the most suitable clustering model, a hyperparameter search was conducted for two model types, with n being the amount of configurations tested: K-Means ($n = 2049$) and Cross-Correlation ($n = 2045$). The Cross-Correlation type computes the correlation of keystroke segements based on the recorded raw audio, MFCC or FFT transformation of the audio, before clustering with K-Means, while K-Means uses the feaature vectors gained from applying MFCC or FFT, directly. This naming distinction is used to be able to talk about and distinguish these model types. To avoid overfitting of the hyperparameters to the whole dataset, skewing recovery results, 20 samples from the participants were picked at random and used in the search, spanning 3 to 5 samples per participant.

The keystroke span 'PR' uses both press and release events, while 'P' uses only the key press. The window size for these events was manually set.

An optional convolutional smoothing step was applied, with window sizes included in the hyperparameter search.

TABLE I. HYPERPARAMETERS FOR K-MEANS AND CROSS-CORRELATION-BASED MODELS.

Hyperparameter	K-Means	Cross-Correlation
Feature	FFT, MFCC, FFT+MFCC	Raw Audio, FFT, MFCC
Smoothing	true, false	
Smoothing Window	5 to 300	
Scaling	true, false	
PCA	true, false	
PCA Components	1 to 20	1 to 12
Keystroke Span	P, PR	

The best models by median score of each type are shown in Table II. Cross-Correlation, using raw audio, outperformed K-Means, which was most effective using MFCC and Principal Component Analysis (PCA).

TABLE II. BEST MODEL SCORES AND THEIR HYPERPARAMETERS.

Hyperparameter	K-Means	Cross-Correlation
Feature	MFCC	Raw
MFCC Components	180	
PCA	True	False
PCA Components	1	
Smoothing	False	False
Scaling	True	False
Keystroke span	PR	P
Median Score	90.27	93.12
Mean Score	88.95	93.21
Max Score	91.77	98.91
Min Score	83.07	85.44

Despite previous works clearly favouring MFCC, FFT was competitive in K-Means models, showing that FFT can achieve comparable performance under the right hyperparameter configurations. The top three models per type, with their respective audio feature processing are summarised in Table III. This shows that with a more extensive hyperparameter search the top models are very close to the same scores.

Cross-Correlation models showed superior performance, especially with raw audio features, while K-Means models using MFCC or FFT performed similarly. This suggests that hyperparameter choices, particularly feature extraction and preprocessing, significantly impact clustering effectiveness for acoustic eavesdropping.

TABLE III. TOP 3 MODELS PER TYPE AND THEIR SCORES.

Model Type	Feature	Median	Mean	Max	Min
K-Means	MFCC	90.27	88.95	91.77	83.07
K-Means	FFT	89.96	88.41	92.47	79.84
K-Means	FFT	89.95	88.62	92.90	79.89
Cross-Correlation	Raw	93.12	93.21	98.91	85.44
Cross-Correlation	Raw	92.85	93.18	98.27	87.29
Cross-Correlation	Raw	92.85	93.52	99.13	88.36

B. Recovering Passphrase Recordings

The best general model, which is of the Cross-Correlation type, from the hyperparameter search on the subset of participant samples was used to cluster a total of 223 samples. The hyperparameter search and selection of the best model is explained in Section VI-A. The top model configuration per type with hyperparameters and scores is shown in Table II. As the recording process was conducted via a custom built website to keep the recording manner similar between participant's, some participants' microphones removed keystroke sounds for the samples due to in-built noise reduction features. Such samples were discarded after listening. For the experiments in-built laptop microphones were used, as this made recording simply feasible via the custom built website. However, in a real-world scenario an attacker would most likely plant their own microphone, as having access to the target machine's microphone would mean the machine has already been compromised, removing such challenges, as built-in noise reduction. Furthermore, an attacker may use more high-end hardware, whereas this study aims to show feasability with even low-cost hardware, such as the built-in microphones used. The usable samples per participant are shown in Table IV.

TABLE IV. SAMPLES PER PARTICIPANT

Participant	Passphrases
1	30
2	30
3	16
4	30
5	19
6	27
7	22
8	30
9	19

In a real-world attack, words from the undemodulated set [1], would have to be checked against a large dictionary to find the correct candidate word, as the words from the undemodulated set likely contain a cluster assignment error, which can be resolved by checking against known English words. To simulate such a dictionary correction, the following Hamming distance per word length was deemed as corrected, by such a dictionary:

$$\text{Hamming Allowance}(w) = \begin{cases} 0 & \text{if } \#w \leq 2 \\ 1 & \text{if } 3 \leq \#w \leq 4 \\ 2 & \text{if } 5 \leq \#w \leq 6 \\ 3 & \text{if } 7 \leq \#w \leq 9 \end{cases}$$

Figure 3 shows the recovery results, where full recoveries are marked with fully coloured rectangles, partial recoveries with partial colouring along with the amount of recovered words, and unrecoverable passphrases with colourless rectangles. Black rectangles represent unusable or samples not recorded by participants. The first two words of each passphrase are shown. The bottom 5 passphrases are 3 words long up to the top 5 passphrases having a length of 8 words. The full passphrase list is listed in the Appendix A.

TABLE V. HARDWARE USED BY PARTICIPANTS.

Participant	Keyboard Model	Microphone Model	Mechanical
1	Tecurs	IdeaPad 5 Pro 14ACN6	✓
2	Laptop	Laptop Webcam	✗
3	Apple Magic (2014)	iMac 2014	✗
4	HIGROUND Base 65	Auna CM 900B	✓
5	Keychron K8 Pro	MacBook Air M1	✓
6	Redragon	Macbook Pro 14	✓
7	Cherry	Laptop	✓
8	Corsair K55 Gaming	Lenovo ThinkPad T14s	✗
9	Cherry	DELL Notebook	✓

Mechanical keyboards were more susceptible, likely due to their louder and more distinct sound profiles, although typing styles, microphone quality, and background noise likely also contributed.

Recovery rates improved using multiple sets of clusters. By applying 10 sets of clusters over a single cluster attempt by the model, shown in Appendix B, full recovery increased from 7 to 19 passphrases, primarily from the same highly susceptible participants. This also boosted partial recoveries. For example, a sample for participant '5' seeing improvements from 3 to 6 recovered words (Figure 3).

In conclusion, a single clustering set achieved partial recovery for all participants, while 10 sets improved full recoveries to 19 and enhanced partial recovery success. A further plot showing the recovery increase for different amount of cluster sets can be seen in Appendix B.

C. Brute-Forcing Combinations of Different Recoveries

An attacker can use the words found by partial recoveries in a brute-force attack by forming the product of these words.

Figure 4 shows the recovery results for brute-forcing combinations of words from partial recoveries, by adding each found word at each index to a set and forming the combinations. The number of combinations needed for a brute-force attack is illustrated in Figure 5, with exponents representing the possible combinations. For example, participant '1' has 2^{38} possible combinations from their partial recoveries for the first passphrase 'finalist caviar cufflink' (bottom left).

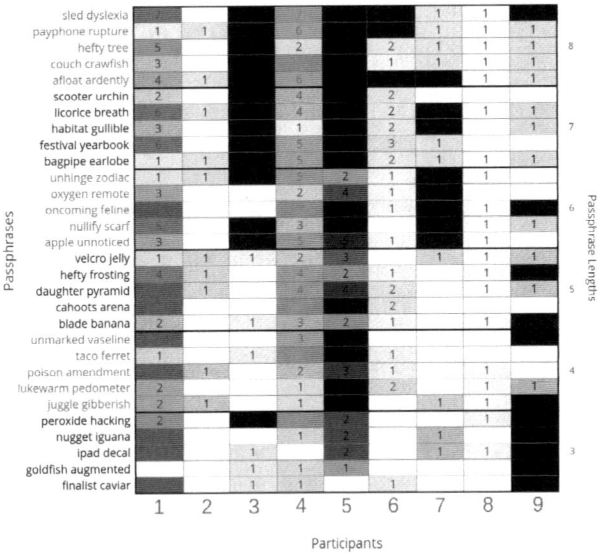

Figure 3. Recovery results using ten clusters.

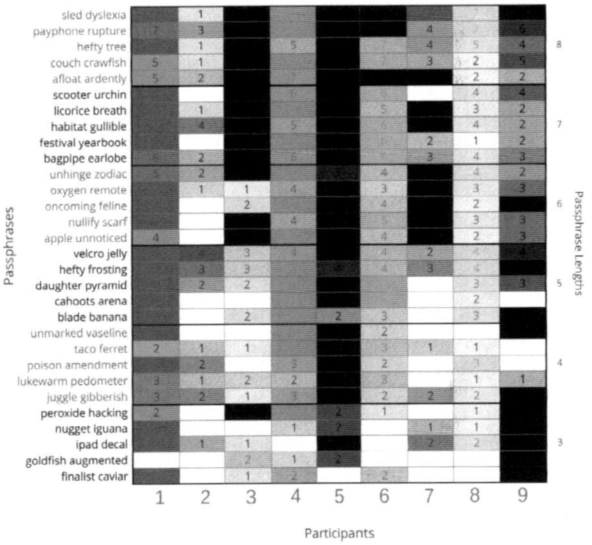

Figure 4. Recoveries brute-forcing combinations of partial recoveries from ten clusters.

However, brute-forcing all combinations naively this way disregards the position of the found words and is still computationally expensive. An alternative approach, starting with the most likely candidate and adding missing words, reduces the number of required combinations (Figure 6). This method, though more efficient, can still fail to fully recover the passphrase, as shown by the red rectangles marking complete successful recoveries. Evidently, there are less full recoveries than in Figure 4, but not all full recoveries in Figure 4, would be computable by even the strongest adversaries, as shown in Figure 5, with multiple recoveries needing more than 2^{80} steps.

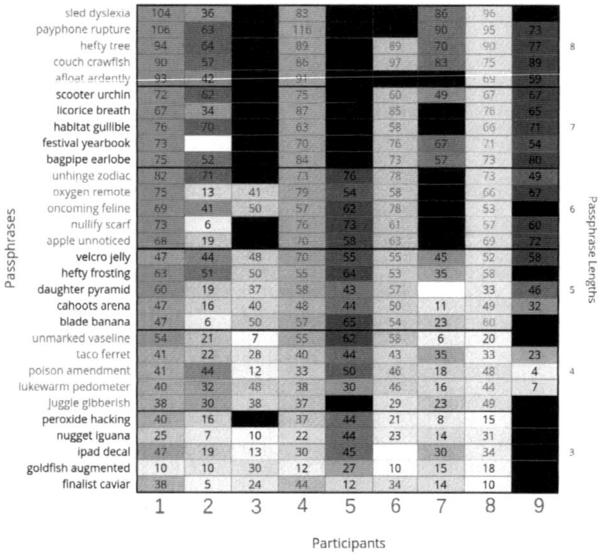

Figure 5. Amount of combinations of demodulated words from ten cluster results. The table shows the exponents to the base of 2.

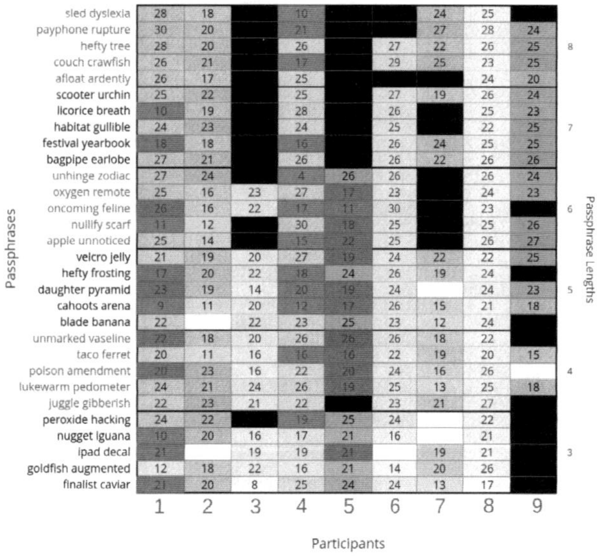

Figure 6. Brute-Force attempts needed, when starting with most likely candidates from ten cluster results. The table shows the exponents to the base of 2. Red marked cells are full recoveries.

In conclusion, starting with partial recoveries and narrowing down candidate words reduces the computational cost of brute-forcing below the border of computational feasibility in terms of complexity theory. This method can be further optimised by leveraging multiple clustering sets to account for errors in the clusters.

VII. Conclusion and Future Work

This study demonstrates that attackers can effectively recover passphrases from audio data, even without direct access to typed text, making the attack a potential non-intrusive and passive part of an attack chain, depending on whether the target has multi-factor authentication in place or not.

The results confirm previous findings [5] [6], showing that cross-correlation outperforms MFCC and FFT for keystroke clustering. However, it also showed that MFCC and FFT remain competitive under certain hyperparameters, suggesting the need for further parameter and model exploration. The hyperparameter search was conducted across 20 audio recordings from nine participants. Additionally, the dictionary attack by Yang et al. [1] was adapted to the acoustic side-channel and an attack exploiting partial passphrase recoveries with significant speed-improvement over naive brute-force attacks, was demonstrated, showing its potential to allow for computable brute-force attempts. Future work should explore further experimentation with different pre- and post-processing techniques, as well as feature combinations to improve clustering accuracy. Additionally, techniques like Metropolis-Hastings for probabilistically improving clusters could be tested, as seen in the Open Source KeyTap2 project [25]. The impact of adding complexity to typing (e.g., special characters, uppercase letters, and backspaces) should also be explored to assess the attack's feasibility under more realistic conditions. Furthermore, the data in this work shows that participants were not equally susceptible to the attack and future work should target specific reasons for why this may be, such as typing style, microphone quality and the used keyboard.

With recommendations from agencies like the NCSC advising three-word passphrases, the attack in this work presents a potential risk, underscoring the need for improved passphrase security through varied delimiters, special characters, and increased randomisation.

References

[1] E. Yang *et al.*, "Wireless training-free keystroke inference attack and defense," *IEEE/ACM Transactions on Networking*, vol. 30, no. 4, pp. 1733–1748, 2022. DOI: 10.1109/TNET.2022.3147721.

[2] D. Asonov and R. Agrawal, "Keyboard acoustic emanations," in *IEEE Symposium on Security and Privacy, 2004. Proceedings. 2004*, ISSN: 1081-6011, May 2004, pp. 3–11. DOI: 10.1109/SECPRI.2004.1301311.

[3] J. Liu *et al.*, "Snooping Keystrokes with mm-level Audio Ranging on a Single Phone," en, in *Proceedings of the 21st Annual International Conference on Mobile Computing and Networking*, Paris France: ACM, Sep. 2015, pp. 142–154, ISBN: 978-1-4503-3619-2. DOI: 10.1145/2789168.2790122.

[4] M. Pleva, E. Kiktova, J. Juhar, and P. Bours, "Acoustical User Identification Based on MFCC Analysis of Keystrokes," en, *Advances in Electrical and Electronic Engineering*, vol. 13, no. 4, pp. 309–313, Nov. 2015, Number: 4, ISSN: 1804-3119. DOI: 10.15598/aeee.v13i4.1466.

[5] Y. Berger, A. Wool, and A. Yeredor, "Dictionary attacks using keyboard acoustic emanations," in *Proceedings of the 13th ACM Conference on Computer and Communications Security*, ser. CCS '06, Alexandria, Virginia, USA: Association for Computing Machinery, 2006, pp. 245–254, ISBN: 1595935185. DOI: 10.1145/1180405.1180436.

[6] T. Halevi and N. Saxena, "A closer look at keyboard acoustic emanations: Random passwords, typing styles and decoding techniques," in *Proceedings of the 7th ACM Symposium on Information, Computer and Communications Security*, 2012, pp. 89–90.

[7] J. Harrison, E. Toreini, and M. Mehrnezhad, "A practical deep learning-based acoustic side channel attack on keyboards," in *2023 IEEE European Symposium on Security and Privacy Workshops (EuroS&PW)*, IEEE, 2023, pp. 270–280.

[8] D. Slater, S. Novotney, J. Moore, S. Morgan, and S. Tenaglia, "Robust keystroke transcription from the acoustic side-channel," in *Proceedings of the 35th Annual Computer Security Applications Conference*, ser. ACSAC '19, San Juan, Puerto Rico, USA: Association for Computing Machinery, 2019, pp. 776–787, ISBN: 9781450376280. DOI: 10.1145/3359789.3359816.

[9] E. Owusu, J. Han, S. Das, A. Perrig, and J. Zhang, "ACCessory: Password inference using accelerometers on smartphones," in *Proceedings of the Twelfth Workshop on Mobile Computing Systems & Applications*, ser. HotMobile '12, New York, NY, USA: Association for Computing Machinery, Feb. 2012, pp. 1–6, ISBN: 978-1-4503-1207-3. DOI: 10.1145/2162081.2162095.

[10] N. Murali and K. Appaiah, "Keyboard side channel attacks on smartphones using sensor fusion," in *2018 IEEE Global Communications Conference (GLOBECOM)*, IEEE, 2018, pp. 206–212.

[11] P. Marquardt, A. Verma, H. Carter, and P. Traynor, "(sp)iphone: Decoding vibrations from nearby keyboards using mobile phone accelerometers," Oct. 2011, pp. 551–562. DOI: 10.1145/2046707.2046771.

[12] A. Barisani and D. Bianco, "Sniffing keystrokes with lasers and voltmeters," in *Proceedings of Black Hat USA*, Black Hat, 2009.

[13] M. Sabra, A. Maiti, and M. Jadliwala, *Zoom on the Keystrokes: Exploiting Video Calls for Keystroke Inference Attacks*, en, arXiv:2010.12078 [cs], Oct. 2020.

[14] M. Vuagnoux and S. Pasini, "Compromising electromagnetic emanations of wired and wireless keyboards.," in *USENIX security symposium*, vol. 8, 2009, pp. 1–16.

[15] K. Ali, A. Liu, W. Wang, and M. Shahzad, *Keystroke Recognition Using WiFi Signals*. IEEE, Sep. 2015. DOI: 10.1145/2789168.2790109.

[16] T. Zhu, Q. Ma, S. Zhang, and Y. Liu, "Context-free attacks using keyboard acoustic emanations," in *Proceedings of the 2014 ACM SIGSAC conference on computer and communications security*, 2014, pp. 453–464.

[17] L. Zhuang, F. Zhou, and J. D. Tygar, "Keyboard acoustic emanations revisited," *ACM Trans. Inf. Syst. Secur.*, vol. 13, no. 1, 3:1–3:26, Nov. 2009, ISSN: 1094-9224. DOI: 10.1145/1609956.1609959.

[18] V. Dhakal, A. Feit, P. O. Kristensson, and A. Oulasvirta, "Observations on typing from 136 million keystrokes," in *Proceedings of the 2018 CHI Conference on Human Factors in Computing Systems (CHI '18)*, ACM, 2018. DOI: https://doi.org/10.1145/3173574.3174220.

[19] A. M. Feit, D. Weir, and A. Oulasvirta, "How we type: Movement strategies and performance in everyday typing," in *Proceedings of the 2016 CHI Conference on Human Factors in Computing Systems*, ser. CHI '16, San Jose, California, USA: Association for Computing Machinery, 2016, pp. 4262–4273, ISBN: 9781450333627. DOI: 10.1145/2858036.2858233.

[20] National Cyber Security Centre, "Top tips for staying secure online," Dec. 2021, [Online]. Available: https://www.ncsc.gov.uk/collection/top-tips-for-staying-secure-online/three-random-words (visited on 08/29/2024).

[21] D. Muth, "Diceware Password Generator," [Online]. Available: https://diceware.dmuth.org/ (visited on 03/16/2025).

[22] Electronic Frontier Foundation, "EFF Dice-Generated Passphrases," Jan. 2023, [Online]. Available: https://www.eff.org/de/dice (visited on 03/16/2025).

[23] R. Morris and K. Thompson, "Password security: A case history," *Commun. ACM*, vol. 22, no. 11, pp. 594–597, Nov. 1979, ISSN: 0001-0782. DOI: 10.1145/359168.359172.

[24] J. Bonneau, "The science of guessing: Analyzing an anonymized corpus of 70 million passwords.," in *IEEE Symposium on Security and Privacy*, IEEE Computer Society, 2012, pp. 538–552, ISBN: 978-0-7695-4681-0.

[25] G. Gerganov, "Keytap2 - acoustic keyboard eavesdropping based on language n-gram frequencies," GitHub Discussions, Dec. 2020, [Online]. Available: https://github.com/ggerganov/kbd-audio/discussions/31 (visited on 03/13/2025).

APPENDIX

A. Generated Passphrases

The following passphrases were used in the experiments:

1) peroxide hacking arena
2) goldfish augmented yoyo
3) nugget iguana nylon
4) finalist caviar cufflink
5) ipad decal uptown
6) lukewarm pedometer litter wreckage
7) juggle gibberish hacking luxurious
8) unmarked vaseline aluminum jasmine
9) poison amendment sizable angelfish
10) taco ferret circle deliverer
11) velcro jelly duplex magazine silicon
12) hefty frosting acid zookeeper patio
13) daughter pyramid onyx pogo palm
14) cahoots arena cement statue mutation
15) blade banana awhile elsewhere tadpole
16) oxygen remote diffuser engine lettuce acid
17) oncoming feline glucose sushi abdomen judiciary
18) nullify scarf deepness modify euphemism grumbling
19) apple unnoticed bullfrog datebook vicinity glove
20) unhinge zodiac movie tadpole tapestry waffle
21) habitat gullible jingling mule envoy device erratic
22) licorice breath thumb navigate saddlebag yahoo voucher
23) festival yearbook fountain underwear nastiness dedicate licorice
24) scooter urchin albatross sneezing itunes gumdrop cubical
25) bagpipe earlobe aerosol aliens ivory clubhouse pantyhose
26) couch crawfish mundane goggles rupture florist rancidity degree
27) hefty tree riverboat sculpture junkyard awhile isotope unveiled
28) sled dyslexia jelly clergyman fruit family blade rancidity
29) payphone rupture awoke virus tuesday upbeat knapsack amnesty
30) afloat ardently fox emission exquisite dagger jersey lubricant

B. Differing amounts of clusters for demodulation

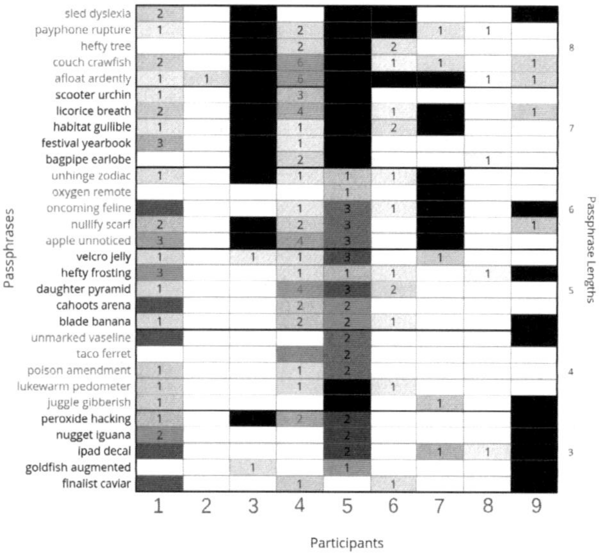

Figure 7. Recovery results using one set of clusters from the best model.

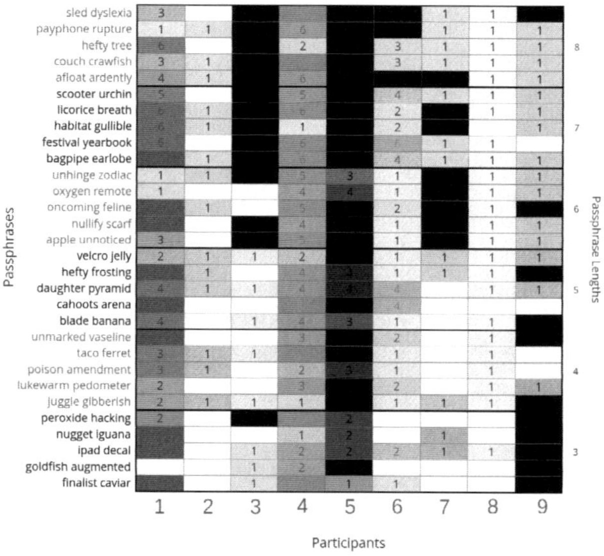

Figure 8. Recovery results using 50 clusters.

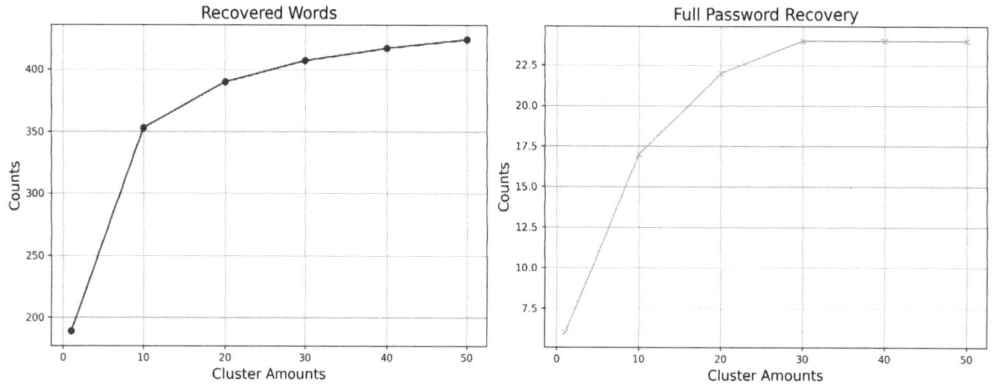

Figure 9. Recovery as a function of clusters.

Graph of Effort: Quantifying Risk of AI Usage for Vulnerability Assessment

Anket Mehra, Andreas Aßmuth, and Malte Prieß
Department of Computer Science and Electrical Engineering
Kiel University of Applied Sciences
Kiel, Germany
e-mail: anket.mehra@student.fh-kiel.de, {andreas.assmuth | malte.priess}@fh-kiel.de

***Abstract*—With AI-based software becoming widely available, the risk of exploiting its capabilities, such as high automation and complex pattern recognition, could significantly increase. An AI used offensively to attack non-AI assets is referred to as offensive AI. Current research explores how offensive AI can be utilized and how its usage can be classified. Additionally, methods for threat modeling are being developed for AI-based assets within organizations. However, there are gaps that need to be addressed. Firstly, there is a need to quantify the factors contributing to the AI threat. Secondly, there is a requirement to create threat models that analyze the risk of being attacked by AI for vulnerability assessment across all assets of an organization. This is particularly crucial and challenging in cloud environments, where sophisticated infrastructure and access control landscapes are prevalent. The ability to quantify and further analyze the threat posed by offensive AI enables analysts to rank vulnerabilities and prioritize the implementation of proactive countermeasures. To address these gaps, this paper introduces the Graph of Effort, an intuitive, flexible, and effective threat modeling method for analyzing the effort required to use offensive AI for vulnerability exploitation by an adversary. While the threat model is functional and provides valuable support, its design choices need further empirical validation in future work.**

***Keywords*-threat modeling; vulnerability assessment; offensive AI.**

I. INTRODUCTION

At the latest since the presentation of ChatGPT (GPT-3.5) by OpenAI in November 2022, the topic of Artificial Intelligence (AI) has also been omnipresent in the general public. As we are now seeing, AI also has an impact on cybersecurity, as the availability of AI services can make known attacks easier or more efficient. The attack itself does not even have to be technical. An employee of a multinational company was tricked into making a bank transfer of 25.6 million US dollars using AI-generated deepfakes [1]. He had taken part in a video conference, supposedly together with the Chief Financial Officer and other employees of the company. In reality, however, all the other people were deepfakes. And this is not an isolated case: Hong Kong police announced that there have been other similar incidents in which deepfakes were used to deceive facial recognition programs. The question arises as to how the availability of AI services and their use in cyberattacks can be quantified and how this aspect can be taken into account in known threat modeling methods.

Several publications deal with the creation of AI models for cybersecurity. A comprehensive overview can be found in [2]. Rising capabilities of AI lead to more complex models, advanced train infrastructure and accessible datasets. Importance for research and understanding it continuously is thus increasing. Since AI is a “dual-use technology” [3], its capabilities can be used in good or malicious directions. For example, using AI can help organizations to enhance their cyber defense mechanisms, but on the other hand and as indicated by the above given example, adversaries can use AI to simplify or improve attacks, as well as to create new and sophisticated attack vectors.

A current gap in research is the quantification of AI threats. To the best of our knowledge, only [4] tried to quantify the threat of offensive AI by a survey with industry experts. Furthermore, in [5] it was identified that there are no methods to quantify factors for the AI threat, namely the motivation. Also, the applicability of AI security research is criticized by [6] because most experiments rely on artificial environments, making the application of research results insufficient.

The latest version 4.0 of the Common Vulnerability Scoring System (CVSS) contains the criterion “automatable” in the new (optional) Supplemental Metric Group. As the term indicates, this criterion is intended to assess the automation potential of an attack, however, it is not intended to address specifically AI-based automation [7]. Furthermore, the CVSS base score examines the severity of a vulnerability by choosing scores between 0 and 10 for different a-priori categories, which are directly related to the vulnerability. External factors are included in the environmental and supplemental metrics. These can be used to quantify the risk of a vulnerability according to different IT system environments. However, in conclusion, none of the metrics examine the AI risk [7].

Being able to quantify the AI threat is important. It allows cyber analysts to prioritize threats and provides support to explain the specific danger of them. Additionally, it allows organizations to proactively implement target-oriented countermeasures.

Furthermore, the importance raises in cloud-based IT systems. These are characterized by having sophisticated connections between multiple components such as deployed web applications or the necessary infrastructure, such as databases and authorization management systems [8]. Any of these components could be vulnerable. With the existence of further offensive AI models, each vulnerability could be automatically exploited. Therefore, quantification during the step of vulnerability assessment give a means of understanding the weak points of a system. This paper addresses the existing research gap of quantifying the risk through AI in vulnerability assessments. It shows the current state of AI in threat modeling and introduces a new method – called Graph of Effort (GOE) – to address the danger of AI attacks in vulnerability assessments. GOE provides the exposure of the vulnerability against AI-based attacks. The method is intuitive, clear to use, and meant to be used by consumers of a given entity potentially affected by a vulnerability. GEO is based on the effort needed to create an AI model to automate the exploitation of a given vulnerability.

The remainder of the paper is structured as follow: After a brief overview of offensive AI (OAI) and AI in threat modeling in Sections II and III, we introduce GOE and calculate the exposure of a given vulnerability of being attacked by AIs in Sections IV and V. Section VII covers a discussion on how to deal with the results of the GOE and integrate it with other vulnerability modeling systems to facilitate prioritizing vulnerabilities. Finally, implications for future work are given.

II. Offensive AI

This Section provides an overview of how AI is offensively used for cyberattacks. According to [4], offensive AI (OAI) can be grouped into two categories: (1) attacks using AI and (2) Adversarial Machine Learning (AML).

In the first category, OAI is used as a tool to assist adversaries in applying their attacks. Potentially, AI could resolve any task as long as it is manually done or requires the use of common thought intelligence used by humans or non-human beings. A key limiting factor for AI training are suitable datasets for training on a given task, so the model can gain experience to perform this task efficiently [9].

The most common uses of OAI as a support tool according to [4], [5] are:

1) Prediction,
2) Generation,
3) Analysis,
4) Retrieval, and
5) Decision Making.

In conclusion, there are several ways to misuse AI for offensive malicious use. On the other hand, AML describes using the knowledge on how an AI model internally works to attack deployed models by organizations or other entities also via AI [10]. Here, the AI model is attacked by an adversary to compromise its security goals, like confidentiality, integrity or availability. This can be achieved, for instance, through data poisoning, wherein adversaries introduce misleading training data to the model, or by launching a Distributed Denial of Service (DDoS) attack to degrade model performance and reduce availability [4] [5].

A categorization of OAI use cases may be found in [2]. They discovered that especially in technical papers and information security briefings OAI use cases can be mostly mapped via the steps defined in MITRE ATT&CK [11]. Meanwhile, non-technical papers mostly categorize OAI into one of the following groups:

- attack in (cyber) warfare,
- attack on society,
- autonomous agents, and
- privacy attack.

This paper aims to prioritize the implementation of countermeasures for specific vulnerabilities, given that the effort required to execute exploits using AI is significantly lower compared to other vulnerabilities. Therefore, the main focus will be on OAI as of the first category of [4] and for all use cases of [2].

III. AI Threat Modeling

AI is discussed in several contexts in the area of threat modeling – this Section gives a brief overview.

Mirsky et al. [4] lists 24 offensive AI-based threats feared by organizations. Furthermore, the authors created a model to quantify the threat of AI by evaluating the harm, profit and achievability of AI-usage, as well as defeatability against it. On the other hand, [6] discovered that – at least on organizational level – no predictors can be found, which describe the threat exposure. However, it has to be emphasized that [6] focused only on AML as subtopic of OAI. Therefore, further work is needed on finding threat exposure predictors on OAI. They also criticize the lack of real-world scenarios in research regarding general security of AI systems.

Malatji and Tolah [5] identified a research gap in the quantification of factors leading to a better understanding of OAI usage. They specified that especially the quantification of the attackers' motivation is missing.

Guembe et al. [12] found out that AI-driven cyberattacks can be done continuously throughout all steps of an attack. In addition, the authors state that current defense mechanisms will become deprecated, as AI enables more sophisticated cyberattacks and detection evasion techniques.

Some publications focused on the creation of threat models for deployed AI systems by organizations. For instance, in [13], the authors created an extension of Microsoft's STRIDE threat model (STRIDE-AI) to identify vulnerabilities of deployed AI systems, approachable by consumers. STRIDE stands for Spoofing, Tampering, Repdudiation, Information Disclosure, Denial of Service and Elevation of Privilege. It aims to assist security analysts to categorize threats. The author of [14] followed a similar approach for threat modeling and risk analysis for AI systems, with a focus on Large Language Models (LLM). In his approach, the author combined the threat classification given by STRIDE with qualitative ratings for each class in the categories of Damage, Reproducibility and Exploitability (DREAD) to add the aspect of risk analysis. DREAD typically also determines the risk for Affected Users and Discoverability. However, these aspects were not analyzed in the proposed threat model in [14].

In [15], the authors created a web application, which assists analysts throughout the threat modeling process for AI-based IT systems. It supports especially threat identification by querying several security related databases, per instance, MITRE Atlas [16]. By means of an underlying graph model with comparable metadata, related assets of an organization and of the databases are found and connected.

A systematic threat modeling procedure for AI software is given in [17]. In their approach, the authors develop a process diagram for the development of AI-based software and furthermore a taxonomy of threats to AI. Based on their given process, the main idea is to sequentially go through it and analyze for all subprocesses and their respective in- and outputs potential threats to AI by means of their taxonomy.

To the best of our knowledge, no paper deals with the creation of a threat modeling method for the exposure of general vulnerabilities against OAI, especially with a focus on being simply applicable and explainable for analysts.

IV. Quantifying Effort of AI-based Attacks

To consider and quantify the potential of AI-based attacks in vulnerability, a new method – graph of effort (GOE) – for analyzing this potential is introduced (see Section IV for details). Foundation of the method is the modified intrusion kill chain as introduced in [18], wherein a cyberattack consists of the four steps (1) Reconnaissance, (2) Weaponization, (3) Delivery, and (4) Exploitation as shown in Figure 1. Reconnaissance describes the tasks needed to find and select victims for the attack. Weaponization is the creation of a transferable package in which malicious code is hidden. Typical weaponized files were PDFs and Microsoft Office documents. The next step, Delivery, describes the transmission of the malicious package to the target network. During the final Exploitation step the, successfully transferred package activates its malicious code often targeting a vulnerability of an application or the host os itself. This kill chain was modified to align with the one used in CVSS v4.0 [7]. The consistent application of identical kill chains between vulnerability assessment frameworks facilitates enhanced coordination of measures during assessments.

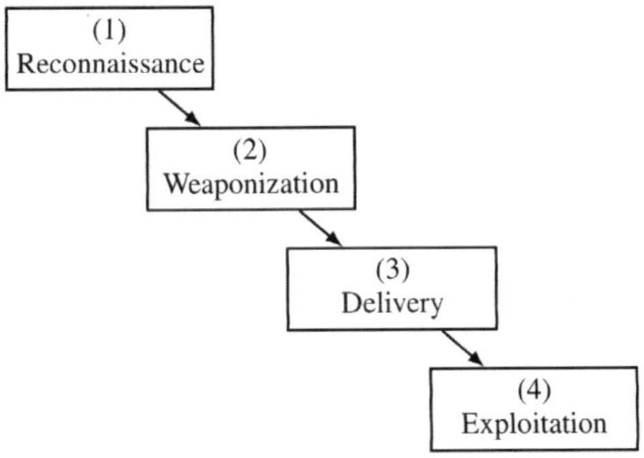

Figure 1. Steps of the intrusion kill chain according to [18].

Based upon the four kill chain steps of [18], our metric answers the following question:

> *What effort is needed to use offensive AI during each kill chain step?*

Our metric calculates a score for each respective step i, $1 \leq i \leq 4$, in the kill chain, see Equation (1):

$$\text{score}_{(i)} \in \{0, \ldots, 3\}. \tag{1}$$

The GOE is visualized in Figure 2 as a binary tree, in which each node describes an advanced level of effort for AI usage the attacker has to muster from top to bottom. The idea of the GOE is to obtain a score based on the answers to three questions: Are there ...

- ... ready to use models or AI-based tools,
- ... datasets to train a suitable model, or
- ... automatisms available to quickly generate suitable data to train an AI model?

The purpose of the questions is to address all relevant aspects of using or training an AI system. The primary assumption is that the simplest way to utilize AI is through ready-to-use systems equipped with a well-designed Graphical User Interface (GUI). In the absence of a GUI, pretrained models can also be quickly deployed.

It is assumed that the adversary possesses broad knowledge of AI and has access to all necessary resources for deployment. Therefore, if a ready-to-use AI system is not available, the adversary could train their own model. This process requires data, which is the most critical asset in training an AI. Without data, AI solutions cannot be developed. Consequently, for the adversary to create an AI system, they must have suitable training data. If such data is not available, the adversary must generate their own dataset. However, given that the provider of a CVE (CVE) is interested in promptly addressing the issue, it is further assumed that the adversary often lacks the time to manually create a high-quality dataset. Instead, they must rely on automated methods to generate data as quickly as possible.

The questions do not cover the detailed sub-aspects related to AI tools and datasets. For instance, AI tools can differ significantly; some are open-source, while others require specialized expertise. The same variability applies to datasets. This design choice is intentional. By avoiding excessive detail, the GOE ensures objectivity. The questions, though simple in design, allow for concise answers, limited to "yes" or "no," thereby minimizing subjective interpretations. For example, if a tool is deemed to require expertise, this perception might initially seem subjective, as individuals have varying definitions of expertise. Other threat assessment systems, such as STRIDE, allow users to select from predefined categorical values like "low/medium/high." However, GOE has intentionally omitted such values to maintain objectivity.

As already indicated in Equation (1), the scores range from 0 (no or low) to 3 (high) to describe the attackers effort; scores depicted on the left-hand side in Figure 2 are always smaller than those on the right-hand side of each level. Starting at the top for each step of the kill chain, the scores and, therefore, the attacker's effort are increasing downwards. The process is stopped when one of the leaves is reached, which are indicated by the term $\text{score}_{(i)}$.

The first question that has to be answered is whether AI-based tools, AI models that are ready to use, or AI-based automatisms already exist. If this the case, then this represents the least possible effort for the attacker ($\text{score}_{(i)} = 0$) because they may directly use these tools to automate their attack. In order to be able to use GOE together with CVSS, we propose a corresponding extension of the vector string. Since GOE only uses binary decisions, we set 0 to `N` and 1 to `H` in order to correspond to the symbols used in CVSS. The first category "**A**utomation **T**ools", `AT:0` or `AT:1`, can thus be noted for the top level of the GOE according to the decision left (0) or right (1) in the binary tree.

Given `AT:1`, so there are neither AI-based tools, ready to use models nor AI-based automatisms available, the next question is whether ready to use datasets or even complete training setups exist which the attacker may use to generate their own AI models. Again, this question may be answered with "yes" (left) which results in the substring `TAI:0` (for **T**rainability of **AI**) and $\text{score}_{(i)} = 1$. If no such datasets or training setups exist (indicated by `TAI:1`), the final criterion, **G**enerability, has to be assessed: Are there APIs or any other tools that enable the automatic creation of data sets to create an AI model? `G:0` means "yes", resulting in $\text{score}_{(i)} = 2$, whereas `G:1` indicates the greatest possible effort for the adversary ($\text{score}_{(i)} = 3$).

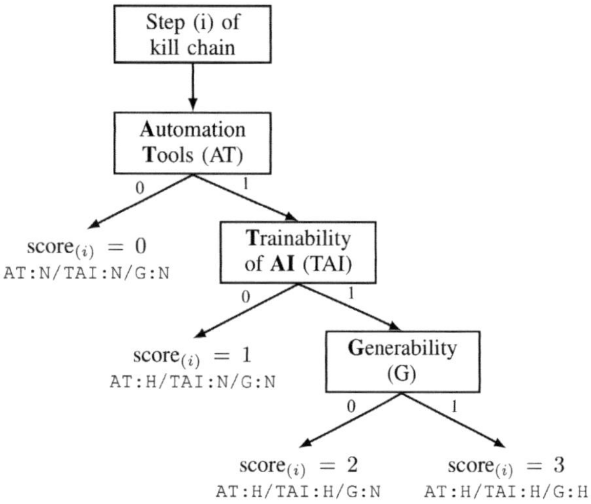

Figure 2. Visualization of the GOE to calculate the effort needed to use AI for an attack step in the intrusion kill chain according to [18].

If the remaining categories, in the order `AT`, `TAI`, and `G`, are set to `N` (which is equivalent to 0), after a leaf has been reached, then the score for step i of the kill chain may also be calculated as the sum of the three categories (`H` is equivalent to 1):

$$\text{score}_{(i)} = \texttt{AT} + \texttt{TAI} + \texttt{G} \quad (2)$$

The proposed threat model determines the AI-based threat with an intuitive approach, which is clearly understandable and easy to visualize. Additionally, GOE is flexible in its usage. Depending on the specific vulnerability or the priorities of security analysts, some of the kill chain attack steps may easily be skipped.

To calculate the overall score $\text{GOE}(v)$ for a given vulnerability v, Equation (3) is used:

$$\text{GOE}(v) = \min_i \left\{\text{score}_{(i)}\right\} \quad (3)$$

Using the minimum score of all steps in the kill chain as the overall score seems most reasonable and intuitive because if one of the steps is easily exploitable through AI, then it effects the exposure of the vulnerability as a whole. But Equation (3) may also be adapted if the analyst prefers, e.g., a weighted average of the scores of the four steps. Additionally, we would like to mention that the assessment of steps of the kill chain may be skipped, if these are of no interest for the analyst. If it is nevertheless desired to use Equation (3), the score of the steps not taken into account can be set to infinity (∞), for example.

The introduction of GOE based on CVSS is intended merely as an example. The universality of GOE allows it to be combined with any method of threat and risk analysis if it is necessary or desired to express whether a vulnerability should be assessed differently due to the availability of AI models. As already indicated, direct integration of GOE in CVSS v4.0 is possible via the "Automatable" criterion in the optional Supplemental Metric Group [7]. If CVSS is combined with GOE, one could assume that if a given vulnerability is completely automatable, indicated via a positive value of the "Automatable" criterion.

To achieve clear and intuitive applicability of the model, some assumptions are made. The adversary is assumed to have unlimited resources and knowledge regarding the considered vulnerability as well as skills in managing and training AI solutions. This assumption ensures that an attacker is not underestimated. Moreover, the proposed GOE does not allow higher scores than 3 (if there is no method of generating data automatically, `AT:H/TAI:H/G:H`). One could now argue that data could be created manually since the adversary according to our first assumption has unlimited resources to do so. However, there is only a small amount of time to create AI-based solutions for vulnerability exploitation because affected service providers are interested to deliver fixes or at least workarounds to their customers or users as soon as possible. Furthermore, if not much data is needed to create a successful AI model, it may be assumed that rule-based automation can easily be created – which is covered by our proposed AT criterion leading to $\text{score}_i = 0$ and, therefore, $\text{GOE}(v) = 0$.

V. EXAMPLE SCORING - CVE-2025-1156

After introducing GOE as an intuitive approach, this Section provides an example modeling for a known vulnerability, namely CVE-2025-1156 listed in the National Vulnerability Database (NVD)[19]:

> "A vulnerability has been found in Pix Software Vivaz 6.0.10 and classified as critical. This vulnerability affects unknown code of the file `/servlet?act=login`. The manipulation of the argument usuario leads to sql injection. The attack can be initiated remotely. The exploit has been disclosed to the public and may be used. The vendor was contacted early about this disclosure but did not respond in any way."

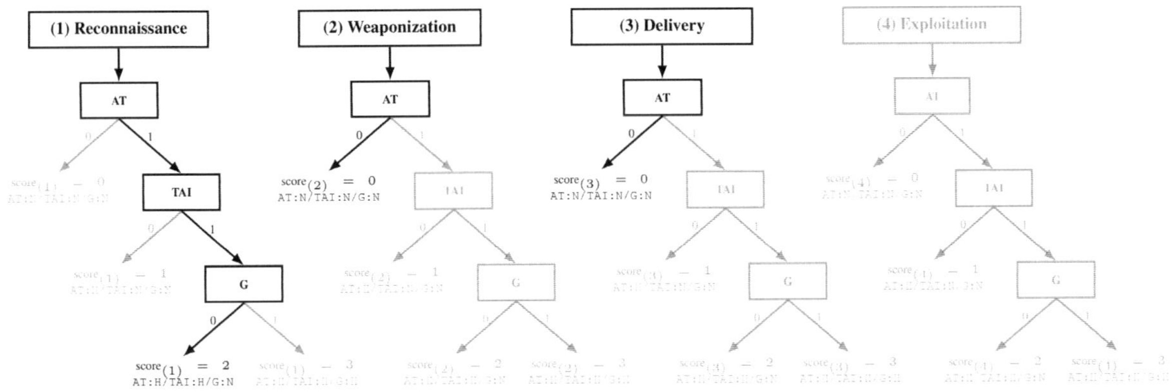

Figure 3. Visualization of the GOE for the known vulnerability CVE-2025-1156 listed in the National Vulnerability Database (NVD), showing the effort needed to use AI in each step of the intrusion kill chain. Given the flexibility of GOE, step (4) of the kill chain is skipped in this case. The overall score is GOE = 0, corresponding to a low effort for exploitation by AI.

Thus, the chosen vulnerability describes an improperly sanitized user input while requesting a given HTTP endpoint for authentication, making it vulnerable to Structured Query Language (SQL) injection. The complexity to launch such an attack is low as only websites using this specific service-desk software need to be found to do the injection [20].

It is worth noticing, that GOE may be used to analyze any given vulnerability. We specifically chose this vulnerability as an example because:

- it is a relatively new entry in the NVD,
- the vulnerability is relevant for cloud services, and
- we can use it to demonstrate that GOE can be used in conjunction with CVSS v4.0 as well as with earlier versions, e.g. CVSS v3.x.

According to the NVD, the vectors for CVE-2025-1156 are as follows:

```
CVSS:3.1/AV:N/AC:L/PR:N/UI:N/S:U/
C:L/I:L/A:L
```

and

```
CVSS:4.0/AV:N/AC:L/AT:N/PR:N/UI:N/
VC:L/VI:L/VA:L/SC:N/SI:N/SA:N,
```

resulting in a base score of 7.3 (criticality "high") for CVSS v3.x and a CVSS-B score of 6.9 (criticality "medium") for CVSS v4.0. We now evaluate the vulnerability using the method described above and calculate the associated GOE, see also Figure 3 for a visualization of the GOE for every single step of the kill chain.

(1) Reconnaissance. An AI model for reconnaissance can detect potential victims (websites) using the given service-desk software. To the best of our knowledge, there are no tools or AI models which could be used to find suitable victims, using the given software. A ready-to-use dataset to train own models is also not available. However, automatically generating training data is possible as it requires only a webcrawler visiting several websites. This crawler has to be capable of finding login pages of the vendor of this service-desk software. This can be done via image recognition or via parsing the Document Object Model (DOM) of the website and comparing the id and class names of the respective HTML elements, for instance. So, the GOE sub-vector looks as follows:

```
AT:H/TAI:H/G:N,
```

resulting in a level score of $\text{score}_{(1)} = 2$, indicating that AI-based attacks are feasible but are connected with a higher score. For this task, models have to be specifically created by the adversary.

(2) Weaponization. A weaponization AI model for this vulnerability needs to create a malicious HTTP request, incorporating the vulnerable query parameter. Basically, this can be done via string interpolation and, therefore, does not need an AI model at all. However, Large Language Models (LLMs) can be used to create malicious HTTP requests. The GOE vector looks as follows:

```
AT:N/TAI:N/G:N
```

and $\text{score}_{(2)} = 0$ indicates, that no effort is needed to incorporate AI to automate the generation of malicious HTTP requests.

(3) Delivery. An AI model for step (3) of the kill chain needs to transport the string used for the SQL injection to the victim network. This is done via a simple HTTP request. Therefore, no AI-based automation is needed. However, AI-based tools, such as LLMs, may be incorporated here which can automate or assist in creating the HTTP request. Therefore, we calculate $\text{score}_{(3)} = 0$, resulting in the same sub-vector as in the previous step:

```
AT:N/TAI:N/G:N
```

It is important to highlight that AI models potentially can be used to evade detection mechanisms [10] for misuse, such as SQL injections. One might thus argue that multiple AI models could be used in this step. In that case, our recommendation is to calculate the GOE sub-vector for each AI model and then use the one with the lowest score to describe it for the respective step since GOE is always meant as a worst case analysis.

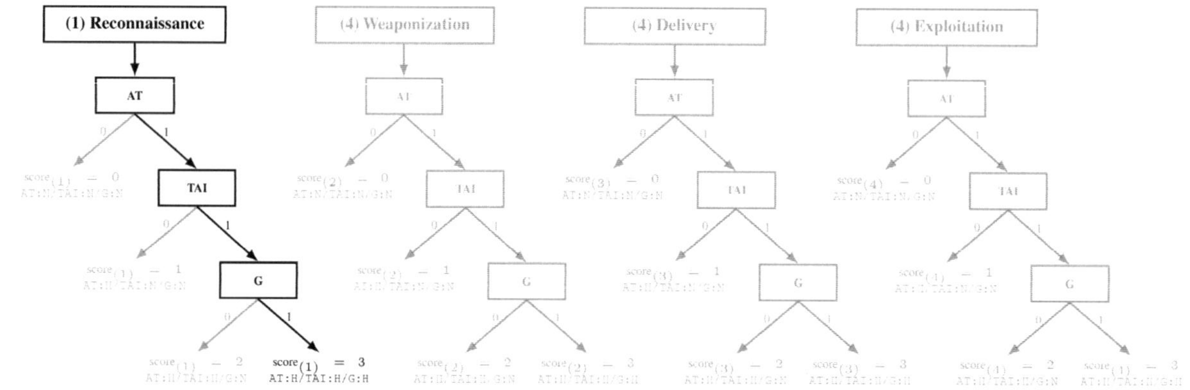

Figure 4. Visualization of the GOE for the vulnerability CVE-2024-30384, showing the effort needed to use AI in each step of the intrusion kill chain. Given the flexibility of GOE, steps (2-4) of the kill chain are skipped in this case. The overall score is GOE = 3, corresponding to a high effort for exploitation by AI and demonstrating the GoE can have values other than 0.

(4) Exploitation. An AI model for exploitation should typically prepare or activate the malicious code after it has been successfully delivered. However, since the malicious code gets inserted into the backend, no further doings are required here for activation. Therefore, this step is skipped. This also highlights the flexible usage of the GOE, since steps can easily be skipped if not needed without effecting the score calculation.

In conclusion, CVE-2025-1156 gets an overall GOE score of

$$\text{GOE(CVE-2025-1156)} = \min\{2, 0, 0, \infty\} = 0.$$

This score means that using OAI to assist in this attack is connected with low effort. As OAI allows for a higher efficiency, scaling and attack automation, this CVE could be more exploited via AI than CVEs with a higher GOE rating. In a real life vulnerability assessment environment, this CVE should be higher prioritized regarding the implementation of AI countermeasures such as, f.e. request rate limiting systems or captchas. Analysts can further combine the high CVSS base score with the low GOE score and could raise the criticality. Thus, to raise the prioritization of dealing with the CVE and enhancing their arguments with the information of the GOE.

VI. Example Scoring - CVE-2024-30384

In this Section, we do another example scoring for CVE-2024-30384 (see Figure 4 for a visualization of the GOE for every single step of the kill chain). The vulnerability is described as follow:

> "An Improper Check for Unusual or Exceptional Conditions vulnerability in the Packet Forwarding Engine (PFE) of Juniper Networks Junos OS on EX4300 Series allows a locally authenticated attacker with low privileges to cause a Denial-of-Service (DoS). If a specific CLI command is issued, a PFE crash will occur. This will cause traffic forwarding to be interrupted until the system self-recovers. This issue affects Junos OS: All versions before 20.4R3-S10, 21.2 versions before 21.2R3-S7, 21.4 versions before 21.4R3-S6."

Hence, the vulnerability is the usage of a preinstalled CLI application in Junos OS on their enterprise switch EX4300 [21]. Junos OS is the operating system based on FreeBSD or Linux of the vendor Juniper Network Devices. The CVSS v3.1 and v4.0 vectors are as follow:

```
CVSS:3.1/AV:L/AC:L/PR:L/UI:N/S:U
/C:N/I:N/A:H
```

and

```
CVSS:4.0/AV:L/AC:L/AT:N/PR:L/UI:N
/VC:N/VI:N/VA:H/SC:N/SI:N/SA:L
```

The base score is 5.5 for v3.1 (criticality "Medium") and 6.8 f or v4.0 (criticality "Medium"). This vulnerability is chosen as second example because it

- needs local access to be exploited,
- shows that AI can sophisticate attacks and therefore, should not always need to be deployed, and
- demonstrates that GOE can have values other than 0.

(1) Reconnaissance. To find suitable victims, an adversary needs to find enterprises which use these switches. The switch can be utilized to work as layer 2 (data link layer) or layer 3 (network layer) device. Hence, not all devices can be found via network exploration. Furthermore, network switches are not open to the internet. Thus, an adversary needs to have physical access or contacts within the victim organization to know if suitable devices are existent within. Acquiring the access or even at least the information is a highly individual process. To the best of our knowledge no tools can assist here. Training a model is insufficient too. Because the process is different each time, we cannot even say what kind of task the model should be trained on, and with what data, to help detect this CVE. We therefore give a reconnaissance score of 3. The GOE sub-vector looks as follows:

```
AT:H/TAI:H/G:H,
```

(2) Weaponization, (3) Delivery. Since the "weapon" in the vulnerability is the pre-installed software itself weaponization and delivery can be skipped.

(4) Exploitation. For the exploitation, an uncertain CLI but preinstalled command needs to be entered. The low attack complexity in the CVSS vectors indicate that it's not a sophisticated attack where timing or patterns needs to be known, even if it's only an assumption. Training an AI seems unreasonable here, therefore this step is also skipped. It would be more suited to use Robotic Process Automation to run the malicious command.

In conclusion, CVE-2024-30384 gets a GOE score of 3 with the following vector:

$$\text{GOE(CVE-2024-30384)} = \min\{3, \infty, \infty, \infty\} = 3$$

It is unlikely that AI is used in any form to assist in exploiting this CVE. In a hypothetical setting in which CVEs were assessed and prioritized only using GOE, this CVE could be ignored.

VII. Conclusion and Future Work

With GOE, an intuitive yet effective method is provided to assess the exposure of AI, based on the effort required for the attacker. GOE offers a flexible approach to quantify and provide a simplistic explanation of AI usage in vulnerability exploitation. After rating vulnerabilities by means of GOE, analysts and other stakeholders can prioritize which vulnerabilities should be assessed first. By combining GOE with well-known and established vulnerability assessment systems such as CVSS, a comprehensive analysis of vulnerabilities can be achieved and more detailed ratings can be done. The current GOE implementation consists of four possible rating values. Therefore, the likelihood is high, that several assessed vulnerabilities will have the same GOE score. By incorporating CVSS or similar systems, the ranking can be made more granular. However, further research is needed if GOE is supposed to get combined with CVSS in such a way that the modified version of CVSS is meant to produce a value between 0 (not critical) and 10 (highest criticality) just like in the default CVSS, but also considers exploitability through AI-driven methods. A discussion within the community is desirable to determine how much a low overall GOE score increases the underlying CVSS score.

The current version of GOE estimates the AI usage based on its effort, the effort is described as how difficult it is to use AI for the respective kill chain step.

The example scores of the last two sections demonstrate that using the GOE is straightforward. The most complex aspect of using it is the research required to assess the questions objectively. Its results further enable security researchers and analysts to strengthen their arguments about why a CVE is easily exploitable via OAI and help them stay updated on the OAI risks associated with a given CVE. Furthermore, it enhances their argumentation for prioritizing mitigating the risk of a vulnerability by means of quantification. By assessing the GOE analysts can get a rough estimation on how many tools, datasets or APIs for the exploitation of a CVE through OAI exist. Therefore, the GOE also quantifies the AI threat. In [5] mentioned that the quantification of the AI threat is missing in current research. However, it needs to be validated, if the GOEs approach of quantification resembles the reality. Field research needs to be done. To validate the GOEs quantification approach, real life vulnerability exploits through OAI have to be verified. Then, it needs to be validated if a higher amount of tools, datasets or APIs lead to a higher amount of CVE exploitation through OAI.

Another implication of our GOE is that it may be necessary to adapt the vulnerability assessment process. Future security analysts will need a broad understanding of AI and the data required to train AI models. However, current teams may lack it. Therefore, it should be investigated whether it is reasonable to augment current vulnerability assessment teams with AI experts who can provide this comprehensive knowledge and help in assessing the GOE.

To extend and conclude, recent research has increasingly focused on threat modeling for the security of deployed AI assets. This work aims to extend existing threat modeling systems by providing an addition that can be used in vulnerability assessments, specifically addressing the threat of OAI against potentially all assets within an organization —- an emerging research area still in its early stages. We hope that this work encourages further research in the field of threat modeling for OAI used to exploit vulnerabilities across all IT system assets.

References

[1] H. Chen and K. Magramo, "Finance worker pays out $25 million after video call with deepfake 'chief financial officer'," 2024, [Online]. Available: https://edition.cnn.com/2024/02/04/asia/deepfake-cfo-scam-hong-kong-intl-hnk/index.html (visited on 02/12/2025).

[2] S. L. Schröer *et al.*, "SoK: On the offensive potential of AI," *arXiv preprint arXiv:2412.18442*, 2024.

[3] S. Ntalampiras, G. Misuraca, and P. Rossel, *Artificial intelligence and cybersecurity research – ENISA research and innovation Brief*, C. Pascu and M. B. Lourenco, Eds. European Union Agency for Cybersecurity, 2023. DOI: 10.2824/808362.

[4] Y. Mirsky *et al.*, "The Threat of Offensive AI to Organizations," *Computers & Security*, vol. 124, p. 103 006, Jan. 2023, ISSN: 0167-4048. DOI: 10.1016/j.cose.2022.103006.

[5] M. Malatji and A. Tolah, "Artificial intelligence (ai) cybersecurity dimensions: A comprehensive framework for understanding adversarial and offensive ai," *AI and Ethics*, Feb. 2024, ISSN: 2730-5961. DOI: 10.1007/s43681-024-00427-4.

[6] K. Grosse, L. Bieringer, T. R. Besold, B. Biggio, and K. Krombholz, "Machine learning security in industry: A quantitative survey," *IEEE Transactions on Information Forensics and Security*, vol. 18, pp. 1749–1762, 2023.

[7] FIRST, *Common vulnerability scoring system version 4.0 specification document*, 1.2, Jun. 2024.

[8] M. Abughazalah, W. Alsaggaf, S. Saifuddin, and S. Sarhan, "Centralized vs. decentralized cloud computing in healthcare," *Applied Sciences*, vol. 14, no. 17, p. 7765, Sep. 2024, ISSN: 2076-3417. DOI: 10.3390/app14177765.

[9] M. Brundage *et al.*, "The malicious use of artificial intelligence: Forecasting, prevention, and mitigation," *arXiv preprint arXiv:1802.07228*, 2018.

[10] C. T. Thanh and I. Zelinka, "A survey on artificial intelligence in malware as next-generation threats," *MENDEL*, vol. 25, no. 2, pp. 27–34, Dec. 2019, ISSN: 1803-3814. DOI: 10.13164/mendel.2019.2.027.

[11] T. M. Corporation, "Mitre att&ck," 2025, [Online]. Available: https://attack.mitre.org/ (visited on 02/14/2025).

[12] B. Guembe *et al.*, "The emerging threat of ai-driven cyber attacks: A review," *Applied Artificial Intelligence*, vol. 36, no. 1, Mar. 2022, ISSN: 1087-6545. DOI: 10.1080/08839514.2022.2037254.

[13] L. Mauri and E. Damiani, "Modeling Threats to AI-ML Systems Using STRIDE," *Sensors*, vol. 22, no. 17, p. 6662, Sep. 2022, ISSN: 1424-8220. DOI: 10.3390/s22176662.

[14] S. B. Tete, "Threat modelling and risk analysis for large language model (llm)-powered applications," *arXiv preprint arXiv:2406.11007*, 2024.

[15] J. von der Assen *et al.*, "Asset-Centric Threat Modeling for AI-Based Systems," in *2024 IEEE International Conference on Cyber Security and Resilience (CSR)*, IEEE, Sep. 2024, pp. 437–444. DOI: 10.1109/CSR61664.2024.10679445.

[16] T. M. Corporation, "Mitre atlas (adversarial threat land- scape for artificial-intelligence systems)," 2025, [Online]. Available: https://atlas.mitre.org/ (visited on 02/14/2025).

[17] V. Kumar, J. Mayo, and K. Bahiss, "Admin: Attacks on dataset, model and input. a threat model for ai based software," *arXiv preprint arXiv:2401.07960*, 2024.

[18] E. M. Hutchins, M. J. Cloppert, R. M. Amin, *et al.*, "Intelligence-driven computer network defense informed by analysis of adversary campaigns and intrusion kill chains," *Leading Issues in Information Warfare & Security Research*, vol. 1, no. 1, p. 80, 2011.

[19] N. I. of Standards and Technology, "Cve-2025-1156 detail," 2025, [Online]. Available: https://nvd.nist.gov/vuln/detail/CVE-2025-1156 (visited on 08/18/2025).

[20] N. I. of Standards and Technology, "Cve-2024-30384 detail," 2024, [Online]. Available: https://nvd.nist.gov/vuln/detail/CVE-2024-30384 (visited on 08/18/2025).

[21] Juniper, "Ex4300 switches," 2025, [Online]. Available: https://www.juniper.net/us/en/products/switches/ex-series/ex4300-enterprise-switch.html (visited on 08/18/2025).

On the Necessity of Measuring Security in IoT

Tobias Eggendorfer
TH Ingolstadt
Faculty of Computer Science
Ingolstadt, Germany
Email: tobias.eggendorfer@thi.de

Katja Andresen
HWR Berlin
Department of Business and Economics
Berlin, Germany
Email: katja.andresen@hwr-berlin.de

Abstract—**While the Internet of things has become ubiquitous, it is mostly populated by former embedded devices, whose software was developed by specialists in the respective field. Hence, security researchers often find issues in those, which some consider to be low hanging fruits. Fixing security flaws in deployed embedded devices is sometimes very complex: In automotive or airborne systems, road- or airworthiness tests need to be passed, in these and e.g. medical devices or industrial Internet of things updates cannot interrupt operation. Therefore, in ideal world, Internet of things and embedded systems would be free from security issues. This could be reached with security metrics, a concept the authors are working on.**

Keywords-Internet of Things; IoT; Embedded Systems; Embedded Security; IoT Security; Security Metrics; Cyber Security; Industrial IoT; Legal Aspects

I. Introduction

In 2017, the United Stated Federal Drug Administration (FDA) recalled St. Jude's pacemakers due to a security issue [1], allowing potentially lethal remote tampering – an issue pre-seen by Holt and Holt's thriller "Flimmer" [2]. In Finland, attackers took down a building complex central heating unit, resulting in frozen pipes and massive restoration costs [3]. The industrial Internet of Things (IoT) controller *SIMATIC* by Siemens has 336 Common Vulnerabilities and Exposures (CVE) entries, 33 of these were issued in 2024 alone [4]. Attacking these might disrupt production processes and even challenge critical infrastructures. Cordless screwdrivers, ovens or coffee appliances may now be configured or used over the Internet, and thus have become a part of the Internet of things – as with the now legendary Miele dishwasher directory traversal [5]. Stealing cars is not short circuiting the ignition any more but gaining access to its Controller Area Network (CAN) bus and pretending by software the key was in the lock [6].

A. IoT and embedded security – Fixing issues

While software security issues are common nowadays, those in IoT and embedded systems are especially nasty: patching and updating the devices is often a tedious process. E.g., for a dash cam, firmware needs to be downloaded on the desktop, copied to a freshly formatted SD card, the dash cam rebooted and the card quick enough removed for the next reboot [7]. The complexity results from the device being offline or not providing an online-update feature.

For some IoT, updating is easier, because devices could download their update. However, there are two issues: On several occasions, updates broke the system, e.g., [8] [9]. Also, the update cannot be installed anytime, an example are cars on ferries updating their system without asking their user. With an update taking longer than the ferry trip, the car cannot be started again and thus blocks unloading the ferry [10]. This could happen to, e.g., a fire truck or an ambulance – those need to be available 24/7, at unpredictable times. Updates would need to be carefully planned with replacement vehicles being set up, as it is for regular maintenance. However, over the air software updates might occur more often, since from a manufacturers point of view, they are easily distributed. This puts an additional burden to an already very resource- and cost-intensive process, affecting update speed and thereby security.

Some devices need to run an approved version of their respective software, e.g., devices deployed in planes need an airworthiness approval, sometimes even by several agencies worldwide. In medical devices, similar rules exist. In neither case a mid air update is recommendable.

Some embedded devices are deployed without reasonable physical access, hindering updates, e.g., pacemakers and internal defibrillators. Some are hardly ever serviced, shifting the task of updating to its user, who is unaware of relevant security patches. In some cases, administrators might even be too careless to install security fixes: Both Hafnium and Heartbleed security issues were observed in the wild years after their respective discovery.

B. Lateral movement

In recent attacks, IoT served as the entry point to corporate networks, moving on from there is called lateral movement. There are reports on using a surveillance web cam [11] or the photovoltaic system's web-interface. In a home environment a smart TV could be the vantage point.

It is often suggested to separate networks, moving IoT devices outside the productive environment. This is only a partial solution, e.g., the Mirai bot net abused infected IoT devices for distributed Denial of Service (dDoS) [12].

C. Motivation for IoT and embedded security metrics

Therefore embedded and IoT-devices should be as secure as possible when deployed, thereby reducing the need for patches. But their manufacturers would always claim that security is of paramount importance to them and their devices underwent rigorous testing. Considering the vast amount of CVE numbers assigned to embedded and IoT-devices this is not plausible. While printers are neither embedded nor IoT, *Hewlett-Packard* provides a very good example for vendor security claims versus reality: On January 29, 2025 they released patches for a CVE issued in 2017 [13] – eight years later.

Due to the absence of security measures in IoT, there is an urgent need for a way to help identify and implement necessary security controls [14].

Search engines like shodan.io support this need. They help identifying IoT-devices and searching for specific devices, software versions or configurations with vulnerabilities.

The authors proposed a security metric [15] to identify a systems level of security as well as to be able to compare devices in order to make an informed procurement decission. This paper discusses how this metric could be applied to IoT and embedded devices in order to increase their security.

D. Structure of this paper

The paper is structured as follows: Section II first defines the concept of embedded systems, IoT and Industrial IoT (IIoT) for the purpose of this paper. It then outlines common security challenges in regular software, how and when they affect IoT systems and how to mitigate them. Based on this, this section provides an overview on software quality management with a focus on security and security metrics outside IoT.

Section III analyses how security metrics could be applied to IoT. Based on this, legal enforcment of the use of security metrics and its potential effects is discussed in Section IV. The last Section V provides a conclusion and gives an outlook on future research.

II. BACKGROUND

The following section provides definitions and an overview on Information Technology (IT), IT-security, security issues and their respective origin as well as counter measures.

A. Embedded Devices, IoT, firm- and software

For this paper, an embedded device is defined as a computer with a specific purpose that is usually integrated into a cyber physical system, interacting with sensors, actors and / or has a specific user interface, but usually not a full keyboard or screen. Their software is optimized for the use case and not meant to be changed by the user, e.g., dashcams, defibrillators, smart TVs, heating controllers or smart locks, but also engine control systems or a lane assistants in cars.

An IoT device is an embedded system connected to the Internet and could either be configured, monitored or controlled remotely. IIoT is IoT monitoring and / or controlling industrial system, such as assembly lines or automated warehouses.

For this paper, software and firmware are considered to be equivalent: While firmware is usually provided "on a chip", which might even be a Read-Only Memory (ROM) module, and comes with a device, from a security perspective it is still a program. With the line between embedded systems and regular computers becoming less clear – a Raspberry Pi could be both – the borderline between soft- and firmware also moves. It becomes relevant, when it comes to potential cyber-physical effects of IoT.

B. IT security in general

Often social engineering (SE) and ransomware are seen as the biggest threads to IT security. From an operational perspective, this explains how the attack has been executed [16] and describes its effects. But technically, each SE attack is a security issue, be it bypassing the need to know or least privileges principle, a flaw in the system, which allowing to inject and execute arbitrary code, or other imperfections. Hence, while SE was supportive, the relevant issue was a faulty system.

For the effect, it is not relevant how the attacker exploits the newly gained access, e.g., to deploy ransomware or part taking in industrial espionage. However, the effects are relevant from an economic and political perspective, as well as for attribution and legal measures; however, this falls outside the technical scope. There, it is only a payload to the actual attack.

The difference between payload, the actual attack, e.g., a buffer overflow or format string issue, and the attack vector, describing how the attack was launched, e.g., through Remote Procedure Call (RPC) or SE, is important: Security measures addressing only the attack vector, e.g., by educating users to prevent SE, do not fix the underlying security flaw. It could still be leveraged through other means.

Security measures could mitigate some attack's effects, e.g., off site backups to prevent ransomware. This reduces the risk, because the damage is lowered. However, the underlying security issue remains unsolved and could still be exploited for activities such as espionage. Hence, the best solution is to fix the cause, the security issue itself, since this is effective for all attack vectors and effects. Only addressing some of them is sometimes called "snake oil" or "security theatre" in the security community, due to their limited effect [17] [18].

C. Typical security issues in IoT and embedded devices

In IoT and embedded devices, there is a huge variety of tasks to perform. While in a Tesla, the systems provide X for the user interface [19] [20], in implanted pace makers a touch screen is not feasible, instead a Bluetooth Low Energy (BLE)-interface could be provided – these having their own security issues, e.g., [21]. Industrial IoT systems often use proprietary protocols to interface with control units, e.g., Supervisory Control and Data Acquisition (SCADA), others have built in web-interfaces, such as the aforementioned dishwasher.

Based on the huge variety of IoT and embedded systems, all security issues in both compiled software as well as those in web applications could occur. For the latter, Open Web Application Security Project (OWASP) provides an overview of potential issues. A regularly updated top ten list indicates the most prevalent, ranging from Cross Site Scripting (XSS) to Lightweight Directory Access Protocol (LDAP)- and Structured Query Language (SQL)-injections, but also including issues like insecure deserialisation of a data stream or authentication bypass [22]. While the list is updated every few years, the issues typically shift positions within the top ten, but rarely disappear entirerly – nor do new issues come up. While at the time of writing, the OWASP Top Ten 2025 list was not yet available, a comparison of the lists from 2017 to

2021 reveals that only three new issues appeared in the top ten. Out of those three that seem to have disappeared, four were merged into two new categories and are still in the top ten, these are: A01:2017 "Injection" and A07:2017 "XSS" merged into A03:2021 "Injection", A04:2017 "XML External Entities" and A06:2017 "Security Misconfiguration" became A05:2021 "Security misconfiguration" [22]. This indicates bad security practice and a non existent web-security learning curve, applicable as well to IoT-web-interfaces.

In regular programs, security issues could be related to memory access, such as with a buffer overflow, out of bounds read or write, format string issue or off by one. These usually result in a program flow alteration or even code injection. Other issues include integer overflows, which might result in a system with an unstable state [23] or as a vantage point for other attacks, such as a buffer overflow [24]. All of which are applicable to IoT as well. Other issues are resemble web attacks, such as an under protected Application Programming Interface (API) or insecure authentication.

These issues either result from insecure programming practice or design flaws. Examples for the former include using `strcpy` instead of `strncpy`. While `strcpy` does not limit its copying to a maximum amount of bytes, `strncpy` does. This prevents – if no other flaws are present, such as integer overflows or off by ones – some buffer overflows, and was introduced in ANSI C in 1989 [25], long after buffer overflows were first described in 1972 [26]. In 1996, the Phrack Magazine in the famous article "Smashing the Stack for Fun and Profit" [27] explained the security issue due to its prevalence in these days. Still now, buffer overflows are of the most often abused security issue. Good programming practice would enforce the use of safer functions. Again an indication of a very slow learning curve, albeit automatic code analysis tools are able to warn [28]. Which points to them not being (properly [29]) used too often.

Design flaws are harder to identify and come by. Whether one considers Central Processing Unit (CPU) microcode software or hardware, both Spectre and Meltdown [30]–[32] are good examples of design issues: They are a result of pipelining in modern CPU architecture. Heartbleed provides an example of a software security issue due to a design flaw: By providing redundant data and not comparing two values, an out of bounds read could be triggered [33], another example "ZUGFeRD", a concept for eXtensible Markup Language (XML) and Portable Document Format (PDF) based e-invoices posing a security risk through redundant, not cross checked data [34] [35]. These logical issues are much harder to automatically detect, and are found in IoT as well.

D. Prevention of security issues

In theory preventing security issues based on bad programming style is well known [15] [36] [37] and easily achieved with static code analysis [28], code reviews, peer programming and other simple quality checking measures.

Identifying design flaws is possible through code reviews and peer programming, however this requires a qualified team. If this was easy, faulty standards such as introducing heartbeat functionality in TLS leading to the aforementioned Heartbleed issue, or the ZUGFeRD issues would not have happened.

E. Relation between software quality management and security

All measures undertaken to increase software quality, such as coding standards, static and dynamic code analysis, code reviews and peer programming have an effect on the amount of security relevant issues in a program. OpenBSD is an example: Due to its quality management, the system only had two remote exploitable security issues in its standard installation "in a heck of a long time" [38], i.e., 30 years.

Quality management will find security issues related to bad programming and some logic flaws. At the same time, it will increase the quality of the code created, since programmers know their code will be reviewed, they will obey the coding standards. If these include safe programming practices, they have an effect on security as well.

F. Measuring software quality

Software quality in general is a broad term, providing many perspectives. ISO 25010 provides eight quality dimensions for software, starting from functionality via portability or usability, but also security. However, in this regard security is restricted to functionality. To the authors, software quality serves as a proxy for security: Quality means the absence of flaws, each flaw could result in a security issue [15] [37].

1) Standards: Standards like the ISO 27000 series only provide a management perspective, but offer little in terms of an operational approach to achieve a high level of software quality, and they cannot measure the quality of the code. To some extent, this aligns with how software quality measurement is discussed in research: So far "software quality" itself lacks a common understanding [15].

2) Formal Verification: Other concepts include more formal specification of software and deriving from this specification a verification. One example are Hoare logics [39]. However for most projects this manual process is cumbersome and very intense. There it is probably only used in environments with high quality and especially safety requirements, such as in space missions. But even then, if the conditions are not updated properly to reflect changes elsewhere, issues could still occur, e.g., the Ariane 5 [23]. In IoT, especially when it comes to high cyber-physical risks, projects like seL4 provide formally verified code [40]–[42].

3) Current concepts: Closer to the market are concepts such as the German's German Federal Office for Information Security (BSI) providing a "software quality seal" based on self assessment of the vendor and easily measurable items such as the time needed to fix issues [43]. The speed of fixing may indicate a learning curve, but is not inherently a quality measure for the software itself. Rather, it serves as an indicator how effective a vendor is in accepting, understanding and resolving reports. This is useful to understand how interested they are in preventing future attacks, it is a measure of the quality of maintenance. But it does not give any indication on whether the bug could have been identified earlier in the development process, which is where software quality stems from. This "software quality seal" is therefore hardly an indication of what it claims to be.

4) Bill of Materials: Another approach to quality is to identify which third party libraries and software is used within a project, including the respective version. If an update becomes available for one of these, it should be easily possible to identify whether it needs to be installed. This idea has been adopted by European Union (EU) Cyber-Resilliance-Act (CRA) by introducing the Software Bill of Materials (SBoM). However a SBoM does not provide a quality measurement in itself and there is no clear path to derive a quality measure from it: Does a short SBoM indicate a higher level or lower level of quality? There are pros and cons for either way. Aside of this, an SBoM is useful in identifying relevant patches. As per [44] IoT projects use less dependencies.

5) Static measures: Khezemi et al. [36] suggest to measure code quality based on statically comparing code by looking at size, code complexity, cohesion, coupling, code readability, and maintainability. These measures have a different understanding of quality than this paper has, in that it does not address security measures.

6) Conclusion: Quality aspects of embedded systems and IoT should address both, hardware as well as software components [45].

G. Measuring software security

Eggendorfer and Andresen [15] provide a detailed overview on currently available methods to measure software security and concludes that there is no commonly accepted method. This applies even more for IoT. However, to achieve a high level of security that is comparable, it is important to capture aspects beyond already existing standards or initiatives related to software quality.

Other initiatives invest in preventive measure, like educating software developers in order to support secure software development [38] [46] [47]. To assess software a broadly understood security metric would offer orientation and guidance. For web applications [48] developed a concept, which however has some minor flaws [15].

Reckhaus [49] compares the invest into IT security to insurance fees to identify an economic value, i.e., metric, for security investments. While this does not assess the security as a quality measure, it helps evaluating security concepts from a economic perspective.

Wuttig [50] analyses IT security in medical IoT devices, albeit without applying a formal metric. His analysis however gives a good impression of minimum requirements that should be included in a formal security test, that could be part of a security metric. A security issue in patient monitors is an example of the relevance [51].

III. Application to embedded and IoT

IoT and embedded systems have different security implications and requirements than desktop software. The following section discusses effects of different development approaches and how this would affect the respective software quality.

A. Differences in software development

Software development for IoT and embedded systems is different to developing other programmes. Embedded systems are designed for special tasks. For that, embedded systems, e.g., laundromats, cameras, smart home equipment, use firmware (software) that directly accesses the hardware of the device to carry out the intended function. Hence, they do not follow the „one fits all“ architecture as the John-von-Neumann approach.

Typical characteristics of these systems have effects on quality, as well as security: Many embedded systems need to process data in real time, i.e., they have an upper limit for computing time. Obvious examples include the Antilock Braking System (ABS) and airbag deployment in cars.

These systems are usually designed for a reliable long term usage – meaning limited maintenance opportunities as well as corrective updates by default.

As they run on special microprocessors and microcontrollers embedded systems use limited resources as computing power and memory – compared with traditional computers. The specific, often restricted hardware might also have an effect on code optimization.

B. Related Work

Corno et al. [44] discuss this in detail for Open Source software, based on an analysis of source code of 30 IoT and 30 non-IoT projects published on github. This is partly because IoT projects are more complex, in that applications need to be fault tolerant, often need to use sensor data, tend to be part of distributed system and require specific domain knowledge [44] [52]–[54]. Also programming languages vary greatly, with memory safe programming languages such as JavaScript being more often used in non-IoT projects, in 18 vs. 4 projects in [44].

Code quality between IoT and non-IoT applications differs massively, software for IoT was "more complex, coupled, larger, less maintainable, and cohesive than non-IoT systems" [36] [55]. This results in some authors suggesting different development processes for IoT [56]–[58].

The unique requirements, specific and open architecture has drawn attention of both malicious attackers and security analysts.

C. Quality assurance

Motoga et al. [59] come to the conclusion that a "diversity of methods" is needed to assure the quality of IoT systems during the development phase. With regard to the lifecycle, "maintainability" is a key goal for the deployment of embedded systems [59], however there is a potential trade off between quality attributes such as security, safety and maintainability [59]. *Müller* [60] also argues that secure IoT development requires its own development process.

Quite interestingly, European Telecommunications Standards Institute (ETSI) issued the standard ETSI EN 303 645 "Cyber

Security for Consumer Internet of Things: Baseline Requirements" representing a collection of rather simple minimum requirements for secure consumer IoT in order to support manufactures to establish security by design. Considering that ETSI is less of an IT but more a telecommunication standardisation body, providing mobile phone network standards such as GSM, EDGE, 3G, 4G and 5G, its IT-security recommendations are not always up to date, ETSI TS 103 523-3 V1.2.1 "CYBER; Middlebox Security Protocol; Part 3: Enterprise Transport Security" even received a CVE number before publication [61]. Not only the authors consider ETSI EN 303 645 problematic, *Morgenstern at al* [62] state the implementation of the standard lacks completeness leading to security risks. Despite this, based on ETSI EN 303 645, the German BSI provides a quality seal for IoT devices, based on voluntary participation [63] [64].

If IoT uses encryption, updating algorithms used for encryption, signing or even hash functions might not be straight forward, since data stored on the device would need to re-encrypted, increasing the complexity of the process. Also interoperability issues with not yet updated systems may occur, if for security aspects downward compatibility has not been implemented.

IV. SUGGESTED LEGISLATIVE SUPPORT

When it comes to security of embedded systems and IoT, at first, security seems to be one attribute among others. However, security is of high importance due to the massive effects of security incidents, the risks of lateral movement of attackers, the abuse of bot nets built upon infected IoT devices and the dangers of cyber-physical effects. Considering this, legislators might support better security by passing more stringent laws, such as the EU did with Directive 2016/1148 of the European parliament and of the council of 6 July 2016 concerning measures for a high common level of security of network and information systems across the Union (NIS)-2 and CRA recently. These, however, would only become efficient if they required measurable IT security, i.e., an objective and neutral way to assess security.

A. The need of a security metric in a legal context

There is a need for objective and measurable security in a legal context, as a real example demonstrates: With an increasing amount of fraudulently manipulated invoices, where attackers swap the recipients bank account against their own, the Higher Regional Court (Oberlandesgericht (OLG)) in Karlsruhe ruled, that sending the invoice encrypted was not a requirement [65], while the OLG Schleswig-Holstein decided encryption is needed [35]. Both based their decision on the same article of the General Data Protection Regulation (GDPR). As a result, in one case, the invoiced party needed to pay again, in the other case not.

The two courts disagreed on two main issues, one was the applicability of the GDPR to a juridical person (Karlsruhe) versus a natural person (Schleswig-Holstein), which could be disputed, and the other on a technical question. According to the respective rulings neither court heard an expert witness on the matter. Both assumed in their own expertise, encryption was efficient to protect integrity, where a digital signature would actually be needed [34] [35] [65]. Karlsruhe found that encryption is not required based on "real world expectations", Schleswig-Holstein considered it as a requirement.

The decision by the OLG Schleswig-Holstein is currently being discussed mainly in the legal community for it basically enforcing email encryption. Some see it as being disruptive and too strict [66]–[68], while others point to a decade of advocacy towards email encryption [35] [65] [69].

The different rulings are a result of allowing room for interpretation of technical requirements by non technical legislators and a non technical judicative. Objectively measured security by contrast allows for consistent court rulings and also consistent expert hearings. Only with a reliable metric, legal concepts such as GDPR have an effect.

B. Economic impact

Procurement decisions should also be made based on a security metric [15]. By providing a legal requirement, it could easier be incorporated in the buying decision, and thereby enhance cyber resilience [15].

C. Labelling

In other domains like electronic devices or textiles labels, batches and seals are accepted and mandatory. For instance the Conformité Européenne (CE) label for electronic goods guarantees that minimum requirements for safety, health and environment have been addressed and fulfilled, albeit the CE label is based on a self assessment [70].

Self assessment has already proven problematic in IT in general, as most software manufactures declare their products to be of high quality, free of security and other flaws, which hardly ever meets reality. Also with the CE-label, these issues occur. If, however, the self assessment is based on a comparable, standardised metric, "fake" assessments could be identified. Still, a legal framework to prevent the abuse of labels – potentially more strict than the one used for CE-labels [71] – is needed.

D. Mandatory Testing

For products that society and lawmakers consider to carry a higher risk, mandatory tests and specific requirements are set up. Examples include cars, aircrafts or medical devices. In special cases regular re-assessments are a legal requirement as well, e.g., the yearly or bi-annual roadworthiness checks for cars or permanent side effect reporting in medicine. In all these cases, security and safety are a requirement, security issues are (almost) unacceptable. The GDPR introduced security requirements – at least in theory: Some consider penetration tests a GDPR requirement [72], however, reality does not agree.

Therefore a security metric would allow efficient, comparable and reliable security comparisons. It would allow any user to make a decision between a more or less secure device apart from other features. With more and more IoT devices connected, chances increase for exploited vulnerabilities.

E. Life cycle

Quality and security management need to addressed throughout the life cycle of an IoT project. Before allowing a product on the marketing, a formal check such as a roadworthiness checks in cars. Therefore a security metric serves as a foundation to measure criteria or attributes (to define) that need to be passed.

Other than with roadworthiness checks, with IoT not the individual device needs to be reevaluated, but only one exemplary device, as other than with cars mechanical wear and tear is not the primary issue. While reevaluation of all IoT devices would be advisable to prevent risks like lateral movement, in a first step it seems to be most important to both apply regular reevaluation to devices with cyber-physical effects as well as to devices used in critical infrastructure.

V. CONCLUSSION AND FUTURE WORK

Security issues are the downside of a technology that surrounds us. This article has shown that embedded systems require special attention to run reliable and secure in an interconnected world. The design and creation of IoT services as well as maintenance tasks along the usage phase appears to be of high complexity.

The authors propose the usage of a metric to measure a software security index that supports the judgement of feasibility for applications in a given context. The metric is therefore addressing the "static" software system with regard to the technical aspects but also considering dynamic aspects. The latter could be part of a penetration test scenario. A metric would allow a judgment in terms of security in IoT environments. Above, a regular validation could be part of a "ready for market" concept. IoT manufacturers would probably have an interest in a better rating leading to quality improvement of the software system.

REFERENCES

[1] ZDNet. (2017) FDA issues recall of 465,000 St. Jude pacemakers to patch security holes. Accessed 2025.03.09. Online: https://www.zdnet.com/article/fda-forces-st-jude-pacemaker-recall-to-patch-security-vulnerabilities/

[2] A. Holt and E. Holt, *Flimmer*. Piratforlaget, 2010.

[3] M. Komar. (2016) DDoS attack takes down central heating system amidst winter in finland. Accessed 2025.03.09. Online: https://thehackernews.com/2016/11/heating-system-hacked.html

[4] cve.org. (2025) CVE.org search for SIMATIC. Accessed 2025.03.09. Online: https://www.cve.org/CVERecord/SearchResults?query=SIMATIC

[5] ——. (2017) Cve-2017-7240. Accessed 2025.03.09. Online: https://nvd.nist.gov/vuln/detail/CVE-2017-7240

[6] K. Tindell. (2023) CAN injection: keyless car theft. Accessed 2025.03.09. Online: https://kentindell.github.io/2023/04/03/can-injection/

[7] AZDOME. (2021) Method of updating the latest firmware. Accessed 2025.03.09. Online: http://forum.azdome.hk/forum.php?mod=viewthread&tid=930&highlight=M300S

[8] S. Harding. (2025) Firmware update bricks HP printers, makes them unable to use HP cartridges. Accessed 2025.03.11. Online: https://arstechnica.com/gadgets/2025/03/firmware-update-bricks-hp-printers-makes-them-unable-to-use-hp-cartridges/

[9] F. Deusch and T. Eggendorfer, "Zur Kompatibilität beim Updating verbundener Systeme (translated: On compatibility when updating interdependant systems)," *K&R*, vol. 2018, no. 7, pp. 456–464, 2018.

[10] M. Zysset. (2025) Wenn das Software-Update beim Auto für Stau sorgt (translated: If the car software update causes a traffic jam). Accessed 2025.03.09. Online: https://www.tagesanzeiger.ch/bls-autoverlad-wenn-das-software-update-fuer-stau-sorgt-135808833029

[11] G. Hull, C. Trivella, and J. Seland. (2025) Camera off: Akira deploys ransomware via webcam. Accessed 2025.03.11. Online: https://www.s-rminform.com/latest-thinking/camera-off-akira-deploys-ransomware-via-webcam

[12] CISA. (2017) Heightened DDoS threat posed by Mirai and other botnets. Accessed 2025.03.09. Online: https://www.cisa.gov/news-events/alerts/2016/10/14/heightened-ddos-threat-posed-mirai-and-other-botnets

[13] Hewlett-Packard. (2025) HP Universal print driver series (PCL 6 and PostScript) - potential security vulnerabilities. Accessed 2025.03.09. Online: https://support.hp.com/us-en/document/ish_11892982-11893015-16/hpsbpi03995

[14] K. Pawar, C. Ambhika, and C. Murukesh, "IoT hacking: Cyber security point of view," *Asian Journal of Basic Science & Research*, 2021. Online: https://api.semanticscholar.org/CorpusID:235194057

[15] T. Eggendorfer and K. Andresen, "Using security metrics to improve cyber-resilience," in *Proceedings of the IARIA Congress 2024*. Porto, Portugal: IARIA, 2024, pp. 152–157. Online: https://www.thinkmind.org/library/IARIA_CONGRESS/IARIA_Congress_2024/iaria_congress_2024_2_210_50107.html

[16] P. Hengge, *Development of a Rule Set for the Defence Against Cyber Attacks by Analysing and Evaluating Attack Vectors in IT Systems*. Hagen: Masterthesis, FernUniversität in Hagen, 02 2025.

[17] B. Schneier. (2025) Entries tagged security theatre. Accessed 2025.03.09. Online: https://www.schneier.com/tag/security-theater/

[18] P. R. Zimmermann. (1991) Beware of snake oil. Accessed 2025.03.09. Online: http://www.philzimmermann.com/EN/essays/SnakeOil.html

[19] J. Michal, *Tesla Model 3 Control Units Security Analysis*. Prag: Masterthesis, CTU Prag, 01 2021.

[20] DragTimes. (2014) Tesla model s ethernet network explored, possible jailbreak in the future? Accessed 2025.03.09. Online: http://www.dragtimes.com/blog/tesla-model-s-ethernet-network-explored-possible-jailbreak-in-the-future

[21] J. Leyden. (2017) Dildon'ts of bluetooth: Pen test boffins sniff out berlin's smart butt plugs. Accessed 2025.03.09. Online: https://www.theregister.com/2017/09/29/ble_exploits_screwdriving/

[22] OWASP. (2021) OWASP top ten. Accessed 2025.03.09. Online: https://owasp.org/Top10/

[23] J.-L. Lions. (1996) Flight 501 failure. Accessed 2025.03.09. Online: http://sunnyday.mit.edu/accidents/Ariane5accidentreport.html

[24] J. Drake. (2015) Stagefright: Scary code in the heart of Android. Zimperium. Accessed 2025.03.09. Online: https://www.blackhat.com/docs/us-15/materials/us-15-Drake-Stagefright-Scary-Code-In-The-Heart-Of-Android.pdf

[25] ISO. (1989) Iso/iec 9899:tc3. Accessed 2025.03.09. Online: https://www.open-std.org/jtc1/sc22/wg14/www/docs/n1256.pdf

[26] J. P. Anderson. (1972) Computer security technology planning study, volume ii. Accessed 2025.03.09. Online: https://csrc.nist.gov/csrc/media/publications/conference-paper/1998/10/08/proceedings-of-the-21st-nissc-1998/documents/early-cs-papers/ande72.pdf

[27] A. One. (1996) Smashing the stack for fun and profit. Accessed 2025.03.09. Online: https://phrack.org/issues/49/1

[28] T. Eggendorfer, "At the source. static code analysis finds avoidable errors," *Admin Magazine*, vol. 2019, no. 53, 2019. Online: https://www.admin-magazine.com/Archive/2019/53/Static-code-analysis-finds-avoidable-errors

[29] A. Lentz and T. Eggendorfer, "Snakes in the grass," in *NLUUG najaarsconferentie 2024*. Utrecht, Netherlands: NLUUG, 2024.

[30] J. Horn *et al.* (2018) Spectre and meltdown. Accessed 2025.03.09. Online: https://spectreattack.com/

[31] M. Lipp *et al.*, "Meltdown: Reading kernel memory from user space," in *27th USENIX Security Symposium (USENIX Security 18)*, 2018.

[32] P. Kocher *et al.*, "Spectre attacks: Exploiting speculative execution," in *40th IEEE Symposium on Security and Privacy (S&P'19)*, 2019.

[33] Synopsis. (2020) Heartbleed. Accessed 2025.03.09. Online: https://heartbleed.com/

[34] T. Eggendorfer, "Schwer verrechnet (translated: Bad computation)," *Linux Magazin*, vol. 2025, no. 04, pp. 50–53, 2025.

[35] F. Deusch and T. Eggendorfer, "E-Rechnung: Verschlüsseln oder Signieren? (translated: E-invoice: Encrypt or sign?)," *K&R*, vol. 2025, no. 4, 4 2025.

[36] N. Khezemi, S. Ejaz, N. Moha, and Y.-G. Guéhéneuc, "Comparison of code quality and best practices in IoT and non-IoT software," *ArXiv*, vol. abs/2408.02614, 2024. Online: https://api.semanticscholar.org/CorpusID:271709982

[37] D. Mathes, *Qualitätsmetriken für Schutzkonzepte (translated: Quality metrics for security concepts)*. Hagen: Masterthesis, FernUniversität in Hagen, 12 2015.

[38] OpenBSD. OpenBSD security. Online: http://www.openbsd.org/security.html

[39] C. A. R. Hoare, "An axiomatic basis for computer programming," *Commun. ACM*, vol. 12, no. 10, p. 576–580, oct 1969. Online: https://doi.org/10.1145/363235.363259

[40] G. Klein *et al.*, "sel4: formal verification of an operating-system kernel," *Commun. ACM*, vol. 53, no. 6, p. 107–115, Jun. 2010. Online: https://doi.org/10.1145/1743546.1743574

[41] D. B. de Oliveira, T. Cucinotta, and R. S. de Oliveira, "Efficient formal verification for the linux kernel," in *Software Engineering and Formal Methods*, Peter Csaba Ölveczky and G. Salaün, Eds. Cham: Springer International Publishing, 2019, pp. 315–332.

[42] SEL4project. (2025) seL4. Accessed 2025.03.09. Online: https://sel4.systems/

[43] F. Deusch and T. Eggendorfer, "Messbarkeit von IT-Sicherheit (translated: Measuring it-security)," *K&R*, vol. 2023, no. 12, pp. 781–786, 12 2023.

[44] F. Corno, L. D. Russis, and J. P. Sáenz, "How is open source software development different in popular IoT projects?" *IEEE Access*, vol. 8, pp. 28 337–28 348, 2020. Online: https://api.semanticscholar.org/CorpusID:211227160

[45] M. Loghi, T. Margaria, G. Pravadelli, and B. Steffen, "Dynamic and formal verification of embedded systems: A comparative survey," *International Journal of Parallel Programming*, vol. 33, pp. 585–611, 2005. Online: https://api.semanticscholar.org/CorpusID:22718479

[46] T. Kölnberger, *Evaluation of effects of security metrics in the software development life cycle*. Hagen: Masterthesis, FernUniversität in Hagen, April 2025.

[47] OWASP. SAMM model overview. OWASP. Online: https://owaspsamm.org/model/

[48] C. Binder, *Entwurf einer Metrik zur Bewertung des IT-Sicherheitsniveaus am Beispiel von Webanwendungen (translated: Design of a metric to measure the IT security level of web applications)*. Hagen: Masterthesis, FernUniversität in Hagen, February 2024.

[49] S. Reckhaus, *IT-Sicherheit und Kosten-Nutzen Analyse von Cyber-Versicherungen (Translated: IT-security and cost-effect analysis of cyber insurance)*. Hagen: Masterthesis, FernUniversität in Hagen, 02 2016.

[50] D. Wuttig, *IT-Sicherheitsprüfung im Internet of Medical Things (Translated: IT-security testing in the Internet of Medical Things)*. Hagen: Masterthesis, FernUniversität in Hagen, 08 2022.

[51] CISA. (2025) Contec Health CMS8000 patient monitor (Update A). Accessed 2025.03.09. Online: https://www.cisa.gov/news-events/ics-medical-advisories/icsma-25-030-01

[52] A. Taivalsaari and T. Mikkonen, "A roadmap to the programmable world: Software challenges in the IoT era," *IEEE Software*, vol. 34, pp. 72–80, 2017. Online: https://api.semanticscholar.org/CorpusID:6751128

[53] ——, "On the development of IoT systems," *2018 Third International Conference on Fog and Mobile Edge Computing (FMEC)*, pp. 13–19, 2018. Online: https://api.semanticscholar.org/CorpusID:44147446

[54] N. Alhirabi, O. F. Rana, and C. Perera, "Security and Privacy Requirements for the Internet of Things," *ACM Transactions on Internet of Things*, vol. 2, pp. 1 – 37, 2021. Online: https://api.semanticscholar.org/CorpusID:231730970

[55] M. Klíma *et al.*, "Selected code-quality characteristics and metrics for Internet of Things systems," *IEEE Access*, vol. PP, pp. 1–1, 2022. Online: https://api.semanticscholar.org/CorpusID:248517759

[56] S. S. Ismail and D. W. Dawoud, "Software development models for IoT," *2022 IEEE 12th Annual Computing and Communication Workshop and Conference (CCWC)*, pp. 0524–0530, 2022. Online: https://api.semanticscholar.org/CorpusID:247230583

[57] J. P. Dias and H. S. Ferreira, "State of the software development life-cycle for the Internet-of-Things," *ArXiv*, vol. abs/1811.04159, 2018. Online: https://api.semanticscholar.org/CorpusID:53282492

[58] X. Larrucea, A. Combelles, J. Favaro, and K. Taneja, "Software engineering for the Internet of Things," *IEEE Software*, vol. 34, no. 1, pp. 24–28, Jan 2017.

[59] S. Motogna, A. Vescan, and C. Şerban, "Empirical investigation in embedded systems: Quality attributes in general, maintainability in particular," *J. Syst. Softw.*, vol. 201, no. C, Jul. 2023. Online: https://doi.org/10.1016/j.jss.2023.111678

[60] M.-C. Müller, *Konzeption eines ganzheitlichen, die IT- und funktionale Sicherheit unter berücksichtigenden IoT-Entwicklungsansatzes (Translated: Concept for a holistic IoT development approach including IT and functional security)*. Hagen: Masterthesis, FernUniversität in Hagen, 06 2018.

[61] CVE.org. (2019) Cve-2019-9191. Accessed 2025.03.09. Online: https://www.cve.org/CVERecord?id=CVE-2019-9191

[62] M. Morgenstern, O. Pursche, and E. Clausing, "Die Sicherheitslage im IoT-Umfeld: Steigende Gefahrenlage und Sicherheit durch Tests (translated: The state of security in IoT: Increased risks and security by testing," *Datenschutz und Datensicherheit - DuD*, vol. 45, pp. 102–106, 02 2021.

[63] BSI. (2022) Consumer IoT. Accessed 2025.03.09. Online: https://www.bsi.bund.de/DE/Themen/Unternehmen-und-Organisationen/Standards-und-Zertifizierung/Consumer-IoT/Consumer-IoT.html

[64] F. Deusch and T. Eggendorfer, "Update IT-Sicherheitsrecht 2021/2022 (translated: Update IT-security-law 2021/2022)," *K&R*, vol. 2022, no. 12, pp. 794–803, 2022.

[65] ——, "Update IT-Sicherheitsrecht 2022/2023 – Teil 2 (translated: Update IT-security-law 2022/2023 part 2)," *K&R*, vol. 2024, no. 4, pp. 242–248, 4 2024.

[66] R. Petrlic. (2025) Remarks on the OLG Schleswig-Decission (Annoucement). Accessed 2025.03.09. Online: https://www.linkedin.com/posts/petrlic_datenschutz-dsgvo-cybersicherheit-activity-7294652352156897280-QMjx/

[67] R. Petrlic and J. Zwerschke, "OLG Schleswig: Ende-zu-Ende-Verschlüsselung ist nach der DSGVO im Geschäftsverkehr regelmäßig erforderlich (translated: OLG Schleswig: End-to-end encryption is a requirement in business communications according to gdpr)."

[68] N. Härting. (2025) Gefährdungshaftung aus Art. 32 DSGVO – OLG Schleswig verirrt sich in die DSGVO und bezeichnet Papier als "Mittel der Wahl" (translated: Liability based on Art. 32 GDPR - OLG Schleswig getting lost in the GDPR and suggesting paper as means of choice). Accessed 2025.03.09. Online: https://www.pingdigital.de/blog/2025/03/03/gefaehrdungshaftung-aus-art-32-dsgvo-olg-schleswig-verirrt-sich-in-die-dsgvo-und-bezeichnet-papier-als-mittel-der-wahl/2528

[69] F. Deusch and T. Eggendorfer, "Verschlüsselte Kommunikation im Unternehmensalltag: Nicetohave oder notwendige Compliance? (translated: Encrypted communications in day-to-day business: Nice-to-have or required compliance)," *K&R*, vol. 2018, no. 04, pp. 223–230, 04 2018.

[70] EU. (1993) Council Directive 93/68/EEC of 22 July 1993. Accessed 2025.03.09. Online: https://eur-lex.europa.eu/legal-content/EN/TXT/HTML/?uri=CELEX:01993L0068-19980812

[71] F. Gronkvis. (2023) What is fake CE marking? Accessed 2025.03.09. Online: https://www.compliancegate.com/fake-ce-marking/

[72] F. Deusch and T. Eggendorfer, "Penetrationstest bei Auftragsverarbeitung (translated: Penetration test with processors)," *K&R*, vol. 2018, no. 04, pp. 223–230, 04 2018.

ACKNOWLEDGEMENTS

The authors like to thank the reviewers for their valuable and useful comments that were helpful in improving and clarifying the paper.

A Forensic Analysis of GNSS Spoofing Attacks on Autonomous Vehicles

Tobias Reichel*, Mathias Gerstner†, Leo Schiller†, Andreas Attenberger*, Rudolf Hackenberg†, Klara Dološ *
*Central Office for Information Technology in the Security Sector
Munich, Germany
e-mail: {tobias.reichel, | andreas.attenberger, | klara.dolos}@zitis.bund.de
†Dept. Informatics and Mathematics, OTH Regensburg
Regensburg, Germany
e-mail: {mathias.gerstner, | leo.schiller, | rudolf.hackenberg}@oth-regensburg.de

***Abstract*—Global Navigation Satellite Systems (GNSSs) are essential for modern technology, enabling precise geographic positioning in aviation, maritime shipping, and automotive systems. In the future, their role will be even more critical for autonomous vehicles, which rely on accurate localization for navigation and decision-making. However, the increasing connectivity of autonomous vehicles exposes them to cyber threats, including GNSS spoofing attacks, which manipulate location data to mislead onboard systems. As reliance on GNSS grows, so does the risk posed by spoofing attacks, making it a critical security concern. This paper describes GNSS spoofing attacks on autonomous vehicles, focusing on their detection both during and after an attack. Furthermore, we analyze data storage strategies to facilitate effective forensic analysis. We highlight the importance of position, signal, and camera data, which should be preserved to ensure a comprehensive forensic investigation. Finally, we suggest a simulation setup that enables studying which data could be used for a forensic investigation. Additionally, we examine established data frameworks and decide whether they are suitable for detecting GNSS spoofing attacks.**

Keywords-GNSS; autonomous driving; forensic; spoofing

I. INTRODUCTION

The ability to determine the geographical location of a device has become an indispensable technology in modern society, finding applications across a wide range of domains. From navigation to resource optimization, location-tracking systems have transformed how individuals and industries operate. Modern mobile phones, for example, enable users to effortlessly navigate unfamiliar locations, access detailed information about their surroundings, and plan their routes efficiently. This constant availability of location data has not only simplified everyday tasks, but has also revolutionized critical sectors such as transportation, logistics, and emergency response [1].

In the transportation industry, precise location tracking has proven to be a cornerstone of operational efficiency and safety. Maritime vessels can optimize their routes to minimize fuel consumption and travel time, while aircraft rely on accurate positioning systems to maintain safe distances between one another and ensure effective coordination in airspace [2]. For cars, location awareness has made traditional paper maps and co-driver navigation obsolete. Instead, Global Navigation Satellite System (GNSS), which encompasses multiple satellite navigation systems, including Global Positioning System (GPS), Galileo, Global Navigation Satellite System (GLONASS) and BeiDou, and related technologies have paved the way for advanced navigation systems, ultimately fostering the evolution of autonomous vehicles [3]. Modern cars increasingly incorporate features aligned with Society of Automotive Engineers (SAE) J3016 autonomy level 3 standards, where the vehicle can control driving in specific conditions, such as on highways. However, these systems still require the driver to take over when requested by the vehicle [4].

Although these advances have brought convenience and efficiency, they have also introduced critical vulnerabilities, particularly in the realm of GNSS-reliant systems. Attacks targeting GNSS receivers in autonomous or semi-autonomous vehicles can compromise their ability to accurately determine a location, potentially leading to catastrophic outcomes, such as collisions or operational failures [5]. These attacks are typically classified into two main categories: jamming and spoofing [6].

GNSS jamming and spoofing, while not new phenomena [7], remain significant threats due to their potential to exploit the dependency of modern systems on precise location data [8]. Jamming involves transmitting high-power interference signals across a wide frequency spectrum, including those used by navigation satellites, effectively disrupting the receiver's ability to interpret legitimate signals [9]. Spoofing, on the other hand, relies on generating and transmitting counterfeit satellite signals to deceive GNSS receivers into calculating an incorrect location. When executed skillfully, spoofing can mislead even sophisticated systems, causing them to accept falsified positions as accurate [10][11].

The motivations behind such attacks are diverse, ranging from malicious intent to sabotage and theft. A conceivable scenario involves targeting a high-profile individual, such as a politician on the way to an important event. By deploying a jamming device, attackers could immobilize the vehicle, potentially preventing the individual from reaching their destination on time. In addition, advances in vehicular technology, such as the Tire Pressure Monitor Sensors (TPMSs), provide attackers with tools to identify specific vehicles [12]. This capability allows for highly targeted attacks, where a jamming or spoofing signal is activated only when the intended vehicle passes by.

The increasing reliance on GNSS systems in critical applications underscores the importance of addressing their vulnerabilities. Understanding the mechanisms and implications of GNSS jamming and spoofing is crucial to develop robust countermeasures that can safeguard the functionality and safety of location-dependent technologies. Additionally, forensic analysis is crucial in examining such attacks after the event, enabling a deeper understanding of methods, impact, and potential attribution to specific actors.

This paper is divided into four main sections. First, we discuss the state of the art and related work in Section II. The fundamentals of GNSS jamming and spoofing are introduced in Section III, outlining key attack methods and their impact on autonomous navigation. Next, we propose a simulation using CARLA [13] and Autoware© [14], replicating realistic spoofing scenarios to analyze attack dynamics and detection challenges in Section IV. Finally, we discuss what is the expected outcome for the simulated data in Section V and comparing it to some established data frameworks, aiming to reconstruct spoofing incidents and extract forensic markers. This methodology is designed to be transferable to real vehicle data in future research, strengthening GNSS-based navigation security.

II. Related Work

GNSS spoofing attacks pose a significant threat to autonomous vehicles, as they can manipulate positioning data and mislead navigation systems. Several of the following studies have addressed the detection and mitigation of such attacks. Bhatti and Humphreys demonstrated how GNSS spoofing could be used to gain hostile control over ships, effectively altering their navigation routes without immediate detection. Their study highlights the broader implications of GNSS deception across various transportation domains, including autonomous vehicles [15].

Further research has focused on spoofing detection methodologies. Dasgupta *et al.* [16] propose a prediction-based GNSS spoofing detection approach using Long Short-Term Memory (LSTM) models to identify anomalies in vehicle position estimates. Similarly, Liu *et al.* [17] assesses the impact of GNSS spoofing on integrated navigation systems by analyzing error covariance in Kalman filtering. A broader survey of spoofing techniques and countermeasures is provided in [18], categorizing current anti-spoofing technologies. In addition, hybrid sensor fusion methods, as demonstrated in [19], integrate GNSS with Inertial Measurement Units (IMUs) and vehicle odometry to detect inconsistencies caused by spoofing attempts.

Recent work [20] explores stealthy "slow-drift" GNSS spoofing attacks in urban environments, highlighting the difficulty of detection when position deviations occur gradually. To improve resilience, [21] presents a physics-based anomaly detection framework, GPS-Intrusion Detection System (IDS), which monitors vehicular behavior to identify spoofing attacks in real time. Furthermore, Radoš et al. provide a comprehensive survey of GNSS jamming and spoofing detection methods, discussing the latest advancements, including machine learning-based approaches for early detection [6].

There are many forensic frameworks [22]–[25] that describe which data should be stored and how it can be preserved for further investigations. Additionally, there are many forensic concepts that define which data is generally relevant for forensic purposes [26]–[28]. Most of them characterize location data as very relevant. In regard to conventional GNSS spoofing detection, in the frameworks for autonomous vehicles, comprehensive data is available to cross-validate the GNSS spoofing. According to Law Enforcement Agencies (LEA), the Event Data Recorder (EDR) plays a central role. The EDR typically has triggers from, for example, a crash or airbag sensor to persist the data. Usually, the last 5 seconds of vehicle speed, steering angle and others will be saved permanently [29]. Caused by the fact that this data is not sufficient for investigations in situations with automated driving functions [30], the conception of a Data Storage System for Automated Driving (DSSAD) is given, where, additionally, data from the driver assistant systems is saved [31]. Data used by an IDS to detect GNSS spoofing in real-time is also relevant for forensic analysis [21]. Due to the non-availability of some data in post-mortem analysis and the difficulty obtaining some data in vehicles, another approach for GNSS spoofing detection must be developed, or volatile data, such as signal strength of satellite signals, must be made available similar to the work in [32] where camera footage is implemented into the EDR.

III. Background and Fundamentals

For a forensic analysis, it is important to understand and document which data points were created and how they were received. In the case of GNSS, it is important to notice that the received signals and their properties depend on, e.g., topology, atmospheric conditions, reflections and it is not feasible to focus on just one of the factors and determine if an attack has occurred [33].

A. How GNSS Works: Principles and Mechanisms

Satellite-based positioning relies on trilateration, where a receiver calculates its location by measuring distances from navigation satellites [34]. Clock synchronization is crucial, as any deviation introduces errors, necessitating additional correction methods.

To determine an accurate three-dimensional position, at least four satellites are required. Three satellites provide an intersection of three spheres, which theoretically yields two possible solutions: one in space and one on Earth's surface. The fourth satellite is necessary to account for timing errors inherent in the receiver's internal clock, ensuring precise positioning by correcting discrepancies in signal travel time. Without this fourth satellite, accurate location determination would be significantly hindered due to clock inaccuracies.

The distance is derived from the travel time of the signal, which in turn is calculated by comparing the relevant send and receive timestamps. This means that perfectly synchronized clocks are required to achieve the highest degree of precision. In practice, it is not unusual that the clocks are not synced as close to one another as desired. Therefore, a pseudo range is being introduced into the system, which has a geometric range and error term. This pseudo-range is based on the clock error and is simply added. This uncertainty complicates the equation in such a way that one needs at least four satellites -the fourth satellite for calculating the time error- to achieve sufficient position accuracy [34].

Determining one's precise location is important, but understanding the current speed of movement is equally crucial. This can be achieved through the Doppler shift, as the signal frequency is proportionally shifted in response to the speed of the receiver [35].

There exist multiple satellite systems. The first operational system, known as Navy Navigation Satellite System (NNSS) or Transit, was decommissioned in 1996. Some older systems, such as the Russian Tsikada from 1974, are still operational but are rarely used in modern society due to their limited positioning accuracy. The oldest widely used system is GPS, developed by the U.S. Army. It was later made accessible for civilian use, but without military-grade security features. Other systems include Global Navigation Satellite System (GLONASS), the Russian alternative to GPS; Galileo, the European navigation network; and BeiDou, which is a Chinese system. These systems operate as down link systems, meaning they use one-way communication from satellites to Earth. [33]

B. The Concept of GNSS Spoofing

Long believed impossible or hard to achieve, GNSS spoofing became reality in 2008, when Humphreys *et al.* demonstrated feasibility under laboratory conditions [36]. Since then, it has become more widespread and bigger attacks have been noticed.

GNSS spoofing is realized by transmitting counterfeit signals that are stronger than the signals from GNSS satellites. Thus, a receiver discards the true signals and computes an incorrect position and timing information. The process is illustrated in Figure 1. There are different possible attacks with a GNSS spoofer. In this paper, we copy the notation and names from sprint [37]. The first possible attack is meaconing, where original GNSS signals are replayed. The attack is successful if the receiver believes the replayed signal instead of the actual satellite signal. The second attack is the code carrier attack, where the GNSS signal is replicated, and the authentic signal is mimicked before adding power and changing the signal. The third attack is the navigation data attack, where the code carrier signal is left intact, but the navigation message will be faked and therefore a denial of service is achieved. The fourth attack is application-level spoofing, which is a man-in-the-middle attack. And the last attack is a multi-method attack, where any number of aforementioned attacks are combined to create a complex attack. Not each attack can be applied successfully on all systems. It depends on the technical capabilities and vulnerabilities of the receiver and vehicle.

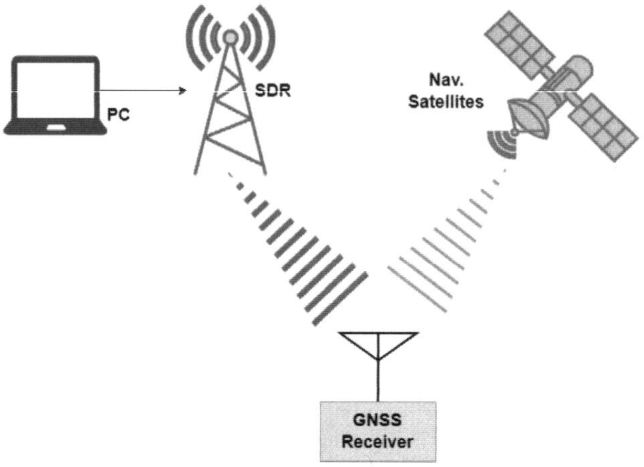

Figure 1. Illustration of GNSS spoofing: The SDR device overpowers satellite signals, deceiving the GNSS receiver with false location data.

It is often helpful to know which receiver is being used and in which state it is. The four distinct states, a receiver can be in, are cold start, warm start, hot or assisted start and reacquisition. While in the state of a cold start, the receiver just starts and has no information. With the warm start, the receiver has the approximated time and position. And with the hot start, the time and last position are known [38]. On the other hand, the reacquisition is not a usual start position, but indicates whether one or more signals from satellites are lost. This can occur naturally, for example in a tunnel, or unnaturally by jamming the frequency of GNSS.

C. Anti Spoofing Mechanisms

There are multiple methods to detect and avoid a GNSS spoofing signal [39] [40]. The simplest to implement is while the receiver has a warm or hot start, which involves obtaining a fix on satellite signals, to verify the location, speed of the vehicle and received timestamps for plausibility. There should be no major sudden jumps in each data type. Another simple solution is to check the authentication of the satellite message. This is not secure for currently deployed systems, as their structure is open knowledge. However, other GNSS systems, which aim to improve security, are in development [41]. By including features from the United States (US) military GPS, an encrypted authentication is being developed as an alternative way for positioning like cell ID.

As spoofing attacks pose significant risks to security-sensitive applications, the development of robust anti-spoofing mechanisms is crucial. Various anti-spoofing methods have recently been developed [6][42][43]. Signal processing-based techniques include correlation peak monitoring, which identifies distortions in the correlation function caused by spoofed signals, and power-based monitoring, which detects anomalies in the Carrier-to-Noise Ratio (C/N0) and Automatic Gain Control (AGC) values that often indicate spoofing attempts [6]. Another approach is to analyze the direction of the arriving signals, which differentiates spoofed signals from legitimate GNSS signals due to their different origins [44].

Data-driven approaches leverage Artificial Intelligence (AI) and Machine Learning (ML) techniques. Supervised learning algorithms classify authentic versus spoofed signals, while deep learning methods extract features from raw signal data for improved detection [45]. Radio Frequency Fingerprinting (RFF) can further enhance security by identifying unique signal characteristics such as phase noise and Doppler shifts[46].

Cryptographic and authentication techniques provide an additional layer of protection. Navigation Message Authentication (NMA) integrates digital signatures into GNSS signals, to ensure data integrity [41].

A promising direction for anti-spoofing involves integrating multiple detection methods. Hybrid approaches that combine signal processing, machine learning, and cryptographic authentication enhance robustness against evolving spoofing threats [6].

D. Digital Automotive Forensics

The digital automotive forensics is a part of the IT-forensics; especially the post-mortem analysis will be examined here. This means that live data is unavailable and only the data which is stored on a device may be used. The Federal Office for Information Security (BSI) gives a six point plan for a standard forensic investigation: strategic preparation, operational preparation, data collection, investigation, data analysis and documentation [26]. The European Network of Forensic Science Institutes (ENFSI) also describes first to validate and test the data with complex examinations [27]. The relevance of data depends on the specific use case. Those are typically given by the organization, which is interested in the investigation and in the technical implementation [47]. For Original Equipment Manufacturers (OEMs), it will often be sufficient to have some sort of hint for a technical conclusion. For the LEAs or insurance provider, where the evidence will be validated in court, it is much more important to have reliable data on the sequence of the event and especially information for attribution. For this, data that can be cross-validated is highly useful. Therefore, data that originates from just one source is considered circumstantial evidence. An example is the National Marine Electronics Association (NMEA) data, which cannot be validated using another data source. With regard to the case where all assistant driving data is acquired, it will be possible to detect the GNSS spoofing by cross-validation. There is a difference between the forensic analysis of stored data in the vehicle and real-time spoofing detection, such as cross-validation of the location provided by a cell tower and the GNSS sensor. Even with possible cross-validation methods, such as visual identification, computing everything in real-time would be challenging. However, in case of an incident, the data could be retrieved and validated.

This can lead to a significant overhead, especially if the dataset is large, distributed across multiple locations, difficult to obtain and unsorted. This is why a forensic framework is necessary. We will consider the data that would be provided by the established forensic framework AVGuard [24] and the legally mandatory or soon to be legally mandatory data storage systems EDR [29] and DSSAD [31]. The forensic framework AVGuard will save the following data: camera Frame per Second (FPS), Light Detection and Ranging (LiDAR)PointCount, GPSFreq, cars, pedestrians, trafficLights, roadsigns, laneDetectionConfidence, undefindedObjects, landmarks,Finite State Machine (FSM), acceleration, brake and steering angle. In the data point FSM it is for example recorded if the vehicle is turning or following a lane. The EDR will save the change in longitudinal velocity, the vehicle speed, the engine throttle, the service brake, the ignition cycle, the drivers safety belt status, the status of the frontal airbag warning lamp, the time of the frontal airbag deployment, if it is a multi event the number of the event and the time to the previous event [48]. The DSSAD is still at the conceptual stage. However it is likely that it will record the state of the Autonomous Driving (AD) system, the transition demand, the human driver take-overs, the minimum risk maneuvers and respective data timestamps [49].

IV. Outline of a GNSS Spoofing Attack Simulation

Since we aim to control all simulation parameters, we propose a simple scenario. For example, an autonomous vehicle is driving on a road with several intersections coming up. According to the users navigation settings, the vehicle is supposed to turn at the second intersection. However, due to a GNSS spoofing attack, the vehicle is being misled into turning early, at the first intersection, instead. Using a real vehicle and executing a successful spoofing attack is not feasible with reasonable resources, and we do not intend to develop a GNSS spoofing attack for state-of-the-art vehicles. Furthermore, for testing purposes of GNSS attacks, a license from the government is needed. Another possibility is conducting testing in a shielded environment. This is feasible but holds some complications, caused by the fact that there is interference with the real world. An alternative is testing with a simulator, which is much easier because the signals can be synchronized in a more straightforward manner [37]. Since our aim is to detect such an attack and conduct a successful forensic investigation, we simply need the resulting digital traces. For this, we expect that a simulation provides us with sufficient data quality for now. Ultimately, we plan to validate our developed workflow on real world data.

The scenario of an autonomous vehicle being misled to an earlier intersection could be simulated using a combination of CARLA [13] and Autoware© [14]. The simulated vehicle in CARLA should be spawned with a camera, two LiDARs sensors, one in the front and one in the back, a GNSS, IMU, lane invasion and a collision sensor. This sensor data will be sent by the Autoware CARLA bridge [50] to Autoware universe, where it can be processed and the vehicle in CARLA will be steered by the control commands of Autoware.

To simulate the signal strength of a GNSS signal, one can produce data in the NMEA 0183 standard [51][52] with help of gps-sdr-sim-realtime by GitHub user gym-487 [53] (Figure 2). This can be used to produce In-Phase and Quadrature (I/Q) data for the true position, called good signal, and the wrong position, called spoofed signal. For spoofing purposes, one has to combine the good and the spoofed signal. This should be done, for example in gnu radio [54], in such way that the spoofed signal is substantially stronger than the good signal. One can reinterpret the signals by GNSS-SDR [55], which provides the full NMEA data. This could be used to see how many satellites are in sight and how fast the vehicle is.

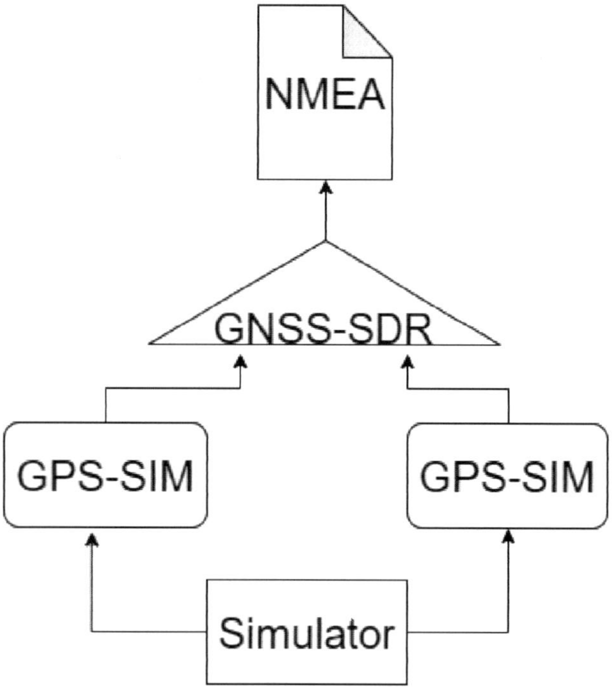

Figure 2. Simulation of GPS signal data

In order to understand the influence of external factors, this scenario should be simulated several times with varying input parameters. The simulation could vary in the following three different manners. The spoofed signal should be varied in the speed with which it is redirected from the original signal. The surroundings should change for easy and hard orientation, and the speed of the target vehicle should be changed.

These simulations will generate data in the vehicle that can be used for incident detection by the IDS as well as for forensics. Importantly, forensics will only be possible if the data is made available by an augmented EDR, DSSAD, the IDS or an elaborated forensic information system. In order to show the relevance of the full GNSS data, it is useful to imagine two different starting points:

1) One investigation with only the location information from the GNSS signal available and
2) another investigation with the full information of the GNSS signal such as signal strength, number of satellites etc.

The second case 2 has already been described in literature and in Subsection III-C. There are many plausibility checks, like changes in speed or C/N0 and AGC values, [6] which uncover such an attack. This data is required to be available for a post-mortem analysis as well, especially after an unclear event. For case 1 it is still possible to compute the GNSS-based speed and compare it to the data given by the speedometer of the vehicle. This plausibility check will likely not have the necessary strength since the GNSS-based speed is calculated on few locations only. Few data points of the GNSS signal and calculated speed will cause high uncertainty, e.g., in terms of wide confidence intervals preventing a test against the speedometer being positive.

To test this hypothesis, we want to generate data similar to the data displayed in the Figure 3. This data is calculated from the GNSS-based speed of the simulated vehicle under the assumption it is locked onto the spoofer, i.e., it ignores all data from the satellites. We can extract the speedometer data from CARLA and can generate the speed data by the real GNSS location and by the spoofed one. We validated this approach by implementing the GPS data creation. For this, we simply used two different GPS sensors, which drifted 10 meters apart over a timespan of 300 seconds. We set the first as the input for the true location and the second for the spoofed location and used the gps-sdr-sim-realtime setup as described and visualized in Figure 2.

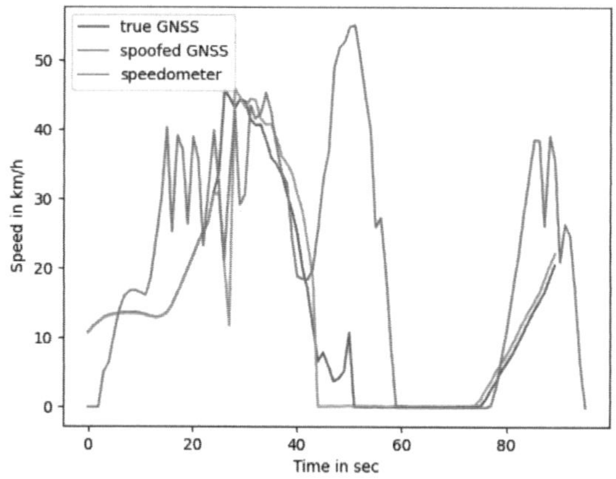

Figure 3. Velocity by GNSS and Speedometer

In this first exemplary simulation, one can see that the speed calculated based on the good GNSS signal also typically lacks behind the speed measured within the vehicle and does not reflect fast changes. And, for our study most interestingly, the spoofed and original GNSS-based speeds are apparently indistinguishable and therefore not viable for GNSS spoofing detection.

V. DISCUSSION

We expect from our simulations that the speed given by GNSS will not significantly differ from the actual speed of the vehicle, and it is thereby not possible to detect GNSS spoofing without additional data. However, caused by the stronger signals that are necessary for GNSS spoofing, in the simulation data a higher number of stronger satellite signals is expected. If the signal strength is recorded, this can aid in detecting an attack. Additionally, we want to consider other sources of information beyond GNSS signals for the in-situ detection as well as the post-mortem analysis of a GNSS spoofing attack. This allows for more elaborate plausibility checks. One option could be to identify street intersections using camera sensor data and AI. This could give a rough estimate of the location of the vehicle in a given street map.

In the currently established forensic frameworks of AV-Guard [24] and the data recorders EDR [29], and DSSAD [31], different types of data are stored. AVGuard [24] will store enough data to have some possible ways to cross-validate GNSS signals. One could test if the acceleration, traffic light and roadsigns could be used for cross-validation. For GPS related data, only the GPS frequency is saved. We do not think any spoofing attack could be detected in that way. The frequency only depends on the band, i.e. one frequency of the GNSS signal. In the simulation, we focused on just the GPS L1 band, which is around 1575.42 MHz. This limitation is not an issue, because the bands are independent. In the future, this should still be tested.

The EDR [29] will only record data in the case of an emergency, i.e., when the airbag gets deployed. In regard to an IDS, like in [21], the data that can be retrieved, is constrained by what is saved. Typically, one wants at least the route data or the satellite data for detecting GNSS spoofing. In contrast, the EDR saves only the vehicle's speed as only parameter for GNSS spoofing detection indicated in [56]. Even if the vehicle crash is caused by a GNSS spoofing attack, in the data recorded by the EDR this would not be recognizable, because no route information or other data associated with GNSS is saved.

Similarly for the DSSAD, which is mandated by United Nations Economic Commission for Europe (UNECE)s United Nations (UN)-R157 [31], there will be data saved regarding the Advanced Driver Assistant Systems (ADASs). The proposal for a DSSAD is not completed yet, so we can only make assumptions about which data might be stored. Interesting data for our use case could be the state of the autonomous driving mode and if the vehicle detected some malicious attacker, which requires the vehicle driver to take over. Both the legally and soon to be legally mandatory data recorders, EDR and DSSAD, are only going to save data in a 5 to 30 seconds interval. Additionally, no data that is typically used in GNSS spoofing detections is recorded.

Looking at the data storage systems, we see the importance of reliable data. Not all data points are interesting, but in the case of autonomous vehicles, attacks like GNSS spoofing should be easily detectable. In the current state this is not the case and one should record more data associated with GNSS. This could include NMEA or other localization data. In the real world there are many ways to identify the location of a vehicle, for example through cell tower ID [57], 3D maps [58] or object detection through Radio Detection and Ranging (Radar) and LiDAR [59].

To conclude which data points are relevant, we will set up a simulation as described above. The simulation will generate data that enables us to analyze the impact of a GNSS spoofing attack on an autonomous vehicle. By evaluating the results, we aim to determine whether our hypothesis is correct, i.e. that current data storage in EDR and DSSAD is insufficient. The findings will help assess whether additional data points are necessary to improve both forensic analysis of such attacks and the security measures used against them.

VI. Conclusion

By evaluating the EDR, DSSAD and AVGuard, we concluded that they will not provide enough data to identify GNSS spoofing attacks. Subsequently, a larger forensic framework needs to be defined, in which sensor data, like images or point clouds going to be saved for a specific period. To determine which data is relevant, we proposed a simulation setup. We plan to expand on this and subsequently publish an analysis of the simulated data. o validate the data from the simulation, we plan to conduct real-world driving tests using a GNSS receiver. These tests will include baseline measurements as well as scenarios where the receiver is intentionally disrupted. The disruptions will be introduced by covering the antenna with metal objects or injecting corrupt signals via a wire to simulate jamming and spoofing. We expect these tests to provide deeper insights into the specific navigation parameters relevant to forensic analysis. We have looked at a very specific case, where the GNSS spoofing worked every time. This should be improved in two different ways. First, the case needs to be closer to the real world, which is more complex and presents further challenges that need to be addressed. For further testing, hardware that more closely replicates real-world complexities should be deployed. On the other hand, there should be more disruptive factors in the simulation like different vehicles, more visible input to clarify the position and different maps, where the angle of the intersections do not line up perfectly. Additionally, it would be interesting to investigate anti spoofing mechanisms. If spoofing is prevented, it would still be possible to detect whether the vehicle has been attacked.

Acknowledgment

The authors would like to thank Conrad Meyer and Dr. Tabea Rosenkranz from the Central Office for Information Technology in the Security Sector (ZITiS). This work was supported by the project 'Digital Forensics in IT Systems (Di-ForIT)', funded by the German Federal Ministry for Economic Affairs and Climate Action (BMWK).

References

[1] Fortune Business Insights, "Globaler Markt für Navigationssatellitensysteme (GNSS) [Global Market for Navigation Satellite Systems (GNSS)]", Jan. 27, 2025, [Online]. Available: https://www.fortunebusinessinsights.com/de/globaler-markt-f-r-navigationssatellitensysteme-gnss–103433 (visited on 02/14/2025).

[2] D. Verma, B. Singh, and F. Zahidi, "Management of GPS Tracking Systems in Transportation", in Mar. 2024, pp. 251–263, ISBN: 978-981-97-0514-6. DOI: 10.1007/978-981-97-0515-3_11.
[3] M. Maurer, J. C. Gerdes, B. Lenz, and H. Winner, Eds., *Autonomous Driving*, en. Berlin, Heidelberg: Springer Berlin Heidelberg, 2016, ISBN: 978-3-662-48845-4 978-3-662-48847-8. DOI: 10.1007/978-3-662-48847-8.
[4] SAE, "SAE Levels of Driving Automation Refined for Clarity and International Audience", 2021, [Online]. Available: https://www.sae.org/site/blog/sae-j3016-update (visited on 01/28/2025).
[5] M. Shabbir, M. Kamal, Z. Ullah, and M. M. Khan, "Securing Autonomous Vehicles Against GPS Spoofing Attacks: A Deep Learning Approach", *IEEE Access*, vol. 11, pp. 105 513–105 526, 2023. DOI: 10.1109/ACCESS.2023.3319514.
[6] K. Rado, M. Brki, and D. Begui, "Recent Advances on Jamming and Spoofing Detection in GNSS", *Sensors*, vol. 24, no. 13, p. 4210, Jun. 2024, ISSN: 1424-8220. DOI: 10.3390/s24134210.
[7] N. O. Tippenhauer, C. Pöpper, K. B. Rasmussen, and S. Capkun, "On the Requirements for Successful GPS Spoofing Attacks", in *Proceedings of the 18th ACM Conference on Computer and Communications Security*, Y. Chen, G. Danezis, and V. Shmatikov, Eds., New York, NY, USA: ACM, 2011, pp. 75–86, ISBN: 978-1-4503-0948-6. DOI: 10.1145/2046707.2046719.
[8] "GNSS Jamming and Spoofing Are a Daily Occurrence", [Online]. Available: https://www.eetimes.eu/gnss-jamming-and-spoofing-are-a-daily-occurrence/ (visited on 02/21/2025).
[9] T. Morong, P. Puricer, and P. Ková, "Study of the GNSS Jamming in Real Environment", *International Journal of Electronics and Telecommunications*, vol. 65, pp. 65–70, Feb. 2019. DOI: 10.24425/ijet.2019.126284.
[10] M. Ceccato, F. Formaggio, N. Laurenti, and S. Tomasin, "Generalized Likelihood Ratio Test for GNSS Spoofing Detection in Devices With IMU", *IEEE Transactions on Information Forensics and Security*, vol. 16, pp. 3496–3509, 2021. DOI: 10.1109/TIFS.2021.3083414.
[11] S. Islam *et al.*, "Impact Analysis of Spoofing on Different-grade GNSS Receivers", in *2023 IEEE/ION Position, Location and Navigation Symposium (PLANS)*, 2023, pp. 492–499. DOI: 10.1109/PLANS53410.2023.10139934.
[12] C. Smith, *The Car Hacker's Handbook: A Guide for the Penetration Tester*. San Francisco: No Starch Press, 2016, ISBN: 978-1-59327-770-3.
[13] A. Dosovitskiy, G. Ros, F. Codevilla, A. Lopez, and V. Koltun, *Carla: An Open Urban Driving Simulator*, 2017. arXiv: 1711.03938.
[14] A. Foundation, "Autoware: Open-Source Software for Autonomous Driving", [Online]. Available: https://github.com/autowarefoundation/autoware (visited on 01/31/2025).
[15] J. Bhatti and E. Humphreys, "Hostile Control of Ships via False GPS Signals: Demonstration and Detection", pp. 51–66, 2016. DOI: https://doi.org/10.1002/navi.183.
[16] S. Dasgupta, M. Rahman, M. Islam, and M. Chowdhury, "Prediction-Based GNSS Spoofing Attack Detection for Autonomous Vehicles", 2020, Publisher: arXiv. DOI: 10.48550/ARXIV.2010.11722.
[17] Y. Liu, S. Li, Q. Fu, and Z. Liu, "Impact Assessment of GNSS Spoofing Attacks on INS/GNSS Integrated Navigation System", *Sensors*, vol. 18, no. 5, p. 1433, May 2018, ISSN: 1424-8220. DOI: 10.3390/s18051433.
[18] L. Meng, L. Yang, W. Yang, and L. Zhang, "A Survey of GNSS Spoofing and Anti-Spoofing Technology", *Remote Sensing*, vol. 14, no. 19, p. 4826, 2022, ISSN: 2072-4292. DOI: 10.3390/rs14194826.
[19] A. Broumandan and G. Lachapelle, "Spoofing Detection Using GNSS/INS/Odometer Coupling for Vehicular Navigation", *Sensors*, vol. 18, no. 5, p. 1305, Apr. 2018, ISSN: 1424-8220. DOI: 10.3390/s18051305.
[20] S. Dasgupta, A. Ahmed, M. Rahman, and T. N. Bandi, *Unveiling the Stealthy Threat: Analyzing Slow Drift GPS Spoofing Attacks for Autonomous Vehicles in Urban Environments and Enabling the Resilience*, Version Number: 1, 2024. DOI: 10.48550/ARXIV.2401.01394.
[21] M. M. Abrar *et al.*, *GPS-IDS: An Anomaly-based GPS Spoofing Attack Detection Framework for Autonomous Vehicles*, Version Number: 2, 2024. DOI: 10.48550/ARXIV.2405.08359.
[22] M. Cebe, E. Erdin, K. Akkaya, H. Aksu, and S. Uluagac, "Block4Forensic: An Integrated Lightweight Blockchain Framework for Forensics Applications of Connected Vehicles", *IEEE Communications Magazine*, vol. 56, no. 10, pp. 50–57, 2018, ISSN: 0163-6804. DOI: 10.1109/MCOM.2018.1800137.
[23] S. Lee, W. Choi, H. J. Jo, and D. H. Lee, "T-Box: A Forensics-Enabled Trusted Automotive Data Recording Method", *IEEE access : practical innovations, open solutions*, vol. 7, pp. 49 738–49 755, 2019. DOI: 10.1109/ACCESS.2019.2910865.
[24] M. A. Hoque and R. Hasan, "AVGuard: A Forensic Investigation Framework for Autonomous Vehicles", in *ICC 2021 - IEEE International Conference on Communications*, Piscataway, NJ: IEEE, 2021, pp. 1–6, ISBN: 978-1-7281-7122-7. DOI: 10.1109/ICC42927.2021.9500652.
[25] M. Hossain, R. Hasan, and S. Zawoad, "Trust-IoV: A Trustworthy Forensic Investigation Framework for the Internet of Vehicles (IoV)", in *2017 IEEE 2nd International Congress on Internet of Things*, M. Parashar, Ed., Piscataway, NJ: IEEE, 2017, pp. 25–32, ISBN: 978-1-5386-2011-3. DOI: 10.1109/IEEE.ICIOT.2017.13.
[26] Bundesamt für Sicherheit in der Informationstechnik [Federal Office for Information Security], *Leitfaden IT-Forensik [Guide to IT-Forensics]*, 2011.
[27] ENFSI, *Best Practice Manual for the Forensic Examination of Digital Technology*, 2015.
[28] L. Ahmeti, K. Dolos, C. Meyer, A. Attenberger, and R. Hackenberg, "A Forensic Approach to Handle Autonomous Transportation Incidents within Gaia-X", *CLOUD COMPUTING 2024*, p. 51, 2024.
[29] Event Data Recorder Committee, "Event Data Recorder", DOI: 10.4271/J1698_202303.
[30] K. Böhm, T. Kubjatko, D. Paula, and H.-G. Schweiger, "New Developments on EDR (Event Data Recorder) for Automated Vehicles", *Open Engineering*, vol. 10, pp. 140–146, Mar. 2020. DOI: 10.1515/eng-2020-0007.
[31] "UN Regulation No 157 Uniform Provisions Concerning the Approval of Vehicles with Regards to Automated Lane Keeping Systems", *Official Journal L 82*, no. 82, pp. 75–137, 2021.
[32] K. Böhm, T. Kubjatko, D. Paula, and H.-G. Schweiger, "New Developments on EDR (Event Data Recorder) for Automated Vehicles", *Open Engineering*, vol. 10, no. 1, pp. 140–146, 2020. DOI: doi:10.1515/eng-2020-0007.
[33] B. Hofmann-Wellenhof, H. Lichtenegger, and E. Wasle, *GNSS: Global Navigation Satellite Systems - GPS, Glonass, Galileo, and More*. Wien and NewYork: Springer, 2008, ISBN: 978-3-211-73012-6. DOI: 10.1007/978-3-211-73017-1.
[34] Y. S. Simamora, N. F. Rachmach, M. Y. Rizqon, K. A. Suseno, and M. N. Hilmi, "Revisiting Trilateration Method Based on Time-of-Flight Measurements for Navigation", *Jurnal Riset Multidisiplin dan Inovasi Teknologi*, vol. 2, no. 01, pp. 207–214, Dec. 2023, ISSN: 3024-8582, 3024-9546. DOI: 10.59653/jimat.v2i01.432.

[35] A. Angrisano, G. Cappello, S. Gaglione, and C. Gioia, "Velocity Estimation Using Time-Differenced Carrier Phase and Doppler Shift with Different Grades of Devices: From Smartphones to Professional Receivers", *Algorithms*, vol. 17, no. 1, 2024, ISSN: 1999-4893. DOI: 10.3390/a17010002.

[36] T. E. Humphreys, B. M. Ledvina, M. L. Psiaki, B. W. O'Hanlon, and P. M. Kintner, "Assessing the Spoofing Threat: Development of a Portable GPS Civilian Spoofer", in *Proceedings of the 21st International Technical Meeting of the Satellite Division of The Institute of Navigation (ION GNSS 2008)*, 2008, pp. 2314–2325.

[37] spirent, "GNSS Signal Spoofing: How to Evaluate the Risks to Safety-Critical and Liability-Critical Systems", *DWP0014 Issue 1-00*, 2020.

[38] R. Goudenove, *Understanding GNSS Receiver Start Modes: Cold, Warm, Hot, Direct*, Nov. 2024.

[39] D.-K. Lee *et al.*, "Detection of GNSS Spoofing using NMEA Messages", in *Proceedings of the European Navigation Conference (ENC)*, Dresden, Germany, 2020, pp. 1–10.

[40] Y.-S. Lee, J. S. Yeom, and B. C. Jung, "A Novel Array Antenna-Based GNSS Spoofing Detection and Mitigation Technique", in *Proceedings of the 2023 IEEE 20th Consumer Communications & Networking Conference (CCNC)*, Las Vegas, NV, USA, 8, 2023, pp. 489–492.

[41] I. Fernández-Hernández *et al.*, "A Navigation Message Authentication Proposal for the Galileo Open Service", *NAVIGATION*, vol. 63, no. 1, pp. 85–102, 2016. DOI: https://doi.org/10.1002/navi.125.

[42] L. Meng, L. Yang, W. Yang, and L. Zhang, "A Survey of GNSS Spoofing and Anti-Spoofing Technology", en, *Remote Sens. (Basel)*, vol. 14, no. 19, p. 4826, Sep. 2022.

[43] P. Papadimitratos and A. Jovanovic, "GNSS-based Positioning: Attacks and Countermeasures", *IEEE MILCOM*,

[44] M. C. Esswein and M. L. Psiaki, "Classification of Authentic and Spoofed GNSS Signals Using a Calibrated Antenna Array", en, *Navigation (Wash.)*, vol. 72, no. 1, navi.675, Jan. 2025.

[45] P. Borhani-Darian, H. Li, P. Wu, and P. Closas, "Detecting GNSS Spoofing Using Deep Learning", en, *EURASIP J. Adv. Signal Process.*, vol. 2024, no. 1, Jan. 2024.

[46] R. Morales-Ferre, W. Wang, A. Sanz-Abia, and E.-S. Lohan, "7Identifying GNSS Signals Based on Their Radio Frequency (RF) Features-A Dataset with GNSS Raw Signals Based on Roof Antennas and Spectracom Generator", *Data*, vol. 2020,

[47] A. Cockburn, *Writing Effective Use Cases* (The Agile Software Development Series), 24. print. Boston: Addison-Wesley, 2012, 270 pp., ISBN: 978-0-201-70225-5.

[48] "EVENT DATA RECORDERS", 2006, [Online]. Available: https://www.ecfr.gov/current/title-49/part-563 (visited on 02/14/2025).

[49] "Data Storage System for Automated Driving", 2019, [Online]. Available: https://wiki.unece.org/download/attachments/87621710/EDR-DSSAD-01-08%20%28CLEPA-OICA%29%20DSSAD%20first%20draft%20for%20discussion%20based%20on%20GRVA-02-21.pdf?api=v2 (visited on 02/14/2025).

[50] G. Kaljavesi, T. Kerbl, T. Betz, K. Mitkovskii, and F. Diermeyer, "Carla-Autoware-Bridge: Facilitating Autonomous Driving Research with a Unified Framework for Simulation and Module Development", 2024.

[51] N. M. E. Association, "NMEA 0183 Version 4.10", 2013, [Online]. Available: https://www.nmea.org/nmea-0183.html (visited on 03/12/2025).

[52] G. Baddeley, "GPS - NMEA Sentence Information", 2001, [Online]. Available: https://aprs.gids.nl/nmea/ (visited on 01/28/2025).

[53] T. Ebinuma, *Gps-sdr-sim-realtime*, GitHub-Repository, 2017.

[54] G. R. Project, "Gnu Radio", [Online]. Available: https://www.gnuradio.org (visited on 01/29/2025).

[55] C. Fernandez-Prades, C. Aviles, L. Estove, J. Arribas, and P. Closas, "Design Patterns for GNSS Software Receivers", in *2010 5th ESA Workshop on Satellite Navigation Technologies and European Workshop on GNSS Signals and Signal Processing (NAVITEC)*, Netherlands: IEEE, Dec. 2010, pp. 1–8, ISBN: 978-1-4244-8740-0. DOI: 10.1109/NAVITEC.2010.5707981.

[56] Electronic Code of Federal Regulations (eCFR), "Event Data Recorders", 2025, [Online]. Available: https://www.ecfr.gov/current/title-49/subtitle-B/chapter-V/part-563 (visited on 01/29/2025).

[57] S. Saleh, A. S. El-Wakeel, S. Sorour, and A. Noureldin, "Evaluation of 5G Cell Densification for Autonomous Vehicles Positioning in Urban Settings", in *2020 International Conference on Communications, Signal Processing, and their Applications (ICCSPA)*, 2021, pp. 1–6. DOI: 10.1109/ICCSPA49915.2021.9385733.

[58] A. Khoche, M. K. Wozniak, D. Duberg, and P. Jensfelt, "Semantic 3D Grid Maps for Autonomous Driving", in *2022 IEEE 25th International Conference on Intelligent Transportation Systems (ITSC)*, 2022, pp. 2681–2688. DOI: 10.1109/ITSC55140.2022.9922537.

[59] J. Koci, N. Jovii, and V. Drndarevi, "Sensors and Sensor Fusion in Autonomous Vehicles", in *2018 26th Telecommunications Forum (FOR)*, Nov. 2018, pp. 420–425. DOI: 10.1109/FOR.2018.8612054.

GFDG: A Genetic Fuzzing Method for the Controller Area Network Protocol

Miguel Stey *, Murad Hachani †, Philipp Fuxen †, Julian Graf †, Rudolf Hackenberg†
Department of Computer Science and Mathematics
Ostbayerische Technische Hochschule Regensburg
Regensburg, Deutschland
* e-mail: miguel1.stey@st.oth-regensburg.de,
† e-mail: {murad.hachani | philipp.fuxen | julian.graf | rudolf.hackenberg}@oth-regensburg.de

***Abstract*—Ensuring the security of modern automotive systems is critical due to their increasing complexity and reliance on interconnected Electronic Control Units. The Controller Area Network still serves as a key communication protocol within these systems, making it a primary target for security testing. Traditional fuzz testing approaches for Controller Area Networks often rely on random or brute-force message generation, not leveraging the system's feedback to improve the generation process. This paper introduces the Genetic Fuzz Data Generator, a fuzzing method that leverages Genetic Algorithms and side-channel analysis to enhance Controller Area Network security testing. The Genetic Fuzz Data Generator dynamically refines its fuzzing strategy by evaluating system responses through side-channel data, such as processing unit temperatures and power supply variations. By structuring Controller Area Network messages as genetic individuals and applying evolutionary principles—including selection, crossover, and mutation—the Genetic Fuzz Data Generator systematically identifies active Controller Area Network IDs and generates targeted fuzz messages. Experimental validation was conducted on a real automotive electronic control unit within a controlled laboratory setup. The first results demonstrated the approach's effectiveness, revealing system anomalies, including a Denial of Service vulnerability that disrupted functions of the investigated Electronic Control Unit. The findings highlight the potential of feedback-driven fuzzing for improving the efficiency of black-box security testing in Controller Area Network-based systems. Future research could further optimize fitness functions or explore additional side-channel metrics.**

Keywords-Automotive Security; Controller Area Network; Fuzz Testing; Genetic Algorithm; Side-Channel Analysis.

I. INTRODUCTION

Modern connected vehicle systems rely on increasingly complex software running on Electronic Control Units (ECUs) that manage critical functions. Ensuring the security of these systems is essential, particularly as the attack surface expands with enhanced connectivity, integration of multiple networked components, and the growing reliance on cloud-based infrastructures for remote diagnostics, software updates, and real-time data processing. Building upon our previous work [1], where we developed a side-channel monitoring setup for fuzz testing automotive systems, we have identified key limitations in traditional random fuzzing approaches—specifically, the challenge of efficiently detecting active Controller Area Network (CAN) IDs. This insight motivated the development of the Genetic Fuzz Data Generator (GFDG), a method that leverages genetic algorithms and side-channel feedback to systematically generate targeted fuzz messages for the CAN protocol.

In conventional fuzz testing, generating a large volume of random messages often results in a low probability of triggering a response from the target system. Our prior research demonstrated that side-channel data could significantly enhance anomaly detection; however, the approach lacked the adaptive capability to focus on active CAN IDs. The GFDG addresses this gap by structuring CAN messages as genetic individuals—each represented by an 11-bit identifier and a payload—and refining them through evolutionary operations, such as selection, crossover, mutation, and migration. Preliminary results suggest that this feedback-driven process can enhance testing efficiency and contribute to identifying subtle vulnerabilities, though further investigation is needed to quantify its full impact.

Given that this paper focuses on the innovative integration of genetic algorithms with side-channel analysis to dynamically target and refine CAN fuzzing, we frame our investigation around the following research questions:

RQ1: How does the integration of genetic algorithms with side-channel feedback improve the identification of active CAN IDs?

RQ2: What are the impacts of evolutionary operations (selection, crossover, mutation, and migration) on the performance and adaptability of the fuzzing process?

This paper is organized as follows. Section II reviews related work, including an analysis of existing fuzzing methodologies and the limitations observed in our 2023 study. Section III describes the underlying concepts and the theoretical foundation of genetic algorithms in the context of fuzz testing. Section IV details the architecture and implementation of the GFDG. Section V presents experimental evaluations conducted on a real automotive ECU, and Section VI discusses the results, highlighting both improvements and remaining challenges. Finally, Section VII concludes with directions for future research.

II. RELATED WORK

Fuzz testing has emerged as a critical technique for identifying vulnerabilities in embedded systems, where conventional random-input approaches often fall short due to limited I/O capabilities, constrained resources, and heterogeneous architectures [2]. These inherent challenges have motivated the development of feedback-driven methodologies that are specifically tailored for embedded environments.

A notable advancement in this area is demonstrated by the Firm-AFL framework, which adapts coverage-guided fuzzing techniques to the constraints of embedded firmware. Firm-AFL shows that by integrating runtime feedback into the fuzzing loop, one can significantly enhance vulnerability detection even in resource-limited settings. This insight underlines the necessity of adapting traditional fuzzing techniques to the particularities of embedded systems [3].

In parallel, side-channel-assisted fuzzing has recently emerged as a promising approach. Sperl and Böttinger propose a method that leverages power consumption measurements as a feedback mechanism, inferring aspects of the target's control flow from power traces. Such side-channel feedback can mitigate the "black-box" limitations inherent in conventional fuzz testing of embedded devices [4].

In the automotive domain, securing the CAN is of paramount importance given its central role in vehicle communications. In "Fuzzing CAN Packets into Automobiles" [5], Lee et al. demonstrate that automotive systems are vulnerable even when attackers inject fuzzed CAN packets without in-depth system knowledge. Their experiments, which involve sniffing CAN traffic and subsequently fuzzing packet fields via wireless channels, reveal that random fuzzing can induce abnormal vehicle behavior. These findings highlight the inherent insecurity of the CAN bus and motivate the need for more systematic, feedback-guided fuzzing strategies in automotive networks.

Building on these insights, our work—the GFDG—applies the Genetic Algorithms (GAs) and side-channel analysis to enhance fuzzing techniques for CAN-based systems. By representing CAN messages as genetic individuals and refining test inputs through evolutionary operations (selection, crossover, and mutation), GFDG leverages runtime and side-channel feedback to focus fuzzing efforts on active CAN IDs. This hybrid approach not only echoes the advantages demonstrated by FIRM-AFL in adapting fuzzing to embedded firmware but also extends the paradigm by integrating the side-channel feedback techniques proposed by Lee et al. [5] and the empirical findings from "Fuzzing CAN Packets into Automobiles".

III. Background

This section provides an overview of key concepts relevant to this work. The CAN protocol is widely used for ECU communication in automotive systems, making it a critical target for security testing. Fuzz testing helps uncover vulnerabilities by generating test inputs and analyzing system responses, but traditional methods struggle with identifying active CAN IDs. GAs offer a potential solution by optimizing test case generation through system feedback.

A. CAN protocol

CAN is a broadcast-based protocol [6] used extensively in the automotive sector to connect ECUs. In the CAN protocol, different types of frames are defined, each serving a specific purpose. The Standard Frame, for example, is used for the regular exchange of messages between ECUs [7]. Typical applications of this frame include transmitting sensor data or sending commands to other ECUs. The Standard Frame consists of several fields that facilitate the transmission process, including the acknowledgment field and the checksum field [7]. For fuzz testing purposes, the most relevant component of the frame is the message it contains. A CAN message is defined by its identifier (ID) and a data field of up to 8 bytes [6]. The primary function of the CAN ID is to define the context of the data, while its secondary role involves enabling message filtering by the nodes on the bus. Since each node broadcasts messages onto the bus, the CAN ID allows each node to determine whether the message is intended for it or should be ignored [8]. In the context of fuzz testing, this means that an ECU will process only those fuzz messages with IDs that it is configured to recognize.

B. Fuzz Testing

Fuzz testing is an automated method for testing the security of information systems. It involves automatically generating input data for the system under test and monitoring its responses [9]. A fuzzer typically consists of two core components: a Fuzz Data Generator (FDG), responsible for producing new fuzz messages, and an Anomaly Monitor, which analyzes the system's reactions to identify potential vulnerabilities [6]. In the context of fuzz testing via CAN, the primary challenges are the large space of possible messages and the fact that an ECU only responds to a subset of CAN IDs. In a black-box fuzzing scenario, the specific active IDs of an ECU are unknown to the tester. Therefore, methods capable of identifying these active IDs are more efficient than non-feedback-based fuzzing approaches. The literature on CAN fuzz testing presents various methods, but most rely on randomly generating messages [10][11] or employing brute-force techniques [12][13][14]. These approaches do not utilize system feedback to identify active IDs, resulting in less efficient fuzzing processes. Consequently, there is a need for more advanced methods that incorporate system feedback to enhance the efficiency of CAN fuzz testing.

C. Genetic Algorithm

The GA is a search algorithm that mimics the principle of evolution from biology to find optimal solutions to problems. GAs can be considered a family of algorithms that utilize the same foundational structure but differ in specific strategies or parameters [15]. To solve a given problem, the first step involves defining an individual, which represents a potential solution. Each individual consists of certain genes that encode potential solutions for the problem. A group of individuals forms a population, and each iteration of the algorithm corresponds to a generation of individuals [15]. The GA begins by generating an initial population that represents Generation 0. The algorithm then iteratively proceeds through several steps for each generation. The core step is the evaluation of individuals based on their fitness, which is a numerical value indicating how well an individual solves the problem. Analogous to survival probability in natural evolution, the fitness score determines the likelihood of an individual contributing to the next generation of solutions [15]. After evaluating the fitness of all individuals, a selection process occurs, where certain individuals are chosen based on their fitness to participate in crossover. Crossover is

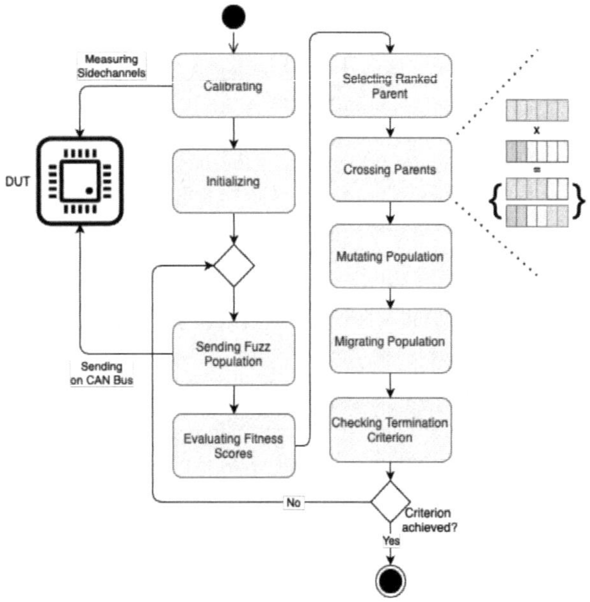

Figure 1. The Process of GFDG.

a genetic operation that combines pairs of selected individuals to generate new offspring, effectively recombining genes to explore new solution spaces [16]. Additionally, during the creation of offspring, mutations can occur. The mutation is typically implemented through bit-flips of genes based on a predefined mutation chance. After generating a new population, the algorithm repeats the cycle of evaluation, selection, crossover, and mutation until a termination criterion is met.

IV. The Genetic Fuzz Data Generator

This section describes the concept for the GFDG that is based on the structure of the GA and uses side-channel information for the evaluation. For this method, additional changes to the GA were taken into account for special requirements of the application to CAN fuzzing. For the GA, it is required to define an individual for the specific problem that the algorithm is applied to. The definition of a CAN Individual in the context of fuzz testing is provided in the following Subsection IV-A. In Subsection IV-B, the developed algorithm for the GFDG is described, including the reasoning in chosen strategies for each operation and all alterations to the standard GA structure. The modified algorithm for the CAN protocol is illustrated in Figure 1 and is further elaborated upon in the subsequent sections.

A. Defining a CAN-Individual

In the GA, each individual in the population represents a potential solution composed of various genes. In the context of fuzzing over the CAN protocol, an individual corresponds to a CAN message. This message must be recognized as a valid CAN message by the receiver of the target ECU. If the message violates protocol rules, the receiver node detects this, resulting in an error frame being sent back to the fuzzer without further processing of the message. Consequently, not all fields of the CAN frame are suitable as mutable genes for the individual. Therefore, the GFDG uses only the message portion of the CAN frame as the genes of an individual. From a broader perspective, an individual in the GFDG is a CAN message consisting of an 11-bit ID and a 64-bit data field. Other fields, such as data length and checksum, are recalculated correctly for transmission and are neither mutated nor inherited. The GA further conceptualizes individuals as collections of chromosomes composed of genes. Here, the CAN ID is treated as a chromosome consisting of 11 genes, each representing one bit of the CAN ID. This chromosome is mutation-resistant and cannot be split during crossover because the CAN ID determines whether the control unit processes the message. One goal of the GFDG is to identify accepting CAN IDs and test different payload data for these IDs. Therefore, IDs are not mutated randomly. Instead, the algorithm strategically generates more or fewer individuals with specific IDs. The second chromosome of a CAN individual represents the payload data, which can contain 0 to 64 bits. Since the payload's interpretation depends on the CAN ID and therefore is not predictable in a black-box scenario, each bit of the payload is treated as an individual gene. In summary, from the perspective of the GA, an individual in the GFDG consists of a non-mutable and non-crossable chromosome representing an 11-bit number and a standard chromosome with up to 64 genes.

B. GFDG Algorithm

The GFDG applies GAs to refine fuzz testing for CAN-based systems. This section details the algorithm's key steps, including initialization, message evaluation, selection, crossover, mutation, and migration. By leveraging system feedback, the GFDG aims to optimize test case generation and improve fuzzing efficiency.

1) Initialization: At the start of the fuzzing process, an initial generation must be created. This initial population is particularly important for the GFDG algorithm as it largely determines the IDs of the first generations. Since IDs do not change when creating new generations and only a few new IDs are introduced through migration, the initial population significantly impacts the performance of a run. In many cases, the standard strategy for GA is to initialize the first generation randomly. However, in this application, random initialization has a low probability of generating IDs in the first generation that trigger a response from the system. If no active IDs are generated, the run's performance depends on how many active IDs are introduced through migration, which constitutes only a small portion of each generation. To address this limitation, a different approach was developed. This method leverages side-channel feedback through the fitness function to actively select the initial population. In the first step, a multitude of CAN messages to the required amount are randomly generated and sent as fuzzing inputs to the target system. As in the normal fuzzing process of GFDG, side-channel data is collected, and a fitness value is calculated for each message. The messages with the highest fitness values are then selected to form the first generation. By prioritizing messages with high fitness scores, this method aims to increase the likelihood of including active CAN IDs in the initial population, which can influence the performance of the GFDG algorithm.

2) Sending and Measuring: After each generation, the main steps of the fuzzing process are performed for each individual. First, the individual is sent to the system under test. Then, the side-channel data of the ECU is measured to evaluate the individual. In the test environment used to evaluate this method, the available side-channels included the temperature of the ECU's three processing units—namely, the Central Processing Unit (CPU), Graphics Processing Unit (GPU), and Automotive Microcontroller (AMC)—as well as the power supply of the associated display of the tested Infotainment System.

3) Evaluation: After an individual is sent to the system under test and the side-channel measurements are collected, these data are used to evaluate the individual. The evaluation is performed similarly to traditional GA, using a fitness function. In the context of optimization problems, the fitness value indicates how well an individual solves the problem. In this application of fuzz testing, the fitness function measures if and to what extent the system reacts to a sent fuzz message. It is important to note that the specific fitness function heavily depends on the system being tested, the chosen side-channels, and their behavior. Therefore, a single, fixed fitness function is not presented here. Instead, the process of identifying an appropriate fitness function for the investigated system is described. When applying this method to other CAN-based systems, it is necessary to analyze the available side-channels to determine which changes indicate a system reaction. This analysis informs the formulation of a suitable fitness function for the specific system.
This method was tested on an ECU controlling the infotainment system of a car. As previously mentioned, the selected side-channels in this setup were the temperatures of the ECU's processing units (CPU, GPU, and AMC) and the power supply of the connected display. The rationale for these side-channels is the assumption that if a fuzz message is processed by an otherwise isolated ECU, the processing units calculating should cause temperature increases. This is especially relevant when the infotainment system displays information, as any change on the display triggered by a fuzz message would require the GPU to render new images, leading to a measurable increase in its temperature. Similarly, the power supply of the display was monitored because potential system reactions, such as turning off the display or adjusting its brightness, would cause detectable changes in power, consumption. Therefore, the fitness function was designed to yield higher scores when the temperature of one or more processing units increased after sending a message or changes in power supply were measured.

4) Selection: After each individual of the current generation has been evaluated, parents for the next generation are selected using Ranked Selection. This method assigns each individual a fixed selection probability based on its rank within the generation according to its fitness score [17]. Ranked Selection was chosen because it ensures that the best-performing individuals have a significantly higher chance of being selected compared to others. This approach is based on the assumption that the fitness function accurately reflects the system's reactions. Consequently, GFDG can prioritize generating more fuzz messages from individuals that triggered the strongest reactions, increasing the likelihood of uncovering system vulnerabilities.

5) Crossover and Mutation: After the parent individuals for the next generation are selected, they are used to create the majority of the next generation through crossover and mutation. This process follows the standard GA approach, using single-point crossover for the payload genes of a message. The resulting offspring are then mutated using a bit-wise mutation strategy, where each bit of the payload is checked for mutation probability, and bit-flips are performed accordingly. As previously mentioned, the CAN ID is not affected by mutation, and its bits are not split by crossover. Instead, the CAN ID is linked to the first gene of the payload. Consequently, a child individual inherits the ID from the parent from which it received its first payload bit. Therefore, this design additionally ensures that the distribution of CAN IDs among the offspring mirrors the distribution present in the parent population.

6) Migration: As previously explained, altering the CAN IDs of parents is avoided because it would most likely result in CAN IDs that the ECU does not respond to. However, this creates a challenge for the GFDG approach, as it restricts each run to generating messages only with the IDs present in the initial generation. The likelihood of the first generation containing at least one active CAN ID is low, especially with small population sizes. This could lead to multiple runs of the GFDG without producing a single CAN message that triggers a response from the system under test. To overcome this limitation, the GFDG introduces an additional step to the standard GA to introduce new IDs into the population without losing the progress made in previous steps. This step is called Migration. During migration, a small portion of the next generation is created using new random individuals. This approach ensures a steady flow of new IDs and payload genes within a single run of the GFDG. Consequently, the algorithm can explore more CAN IDs in one run, increasing overall efficiency.

7) Termination Criteria: Every GA requires a termination criterion, which is checked after each generation. The common approach is to set a maximum number of iterations, which the GFDG also employs. Tests of the GFDG evaluated different iteration limits, identifying 50 to 100 generations as the optimal range. A lower limit prevents the algorithm from fully leveraging its evolutionary process, while a higher limit leads to a rapid increase in duplicate messages. Notably, this effect correlates with mutation probability—higher mutation rates can reduce the likelihood of duplicate messages within a single run, potentially allowing for a greater number of generations.

Algorithm 1 GFDG Algorithm

Input: POP_SIZE, MAX_ITER, CROSSOVER_RATE, MUTATION_RATE, MIGRATION_COUNT

$population \leftarrow initialize\_population()$
$generation \leftarrow 0$
while $generation < MAX\_ITER$ **do**
  for each $individual$ in $population$ **do**
    $individual.fitness \leftarrow send\_and\_evaluate(individual)$
  end for
  if $termination\_criteria\_met(population)$ **then**
    break
  end if
  $mating\_pool \leftarrow ranked\_selection(population)$
  $new\_population \leftarrow \{\}$
  while $|new\_population| < POP\_SIZE - MGRATION\_COUNT$ **do**
    $(parent1, parent2) \leftarrow pick\_two(mating\_pool)$
    $(child1, child2) \leftarrow crossover\_and\_mutate(parent1, parent2, CROSSOVER\_RATE, MUTATION\_RATE)$
    $new\_population \leftarrow new\_population \cup \{child1, child2\}$
  end while
  for $i \leftarrow 1$ **to** $MIGRATION\_COUNT$ **do**
    $new\_population \leftarrow new\_population \cup generate\_CAN\_message()$
  end for
  $population \leftarrow new\_population$
  $generation \leftarrow generation + 1$
end while

V. Experiments

The previously described GFDG algorithm was implemented and tested on an ECU in a laboratory setup to evaluate its performance. The tested system is an automotive ECU used in certain 2020 vehicle models to control various cockpit functions. Testing focused on the ECU's dedicated CAN channel for controlling the Infotainment System. Temperature sensors and an oscilloscope were used to monitor the previously mentioned side-channel signals. Before fuzz testing, multiple baseline measurements of the ECU were conducted to establish reference data representing its normal operating state. This baseline was then used for comparison with measurements taken during fuzz testing. For evaluation, multiple fuzz testing runs with the GFDG were performed under different ECU states, including while Navigation or Radio functions were active and while a mobile device was connected to the Infotainment System via Bluetooth. Each test run was performed with a population size of 16, a migration count of 4, and a maximum iteration count of 50. After each test run, the ECU was properly shut down, and a waiting period was observed to allow the processing units to cool. After each test, the GFDG log file—containing all sent CAN messages, associated fitness scores, and timestamps—was documented along with the side-channel measurements. Additionally, the display of the Infotainment System was manually monitored, and any visual effects were recorded.

VI. Results

After the experiments, the initial analysis compared side-channel measurements with and without fuzzing to identify anomalies. Without fuzz testing, the temperature of all three processing units remained stable within a 0.1 to 0.2°C range across all tests, and the display's power supply remained consistent. During fuzz testing with the GFDG, multiple anomalies were observed. These included temperature increases of 1 to 2°C in one or more processing units in a short period, which were reproducible by resending the same fuzz messages. Notably, temperature spikes were most pronounced when fuzz messages triggered visual changes on the display, confirming the hypothesis that rendering new images requires GPU processing, leading to increased temperature. Additionally, certain CAN messages generated by the GFDG caused a temporary decrease in display brightness, resulting in a measurable voltage drop of at least 50 percent. Some fuzz messages also led to short-term temperature spikes in the AMC. However, no visible changes in the user interface were observed for these cases, making it unclear what system behavior they triggered. Overall, multiple CAN messages were identified that caused observable changes in the system under test. Several messages with different CAN IDs triggered notifications on the display, including warning and error messages. Analyzing the GFDG log file confirmed that all fuzz messages with a measurable system impact were correctly identified by the fitness function. Furthermore, multiple child messages—generated from the same parent ID but with modified payloads—elicited distinct system reactions. A notable case involved a message generated through the migration step, which triggered a "Goodbye" message on the display. The GFDG detected this message as active due to a significant GPU temperature increase and selected it as a parent for further genetic operations. The resulting three child messages with the same ID exhibited different behaviors: two had no visible effect and were confirmed inactive through side-channel measurements, while the third caused the system to reboot the Bluetooth function and display an error message. Further testing revealed that sending this message twice in quick succession caused multiple infotainment functionalities to crash. Specifically, the Media, Radio, and Telephone menus became inaccessible through the user interface. Although the Bluetooth settings menu remained available, users could no longer modify any settings, turn Bluetooth on/off, or connect new devices to the vehicle's Infotainment System. This behavior was classified as a Denial of Service (DoS) vulnerability.

VII. Conclusion and Future Work

This research introduced the GFDG, a fuzzing approach for the CAN protocol that leverages GAs with the goal of enhancing testing efficiency. Unlike conventional CAN fuzzing methods, the GFDG incorporates system feedback through side-channel analysis, enabling the identification of active CAN IDs and the generation of targeted fuzz messages. By structuring CAN messages as genetic individuals and applying evolutionary operations, such as selection, crossover, and mutation, the GFDG dynamically refines its test cases to increase the likelihood of triggering system responses and uncovering vulnerabilities. Experimental results suggest that this approach is capable of identifying system anomalies within an automotive ECU, though further analysis is needed to fully assess its effectiveness. Notable findings included measurable increases in processing unit temperatures and power supply variations, confirming the correlation between system reactions and observable changes in side-channels. Furthermore, the GFDG successfully uncovered a DoS vulnerability capable of disrupting multiple Infotainment functions, highlighting its potential for real-world security assessments. However, this method has certain limitations. The performance of the GFDG heavily depends on the accuracy of the defined fitness function, which, in turn, relies on the availability and quality of side-channel data for recognizing system reactions. Additionally, parameters, such as mutation probability, population size, and migration proportion influence its overall effectiveness. These aspects require further research to refine this method.

Despite these limitations, the experimental results indicate that integrating genetic algorithms with side-channel feedback can enhance the identification of active CAN IDs (RQ1) and can contribute to the efficiency and accuracy of vulnerability detection in automotive ECUs. Additionally, the application of evolutionary operations—selection, crossover, mutation, and migration—appeared to help refine fuzz messages, potentially enhancing the adaptability of the fuzzing process (RQ2), though further analysis is required to quantify this effect.

REFERENCES

[1] P. Fuxen, M. Hachani, J. Schmidt, P. Zaumseil, and R. Hackenberg, "Side channel monitoring for fuzz testing of future mobility systems", *CLOUD COMPUTING 2023*, p. 24, 2023.

[2] J. Yun, F. Rustamov, J. Kim, and Y. Shin, "Fuzzing of embedded systems: A survey", vol. 55, no. 7, 2022, ISSN: 0360-0300. DOI: 10.1145/3538644.

[3] Y. Zheng *et al.*, "FIRM-AFL: High-throughput greybox fuzzing of IoT firmware via augmented process emulation", presented at the 28th USENIX Security Symposium (USENIX Security 19), 2019, pp. 1099–1114, ISBN: 978-1-939133-06-9.

[4] P. Sperl and K. Böttinger, "Side-channel aware fuzzing", in *Computer Security–ESORICS 2019: 24th European Symposium on Research in Computer Security, Luxembourg, September 23–27, 2019, Proceedings, Part I 24*, Springer, 2019, pp. 259–278.

[5] H. Lee, K. Choi, K. Chung, J. Kim, and K. Yim, "Fuzzing can packets into automobiles", in *2015 IEEE 29th International Conference on Advanced Information Networking and Applications*, IEEE, 2015, pp. 817–821.

[6] H. Zhang, K. Huang, J. Wang, and Z. Liu, "CAN-FT: A fuzz testing method for automotive controller area network bus", in *2021 International Conference on Computer Information Science and Artificial Intelligence (CISAI)*, Sep. 2021, pp. 225–231. DOI: 10.1109/CISAI54367.2021.00050.

[7] "Iso 11898-1:2024 road vehicles — controller area network", International Organization for Standardization, Standard, version 3, May 2024.

[8] F. Pölzlbauer, R. I. Davis, and I. Bate, "Analysis and optimization of message acceptance filter configurations for controller area network (CAN)", in *Proceedings of the 25th International Conference on Real-Time Networks and Systems*, ser. RTNS '17, New York, NY, USA: Association for Computing Machinery, Oct. 4, 2017, pp. 247–256, ISBN: 978-1-4503-5286-4. DOI: 10.1145/3139258.3139266.

[9] A. Singhal, T. Winograd, and K. A. Scarfone, "Guide to secure web services", National Institute of Standards and Technology, Gaithersburg, MD, NIST SP 800-95, 2007, Edition: 0, NIST SP 800–95. DOI: 10.6028/NIST.SP.800-95.

[10] D. S. Fowler, J. Bryans, S. A. Shaikh, and P. Wooderson, "Fuzz testing for automotive cyber-security", in *2018 48th Annual IEEE/IFIP International Conference on Dependable Systems and Networks Workshops (DSN-W)*, ISSN: 2325-6664, Jun. 2018, pp. 239–246. DOI: 10.1109/DSN-W.2018.00070.

[11] T. Werquin, R. Hubrechtsen, A. Thangarajan, F. Piessens, and J. T. Mühlberg, "Automated fuzzing of automotive control units", in *2019 International Workshop on Secure Internet of Things (SIOT)*, ISSN: 2690-8557, Sep. 2019, pp. 1–8. DOI: 10.1109/SIOT48044.2019.9637090.

[12] A. Anistoroaei, B. Groza, P.-Ş. Murvay, and H. Gurban, "Security analysis of vehicle instrument clusters by automatic fuzzing and image acquisition", in *2022 IEEE International Conference on Automation, Quality and Testing, Robotics (AQTR)*, May 2022, pp. 1–6. DOI: 10.1109/AQTR55203.2022.9802024.

[13] D. S. Fowler, J. Bryans, M. Cheah, P. Wooderson, and S. A. Shaikh, "A method for constructing automotive cybersecurity tests, a CAN fuzz testing example", in *2019 IEEE 19th International Conference on Software Quality, Reliability and Security Companion (QRS-C)*, Jul. 2019, pp. 1–8. DOI: 10.1109/QRS-C.2019.00015.

[14] M. Li, Y. Wang, H. Zhang, and J. Wang, "PRFT: A fuzz testing method for tire pressure monitoring system based on protocol reverse", in *2023 2nd International Conference on Big Data, Information and Computer Network (BDICN)*, Jan. 2023, pp. 248–252. DOI: 10.1109/BDICN58493.2023.00058.

[15] S.-J. Wu and P.-T. Chow, "Steady-state genetic algorithms for discrete optimization of trusses", *Computers & Structures*, vol. 56, no. 6, pp. 979–991, Sep. 17, 1995, ISSN: 0045-7949. DOI: 10.1016/0045-7949(94)00551-D.

[16] A. Lambora, K. Gupta, and K. Chopra, "Genetic algorithm- a literature review", in *2019 International Conference on Machine Learning, Big Data, Cloud and Parallel Computing (COMIT-Con)*, Feb. 2019, pp. 380–384. DOI: 10.1109/COMITCon.2019.8862255.

[17] A. Shukla, H. M. Pandey, and D. Mehrotra, "Comparative review of selection techniques in genetic algorithm", in *2015 International Conference on Futuristic Trends on Computational Analysis and Knowledge Management (ABLAZE)*, Feb. 2015, pp. 515–519. DOI: 10.1109/ABLAZE.2015.7154916.

Intrusion Detection using Peer-to-Peer Distributed Context-Information for Electric Vehicle Supply Equipment

Julian Graf, Christoph Moser, Philipp Fuxen, Rudolf Hackenberg
Faculty of Computer Science and Mathematics
Ostbayerische Technische Hochschule Regensburg
Regensburg, Germany
e-mail: {julian.graf | christoph.moser | philipp.fuxen | rudolf.hackenberg}@oth-regensburg.de

***Abstract*—In this paper, we present a decentralized approach to securing charging infrastructure in the private and semi-public sector. The goal is strengthening the resilience of charging infrastructure through enhanced security mechanisms based on sharing context information. Therefore, an architecture was developed that combines concepts of data acquisition, information exchange and analysis methods to efficiently monitor Electric Vehicle Supply Equipment systems. The "Resiliente und Sichere Ladeinfrastruktur" research project architecture connects the interfaces between charging hardware, a highly scalable Peer-to-Peer cybersecurity mesh network and the static and Artificial Intelligence-supported analysis processes on the top layer. The most important tasks across the domains of detection, reaction, attribution and prevention are taken into account. A large information space, which aggregates the content of the individual domains, is created and made available in the network. The context data of the information space is obtained from the individual peers and used for the analysis. Context-based data regarding loading procedures, network communication parameters, system loads, Open Charge Point Protocol parameters, and other domain data clusters are recorded. The extended local and central analysis use the context information for monitoring and attack classification. The context information is transmitted via an InterPlanetary File System-based Peer-to-Peer mesh network.**

Keywords-EVSE; Charging Station; Security; Peer-to-Peer; P2P; Context Information; Resilience; Attack Detection; IDS; Security-Architecture.

I. INTRODUCTION

The increasing uptake of Electric Vehicles (EVs) is a crucial step towards sustainable mobility. Governments and organizations around the world are setting ambitious targets to reduce CO2 emissions, with the development of a nationwide charging infrastructure playing a central role [1]. A reliable, safe and efficient charging infrastructure is crucial to increase the adoption of electric vehicles and enable a sustainable transition to transportation. However, while charging infrastructure is growing exponentially, the security of these systems often falls short of requirements. Cyberattacks on charging stations can not only affect individual users but, in the worst case, destabilize the entire energy grid and cause significant economic damage [2]. The charging infrastructure for electric vehicles is complex and consists of a large number of components, including hardware, software and communication interfaces. This heterogeneity opens up numerous attack surfaces for cyber threats. Existing studies have already revealed serious security vulnerabilities in current systems. For example, the widely used Open Charge Point Protocol (OCPP) 1.6 has significant vulnerabilities that allow attackers to carry out Man in the Middle (MitM) attacks or energy theft [3]. Other threats include Denial of Service (DoS) attacks, inadequately protected interfaces and the risk of malware spreading via compromised charging stations [4][5]. Despite the existing security measures, a fundamental problem remains: Current protection mechanisms are mostly centralized and reactive, which leaves them vulnerable to coordinated attacks and makes it difficult to efficiently detect and defend against threats. To minimize security risks, we propose a new type of decentralized architecture with the ReSiLENT approach. An additional detection unit is integrated into an Electric Vehicle Supply Equipment (EVSE), which gathers local data, conducts a series of analysis on behalf of intrusion detection and connects the EVSE to the cybersecurity mesh (a network of many individual EVSE). This allows the charging stations to communicate securely with each other and exchange contextual information. This distributed structure enables faster detection of anomalies and attacks and improves the resilience of the overall system. By integrating a cybersecurity mesh based on the principles of the cybersecurity domains of prevention, detection, reaction and attribution, a scalable and economically viable security solution for EVSE is created. As this paper introduces the concept of the ReSiLENT approach, the following research questions focus on its theoretical foundations and possible implications:

- **RQ1:** How can a decentralized peer-to-peer architecture effectively contribute to the detection and prevention of cyberattacks on EVSE?
- **RQ2:** Can contextual information be used to improve the prevention, detection, response and attribution of attacks on the charging infrastructure?

Following this introduction, Section II analyzes the relevant literature and existing work on security problems in the charging infrastructure. Section III describes the current threat situation for EVSE and highlights specific attack scenarios. Section IV provides an overview of the ReSiLENT system and its architecture. The details of the peer-to-peer network technology and its security advantages are discussed in Section V. Section VI presents the Cybersecurity Mesh, which enables efficient threat detection and defense. Section VII describes the ReSiLENT cybersecurity stack with its four core areas: Detection, Reaction, Prevention and Attribution. Finally, Section VIII discusses further research questions and future challenges.

II. Related Work

The security of EVSE is an increasingly relevant area of research as the number of connected charging stations continues to grow and potential attack vectors increase. Existing work is investigating various security-critical aspects, from vulnerabilities in communication and authentication to approaches for detecting and preventing cyberattacks. This section presents relevant studies that deal with security risks, attack detection and possible countermeasures in the charging infrastructure. It then discusses the extent to which existing solutions are sufficient and what research gaps still exist.

The security of EVSE is increasingly becoming a focus of research, as networked charging stations offer new opportunities for attacks. Existing work identifies vulnerabilities in communication, authentication and hardware. Skarga-Bandurova et al. [6] highlight various security vulnerabilities in charging stations, including lack of authentication for API access, insecure firmware updates and insufficiently protected data, and recommend secure communication, encryption and intrusion detection systems as countermeasures. Gottumukkala et al. [4] analyze vulnerabilities in the cyber-physical security of charging stations and identify attacks on network interfaces such as Bluetooth, Wi-Fi and wired connections, including spoofing, MitM, DoS and SQL injection. In addition, they show that physical access enables attacks on chip components, side-channel attacks and tampering. As a countermeasure, they propose a secure system design that includes a comprehensive assessment of threat vectors in hardware and software. Gottumukkala et al. [4] expand their recommendations on hardware and software security by focusing on the elimination of existing vulnerabilities and the preventive development of secure systems. Pratt et al. [5] address the growing threat to electric vehicle charging infrastructure and develop security paradigms to defend against potential cyberattacks. The large number of components, the heterogeneity of the systems and the decentralized distribution of critical infrastructures pose a particular security challenge. Although Pratt et al. [5] emphasize the independence of the various players in the charging system, they also point out the need for a coordinated exchange of information to defend against threats. They also emphasize the importance of continuous monitoring and diagnostics of all system components, focusing in particular on the role of EVSE monitoring from the provider's perspective. They classify key data such as billing information, location data and charging performance managed by a central entity. They also discuss mechanisms for checking the consistency between the physical and digital state of the charging infrastructure in order to detect deviations at an early stage. In the event of an attack, the response strategy should take into account both the security requirements of the affected component and the potential impact. Particularly critical incidents, such as attacks on the power grid, require differentiated measures compared to targeted attacks on individual units. Security is restored primarily through regular software and firmware updates of the vehicle and EVSE systems.

Securing charging infrastructure requires not only addressing existing vulnerabilities but also effective attack detection. Various research efforts have explored different methods to enhance security in this domain. While the integration of multilayered intrusion detection system architectures [7] enables the analysis and evaluation of several AI-supported procedures by providing large information spaces and thus optimizes the results. Buedi et al. [8] contribute a multidimensional dataset containing charging information and its evaluation. Their study focuses on EVSE in both charging and idle states, analyzing power consumption, network traffic, and host activities to support anomaly detection. Similarly, Kim et al. [9] provide a DoS-specific dataset that includes four attack scenarios related to vehicle authentication. Another approach is introduced by Purohit and Govindarasu [10], who utilize data collected from charging infrastructure entities. Instead of sharing raw data, their method relies on exchanging model parameters, enabling a federated learning framework for enhanced security. Additionally, Mavikumbure et al. [11] propose Cy-Phy ADS, an anomaly detection framework that integrates CAN data with machine learning to identify potential threats in charging systems. While many studies focus on anomaly detection and machine learning-based models for attack identification, our approach takes a broader, more comprehensive security perspective on EVSE. While existing work mainly focuses on specific security domains, Fuxen et al. [12][13] focus on a decentralized, graph-based architecture for Cyber Threat Intellgence (CTI) analysis and privacy-preserving threat intelligence sharing. The ReSiLENT approach, on the other hand, deals specifically with the security-critical EVSE. The challenges in this area differ from those of classic IT systems, as EVSE offers not only digital but also physical attack vectors that can have a direct impact on the power grid and transportation infrastructure. While Fuxen et al. [12][13] focus on cross-organizational threat detection and networking, our focus is on the local, decentralized security architecture of charging stations and their resilience against coordinated attacks. Our approach integrates specific protection measures for EVSE, including secure communication between charging points, protection in the OCPP, and attack detection based on real EVSE usage data. In summary, the security of EVSE is becoming an increasingly important area of research as the number of connected charging stations rises, creating new attack vectors. Various studies have identified vulnerabilities in communication, authentication, and hardware, proposing countermeasures such as secure communication, encryption, and intrusion detection systems. While existing solutions provide valuable insights, there is still room for improvement, particularly in the development of secure, decentralized systems, as most solutions currently rely on centralized systems. Furthermore, existing research tends to focus on either detection or prevention of cyberattacks instead of taking a comprehensive approach including the domains of reaction and

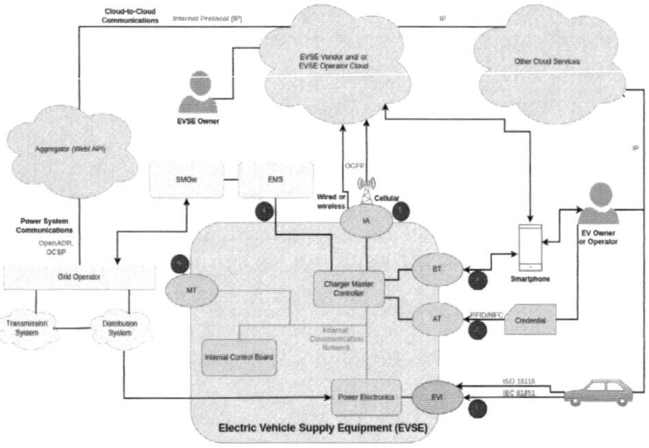

Figure 1. Electric Vehicle Infrastructure Landscape [15].

attribution.

III. EVSE Threat Landscape

EVSE faces numerous cybersecurity vulnerabilities that could compromise the integrity of the charging infrastructure and the power grids. These vulnerabilities include weak authentication mechanisms, unsecured communications, and potential exploits in connected systems [14]. Attacks on EVSE could lead to consequences ranging from localized disruptions to long-term national impacts [15]. The cyber-physical nature of EVSE systems, involving sensing, communication, and computational components, makes them susceptible to various threats [4]. As Electric Vehicle (EV) adoption grows, securing the charging infrastructure becomes crucial to prevent potential political, social, and financial consequences [16]. To address these challenges, researchers emphasize the need for comprehensive cybersecurity approaches, including threat modeling, risk assessments, and the development of effective countermeasures [14], [15]. Implementing Information Technology (IT) and Operational Technology (OT) cybersecurity best practices can help mitigate these risks and ensure the resilience of EVSE systems [15]. Before delving into the concepts and ideas that underlie the ReSiLENT project, it is essential to first establish the necessity of these efforts. Therefore, taking a look at current threats concerning Electric Vehicle Infrastructure (EVI) and especially EVSE.

ReSiLENT identifies attack vectors at a more granular level. As shown in Figure 1 designations 1-6, the interfaces EVI (ev-to-evse) via powerline communication, authentication (AT) via RFID / NFC, Bluetooth, EVSE Internet Access, SmartMeter Gateway (SMGw) and the maintenance terminal alone and in combination are identified as possible entry points. Effectively addressing each attack vector requires the identification, monitoring, and integration of countermeasures, ensuring an understanding of potential threats and the deployment of dedicated solutions to safeguard the resilience of the EVSE ecosystem.

IV. Overview of the ReSiLENT System

Given the current security landscape, there is a clear need to enhance EVSE cybersecurity. ReSiLENT introduces a novel architecture leveraging the distribution of cybersecurity information and assets across various actors and components within a connected charging infrastructure using a Peer-to-Peer (P2P) mesh network. Covering the domains detection, reaction, prevention, and attribution, the goal is to create a scalable and flexible security ecosystem for various e-mobility market segments, including private, commercial, and public high-power charging. Furthermore, our approach aims to ensure the economic viability of cybersecurity measures in low-cost charging infrastructure through automation.

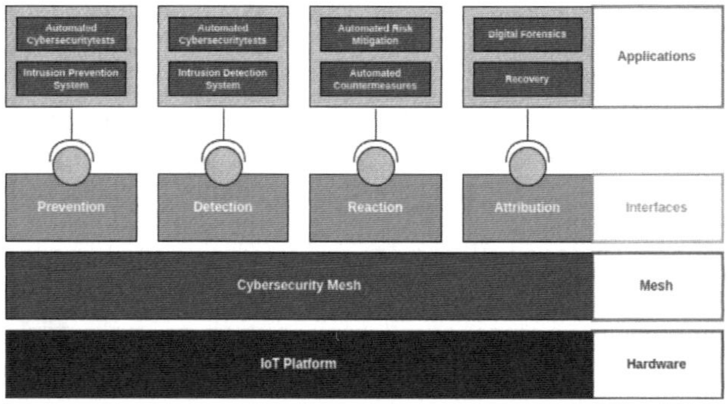

Figure 2. ReSiLENT High-Level Architecture.

As shown in Figure 2, the high-level ReSiLENT architecture consists of three core levels. Starting with the hardware level, which is mapped via the so-called IoT platform. The hardware level forms the interface to the firmware of the local charging controllers and to other hardware elements installed in the charging station. It enables the collection of information on specific system parameters, such as the current and voltage during a charging process or the utilization of the controller CPU. It also enables safety measures to be carried out on the charging station. Possible reactions here are, for example, canceling the charging process or closing communication connections. The second level, also known as the mesh level, is responsible for connecting the charging stations. A P2P mesh network is established at this level. Each charging station is considered a peer in this network and can provide and request information after authentication. The mesh network offers the possibility to share information in a decentralized manner. Charging stations can specifically request information that is required for local analyses. The creation, networking and distribution of a context-based information space is essential for advanced attack classification, derivation of response measures, prevention and attribution. The top level, also known as the application level, is supplied with the required data space via the domain-specific interfaces. It integrates the cybersecurity applications, which carry out certain analyses, measures or the provision of information depending on the domain. Through this architecture, we establish a robust security system that enhances the resilience of EVSE against cyber threats while ensuring practical and cost-efficient implementation.

V. Peer-to-Peer Mesh-Network

The essence of the ReSiLENT project is to identify an effective method for distributing context information while simultaneously ensuring security. In the realm of Internet of Things (IoT) networks, application protocols such as Message Queueing Telemetry Transport (MQTT) have gained significant popularity due to their lightweight nature and efficiency in distributing data. MQTT is particularly well-suited for resource-constrained environments, offering publish-subscribe communication that minimizes bandwidth and computational overhead. However, its architecture relies on centralized brokers, which may introduce single points of failure and increasing complexity when scaled up [17]. Therefore, and because of the reasons mentioned below, a P2P approach was taken in the ReSiLENT-System. More specifically, the InterPlanetary File System (IPFS) protocol stack was chosen, as it combines peer-to-peer communication (via libp2p) with robust data storage capabilities, enabling distributed systems to share and store content without the need for centralized servers. The ReSiLENT P2P mesh network offers the following advantages:

- **Resilience Against Failures and Attacks:** ReSiLENT follows a security-by-design approach, prioritizing decentralization to enhance resilience. Unlike centralized models, where data is stored on a single server, ReSiLENT distributes data across multiple nodes. When a node requests data, it caches a copy and serves it to others, ensuring continued availability even if the original source goes offline.
- **Data Integrity and Tamper Resistance:** One of the key security aspects of ReSiLENT is ensuring data integrity and protection against tampering. In contrast to Hypertext Transfer Protocol (HTTP), data in IPFS is addressed by content rather than location. Instead of being found through a Uniform Resource Locator (URL), files are retrieved via their cryptographic hash. This ensures that each file is uniquely identified by its content rather than its address.
- **Secure and Reliable Data Distribution:** Traditional server-client models often experience performance degradation when too many users access a server simultaneously. In contrast, P2P networks such as IPFS allow nodes to retrieve files from the nearest available peers, optimizing data transfer efficiency.
- **Anonymity and Privacy Protection:** Privacy is a critical aspect of cybersecurity, and P2P networks offer inherent advantages in this regard. Depending on the protocol, P2P communication can provide a certain degree of anonymity, as data requests and transmissions are relayed through multiple nodes. This obfuscation makes it more difficult to trace data streams and provides an added layer of privacy protection. Within ReSiLENT, this feature can be leveraged for secure sharing of anonymized cyber threat intelligence, ensuring that sensitive data remains protected while enabling collaborative security efforts among distributed nodes.

VI. Context Distribution

With the possibility of distributing data, it is necessary to evaluate which data must be passed on and which node has an interest in receiving it. In the ReSiLENT-System, the contextual information disseminated through a private IPFS network enables each node to conduct a series of analytical processes. The goal is to determine which context information needs to be distributed to positively impact existing CTI processes and to develop new approaches based on this foundation.

A. Conventional Approaches vs ReSiLENT

Traditionally, cyber threat intelligence relies on a centralized server model, where all data is collected and processed in one location. This approach, while effective, introduces single points of failure, scalability limitations, and potential privacy concerns. ReSiLENT employs a hybrid P2P model, where each node contributes to CTI by analyzing and sharing context information. A specialized centralized node, with greater computational power, augments the P2P network by performing complex calculations. Figure 3 illustrates the context distribution and analysis in the ReSiLENT system. The nodes $P_1 - P_4$ represent individual charging stations, where the IoT platform within each EVSE gathers local hardware and network data, shares relevant information, and conducts analysis before publishing results back into the network. The central node P_M leverages additional information, e.g. from a Charging Station Managemant System (CSMS), for its analysis.

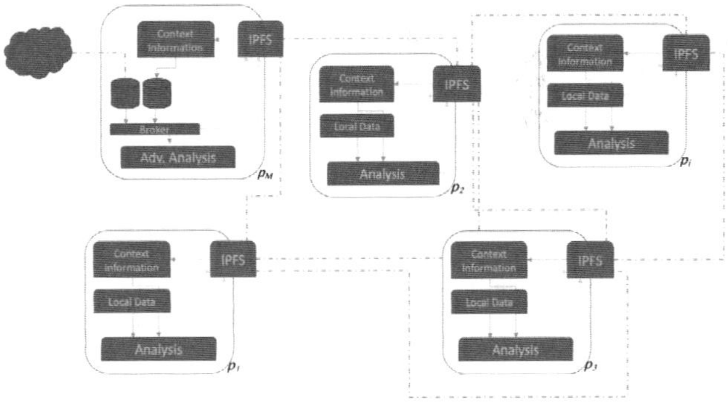

Figure 3. Overview of ReSiLENT P2P context distribution and analysis.

B. Distribution of Context Information

To effectively distribute context information within the network, ReSiLENT leverages a combination of IPFS functionalities:

- **Distributed Hash Table (DHT)** Enables efficient storage and retrieval of data.
- **PubSub Mechanism:** Facilitates real-time notifications about publication of files in the DHT.

- **Topic-based Channels:** Nodes subscribe to relevant topics, such as detection methods or threat reports, ensuring focused information exchange.

C. Types of Distributed Information

s shown in Table I, ReSiLENT distributes various forms of context information, including EVSE charging session data, network traffic, hardware status and threat reports generated by local analysis. This is not a comprehensive list yet, as further information can be relevant based on future development of CTI-Applications.

TABLE I. TYPES OF DISTRIBUTED INFORMATION IN RESILENT

Data Type	Description
Threat Reports	Periodically generated by each EVSE to document anomalies, vulnerabilities, and security states.
IPFS Metrics	Insights into neighboring peers, network traffic, detection of malicious nodes, and integrity verification.
EVSE Profiles	Summarizing charging behavior, station usage, and proximity relationships.
User Profiles	Capturing behavioral patterns, such as charging station preferences and consumption trends.

VII. RESILENT CYBERSECURITY-STACK

The ReSiLENT cybersecurity stack combines methods and procedures from the domains of **detection**, **reaction**, **prevention** and **attribution**, making efficient use of overarching synergy effects. Focused and classified attack detection makes it possible to generate targeted information that enables dedicated response measures to be activated and provides information on balanced preventive measures. Attributive operations can be efficiently identified based on the results of other domains.

A. Detection

To detect attacks on EVSE, it is necessary to combine different monitoring methods and systems. For the protection and detection of ReSiLENT, procedures from the following areas are to be included:

- Network traffic monitoring
- Intrusion Detection and Prevention System (IDS/P)
- Signature-based Intrusion Detection System (IDS)
- Behaviour-based IDS
- Firmware integrity checks, e.g. secure boot
- Secure updates, e.g. code signing
- Physical tamper detection
- Protocol and log analysis, e.g. correlation of events
- Authentication and access control
- Anomaly Detection using Artificial Intelligence (AI)
- Threat Intelligence, e.g. information sharing

In order to regularly monitor and evaluate the systems, it makes sense to carry out additional stress tests and penetration tests. Blackbox fuzzing attacks should also be included.

A crucial aspect of the ReSiLENT detection approach is the usage of context information shared by individual nodes and distributed over the IPFS mesh. The threat detection mechanisms specifically using this shared data fall into three categories:

- **Complementary**: Using data and results from multiple nodes in order to gain a broader view of the whole system, even on single nodes.
- **Consensus-Oriented**: Cross-verifying results from different nodes to increase detection reliability.
- **Comparative**: Analyzing deviations from normal behavior based on historical data and comparing results of multiple nodes.

B. Reaction

With regard to response measures, a distinction must be made between automated measures and manual or person-controlled measures.

Automated measures:

- Segmentation or isolation of components
- Automated blocking, e.g. IP- / MAC-addresses or traffic
- Rollbacks to previous firmware or software versions
- Automated lockouts, e.g. failed authentication

Manual interventions:

- Security incident response teams
- Forensic investigations
- Replacing hardware and software

A structured evaluation should be carried out after each prevented or successful attack. Based on that, security guidelines should be updated and findings should be incorporated into the ongoing security strategy.

C. Attribution

Attribution is often a major challenge in the field of cybersecurity. The same applies to attacks on charging stations for electric vehicles: Although technical traces can be collected, a clear attribution to specific actors is usually only possible with considerable effort and probability statements. Nevertheless, there are various measures and methods to support the best possible attribution. Attribution benefits from the most accurate attack classification possible, which includes, among other things, information gathering methods with or for digital forensics. The use of synergy effects of the ReSiLENT cybersecurity stack based on context information plays a central role here.

D. Prevention

While detection, response and attribution tend to intervene when a security event has already taken place or is actively underway, prevention starts before the actual incident. Prevention refers to all measures aimed at preventing attacks from the outset or significantly reducing their chances of success. The aim is to reduce the attack surface, minimize vulnerabilities and make access as difficult as possible for attackers A basic distinction is made between three preventive measures: technical, organizational and process-related preventive measures:

Technical prevention measures:

- Secure system and software architecture
- Security aspects during development phase

- Use of secure configurations
- Secure key management
- Encrypted communication
- Authentication and access controll
- Network segmentation
- Patch and update management
- Physical safety

VIII. Conclusion and Future Work

The security system for hardening the resilience of charging infrastructure presented in this paper demonstrates technology-based, modern approaches for collecting, distributing and analyzing EVSE-relevant data. In addition to recording Vehicle-to-EVSE transmissions, the interface between the IoT platform to the charging station also enables the monitoring of relevant charging process data, back-end communication, as well as the hardware status. The cybersecurity mesh network that builds on this enables the collected context information to be distributed securely, quickly and in a scalable manner. The extended analysis methods can integrate complex context-based analyses through the decentralized networking of the charging stations and thus also their data. Attacks can be detected and classified via the detection domain with your applications. Dedicated security measures can be selected, implemented and transmitted to the prevention applications for further preventive steps using the methods and procedures of the reaction domain. And finally, the decentralized distributed information space can be used for attributive measures.

In the future, it is intended to further expand the collection of context information and thus enlarge the information space. This will increasingly include EVSE-related communication patterns from Vehicle-to-EVSE. Furthermore, the response measures will be cyclically adapted and expanded in line with the progress made in the development of detection analyses. An automated derivation of preventive security measures is to be integrated on the basis of the information space of the detection and response domains and visualized for users. In addition, attributive measures are to be finally integrated based on the results of the three preliminary domains. The developments will be accompanied by tests using a laboratory test setup and the integration of the software into real charging stations to evaluate the functionality.

References

[1] E. Parliament, "'fit for 55' legislative package: Strengthening the co2 emission performance standards for new passenger cars and new light commercial vehicles," [Online]. Available: https://www.europarl.europa.eu/RegData/etudes/BRIE/2021/694249/EPRS_BRI(2021)694249_EN.pdf (visited on 12/13/2024).

[2] S. H. Ahmed and F. M. Dow, "Electric vehicle and charging station technology as vulnerabilities threaten and hackers crash the smart grid," 2016.

[3] C. Alcaraz, J. Lopez, and S. Wolthusen, "Ocpp protocol: Security threats and challenges," *IEEE Transactions on Smart Grid*, 2017. DOI: 10.1109/TSG.2017.2669647.

[4] R. Gottumukkala *et al.*, "Cyber-physical system security of vehicle charging stations," in *2019 IEEE Green Technologies Conference(GreenTech)*, 2019. DOI: 10.1109/GreenTech.2019.8767141.

[5] R. M. Pratt and T. E. Carroll, "Vehicle charging infrastructure security," in *2019 IEEE International Conference on Consumer Electronics (ICCE)*, 2019. DOI: 10.1109/ICCE.2019.8662043.

[6] I. Skarga-Bandurova, I. Kotsiuba, and T. Biloborodova, "Cyber security of electric vehicle charging infrastructure: Open issues and recommendations," in *2022 IEEE International Conference on Big Data (Big Data)*, 2022. DOI: 10.1109/BigData55660.2022.10020644.

[7] J. Graf, K. Neubauer, S. Fischer, and R. Hackenberg, "Architecture of an intelligent intrusion detection system for smart home," in *2020 IEEE International Conference on Pervasive Computing and Communications Workshops (PerCom Workshops)*, 2020, pp. 1–6. DOI: 10.1109/PerComWorkshops48775.2020.9156168.

[8] E. D. Buedi, A. A. Ghorbani, S. Dadkhah, and R. L. Ferreira, "Enhancing ev charging station security using a multi-dimensional dataset: Cicevse2024," in *Data and Applications Security and Privacy XXXVIII*, 2024. DOI: 10.1007/978-3-031-65172-4_11.

[9] Y. Kim, S. Hakak, and A. Ghorbani, "Ddos attack dataset (cicev2023) against ev authentication in charging infrastructure," in *2023 20th Annual International Conference on Privacy, Security and Trust (PST)*, 2023. DOI: 10.1109/PST58708.2023.10320202.

[10] S. Purohit and M. Govindarasu, "Fl-evcs: Federated learning based anomaly detection for ev charging ecosystem," in *2024 33rd International Conference on Computer Communications and Networks (ICCCN)*, 2024. DOI: 10.1109/ICCCN61486.2024.10637543.

[11] H. S. Mavikumbure *et al.*, "Cy-phy ads: Cyber-physical anomaly detection framework for ev charging systems," *IEEE Transactions on Transportation Electrification*, 2024. DOI: 10.1109/TTE.2024.3363672.

[12] P. Fuxen *et al.*, "Mantra: A graph-based unified information aggregation foundation for enhancing cybersecurity management in critical infrastructures," in *Open Identity Summit 2023*, Bonn: Gesellschaft für Informatik e.V., 2023, pp. 123–128, ISBN: 978-3-88579-729-6. DOI: 10.18420/OID2023_10.

[13] P. Fuxen, M. Hachani, R. Hackenberg, and M. Ross, "Mantra: Towards a conceptual framework for elevating cybersecurity applications through privacy-preserving cyber threat intelligence sharing," *IARIA Cloud Computing 2024*, 2024. DOI: 10.18420/OID2023_10.

[14] G. Vailoces, A. Keith, A. Almehmadi, and K. El-Khatib, "Securing the electric vehicle charging infrastructure: An in-depth analysis of vulnerabilities and countermeasures," in *Proceedings of the Int'l ACM Symposium on Design and Analysis of Intelligent Vehicular Networks and Applications*, ser. DIVANet '23, New York, NY, USA: Association for Computing Machinery, 2023, pp. 31–38. DOI: 10.1145/3616392.3623424.

[15] J. Johnson, T. Berg, B. Anderson, and B. Wright, "Review of electric vehicle charger cybersecurity vulnerabilities, potential impacts, and defenses," *Energies*, vol. 15, no. 11, p. 3931, May 26, 2022, ISSN: 1996-1073. DOI: 10.3390/en15113931.

[16] J. Johnson, "Securing vehicle charging infrastructure," SAND–2020-11971R, 1706221, 691697, Nov. 6, 2020, SAND–2020–11971R, 1706221, 691697. DOI: 10.2172/1706221.

[17] M. A. Spohn, "On MQTT scalability in the internet of things: Issues, solutions, and future directions," *Journal of Electronics and Electrical Engineering*, p. 4, Oct. 19, 2022, ISSN: 2972-3280. DOI: 10.37256/jeee.1120221687.

A Transformer-Based Framework for Anomaly Detection in Multivariate Time Series

Fabian Folger*, Murad Hachani†, Philipp Fuxen†, Julian Graf†,
Sebastian Fischer†, Rudolf Hackenberg†
Department of Computer Science and Mathematics
Ostbayerische Technische Hochschule Regensburg
Regensburg, Deutschland
* e-mail: fabian1.folger@st.oth-regensburg.de,
† e-mail: {murad.hachani | philipp.fuxen | julian.graf |
sebastian.fischer | rudolf.hackenberg}@oth-regensburg.de

***Abstract*—This paper introduces a comprehensive Transformer-based architecture for anomaly detection in multivariate time series. Using self-attention, the framework efficiently processes high-dimensional sensor data without extensive feature engineering, enabling early detection of unusual patterns to prevent critical system failures. In a subsequent laboratory setup, the framework will be applied using fuzzing techniques to induce anomalies in an Electronic Control Unit, while monitoring side channels, such as temperature, voltage, and Controller Area Network messages. The overall structure of the architecture, as well as the necessary preprocessing steps, such as temporal aggregation and classification up to the optimization of the hyperparameters of the model, are presented. The evaluation of the model architecture with the postulated restrictions shows that the model handles anomaly scenarios in the dataset robustly. It is necessary to evaluate the extent to which the model can be used in practical applications in areas, such as cloud environments or the industrial Internet of Things. Overall, the results highlight the potential of Transformer models for the automated and reliable monitoring of complex time series data for deviations.**

***Keywords-AI*; *Transformer*; *Time Series*; *Anomaly Detection*; *ECU*; *Temporal Aggregation*.**

I. INTRODUCTION

Transformer architectures have seen a surge in popularity recently, largely driven by the success of Large Language Models (LLMs) like ChatGPT, Gemini, and Claude. Initially focused on natural language processing tasks, these models have demonstrated that the underlying self-attention mechanisms can be beneficial in other domains as well. This trend is supported by the rapid increase in computing power in cloud and GPU environments, which now makes it possible to train and use models with a large number of parameters quickly and reliably.

A prime example is NVIDIA's recent presentation at CES, where new graphics cards and "DLSS 4" were introduced [1]. These products utilize transformer-based components to generate high-resolution pixels and entire frames, replacing the previously dominant Convolutional Neural Network (CNN) architectures with transformers that excel in parallel, context-sensitive processing.

Transformers are also becoming increasingly relevant for time series analysis, particularly when handling complex or multivariate sensor data. Their ability to capture long-range dependencies within signals is especially advantageous for anomaly detection—a critical need in industrial and Internet of Things (IoT) applications, such as machine, sensor, or network monitoring. Traditional methods like Recurrent Neural Networks (RNNs), Long Short-Term Memory (LSTM) models, or CNNs often struggle with modeling long-term dependencies, making the self-attention mechanism of transformers a powerful alternative [2].

This work develops and evaluates a specialized transformer approach for anomaly detection on multivariate, labeled sensor data. The goal is to create a fully automated framework that can be applied to a variety of multivariate datasets, demonstrating how transformer models can detect rare abnormal states and outperform classical methods, such as LSTM autoencoders and Isolation Forests. Due to its ability to detect anomalies in complex sensor environments, this approach is particularly suitable for safety-critical applications, including its potential use in fuzz testing scenarios. The model is designed to support the automatic detection of anomalies in different domains; its effectiveness in fuzz testing environments will be evaluated in future work.

The paper is organized into seven sections. The Introduction provides an overview of the research topic and objectives. The Section II examines relevant approaches and previous studies. The Section III outlines the data sources and preprocessing steps. The Section IV details the model's design. The Section V reviews and interprets the results. The Section VI compares the model presented with other common methods in this domain. Finally, the Section VII summarizes key insights, highlights potential applications, and suggests directions for future research.

II. RELATED WORK

The detection of anomalies in technical systems is a comprehensive field of research that has gained considerable importance in recent years due to advances in the field of machine learning and, in particular, the use of neural networks. Various methods are employed, differing depending on the domain and data structure. This section presents related work from the fields of fuzz testing, transformer-based anomaly detection on time series data, and a platform for monitoring Electronic Control Units (ECUs) using side-channel analysis, which together provide a background for our research.

M. Böhme et al. have analyzed the challenges and opportunities of fuzzing and emphasize the problem of "human-in-the-loop", where test auditors have to invest considerable effort in analyzing the fuzzing results. Their research focuses on automating these processes through Artificial Intelligence (AI) [3]. L. McDonald et al. classify fuzzing methods and investigate hybrid approaches that combine static analysis, runtime error detection, and machine learning. They identify side-channel fuzzing as a promising extension for black-box fuzzing in the field of embedded [4]. One of the main problems with black box fuzzing is the lack of direct insight into the internal processes of the system under test. One solution to this is side-channel fuzzing, in which physical side channels, such as power consumption, electromagnetic emissions, or temperature curves are analyzed [5] [6]. P. Sperl et al. show that power trace analyses are suitable for optimizing fuzzing processes by drawing conclusions about the internal processes of a system [5]. This method has been successfully applied to embedded systems to identify unexpected behavior and detect error states more efficiently.

Transformer models have achieved outstanding performance in many tasks in the field of natural language processing and computer vision [7]. Transformer models have also demonstrated outstanding results in the analysis and forecasting of time series data [8][9]. Furthermore, it is important to point out that there is no obvious need to use transformer models for long-term time series predictions, since even simple MLP models can outperform transformers, such as DLinear in the analysis of long-term time series predictions [10]. However, the results of transformers, such as PatchTST [11] already show significant improvements. Xu et al. [2] were able to prove that transformer models also offer advantages in the detection of time series anomalies, since temporal dependencies can be represented by the model, which leads to a high detection performance. Although there are different transformer architectures that have already been applied to time series-based data with different focused objectives, such as lightweight [12] [13] or cross-block connectivity [14] or adaptive computation time [15], it is still a future task to adapt and evaluate different architectural approaches to time series data [7]. However, Zerveas et al. [16] have shown that there is little work on pre-trained transformers for time series data and the existing studies focus mainly on the classification of time series data. In various system architectures and frameworks that rely on the combined analysis of static and dynamic AI-based methods, such as [17], research into modern approaches to processing and anomaly detection of time series to improve the recognition rates of these systems and frameworks are important.

The monitoring and anomaly detection used in this work is based on the platform of Fuxen et al. [18] who have developed a system for monitoring ECUs using side-channel analysis for fuzz testing in future mobility systems. Based on this platform, our transformer model was developed and will be evaluated in a fuzz testing scenario as part of future work. The combination of monitoring, fuzzing and AI-supported analysis offers an innovative approach to safeguarding safety-critical systems and uses the findings of Fuxen et al. as a foundation.

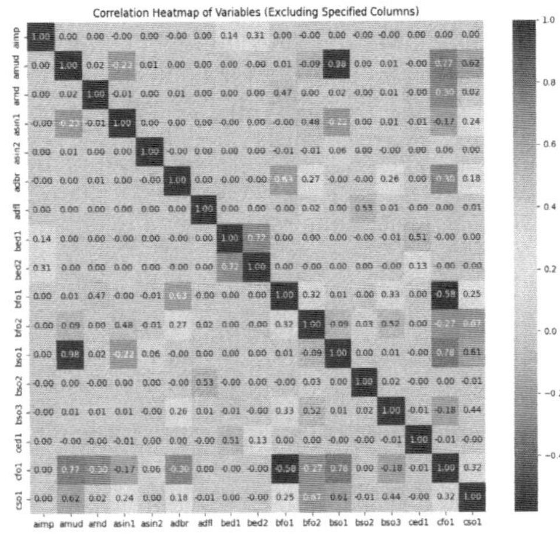

Figure 1. Correlation Heatmap

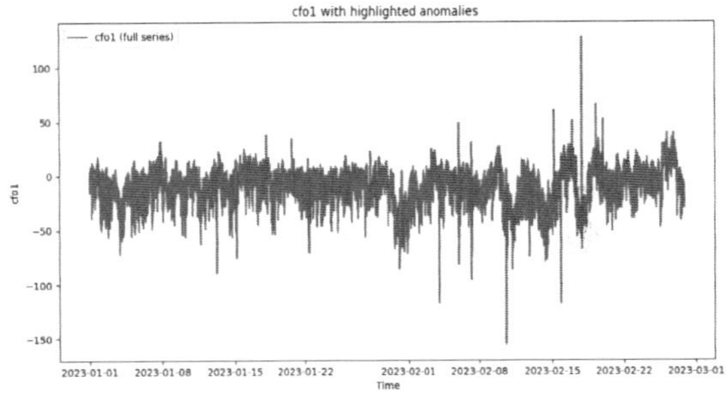

Figure 2. Time series variable cfo1 plotted with anomalies highlighted in red

III. DATASET

The primary criterion in selecting the dataset was its applicability to real-world scenarios, particularly for deploying the AI on real-time measurements in a laboratory environment. The Controlled Anomaly Time Series (CATS) dataset [19] from Solenix Engineering GmbH was chosen for its rich features that enable a realistic simulation of complex dynamic systems. This dataset comprises synthetically generated multivariate time series with 17 variables, including control commands, environmental influences, and sensor data, such as temperature and voltage.

At the outset of the data analysis, a correlation matrix was created in the form of a heatmap. This heatmap shown in Figure 1, depicts the complete dataset and reveals strong interdependencies among several variables. The color coding indicates negative correlations in blue and positive correlations in red—both types being crucial for the transformer when dealing with multivariate datasets. It is particularly noticeable that the characteristics *bso1* and *cfo1* with 0.98, and 0.77 show a relatively strong correlation with *amud*.

Figure 2 presents an example of injected anomalies in the variable CFO1, with anomalies highlighted in red. The plot was generated prior to data cleaning and scaling, showing raw measurement values on the Y-axis and the temporal progression

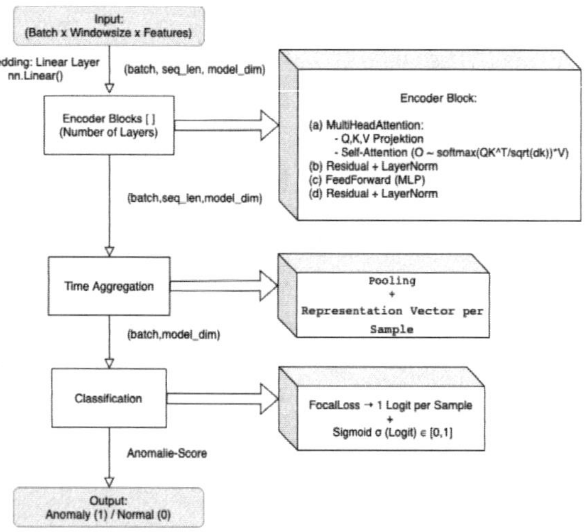

Figure 3. Transformer Architecture

(dates) on the X-axis, as the data were collected over several days.

A critical consideration for this dataset is the "root cause" of the anomalies, which initially manifests in other variables. Therefore, the dataset must not be truncated or abstracted, as doing so would eliminate these dependencies and prevent the transformer from learning the inherent patterns present in the original variables.

Notably, the dataset contains 200 carefully injected and annotated anomalies, which cover both obvious and context-dependent cases, making it an excellent benchmark for training the transformer-based anomaly detection system. With a resolution of 1 Hz over 5 million timestamps, the dataset offers data to learn normal system behavior and to develop robust anomaly detection models. An accompanying metadata file lists the time intervals of the anomalies, facilitating the removal of these segments during data preparation to expand the training set of normal data.

This dataset mirrors the physical measurement parameters expected in the laboratory. By applying the transformer model—known for its ability to capture both local and global temporal dependencies and to model complex multivariate correlations—to this synthetic data, the anomaly detection system can be evaluated and optimized under conditions that closely resemble practical scenarios.

IV. ARCHITECTURE

In the following section, we provide an in-depth description of the implemented Transformer architecture. This section covers the core structure, the underlying mathematical principles. Figure 3 illustrates the overall Transformer architecture, which is designed to classify time series segments based on their anomaly probability. The architecture is structured into the following steps:

1) Input Layer: The initial processing stage for incoming time series segments.
2) Linear Embedding (Embedding-Layer): Transforms raw sensor data into a higher-dimensional representation.
3) Batch Normalization: Enhances training stability by normalizing feature distributions.
4) Transformer Encoder: Implements multi-head self-attention and feedforward networks to capture temporal dependencies.
5) Global Aggregation (Mean over Time): Condenses the time-dependent representations into a single feature vector per segment.
6) Classification Head (Linear Output): Projects the aggregated features into a scalar output for anomaly detection.

A. Input Layer and Batch Normalization

The model begins by processing time series segments, each with dimensions [BatchSize, WindowSize, Features]. A linear embedding layer transforms raw sensor data (17 features) into a higher-dimensional space (e.g., 128 dimensions) using the formula:

$$y = xA^T + b \tag{1}$$

where x is the input, A represents the weight matrix (initialized uniformly with

$$k = \frac{1}{\text{in\_features}} \tag{2}$$

and b the bias. This step is crucial in mapping the raw input data into a format suitable for the self-attention mechanism.

Batch normalization is applied to maintain a stable distribution of features across each sliding window. This normalization improves the model's robustness during training.

B. Attention and Encoder Layer

In our model, we adopt the vanilla Transformer architecture as described in Attention is All You Need [20]. The attention mechanism begins by projecting the input into three distinct representations—queries, keys, and values—via learned linear transformations. These projections are then used in a scaled dot-product attention computation, where the dot product of queries and keys is scaled by the inverse square root of the key dimensionality to ensure numerical stability. The resulting attention weights are applied to the values, allowing the model to focus on relevant parts of the input.

Building upon this, the encoder layer integrates multi-head self-attention with a position-wise feed-forward network. Each encoder block applies residual connections and layer normalization both after the multi-head self-attention and the feed-forward network, which enhances gradient flow and stabilizes training. This combination of attention and encoder components forms the core of the Transformer model, enabling it to capture complex dependencies in sequential data.

C. Temporal Aggregation

After processing the sequence through the Transformer encoder layers, a temporal aggregation step is applied to condense the time-dependent representations into a single vector per input segment. This is achieved using an element-wise mean pooling operation across the time dimension:

$$\mathbf{z} = \frac{1}{T}\sum_{t=1}^{T}\mathbf{x}_t,$$

where $\mathbf{x}_t \in \mathbb{R}^{d_{\text{model}}}$ is the output for each time step t and z represents the aggregated feature vector. Although alternatives, such as max pooling or token-based representations (e.g., using a `[CLS]` token) exist, average pooling is chosen here for its simplicity and its ability to equally represent all time steps [21][22].

D. Classification

The final stage of the architecture is the classification head. The aggregated vector z is passed through a linear layer to produce a scalar output:

$$o = \text{Linear}(\mathbf{z}) \in \mathbb{R}.$$

A sigmoid activation is then applied to convert the scalar into a probability score between 0 (normal) and 1 (anomalous) [21][22]:

$$\sigma(\text{Logit}) = \frac{1}{1 + \exp(-\text{Logit})}$$

A threshold value determines the final binary classification. For handling class imbalances typical in anomaly detection, a Focal Loss is used instead of standard binary cross entropy [23]. The Focal Loss formula is:

$$\text{FL}(\hat{y}, y) = \alpha\left(1 - \hat{y}\right)^{\gamma}\text{BCE}(\hat{y}, y),$$

this is set to emphasize hard-to-classify examples.

Anomaly detection typically involves highly imbalanced data, where anomalous events are extremely rare compared to normal instances. Traditional loss functions like Binary Cross Entropy (BCE) treat all samples equally, often causing the model to be biased toward the majority class and overlook the few but critical anomalies. Focal Loss addresses this challenge by dynamically down-weighting the loss contribution of well-classified normal samples and up-weighting the misclassified or harder-to-classify anomalous examples. In practice, this means that the model is encouraged to learn more from the sparse anomaly examples, enhancing its sensitivity and overall detection performance in an imbalanced dataset [23].

E. Training

In preparation for training, suitable hyperparameters for the Transformer model are determined using Optuna [24]. This process follows a semi-supervised approach: while the model is mainly trained on normal (non-anomalous) data, the validation set contains a few anomalies. This setup enables the optimization process to favor parameter combinations that effectively detect anomalies, optimizing for metrics, such as the F1 score.

Once Optuna identifies the best hyperparameters, the model is retrained on normal data in an unsupervised manner—meaning it does not explicitly see any anomaly examples during training. The final evaluation, however, is performed on a test set containing both real and synthetically generated anomalies, thereby assessing the model's true capability to detect unusual patterns.

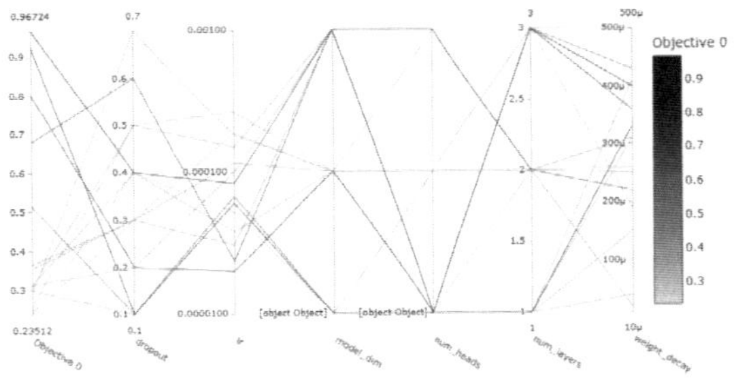

Figure 4. Evaluation of Hyperparameters using Optuna

The hyperparameter tuning is managed via an Optuna Optimizer class (see Figure 4), which integrates several DataLoader instances for training, validation, and test data (both normal and anomalous). During each trial in the process, hyperparameters (e.g., model dimension, number of attention heads, encoder layers, dropout, learning rate, and weight decay) are sampled from predefined ranges.

V. EVALUATION

To assess the model's performance, we applied standard binary classification metrics—such as the confusion matrix, F1-score, and ROC-AUC—among others. In this section, we analyze the results on the CATS dataset using these metrics, and we detail the hyperparameter configuration of the best performing model as identified through OPTUNA [25][26].

TABLE I
MODEL RESULTS

Transformer Metrics	Values
Optimal threshold	0.0117
ROC-AUC	0.9993
F1-Score	0.9717
Precision	0.9585
Recall	0.9853
Accuracy	0.9921
Anomalies detected (all Labels)	11731/83558 (14.04%)
Anomalies detected (Anomaly-Labels)	11244/11413 (98.52%)

Table I summarizes the overall performance of our anomaly detection model. The high ROC-AUC of 0.9993 and F1-Score of 0.9717 indicate that the model is effective in discriminating between normal and anomalous instances in the CATS dataset while being trained with an unsupervised method. The model achieves a precision of 0.9585 and a recall of 0.9853, which reflects its balanced capability to correctly identify anomalies while minimizing false positives. Overall the accuracy is reported at 0.9921, and the confusion matrix confirms that 98.52% of the true anomaly labels are correctly detected. These metrics underscore the robustness of our approach in handling complex multivariate time series data and highlight its potential for reliable anomaly detection in practical applications. The confusion matrix confirms these results, with the model detecting 98.52% of true anomalies.

Key hyperparameters for the CATS dataset and optimized via Optuna include:

- **Dropout:** 0.2
- **Learning Rate:** 2.0075e-05
- **Model Dimension:** 128
- **Attention Heads:** 8
- **Encoder Layers:** 3
- **Weight Decay:** 0.00036
- **Batch Size:** 128

VI. Comparison With Other Architectures

In this section, we provide a preliminary comparative analysis of our Transformer-based anomaly detection model with the established methods evaluated in the publication *Anomaly Detection in Time Series: A Comprehensive Evaluation* [26]. It should be noted that our evaluation is currently limited to the CATS dataset, which was chosen due to its close resemblance to our laboratory setup. This selection enables us to investigate the model's performance under controlled conditions that reflect our specific experimental environment.

While a direct comparison is inherently challenging due to the use of different datasets across studies, we have compared our model's performance with established architectures by benchmarking key metrics (ROC-AUC, F1-Score, Precision, and Recall) against those reported in the literature. We acknowledge that such indirect comparisons have limitations, however, on the Timeeval website, the CATS dataset is already listed and integrated on GitHub [27]. This availability opens up opportunities for further evaluation, either by our team or by the broader research community. In future work, we plan to leverage this integration to perform additional assessments and comparisons. Furthermore, benchmarking our Transformer-based model using the datasets available on Timeeval could provide a standardized framework to rank and compare its performance against other state-of-the-art approaches in [26].

Custom aspects of our framework include:

- **Focal Loss with Self-Attention:** This combination, while less common in time series applications, effectively addresses class imbalance by emphasizing the misclassified anomaly cases.
- **Flexible Time Window Segmentation:** The model adapts its sequence length and optimizes the number of attention heads, allowing it to better capture diverse temporal characteristics.
- **Tailored Binary Anomaly Classification:** By focusing on binary labels (normal vs. anomalous) and leveraging a specialized loss function, our approach directly targets the detection of rare anomaly labels.

A key discussion point is the generalizability of the results. Although the dataset used in this study contains carefully embedded anomalies, it remains an open question whether these findings can be directly transferred to more complex, real-world scenarios. Future experiments with time series data from various domains—such as industrial processes or medical applications—are needed to fully assess the model's robustness under varying conditions.

Another important aspect is the sensitivity to preprocessing choices. For instance, the window size used in the sliding-window technique has a significant impact on the patterns that are detected based on our experiments. Similarly, strategies for handling missing data and the specifics of hyperparameter tuning (e.g., via Optuna) can greatly influence the reliability and speed of anomaly detection. Sensitivity analyses, such as systematically varying the window size or testing different missing-data methods, would help ensure that the model's performance is not overly dependent on narrow parameter settings.

Compared to traditional methods, the Transformer—especially in its encoder-only configuration—offers potential advantages in terms of flexibility and performance. While decoder layers might be beneficial for forecasting or reconstruction tasks, they also increase complexity and resource requirements without necessarily improving pure anomaly detection. In contrast, older methods like classical autoencoders or statistical approaches (e.g., Isolation Forest) can sometimes achieve similar results with less effort but often struggle to capture the complex, nonlinear dependencies in high-dimensional time series data.

VII. Conclusion and Future Work

The Transformer-based architecture presented in this work has proven to be a potential approach for anomaly detection in multivariate time series. By leveraging self-attention mechanisms, the model was able to capture relationships in the dataset and accurately predict potential anomalies with minimal feature engineering. The flexible data pipeline—including missing-value handling, scaling, and segmentation—enables rapid adaptation to new datasets and application scenarios.

Optimized hyperparameter optimization has shown that a systematic, semi-supervised approach can identify optimal settings that effectively support the final unsupervised training. However, the validity of these results is highly dependent on the quality and representativeness of the underlying data. Therefore, it is necessary to perform future evaluations on different real data sets from different domains using time series data to finally confirm the generalizability and robustness of the model.

Overall, the experiments highlight the potential of transformer architectures for anomaly detection and provide valuable insights for future research.

In practice, the Transformer-based approach offers the advantage of capturing high-dimensional relationships between sensor variables. This capability enables the reliable identification of unusual patterns even in noisy environments or under changing data distributions. It can be concluded that the demonstrated method has some relevance for industrial or safety-critical scenarios in which multi-sensor data must be continuously monitored for deviations. However, further development is required to provide a productive model for this.

Comparing models across heterogeneous datasets remains challenging. Our preliminary benchmarking using key metrics underscores the potential of our approach. The integration of the CATS dataset into Timeeval offers a promising avenue for future standardized evaluations of our Transformer-based model alongside other state-of-the-art techniques [26].

Moreover, Transformer-based anomaly detection is finding increasing application in other fields, such as medicine, where it can identify abnormal patterns in complex biosignals. In our laboratory setup, an ECU combined with a fuzzer is used to deliberately induce anomalous states on the Controller Area Network (CAN) bus while simultaneously capturing side-channel data, such as temperature and voltage. This integrated approach not only delivers a comprehensive view of the system state but also provides feedback to progressively enhance the fuzzing algorithm [18].

The results of the presented methodology for time-series-based anomaly detection confirm the effectiveness of the developed model within the limitations. This provides a solid basis for further investigations and evaluations in laboratory environments and beyond. The flexible exploration of different use cases within the research group with regard to automotive security and IoT security is a focused goal.

REFERENCES

[1] NVIDIA, "Dlss 4: Multi-frame generation and ai innovations", Accessed: 2025.03.19, NVIDIA Corporation, 2024, [Online]. Available: https://www.nvidia.com/en-us/geforce/news/dlss4-multi-frame-generation-ai-innovations/.

[2] J. Xu, H. Wu, J. Wang, and M. Long, "Anomaly transformer: Time series anomaly detection with association discrepancy", *CoRR*, vol. abs/2110.02642, 2021. arXiv: 2110.02642.

[3] M. Böhme, C. Cadar, and A. Roychoudhury, "Fuzzing: Challenges and reflections", *IEEE Software*, vol. 38, no. 3, pp. 79–86, 2021.

[4] L. McDonald, M. I. U. Haq, and A. Barkworth, "Survey of software fuzzing techniques", Dec. 2021.

[5] P. Sperl and K. Böttinger, "Side-channel aware fuzzing", in *Computer Security–ESORICS 2019: European Symposium on Research in Computer Security*, Springer, vol. 24, Sep. 2019, pp. 259–278, ISBN: 978-3-030-29958-3. DOI: 10.1007/978-3-030-29959-0_13.

[6] M. Muench, J. Stijohann, F. Kargl, A. Francillon, and D. Balzarotti, "What you corrupt is not what you crash: Challenges in fuzzing embedded devices", *NDSS Symposium 2018*, 2018. DOI: 10.14722/ndss.2018.23176.

[7] Q. Wen *et al.*, *Transformers in time series: A survey*, 2023. arXiv: 2202.07125.

[8] S. Li *et al.*, "Enhancing the locality and breaking the memory bottleneck of transformer on time series forecasting", *Advances in neural information processing systems*, vol. 32, 2019.

[9] T. Zhou *et al.*, "Fedformer: Frequency enhanced decomposed transformer for long-term series forecasting", in *International conference on machine learning*, PMLR, 2022, pp. 27 268–27 286.

[10] A. Zeng, M. Chen, L. Zhang, and Q. Xu, "Are transformers effective for time series forecasting?", in *Proceedings of the AAAI conference on artificial intelligence*, vol. 37, 2023, pp. 11 121–11 128.

[11] Y. Nie, N. H. Nguyen, P. Sinthong, and J. Kalagnanam, *A time series is worth 64 words: Long-term forecasting with transformers*, 2023. arXiv: 2211.14730 [cs.LG].

[12] Z. Wu, Z. Liu, J. Lin, Y. Lin, and S. Han, "Lite transformer with long-short range attention", *CoRR*, vol. abs/2004.11886, 2020. arXiv: 2004.11886.

[13] S. Mehta, M. Ghazvininejad, S. Iyer, L. Zettlemoyer, and H. Hajishirzi, "Delight: Very deep and light-weight transformer", *CoRR*, vol. abs/2008.00623, 2020. arXiv: 2008.00623.

[14] A. Bapna, M. X. Chen, O. Firat, Y. Cao, and Y. Wu, "Training deeper neural machine translation models with transparent attention", *CoRR*, vol. abs/1808.07561, 2018. arXiv: 1808.07561.

[15] M. Dehghani, S. Gouws, O. Vinyals, J. Uszkoreit, and L. Kaiser, "Universal transformers", *CoRR*, vol. abs/1807.03819, 2018. arXiv: 1807.03819.

[16] G. Zerveas, S. Jayaraman, D. Patel, A. Bhamidipaty, and C. Eickhoff, "A transformer-based framework for multivariate time series representation learning", in *Proceedings of the 27th ACM SIGKDD conference on knowledge discovery & data mining*, 2021, pp. 2114–2124.

[17] J. Graf, K. Neubauer, S. Fischer, and R. Hackenberg, "Architecture of an intelligent intrusion detection system for smart home", in *2020 IEEE international conference on pervasive computing and communications workshops (PerCom Workshops)*, IEEE, 2020, pp. 1–6.

[18] P. Fuxen, M. Hachani, J. Schmidt, P. Zaumseil, and R. Hackenberg, "Side channel monitoring for fuzz testing of future mobility systems", *CLOUD COMPUTING 2023*, 2023.

[19] Patrick Fleith, *Controlled anomalies time series (CATS) dataset*, version 2, Sep. 14, 2023. DOI: doi.org/10.5281/zenodo.7646896.

[20] A. Vaswani *et al.*, "Attention is all you need", *CoRR*, vol. abs/1706.03762, 2017. arXiv: 1706.03762.

[21] S. Song, N.-M. Cheung, V. Chandrasekhar, and B. Mandal, "Deep adaptive temporal pooling for activity recognition", in *Proceedings of the 26th ACM international conference on Multimedia*, Oct. 15, 2018, pp. 1829–1837. DOI: 10.1145/3240508.3240713. arXiv: 1808.07272[cs].

[22] G. Zerveas, S. Jayaraman, D. Patel, A. Bhamidipaty, and C. Eickhoff, *A transformer-based framework for multivariate time series representation learning*, Dec. 8, 2020. DOI: 10.48550/arXiv.2010.02803. arXiv: 2010.02803[cs].

[23] T.-Y. Lin, P. Goyal, R. Girshick, K. He, and P. Dollár, *Focal loss for dense object detection*, Feb. 7, 2018. DOI: 10.48550/arXiv.1708.02002. arXiv: 1708.02002[cs].

[24] T. Akiba, S. Sano, T. Yanase, T. Ohta, and M. Koyama, "Optuna: A next-generation hyperparameter optimization framework", in *Proceedings of the 25th ACM SIGKDD International Conference on Knowledge Discovery & Data Mining*, ser. KDD '19, New York, NY, USA: Association for Computing Machinery, Jul. 25, 2019, pp. 2623–2631, ISBN: 978-1-4503-6201-6. DOI: 10.1145/3292500.3330701.

[25] P. Wenig, S. Schmidl, and T. Papenbrock, "TimeEval: A benchmarking toolkit for time series anomaly detection algorithms", *Proc. VLDB Endow.*, vol. 15, no. 12, pp. 3678–3681, Aug. 1, 2022, ISSN: 2150-8097. DOI: 10.14778/3554821.3554873.

[26] S. Schmidl, P. Wenig, and T. Papenbrock, "Anomaly detection in time series: A comprehensive evaluation", *Proceedings of the VLDB Endowment*, vol. 15, no. 9, pp. 1779–1797, May 2022, ISSN: 2150-8097. DOI: 10.14778/3538598.3538602.

[27] T. Project, "Timeeval - datasets overview", Accessed: 2025.03.19, 2022, [Online]. Available: https://timeeval.github.io/evaluation-paper/notebooks/Datasets.html.

Theoretical Integration of Hyperledger Fabric in Gaia-X: Towards an Approach for Federated Data Access

Liron Ahmeti*, Klara Dolos*, Conrad Meyer*, Andreas Attenberger*, Rudolf Hackenberg†
*Research Unit, Central Office for Information Technology in the Security Sector
Munich, Germany
Email: poststelle@zitis.bund.de
†Dept. Informatics and Mathematics, OTH Regensburg
Regensburg, Germany
Email: rudolf.hackenberg@oth-regensburg.de

Abstract—**Securing and managing distributed data in federated ecosystems is a key challenge when data protection, sovereignty and interoperability need to be guaranteed at the same time. Previous blockchain-based solutions often reach their limits in terms of integration capability and fine-grained access mechanisms. This theoretical paper presents a multilayered architecture concept that integrates Hyperledger Fabric into the Gaia-X ecosystem. Advanced encryption methods and a smart-contract-based reassembly logic are used to securely distribute fragmented data and make it accessible only to authorized actors. The approach promotes digital sovereignty and scalability within Gaia-X-compliant data spaces and serves as an initial conceptual basis that will be technically validated and further developed in future work.**

Keywords-Gaia-X; blockchain; architecture concept; federated data spaces

I. Introduction

Incorporating blockchain technology into existing and new digital ecosystems can promote a secure and decentralized method for storing and managing data while creating new opportunities for effective data governance and interoperability. Gaia-X, a European initiative, aims to create a secure and federated data ecosystem in Europe, allowing participants to share information interoperably while maintaining their digital sovereignty [1]. In this context, Hyperledger Fabric is presented as a blockchain platform that provides a flexible basis for such integrations through its permission-based architecture and the ability to implement smart contracts. The main goal of this paper is to develop an architecture to merge Hyperledger Fabric and the Gaia-X ecosystem to implement an interoperable private blockchain. These requirements include the ability to store data in an encrypted and partitioned manner and to reassemble and make this data accessible. The research will focus on the following key questions:

- i How can blockchain be designed to be compatible with Gaia-X to store and reassemble encrypted, split data?
- ii What security measures are necessary to ensure the integrity and confidentiality of the data?
- iii What challenges and opportunities arise from integrating blockchain technology into the Gaia-X ecosystem?

By answering these questions, this approach will help promote digital sovereignty and improve interoperability within the Gaia-X ecosystem. The remainder of the paper is organized as follows: Section II analyses the current state of the art and associated challenges. Section III presents the conceptual model, explaining the multi-layered structure of the system. Finally, Section IV discusses the advantages and disadvantages of the proposed approach and provides an outlook on future empirical validations and further developments.

II. Related Work

Secure and decentralized data management is becoming increasingly important, especially in trustworthy data ecosystems. Blockchain technology, particularly Hyperledger Fabric, offers promising approaches for secure data management through decentralization, transparency and tamper-proofing. At the same time, Gaia-X is pursuing the goal of establishing a federated and interoperable European data infrastructure. Integrating blockchain into Gaia-X could create new opportunities for trustworthy and privacy-compliant data spaces. A key aspect is data encryption and sharing to meet data protection requirements while ensuring efficient use and storage of sensitive information. This section provides an overview of the current state of research on blockchain technology, Gaia-X and data encryption and sharing methods in the context of distributed systems.

A. Blockchain

Blockchain technology has emerged as a transformative innovation, initially conceptualized by Nakamoto as the framework for Bitcoin [2]. Since then, it has evolved beyond cryptocurrencies to become a foundation for secure, decentralized, and transparent data exchange [3]. As a distributed ledger technology, blockchain enables immutable, trustless transactions without intermediaries [4]. Its applications span various sectors, including finance, healthcare, supply chain management, and identity verification [5][6]. Blockchains are typically classified into three categories: public, private, and consortium [7]. Public blockchains, like Bitcoin and Ethereum, operate in open, permissionless environments but face challenges, such as high energy consumption and scalability [3]. In contrast, private blockchains restrict access to authorized entities, which enhances efficiency and security [8]. Current research is focused on optimizing consensus mechanisms and improving interoperability with existing digital infrastructures to fully realize the transformative capabilities of blockchain [8]. Current research focuses on optimizing consensus and improving interoperability with established infrastructures, aiming to harness blockchain's transformative potential [8] fully. However, many existing solutions concentrate on single-use cases or rely on built-in cryptocurrencies, reducing flexibility in more complex enterprise scenarios [5].

B. Hyperledger Fabric

Hyperledger Fabric is an open-source blockchain framework tailored for enterprise use. It processes transactions in three phases: Execution, Ordering, and Validation. Initially, transactions are simulated to assess their impacts, then ordered by a dedicated group of nodes, and validated by peer nodes before updating the ledger. This design reduces bottlenecks typical in 'order-execute' systems, enhancing modularity and scalability. In a Fabric network, nodes called peers carry out various roles. Endorsing peers execute chain code to simulate and sign transactions, which are then sent to the ordering service for final arrangement. After consensus, participants validate endorsements and check for conflicts before adding transactions to the ledger. With verifiable identities issued by the Membership Service Provider (MSP), Hyperledger Fabric operates as a permissioned system. This eliminates the need for an internal cryptocurrency and allows users to choose a suitable consensus mechanism. By isolating chain code in Docker containers, Fabric increases security and supports fine-grained data control, enabling channels to restrict information sharing to specific participants. These features make Hyperledger Fabric a robust option for enterprise applications [9], nonetheless, cross-platform interoperability, off-chain data integration, and performance tuning remain challenges [9].

C. Gaia-X

Gaia-X is an initiative to create a federated, secure data infrastructure that promotes data sovereignty and interoperability. This is done by setting up so-called data spaces, i.e. digital representations of different sectors, such as health, agriculture or mobility, which enable secure and transparent data exchange between multiple stakeholders [10]. The architecture is based on three principles: Federation, decentralization and openness [11]. Federation allows different actors to retain their autonomy and interact in the ecosystem. Decentralization ensures no central body controls all processes, strengthening scalability and flexibility. Openness makes all Gaia-X components visible and accessible. A central element is the federation services, which include identity and trust management and support the federated catalogue to find suitable providers and services [11]. Providers register self-descriptions transferred as linked data into a knowledge graph so that users can query and filter them [11]. The Gaia-X Trust Framework also ensures security and compliance so all participants can operate in a protected environment [11]. A Trust Anchor instance acts as the issuing authority for digital identities [12] and confirms the identity of persons, organizations and devices [13]. These identities are based on the Self-Sovereign Identity (SSI) concept, which allows users to manage their digital credentials without central services [13]. An SSI wallet enables the secure storage of identity data and direct, trustworthy exchange.

D. Data encryption and splitting

Encryption and splitting techniques have long been essential for secure data distribution. Modern approaches, such as threshold cryptography and Content-Defined Chunking(CDC), aim to reduce single points of failure and permit partial reassembly only by authorized users. However, these solutions typically focus on data at rest within specialized storage systems and do not adequately consider interactions with external clouds or global consortia like Gaia-X. Additionally, the complexities of key management and vulnerabilities related to side channels, such as deduplication leaks, further complicate their implementation in real-world scenarios.However, most of these approaches focus solely on data security measures and do not fully address how to integrate external cloud infrastructures or handle large-scale federation requirements (e.g. in Gaia-X scenarios) [1][6]. Many solutions rely on a single blockchain domain, leaving a gap in unified, end-to-end architectures that connect on-chain trust mechanisms with off-chain systems. Current research highlights the potential of Hyperledger Fabric for secure, tamper-proof data management and the capabilities of Gaia-X for federated trust and service discovery. However, few comprehensive approaches integrate these two technologies to create a unified architecture. Specifically, such an architecture should provide on-chain trust, align with Gaia-X's identity and trust framework, and incorporate strong encryption and data segmentation for sensitive information. Our work addresses this gap by proposing an integrated solution that connects Fabric and Gaia-X while leveraging best practices in data protection for scalable, multi-stakeholder scenarios.

III. Conceptual Model

A. Requirements

Integrating a private Hyperledger blockchain into secure data infrastructures in the context of Gaia-X requires both functional and non-functional requirements, focusing on data security, scalability, data splitting and reunification. Functionally, the system must protect data during storage and transmission using modern encryption methods by splitting it into smaller, encrypted units before distribution to different nodes and securely reuniting it later. Non-functionally, it must be ensured that the system remains performant even with an increasing number of transactions and participants by distributing efficient, decentralized storage across a network and, at the same time, acting interoperably with the Gaia-X Trust Framework, which enables access for all users with a Gaia-X identity.

B. Proposed Architecture

The proposed architecture is built on a private Hyperledger Fabric blockchain, which is accessible through the Gaia-X Trust Framework for all participants who possess a valid Gaia-X identity. This architecture adopts a multi-layered approach. The following Figure 1 illustrates the architecture.

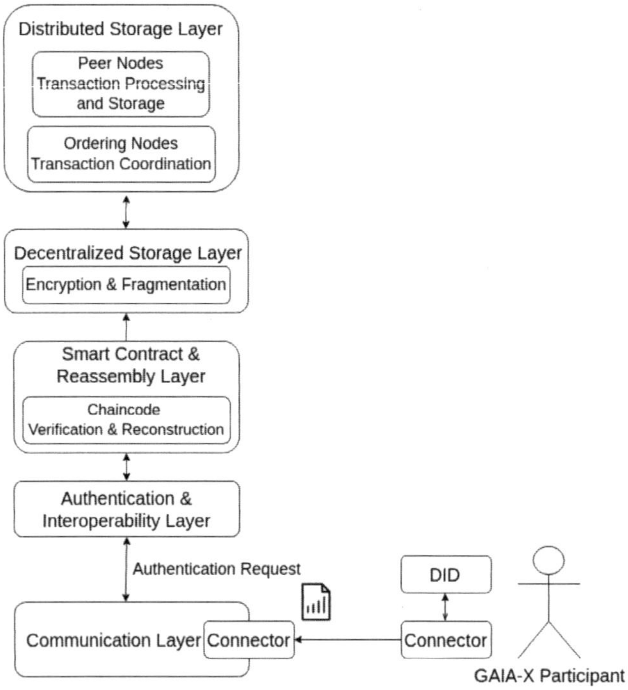

Figure 1. Hyperledger-GaiaX-Architecture

1) Decentralized Storage Layer: At the base, raw data is first secured using symmetric encryption. Following encryption, a threshold cryptography approach—employing Shamir's Secret Sharing—is applied to fragment the encrypted data into n pieces, where only a subset (k-out-of-n) is required for complete reassembly [14]. This layer guarantees that even if individual fragments are compromised, they alone reveal no sensitive information.

2) Distributed storage layer: The fragmented data is then distributed across a network of decentralized nodes within the Hyperledger Fabric framework. Each peer stores only a portion of the total data, reducing the risk of a complete data breach. Integrity is maintained by employing cryptographic hash functions (e.g., SHA-256) to monitor that fragments remain unaltered during storage.

3) Smart contract and Reassembly layer: Smart contracts, implemented as chaincode, serve as the control centre for data reassembly. These smart contracts are programmes that automatically check whether all the necessary conditions have been met - similar to an automated system that only acts once all the security checks have been passed [9]. In our approach, they ensure that all necessary data fragments are present and intact and that the requesting user has the necessary authorisations before the reassembly process is started. By automatically initiating and managing the reassembly process, smart contracts ensure that only fully verified and authorised reassembly events occur, thereby tightly coupling the fragmentation and storage layers with the access control mechanism.

4) Authentication and Interoperability layer: This layer collaborates with the Gaia-X connector, the communication layer, to facilitate optimized, standards-based authentication. The connector performs external identity checks using decentralized identifiers (DIDs) and verifiable credentials (VCs) from the Gaia-X ecosystem [1]. Meanwhile, this layer manages internal policy enforcement and session management. Once the connector verifies a Gaia-X identity, the authentication layer can assign it to local roles or authorizations and oversee tasks, such as renewing approvals or reassigning keys. This system ensures that only entities with valid Gaia-X credentials, confirmed by the connector, are granted access to data and the reassembly processes.

5) Communication layer: All layers are interconnected through a secure communication infrastructure that utilizes protocols, such as TLS and VPN. This setup ensures that all data exchanges between processing nodes, storage nodes, smart contracts, and authentication systems occur over encrypted channels, protecting against unauthorized interception or tampering. Additionally, the Gaia-X connector, responsible for processing all incoming and outgoing requests to the Gaia-X ecosystem, is defined within this layer. The connector verifies the identity of external participants to ensure that only authorized data exchanges occur. It also serves as a protocol bridge by adapting internal data formats and processes to maintain interoperability with Gaia-X standards. This layer consolidates all network communication—including secure node-to-node interaction and external Gaia-X requests—to ensure consistent encryption, manage potential VPN segments, and prevent the unauthorized interception or tampering of sensitive data.

6) Interlayer Interactions and Data Flow: The Communication Layer receives an incoming request to store data at the initial stage. This layer verifies the request and forwards it to the Authentication and Interoperability Layer, where the requester's credentials are validated. Upon successful authentication, the request is forwarded to the Smart Contracts and Reassembly Layer, where smart contracts are triggered to initiate the data processing pipeline. The Data Processing and Fragmentation Layer then encrypts the raw data using symmetric encryption techniques and partitions it into secure fragments using Shamir's Secret Sharing. These encrypted and fragmented data pieces are subsequently distributed across the Distributed Storage Layer, ensuring that each storage node holds only a portion of the fragmented data alongside cryptographic hashes for integrity verification. When an access request is made to retrieve stored data, the Communication Layer first receives the request and forwards it to the Authentication and Interoperability Layer for identity verification. The request moves forward if the requester is authorized to access the requested data. The Smart Contracts and Reassembly Layer then autonomously verifies the required fragments' presence and integrity before triggering the reassembly process. The required encrypted data fragments are retrieved from the Distributed Storage Layer and reassembled, ensuring data integrity. The reassembled encrypted data is then securely transmitted to the requester. Throughout these stages, the Secure Communication Infrastructure ensures that all interlayer data exchanges are protected by protocols, such as TLS, thereby maintaining confidentiality and preventing tampering. This structured approach ensures data storage and retrieval under strictly verified and secure conditions.

IV. Discussion

The proposed model is built on a private Hyperledger Fabric blockchain and utilizes the Gaia-X Trust Framework to facilitate secure, decentralized data storage. While it introduces several approaches, it also brings forth critical issues that warrant discussion in current research. One of the key advantages of this model is its combination of data encryption, secret sharing, and distributed storage. The model achieves robust security by employing AES-256 alongside Shamir's Secret Sharing. This ensures that complete data is not disclosed even if individual nodes are partially compromised, significantly reducing the risk of data leaks and providing mathematically sound security. Additionally, the decentralized storage of data fragments enhances resilience and scalability, as the load is distributed across multiple nodes. The Gaia-X Trust Framework establishes W3C Verifiable Credentials and self-descriptions as essential components for creating interoperable identity and access controls within Gaia-X ecosystems [12]. This ensures that only participants with a validated Gaia-X identity can access the system, promoting security, transparency, and traceability of data access within a federated ecosystem. This model encounters several significant challenges. Lessons learned so far indicate that integrating hybrid encryption and secret-sharing mechanisms is complicated and requires careful coordination to prevent performance bottlenecks or potential security vulnerabilities. In real-time applications, cryptographic operations can drastically impact throughput and scalability as the number of participants increases. Interoperability is also a critical concern; differing implementations and standard versions can result in practical inconsistencies. Furthermore, developing smart contracts for the secure reassembly of fragmented data is a complex task. Recent blockchain research has highlighted considerable security risks associated with insufficiently validated smart contract code, underscoring the importance of thorough testing and formal verification. In terms of future use cases, potential domains include Healthcare, enabling secure patient record exchange and real-time collaboration among hospitals, although large file sizes may require specialized data-splitting and off-chain indexing solutions; Supply Chain, verifying product provenance across multiple organizations, where Gaia-X can standardize participant identity while Fabric ensures transaction immutability and private data channels; and Automotive Mobility Services, supporting distributed sensor data or usage-based insurance under a federated yet privacy-preserving environment. By providing more technical details on these potential domains, we clarify how advanced encryption, threshold cryptography, and trusted identities interact in real multi-stakeholder ecosystems. Ultimately, bridging the gap between blockchain's decentralized trust model and Gaia-X's federated governance will pave the way for scalable and secure data spaces.

V. Conclusion and Future Work

This approach introduces a theoretical concept for integrating a private Hyperledger Fabric blockchain into the Gaia-X ecosystem. The proposed approach employs hybrid encryption, secret sharing, and decentralized storage to guarantee high levels of data security and sovereignty. Throughout the research, the following questions were specifically addressed:

i Compatibility between blockchain and Gaia-X was established through a multi-layered architecture, facilitating the storage and secure reassembly of encrypted, fragmented data using smart contracts.

ii Necessary security measures for ensuring integrity and confidentiality—including AES-256 encryption, Shamir's Secret Sharing, and cryptographic hashes—were defined

iii Opportunities, such as increased digital sovereignty and enhanced interoperability, and challenges, like performance limitations, complex smart contract validations, and interoperability constraints, were identified and discussed.

This integrated approach provides a strong foundation for building high-assurance federated ecosystems. However, the lessons learned emphasize the importance of thorough testing, rigorous performance optimization, and formal verification of chain code to address the complexities identified during the initial theoretical analysis. Future expansions of this research will include extended pilot projects involving various domain partners, deeper evaluations based on metrics, such as latency with large participant pools, targeted performance enhancements, rigorous validation of smart contracts, and ongoing standardization of cryptographic operations within the Gaia-X environment. Practical validation and empirical studies will be essential to confirm whether current security, performance, and interoperability expectations are fully met or require adjustments.

Acknowledgements

This paper was written as part of the project GAIA-X 4 Advanced Mobility Services in the project family Future Mobility funded by the Federal Ministry of Economics and Climate Protection (BMWK).

References

[1] G.-X. H. Austria, *Building a dataspace: Technical overview*, Available from https://www.gaia-x.at/wp-content/uploads/2023/04/WhitepaperGaiaX.pdf, 2023. (retrieved: 2025-03-04).

[2] F. Salzano, L. Marchesi, R. Pareschi, and R. Tonelli, "Integrating blockchain technology within an information ecosystem," *Blockchain: Research and Applications*, vol. 5, no. 4, p. 100225, 2024, Available from https://www.sciencedirect.com/science/article/pii/S2096720924000381, ISSN: 2096-7209. DOI: https://doi.org/10.1016/j.bcra.2024.100225.

[3] N.Arunkumar and P.Sivaprakasam, "Blockchain technology in data management," in *2020 Fourth International Conference on Computing Methodologies and Communication (ICCMC)*, 2020, pp. 199–206. DOI: 10.1109/ICCMC48092.2020.ICCMC-00039.

[4] D. V. Dimitrov, "Blockchain applications for healthcare data management," *Healthcare Informatics Research*, vol. 25, pp. 51–56, 2019, Available from https://api.semanticscholar.org/CorpusID:67771752. (retrieved: 2025-03-04).

[5] M. Hasnain, F. R. Albogamy, S. S. Alamri, I. Ghani, and B. Mehboob, "The hyperledger fabric as a blockchain framework preserves the security of electronic health records," *Frontiers in Public Health*, vol. 11, 2023, Available from https://api.semanticscholar.org/CorpusID:265576007. (retrieved: 2025-03-04).

[6] S. Wong, J.-K.-W. Yeung, Y.-y. Lau, T. Kawasaki, and R. Kwong, "A critical literature review on blockchain technology adoption in supply chains," *Sustainability*, 2024, Available from https://api.semanticscholar.org/CorpusID:270607203. (retrieved: 2025-03-04).

[7] W. Gao, X. Hei, and Y. Wang, "The data privacy protection method for hyperledger fabric based on trustzone," *Mathematics*, vol. 11, no. 6, 2023, Available from https://www.mdpi.com/2227-7390/11/6/1357, ISSN: 2227-7390. (retrieved: 2025-03-04).

[8] A. Shukla, P. Jirli, A. Mishra, and A. K. Singh, "An overview of blockchain research and future agenda: Insights from structural topic modeling," *Journal of Innovation Knowledge*, vol. 9, no. 4, p. 100605, 2024, Available from https://www.sciencedirect.com/science/article/pii/S2444569X24001446, ISSN: 2444-569X. DOI: https://doi.org/10.1016/j.jik.2024.100605. (retrieved: 2025-03-04).

[9] E. A. et al., "Hyperledger fabric: A distributed operating system for permissioned blockchains," in *Proceedings of the Thirteenth EuroSys Conference*, ser. EuroSys '18, Porto, Portugal: Association for Computing Machinery, 2018, pp. 1–15, ISBN: 9781450355841. DOI: 10.1145/3190508.3190538.

[10] T. Coenen et al., "Gaia-X and European Smart Cities and Communities," Gaia-X, White Paper, Oct. 2021, Version 21.09.

[11] "Gaia-x Architecture Document - 22.04 Release," Gaia-X, Architecture Documentation, version 22.04, Apr. 2022.

[12] "Gaia-X Trust Framework - main version (fb420580)," Gaia-X, 2022, Available from https://gaia-x.gitlab.io/policy-rules-committee/trust-framework/trust%5Fanchors/. (retrieved: 2025-03-04).

[13] B. Maier and N. Pohlmann, "Gaia-X Secure and Trustworthy Ecosystems with Self Sovereign Identity," Gaia-X European Association for Data and Cloud AISBL, White Paper, 2022.

[14] A. Shamir, "How to share a secret," *Communications of the ACM*, vol. 22, no. 11, pp. 612–613, 1979.

PERTD - Cloud Application Threat Modeling

Aspen Olmsted
School of Computer Science and Data Science
Wentworth Institute of Technology
Boston, MA 02115
olmsteda@wit.edu

Abstract— **This research work investigates the problem of developing secure cloud software applications. Currently, proposed solutions focus on data flow across so-called trust boundaries. The challenge with the current approach is that many of our applications' threats are not from malicious users. Many threats come from poor design, misunderstanding of use cases, and a lack of planning for environmental changes. This research focuses on the challenges of developing secure cloud software applications through a modeling process that allows us to identify risks to the cloud software during the design phase and implement strategies to mitigate those risks in the coding and implementation phase.**

Keywords- cyber-security; software engineering; software development lifecycle

I. INTRODUCTION

Secure software development stands at the intersection of innovation and protection, emphasizing the design, implementation, and maintenance of software systems with a robust focus on security. By embedding security measures and best practices throughout the development lifecycle, we can transform vulnerabilities into resilient defenses against potential threats. Here are some inspiring research areas in secure software development:

1. Secure Coding Practices: This area champions identifying and promoting vital coding techniques that empower developers to write secure code. By exploring common programming errors and vulnerabilities, we can equip ourselves with tools like static code analysis and automated vulnerability detection, paving the way for robust software security.

2. Threat Modeling: In a proactive approach, threat modeling illuminates potential threats and vulnerabilities early in development, giving you a sense of preparedness and control. This research area enables developers to refine their techniques and effectively chart pathways to improved security through tools like attack tree analysis and risk assessment methodologies.

3. Security Testing: Evaluating software for weaknesses becomes a quest for excellence, driving us to improve constantly. Innovative techniques such as penetration testing and fuzz testing serve as guardians of security, while automated processes revolutionize how we ensure the integrity of our software systems.

4. Secure Software Architectures: Research in this field aspires to design architectures that withstand attacks, safeguarding sensitive information with secure component integration and effective communication protocols.

5. Secure Software Development Processes: Methodologies become a fortress by embedding security at every stage of the software development lifecycle, from requirements engineering to incident response planning, forming an unshakeable foundation of trust.

6. Secure DevOps and Agile Development: In the fast-paced realms of DevOps and agile methodologies, research navigates the exciting intersection of speed and security, integrating practices that ensure rapid innovation without compromise.

7. Secure Software Analytics: This area of research uncovers patterns and anomalies in software-related data, harnessing the power of machine learning and data mining to predict vulnerabilities and bolster our defenses.

8. Security Education and Training: Elevating security education for developers transforms knowledge into action, fostering a culture of security awareness that resonates within software development teams.

These research areas advance secure software development and inspire a collective drive to protect our digital world and mitigate risks associated with cyber threats and attacks. Our paper's focus on threat modeling is a call to action, aiming to reduce risks to software functionality, regardless of the source of potential danger.

The organization of the paper is as follows. Section II describes the related work and the limitations of current methods. Section III describes workflow engines used in our motivating example of a distributed cloud application. Section IV discusses a current Threat Modeling technique called STRIDE. Section V discusses an alternative Threat modeling technique called DREAD. In Section VI, we give a motivating example from our study. Section VII describes our modeling methodology. We conclude and discuss future work in Section VIII.

II. RELATED WORK

Functional requirements can be defined and represented in various ways. While these requirements serve as the foundation for software development, non-functional requirements (NFRs) provide the essential guidelines for coding implementation. Many authors have examined NFRs and the challenges of incorporating them into the design process. Pavlovski and Zou [1] NFRs are defined as specific behaviors and operational constraints, including performance expectations and policy limitations. Despite many discussions surrounding them, they are often not given the attention they deserve.

Glinz [2] suggests categorizing functional and non-functional requirements to ensure their groups are inherently considered during application development. Alexander [3] points out that the language used to describe requirements is essential, noting that words ending in "-ility," such as reliability and verifiability, often refer to NFRs. Much of this research focuses on identifying NFRs. Our work builds on these foundations by applying domain-specific models using our proposed modeling technique.

Ranabahu and Sheth [3] explore four different modeling semantics to represent cloud application requirements: data, functional, non-functional, and system. Their work primarily addresses functional and system requirements, with some overlap in non-functional requirements from a system perspective. They built upon research conducted by Stuart, who defined semantic modeling languages for modeling cloud computing requirements throughout the three phases of the cloud application life cycle: development, deployment, and management. Our work fills in the gap regarding the semantic category of non-functional requirements.

Ranabahu and Sheth [3] use Unified Modeling Language (UML) to model only functional requirements. UML [5] is a standardized notation for representing software systems' interactions, structures, and processes. It consists of various diagram types, with individual diagrams linked to different perspectives of the same part of a software system. We utilize UML to express non-functional requirements as a secondary step following the PERTD models.

Integrating UML Sequence, Activity, and Class diagrams can enhance the semantics of our models. UML offers extensibility mechanisms that allow designers to add new semantics to a model. One such mechanism is a stereotype, which helps extend the vocabulary of UML to represent new model elements. Traditionally, software developers interpret these semantics and manually translate them into program code in a hard-coded manner. In our book [6], we marry the models generated by each phase of the software development lifecycle into with threat modeling and risk mitigation techniques.

The Object Constraint Language (OCL) [7] is part of the official Object Management Group (OMG) standard for UML. An OCL constraint specifies restrictions for the semantics of a UML specification and is considered valid as long as the data is consistent. Each OCL constraint is a declarative statement in the design model that signifies correctness. The expression of the constraint occurs at the class level, while enforcement happens at the object level. Although OCL has operations to observe the system state, it does not include functions to modify it.

JSON [8] stands for "JavaScript Object Notation," a simple data interchange format that began as a notation for the World Wide Web. Since most web browsers support JavaScript, and JSON is based on JavaScript, it is straightforward to support there, which stands for "JavaScript Object Notation," a simple format used for data interchange that originated as a notation for the World Wide Web. Since most web browsers support JavaScript and JSON is based on JavaScript, it is easy to work with in web environments. Many cloud-based web services now exchange data in JSON format. JSON Schemas [9] define correctness for data passed in JSON format. We utilize an extended form of JSON schemas on the aggregated data from several web services.

Our contribution to secure software development for cloud applications involves a new Threat Modeling technique, coupled with modeling standards, such as UML and OCL, utilizing their extensibility mechanism of stereotypes to model non-functional requirements effectively. We allow for an aggregated JSON Schema with our extensions to validate the combined data format.

III. WORKFLOW ENGINES

Workflow engines like Zapier [10] and Power Automate [11] are powerful automation tools that enable users to create and manage workflows for integrating and automating tasks across various applications and services, whether in the cloud or on-premises.

Zapier is a popular cloud-based automation platform that allows users to connect to different web applications and automate their workflows. It operates on a simple "trigger-action" model, where an event in one application triggers an action in another. Users can create "Zaps" (automated workflows) by selecting a trigger and defining the subsequent actions. For example, when a new email arrives in Gmail (trigger), the attachments can be automatically saved to Google Drive (action).

Zapier supports numerous apps and services, including well-known ones like Gmail, Slack, Salesforce, and Trello. It features a user-friendly interface, pre-built Zap templates for everyday use cases, and advanced options like filters, delays, and data transformations. Additionally, Zapier allows for multi-step Zaps, making it possible to create complex workflows with multiple actions and conditions.

Power Automate is a cloud-based service from Microsoft that allows users to automate workflows and integrate applications and services within the Microsoft ecosystem and beyond. It offers connectors for various applications, including Microsoft 365 apps (such as Outlook and SharePoint), Dynamics 365, Azure services, and third-party services like Salesforce, Dropbox, and Twitter.

Power Automate features a visual design interface where users can create workflows by combining triggers, actions, and conditions. Available triggers include email arrivals, button clicks, data changes, and scheduled events. Actions can involve sending emails, creating tasks, updating records, etc. Power Automate offers advanced capabilities like loops, parallel branches, and approval processes.

Both Zapier and Power Automate provide extensive libraries of pre-built templates and connectors, making it easier for users to begin automating tasks. They offer options to monitor and manage workflows, handle errors, and track activity logs. These platforms cater to users with varying technical expertise, from business users to developers, and help automate repetitive tasks, streamline processes, and enhance productivity.

IV. STRIDE THREAT MODELING

STRIDE [12] is a threat modeling framework that offers a structured approach for identifying and analyzing threats in software systems. It aids security practitioners and developers in understanding potential risks and implementing appropriate security controls. STRIDE is an acronym representing six categories of threats:

1. Spoofing Identity: This category involves attackers impersonating legitimate users or entities to gain unauthorized access or deceive the system. For instance, attackers may spoof

a user's identity by stealing credentials or manipulating authentication mechanisms.

2. Tampering with Data: Tampering threats involve the unauthorized modification or alteration of data within the system. Attackers may tamper with data in transit, modify stored data, or manipulate system parameters to achieve desired outcomes. For example, an attacker could alter the contents of a database, inject malicious code into an application, or change parameters to bypass security checks.

3. Repudiation: Repudiation threats allow users to deny their involvement in specific transactions or activities, posing challenges for auditing and accountability. For instance, an attacker might modify logs or manipulate transaction records to evade detection or deny their actions.

4. Information Disclosure: This category addresses threats related to unauthorized exposure or disclosure of sensitive information. Attackers may exploit vulnerabilities to access confidential data, such as personal information, financial records, or intellectual property. This can happen through insecure data transmission, weak access controls, or information leakage via error messages.

5. Denial of Service: Denial of Service (DoS) threats aim to disrupt or degrade a system's availability or performance. Attackers may overload resources, exhaust system capacity, or exploit vulnerabilities to cause a service outage, rendering the system unresponsive or unusable for legitimate users.

6. Elevation of Privilege: Elevation of Privilege threats involve attackers gaining unauthorized access to higher privileges or permissions than they should have. By exploiting vulnerabilities or design flaws, attackers can bypass security controls and gain elevated access rights, leading to unauthorized data access, system compromise, or further exploitation.

When applying the STRIDE framework, security practitioners and developers analyze the software system from the perspective of each threat category. They identify potential vulnerabilities and develop corresponding mitigation strategies to address the threats. This analysis facilitates informed decisions regarding security controls, system design improvements, and the prioritization of security efforts.

V. DREAD THREAT MODELING

DREAD is a threat modeling framework designed to assess and prioritize software vulnerabilities based on their potential impact. The acronym DREAD stands for five key factors used to evaluate threats:

1. Damage Potential: This factor refers to the extent of harm that could be caused if a vulnerability is exploited. It evaluates the impact, which can range from minor inconveniences to severe consequences like data breaches, system compromises, or financial losses.

2. Reproducibility: This measures how easily an attacker can reproduce or exploit a vulnerability. Vulnerabilities that are consistently easy to exploit are considered more dangerous than those that require complex or unpredictable conditions for exploitation.

3. Exploitability: This factor assesses the level of skill or effort needed to exploit a vulnerability. Vulnerabilities easily exploited with readily available tools or techniques pose a higher risk. Conversely, vulnerabilities that are difficult to exploit or require specialized knowledge are considered lower risk.

TABLE 1 - UPLOAD ACTIVITY STRIDE MODEL

Action	S	T	R	I	D	E
Timerfires						
PrepareDataForUpload						
SendData	X	X		X	X	
ReceieveData						
LoadData						
BuildViews						

4. Affected Users: This evaluates the number of users or systems a vulnerability could impact. A vulnerability affecting numerous users or critical systems is considered more significant than one impacting only a limited subset of users.

5. Discoverability: This assesses how likely an attacker is to find the vulnerability. Vulnerabilities that are easily discoverable—through public disclosures, known attack techniques, or automated scanning tools—are riskier than those that are harder to find or require advanced reconnaissance.

Using the DREAD framework, each factor is scored on a scale from 0 to 10, with 0 being the least concerning and ten being the most critical. These scores help prioritize vulnerabilities and allocate resources for mitigation efforts. Higher scores indicate a higher priority for addressing the identified vulnerabilities.

While DREAD is a valuable tool for assessing and prioritizing vulnerabilities based on their potential impact, it should be used alongside other threat modeling techniques and considerations to ensure a comprehensive security analysis and informed decision-making.

VI. MOTIVATING EXAMPLE

The challenge with the STRIDE and DREAD threat models is that they primarily focus on vulnerabilities associated with malicious user activities. However, many risks arise from architecture, the environment, or human error.

Consider a common architecture used by many businesses today: data generated by an online transaction processing (OLTP) system, either stored on-premises or logically on-premises, is synchronized to a cloud system considered off-premises and beyond the organization's control. This scenario is not uncommon in today's business landscape.

Consider a large performing arts venue employing a local SQL Server-based system for ticketing and donation transactions. Meanwhile, its marketing department uses a cloud-based email and SMS marketing system. The OLTP data must be extracted, translated, uploaded, and loaded regularly for the marketing system to function correctly.

Various issues can arise when multiple processes and data are transferred across networks that span domain boundaries. A UML activity diagram illustrates the steps involved in moving data from the on-premises OLTP system to the cloud-based system used by the marketing team. This model shows that activities occur in both environments. The challenge with the STRIDE and DREAD threat models is that the vulnerabilities modeled and the matching remediations target malicious user activities. Many times, risks come from architecture, environment, or human error.

A motiving example is an architecture that is used in many businesses today where data that is generated in OLTP systems that are either stored on-premises or logically on-premises is synchronized to a cloud system that is considered off-premises and outside the domain of control of the organization. To understand this better, consider a large performing arts venue that utilizes a local SQL Server-based system to process ticketing and donation transactions. The marketing department uses a cloud-based system for email and SMS marketing. The OLTP data must be extracted, translated, uploaded, and loaded regularly for the marketing system to be functional.

Understanding the data transfer process is crucial to prevent

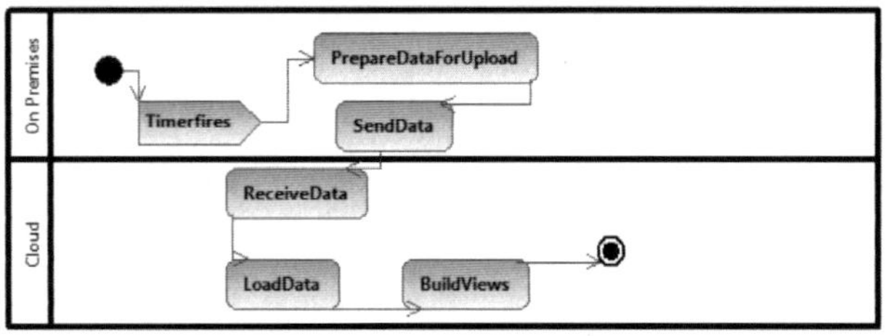

Figure 1 - Upload Activity

potential risks. Figure 1 shows a UML activity diagram executed to move data from the OLTP system on-premises to the system in the cloud used by the marketing folks. In the model, you will see that activities happen in both partitions.

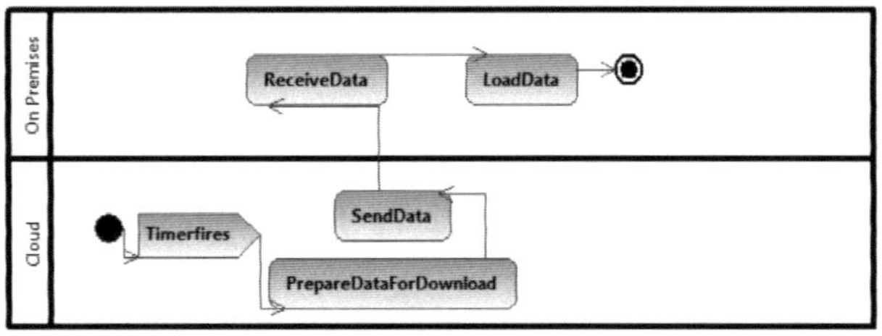

Figure 2 - Download Activity

Figure 2 presents a model that outlines the execution path when data is retrieved from the cloud system. The data includes sending activity for both emails and SMS text messages. This sending activity can be substantial, encompassing tuples for sends, opens, clicks, and bounces. Additionally, information regarding communication preferences and unsubscribed data is retrieved.

The marketing department requires service availability and data integrity for its business operations. For instance, NFRs could specify that the system must be available 99.999% of the time or that the data must be no more than 24 hours old. Whenever a distributed system is proposed, a model should be developed to represent these NFRs and the threats to the system's ability to meet them.

Unfortunately, the focus of STRIDE and DREAD on malicious users does not adequately address many of the risks in our motivating example. Table 1 illustrates a STRIDE model corresponding to the update activity depicted in Figure 1, while Table 2 shows the STRIDE model related to the download activity from Figure 2. In the STRIDE model, actions are at risk from malicious users; however, many steps are also vulnerable to environmental issues that can impact the system's availability and integrity. Examples of these issues include network and system outages, concurrent computational usage on equipment, and lack of control of the quality of source data.

VII. PERTD MODEL

We developed the PERTD Model to assess better the risks associated with distributed applications. This model addresses four main environmental risk categories for distributed systems:

1. Partition

Activities vulnerable to partition errors will fail if a network is partitioned between on-premises devices and the cloud. Risk reduction strategies include:

- Pausing the complete workflow and retrying
- Utilizing previous execution data
- Employing alternative data sources

TABLE 2 - DOWNLOAD ACTIVITY STRIDE MODEL

Action	S	T	R	I	D	E
Timerfires						
PrepareDataForDownload						
SendData	X	X		X	X	
ReceieveData						
LoadData						

2. Execution

Activities that are susceptible to execution errors may fail due to ambiguous code requirements, which can lead to runtime or tooling errors. For example, queries that generate data might fail with future datasets. Risk reduction measures include:

- Utilizing previous execution data (most systems create a copy before execution)
- Using alternative data sources

3. Requisite

TABLE 4 - UPLOAD ACTIVITY PERTD MODEL

Action	P	E	R	T	D
Timerfires		X			
PrepareDataForUpload		X			
SendData	X	X	X	X	
ReceieveData	X	X	X	X	
LoadData		X	X	X	X
BuildViews		X	X		

Activities with requisite vulnerabilities depend on prerequisite activities. If a prerequisite fails, the dependent activity becomes stale. Risk reduction can involve:

- Utilizing previous execution data

- Employing alternative data sources

4. Timing

Activities at risk due to timing need to finish within a specific time window or under a threshold duration. Risk reduction strategies include:

- Utilizing previous execution data (most systems create a copy before execution)

- Using alternative data sources

5. DATA

Activities are at risk due to data often being combined from different sources. Unfortunately, schema correctness specifiers only apply to one data source. Risk reduction strategies include:

- Additional workflow steps to verify correctness

In Tables 3 and 4, we apply our PERTD model to analyze the risks related to uploading and downloading activities. The PERTD model captures significantly more risks than the STRIDE model.

After identifying NFRs in the PERTD model, we develop standard UML Class, Sequence, and Activity Diagrams. The threats to the system are modeled using UML stereotypes. UML stereotypes extend the standard UML language by introducing custom or specialized elements, properties, and behaviors. They allow the addition of domain-specific annotations, constraints, or semantics to UML elements, enhancing expressiveness and tailoring modeling for specific contexts. Stereotypes are indicated by guillemets (<< >>) placed above the name of the stereotyped element.

Stereotypes can be attached to classes, messages, attributes, and activities. With the PERTD model, we incorporated the four risk categories as stereotypes: <<PARTITION>>, <<EXECUTION>>, <<REQUISITE>>, <<TIMING>> and <<DATA>>. These stereotypes are then tagged to messages in UML Sequence and Activity diagrams, while data classes and

TABLE 3 - DOWNLOAD ACTIVITY PERTD MODEL

Action	P	E	R	T	D
Timerfires		X			
PrepareDataForDownload		X			
SendData	X	X	X	X	
ReceieveData	X	X	X	X	
LoadData		X	X		X

individual attributes can also be tagged if they are susceptible to these risks.

Additionally, OCL is included to specify invariants that can define additional semantics related to the correctness of method calls, classes, or attributes. For instance, if data in a particular class must be no older than three days, this can be expressed using the last_update attribute.

To verify data from when it is vulnerable, we utilize an extended version of JSON Schemas [9]. Our extension allows the Schema to reference different data sources. JSON schema supports a CONTAINS operator to verify the existence of an element in a collection. We added a CONTAINEDIN operator to span across schemas represented by different data sources in the distributed system. We also added a NOTCONTAINEDIN to verify the absence of an element. Figure **3** shows two sample schemas. The top schema is a simplified version of a patron, the bottom schema is a simplified version of a ticket. They share an email field which is designated in the tickets schema to require the existence in the patron data.

```
{
  "$id": "https://aspenolmsted.com/patron.schema.json",
  "$schema": "https://json-schema.org/draft/2020-12/schema",
  "type": "array",
  "items": {
    "type": "object",
    "properties":{
      "name": {"type": "string" },
      "email": {"type": "string" }
    },
  }
}

{
  "$id": "https://aspenolmsted.com/tickets.schema.json",
  "$schema": "https://json-schema.org/draft/2020-12/schema",
  "type": "array",
  "items": {
    "type": "object",
    "properties": {
      "event": {"type": "string" },
      "email": {"type": "string",
        "containedin' : "https://aspenolmsted.com/patron.schema.json"},
      "tickets": {"type": "integer"}
  },
  }
}
```

Figure 3 - Sample Schema

To mitigate the risk of data integrity issues, we validate the data against the specified schemas as part of the data workflow.

VIII. Conclusions and Future Works

In this work, we provide a modeling methodology to handle issues in cloud software development related to NFRs in distributed systems. We show that in this work, we present a modeling methodology aimed at addressing issues related to NFRs in distributed systems during software development. Our PERTD model enables us to identify significantly more fine-grain risks associated with distributed systems. Additionally, we have enhanced the modeling of functional requirements by employing UML stereotypes to represent the NFRs identified in the PERTD model. Future work will incorporate code generation to mitigate the risks identified and modeled throughout this process. Utilizing our PERTD model makes identifying many more risks to a distributed system possible. We extended the modeling of functional requirements by using UML stereotypes to model the NFRs identified in the PERTD model. Implementation of cross-data source validation is provided to ensure data integrity. In our future work, we will add code generation to reduce the risks identified and modeled in the process.

References

[1] C. J. Pavlovski and J. Zou, "Non-functional requirements in business process modeling," *Proceedings of the Fifth on Asia-Pacific Conference on Conceptual Modelling, vol. 79,* pp. 1-10, 2008.

[2] M. Glinz, "Rethinking the Notion of Non-Functional Requirements," *Third World Congress for Software Quality, Munich, Germany,* pp. 1-10, 2005.

[3] Alexander, I, "Misuse Cases Help to Elicit Non-Functional Requirements," *Computing & Control Engineering Journal, 14, 40-45,* pp. 1-10, 2003.

[4] R. Ajith and A. Sheth, "Semantic Modeling for Cloud Computing, Part I," *Computing,* vol. May/June, pp. 81-83, 2010.

[5] Object Management Group, "Unified Modeling Language: Supersturcture," 05 02 2007. [Online]. Available: http://www.omg.org/spec/UML/2.1.1/. [Accessed 20 Feb 2025].

[6] A. Olmsted, Security-Driven Software Development: Learn to analyze and mitigate risks in your software projects, Birmingham, UK: Packt Publishing, 2024.

[7] Object Management Group, "OMG Formally Released Versions of OCL," 02 2014. [Online]. Available: http://www.omg.org/spec/OCL/. [Accessed 20 02 2025].

[8] JSON.org, "Introducing JSON," 2024. [Online]. Available: https://www.json.org/json-en.html. [Accessed 20 Feb 2025].

[9] Open Collective, "JSON Schema," 2024. [Online]. Available: https://json-schema.org/. [Accessed 20 Feb 2025].

[10] Zapier Inc., "Automate without limits," 2024. [Online]. Available: https://zapier.com/. [Accessed 20 Feb 2025].

[11] Microsoft, "Power Automate," 2024. [Online]. Available: https://www.microsoft.com/en-us/power-platform/products/power-automate. [Accessed 20 Feb 2025].

[12] R. Khan, D. Laverty, D. McLaughlin and S. Sezer, "STRIDE-based threat modeling for cyber-physical systems,," in *2017 IEEE PES Innovative Smart Grid Technologies Conference Europe (ISGT-Europe),* Turin, Italy, 2017.

Trends for Pulling HPC Containers in Cloud

Vanessa Sochat
Lawrence Livermore National Laboratory
e-mail: sochat1@llnl.gov

***Abstract*—Container technologies are foundational for cloud orchestration and have captured the interest of the High Performance Computing (HPC) community. While much work has been done to demonstrate that there is no additional overhead when using a container technology, strategies for building and pulling scientific containers to cloud environments and the cost implications of those choices have not been fully studied. Due to the importance and predominance in the ecosystem, considerations that minimize the time of operations, such as pulling and staging, are essential. This understanding and innovation in the space is becoming more important as more scientific applications are ported to cloud environments. In this study, we first aim to understand the landscape of containerized scientific applications, assembling a sample of more than 77K Dockerfile recipes discovered from repositories in a research software engineering database and across a set of well-known machine learning organizations. We assess these data for trends in building strategy and resulting containers, and show that applying best practices to a set of 10 application containers can lead to improvements in layer redundancy and thus lower time and cost to use the set. Finally, we develop a simulation tool that creates containers for controlled experiments that vary the total size, and the number and size of layers. With this tool, we run an experimental study that varies layer size and count across several scales to better understand the trade-off between layer count and size and the subsequent cost. In this experimental work, we find that total image size is a dominating variable during provisioning, and that strategies to improve I/O and enable lazy loading of images can lead to improvements of 3-15x. This work is valuable to inform the HPC community moving to the cloud about best practices for building and pulling containers.**

Keywords-cloud; containers; Kubernetes; HPC; trends.

I. Introduction

Capturing application logic in containers is a strategy to ensure reproducibility and automation of modern workflows [1]. The dominant force of cloud, and specifically container orchestration in cloud [2], has further incentivized the High Performance Computing (HPC) community to investigate and pursue strategies for optimally running HPC applications there, requiring a different mindset to consider not just optimizing performance [3]–[5] but also minimizing monetary cost. One component of this cost is the action of moving a container from a registry [6] to the cloud environment, an action often referred to as "pulling" that can add additional time to a workload, and thus incur additional monetary costs.

The process of pulling a container from a registry is governed by the Open Containers Distribution Specification [7], where first a container runtime makes a request to a registry Application Programming Interface (API) for a specific image identifier and tag, and a successful response returns an image manifest list [8]. The manifest list is parsed until a matching image platform is found, and then the container runtime tool can download the final image manifest, which includes a list of layers for download. Each layer is typically a compressed archive of a piece of the image filesystem, created as one command line in the build file called a Dockerfile [9]. While layers are downloaded in parallel and validated, the extraction is sequential due to the need to assemble the filesystem in the order mandated by the image configuration [10]. This entire process involves multiple interactions with the registry, and the download and extraction steps that encompass the pull can take upward of 76% of the container startup time [11].

Running a containerized workload using Kubernetes [12] starts with the pull of an application container. If all containers need to be started at the same time, node coordination is important. As container sizes grow larger and require more time to pull, this step could incur larger monetary costs. The design of the container and strategy for pulling can contribute to the efficiency of this step. If layers are assembled in a way to clean up unused files or take advantage of multi-stage builds, image size can be minimized [13]. The choice of filesystem and content retrieval and extraction strategy can further influence the time from initial pull to application start. This calls for an assessment of best practices when building and pulling containers, and the extent to which they are followed. If there is little time and incentive in the scientific community to optimize building and pulling strategies, the result can be a setup that is more monetarily costly.

While work has been done to assess all images in a registry [14] and pulling for common service containers [15], to our knowledge, no work has focused on images built in the scientific community. In this work, we do a temporal and quantitative analysis on the scientific community container ecosystem from 2014 until present day. In Section II we assess trends and practices for building containers, and look at changes in size, number of layers, base images used, and reuse. We develop an open-source tool to run simulations of container pulling across sizes and number of layers. We perform experiments across different cluster and container sizes with simulated and real application containers to identify ideal pulling strategies (Section III). We show that the total image size is the dominant variable related to pulling time, make suggestions based on our experimental results for effective pulling strategies, and develop two new pieces of software to support pulling experimentation and cluster deployment [16], [17]. Finally, in Section IV we review interesting findings, limitations, and follow-up work. Starting on the premise that the HPC community desires to move application containers from on-premises to the cloud and pulling is a required step that incurs monetary costs, this work is a starting point to define good practices and areas of future work.

II. Methods

A. Analysis of Container Images

Deployment of container images to HPC systems or cloud requires pulling the container images from registries, a task that can increase in time and thus be more costly for a workflow. Thus, understanding the sizes of images and change over time can provide insight into current practices and suggestions for improvement.

B. Dockerfile Ecosystem

We aim to use build recipes for containers to assess image and layer sizes and content. Larger sizes will take longer to pull, incurring higher monetary costs, and this can be associated with good and bad practices in the build recipes themselves [18]. The first task was to assemble a database of container image references, often called unique resource identifiers (URIs). A URI is a unique identifier that includes the registry, repository, and tag associated with a specific digest that indicates a version (e.g., docker.io/library/ubuntu:latest). While registries can expose a catalog endpoint to retrieve a catalog of all containers, most do not as it would increase load on already busy registries. Thus, we opt for a programmatic approach using the Research Software Encyclopedia, a meta-software database of over 5.6K curated research software projects [19], to discover Dockerfile recipes from established research software and machine learning projects. We can use this set to identify common underlying base images, and do an analysis of container and layer sizes.

C. Image and Layer Sizes

The container registry can provide manifests – JSON documents that detail the contents of the images, namely layers and digests, and the configurations. We are first interested in using this metadata to better understand the number of layers across images and tags, and how this has changed across time. Seeing that the number of layers has changed over time might reflect a change in build practices. We then can assess similarity of images by way of pure digests of images and content of the layers themselves.

D. Image Similarity

1) Content Similarity

A single Dockerfile provides three ways to assess similarity – the similarity of the base images used to build the container, the similarity of the Dockerfile build instructions themselves, and the similarity of the exact digests of the layers. The choice of a base image reflects a user preference, as different bases bring different package managers and potential needs for building software. The content similarity reflects layers having similar functionality, and the exact matching of digests is directly related to reuse, as a digest match indicates a cache hit and not needing to pull a new layer [14].

Similarity of container images by way of content can be done for both our Dockerfile database and the base images they are built from. For each, we treat the image build instructions as a document, where each line that builds a layer is parsed as a single sentence. To derive the build instructions for the base images, we parse the FROM directives of the Dockerfiles, and retrieve build instructions from the "history" section of the image manifest in the registry. For our Dockerfile database, we simply need to parse the RUN directives directly in the Dockerfile. For each of these sets of build instructions, we apply the following approach. If we consider a grouping of layers that encompasses a Dockerfile (and image) to be akin to paragraphs or sentences that make up a document, we can use these build instructions as a corpus. For each document, we pre-process the instruction lines to remove a subset of punctuation, and replace other punctuation with a space (e.g., underscores and dashes) and tokenize the result. We can then derive word2vec embeddings [20] each of length 300 for each image or Dockerfile, and do a pairwise similarity of these vectors using cosine similarity to derive a similarity matrix. These similarity values reflect the degree to which build instructions (from base images or Dockerfiles) are built with common logic.

2) Digest Similarity

While our similarity analysis primarily aimed to reflect on similarity of content, a different goal is to better understand the impact of build strategies on resulting digest similarity. The exact digest is the unique identifier for a layer, and the decision point about whether a container runtime needs to pull a layer. Since layers are saved to a cache [21], it follows that a strategy that minimizes redundancy of layer digests requires fewer pulls, both taking up less space on the filesystem and time to do the pulls.

Toward the goal of understanding digest similarity "in the wild" and similarity when care is taken to ensure redundancy, we can first assess the similarity of digests across our set of unique resource identifiers for base images. We will calculate the Jaccard coefficient between pairwise images, which is the ratio of the number of intersecting digests divided by the union of all digests. A Jaccard coefficient of 1 indicates most similar, and 0 most dissimilar. This value is expected to be low, as each digest reflects not only the content within it, but the previous layers [22]. We can then compare these scores against equivalently calculated values for different sets of images that are intentionally built with different redundancy strategies in mind:

1) A reasonable effort to create redundancy
2) A best effort to create redundancy
3) Little effort to create redundancy.

For each of these sets, we aim to compare a set of $\tilde{1}0$ containerized HPC proxy applications (and new builds of the same applications with an improved strategy) based on a real-world performance study [23]. For (1) we will use a derivative of the containers from the study where a reasonable effort was taken to ensure redundancy, however some images used an entirely different build strategy to achieve more ideal performance. Best-effort builds of the same applications (2), and a highly redundant set of the same applications (3) using spack [24] "containerize" to generate multi-stage builds with one large layer that included a main application and all dependencies. This exercise will demonstrate the impact to building strategy on overall image similarity, and consequently, redundancy of layers that can influence cost. All container Dockerfiles are available [25].

E. Image Bases

For our next analysis, we want to classify our images for the underlying base image, which typically falls in the set of operating systems including debian, alpine, ubuntu, centos, fedora, rockylinux, and busybox. This task requires the unique resource identifier that can be used to pull the actual image layers for analysis. To do this assessment, we first reduce our entire set of images to inspect just one tag for each, choosing either "latest" or (if not available), the newest dated tag. We do this because different tags belonging to the same URI do not typically vary with respect to the base operating system, and we can estimate the unique resource identifier of the image from one single tag. We also have to be selective due to the need to pull the entire image and extract the contents to the filesystem, which can be both expensive in time and cost for internet bandwidth.

Since there is no single, reliable way to derive a base operating system, we will use a simple strategy to compare the extracted filesystem paths in the image to a known database of operating system paths. This approach is enabled by the "guts" software [26] to extract the container image to the filesystem, and generate a complete manifest of file paths and environment paths. Using this manifest, we can compare each extracted image fileystem against a database of 46 base extractions across tags of those named base images [27]. This means that, given a contender image A that needs classification and a set of base images B:

- Extract paths from A (PA)
- Generate a set (intersection) of paths across B. This represents shared paths in the base images B that could not be used to distinguish them (PB)
- Subtract this set of paths from A.
- This provides distinct paths in A. (PA - PB = AP)
- AP is a combination of application-specific additions to the base image, and non-shared base image paths.
- Compare each base image paths Bi with AP to generate a score Si (Si = intersection(AP, Bi) / len(AP))

By scoping the denominator to the set of paths in AP, paths in Bi shared with other base images are again discarded. (Si = intersection(AP, Bi) / len(AP)). The score calculated above represents the percentage of extracted filesystem paths in A that are also present in Bi, a given base image set of filepaths after removing any shared paths between base images. While some of these paths will be added software installs, the remainder will be paths that identify a base image family. Given no additional software installs, all of these paths will be derived from the base image, and the maximum similarity score is 1. Given no overlapping paths between AP and Bi, the minimum score is 0. When we calculate similarity of our contender image A with all base images Bi, the maximum score is declared the matching base image.

F. Building Best Practices

In addition to word2vec embeddings generation for similarity calculations, the Dockerfile database can be used to make observations about image building best practices.

G. Image Pulling Strategy

a) Number of Layers

While the maximum number of layers for a Docker image is known to be 127, the implemented maximum set by the Docker client is in fact 125 [28]. In practice this limit is determined by the kernel version, and so different container building tools can vary in allowances. For the purposes of this work, we will test an upper limit of 125 layers, as a majority of scientific container developers build with docker [29]. The question remains for build practices, given a constant size, whether it is a better strategy to choose few large layers, or more smaller layers. And secondly, given some number of layers, how does pull time vary with image size and choice of network or registry? Toward this goal, we developed a docker building tool to generate images with a controlled total size, and number of unique layers [17]. We used the Dockerfile database to calculate a range of image sizes based on percentiles between the 25th and 100th (Table I) as a strategy to reflect images being used by the community. For each of these sizes, we will perform a container pulling study that generates the respective size at a range of layer counts that are equivalently derived from the data. The sizes were chosen at percentile increments of 5, with the exception of the range between the 95th and 100th percentile, which was broken into an additional set of three ranges due to the larger span between the values.

For the study, we chose two values for the number of layers – the median (9) of the dataset, along with the upper max of 125. For each pair of image size and layer count, the size of the layer is calculated as the total size stated above divided by the number of layers. We will only build images for which the minimum size is within the allowances of a standard registry (10MB or smaller).

The experiment will use Kubernetes, the de facto standard container orchestration framework for cloud and Fortune 500 companies [2] and be run on Google Kubernetes Engine (GKE). As each container is assembled from layers with a different generation command, there is no chance for overlap of file names so the cache can never be used when pulling images. The study will be run on each of 4, 8, 16, 32, 64, 128, and 256 n1-standard-16 nodes on Google Cloud, with 16 vCPU and 60GB RAM per node. Initial testing was done to pull containers on the n1-standard-16 and a larger instance, n1-standard-64 (64 vCPU and 240GB memory), and n1-standard-16 was chosen as the n1-standard-64 was only

TABLE I. IMAGE SIZES CHOSEN FOR PULLING STUDY

Image Size (bytes)	Human readable	Percentile from Database
53702097.0	(53.7 MB)	25th
58049507.8	(58.05 MB)	30th
71460665.0	(71.46 MB)	35th
91388866.2	(91.39 MB)	40th
108513992.4	(108.51 MB)	45th
132399102.0	(132.4 MB)	50th
163049655.0	(163.05 MB)	55th
218665412.8	(218.67 MB)	60th
271728773.4	(271.73 MB)	65th
320018606.2	(320.02 MB)	70th
392602448.0	(392.60 MB)	75th
496514346.8	(496.51 MB)	80th
687439577.6	(687.44 MB)	85th
1181249324.6	(1.18 GB)	90th
2775722493.4	(2.78 GB)	95th
6841726027.3	(6.84 GB)	96.25th
10907729561.2	(10.91 GB)	97.5th
14973733095.1	(14.97 GB)	98.75th
19039736629.0	(19.04 GB)	100th

1.028x faster, but 3.87x more expensive. For each container, a Job [30] will be created that requires pulling the container to all nodes, and the Kubernetes Event Exporter [31] will be used to capture all events from which pull times and errors can be derived. Importantly, this tool requires setting the max age of events to a large value (1200 seconds) or else events can be dropped. The experiment will be conducted multiple times, each time optimizing a different part of the setup to give actionable advice about pulling practices. At the end of this first experiment, there will be data for deciding on one or more image sizes and number of layers for subsequent experiments to assess pulling strategies across nodes [32], discussed next.

b) Local vs. Remote Registry

The location of the registry relative to the final destination of the pull can be a salient factor to pulling latency, where sources that are physically closer to their destination might see improvements in latency and pulling time. To test this approach, we will pull the application container set from GitHub packages (ghcr.io) and then directly from the registry provided by the cloud where the experiments are run, Google Artifact Registry (gcr.io).

c) Filesystem Latency

Input/Output operations per second (IOPS) and throughout can be hugely influenced by the filesystem available to the Kubelet, resulting in a 3x improved throughput [32] and thus, faster image pulls as the layers are streamed to the filesystem and then extracted. With this knowledge, we aim to test adding a single 375GB LocalSSD to each node in the cluster to which the images will be pulled.

d) Streaming Images

While our experiment containers did not contain a real application (they start and complete) it is worth testing image streaming, where images are allowed to enter a running state before the entire image is downloaded. This is done by way of starting containers with content that is recorded to be accessed at the onset of the container running, and then loading content that is needed on demand – a strategy called lazy loading [33]. While it cannot be known exactly how Google Cloud has implemented this approach, an open source tool to perform this task is the SOCI (Seekable OCI) snapshotter [33], a containerd plugin that creates an index of image contents, and then is able to start the container before download finishes. This is possible because, as Harter et. al showed [11], only 6.4% of container data is needed for this step. In a real-world application scenario, this would hugely reduce costs because, although the image pull still needs to complete, the pull itself does not slow down the starting time of the workload. While we cannot determine if Google Cloud is using this exact snapshotting, the project that SOCI derives from, the stargz snapshotter [34] came from a project developed by Google engineers. The lazy loading approach has been documented to speed up a workload start time by 6.3x [32]. On Google Cloud, image streaming requires using Google's Artifact Registry, which does incur additional costs.

e) Real-World Application Test

Given a pulling strategy that is shown to be optimal in the previously stated experiments, we would finally want to test the approach with real applications. The reason is, especially for the image streaming strategy previously mentioned, the ability for the container to start depends on the logic of the entrypoint. As our simulated containers do not have real entrypoints or applications, the times for the streaming images could be unusually or unrealistically fast. Toward this goal, we can use a subset of the spack containers described in Section II-D1 (LAMMPS, OSU All Reduce, AMG, and Minife) that can guarantee that the application and dependencies are contained within one layer, and the experiment is testing actual applications that can be validated to run and return a result.

f) Node Coordination

As a final investigation in the study, we want to investigate the extent to which nodes in the cluster are coordinated for events, including a pod being scheduled, a container pulling, pulled, created, and started. If these events are not orchestrated in unison, given a workload that requires all containers running at the same time, it could further delay the application start and incur additional cost.

III. RESULTS

A. Dockerfile Ecosystem

We used the Research Software Encyclopedia to identify 4,621 associated GitHub repositories. Of that set, 694 had at least one Dockerfile. In total, we find 77,449 Dockerfile across research software engineering and machine learning projects to further explore.

B. Image and Layer Sizes

For each of our 77,449 Dockerfile, we retrieve complete metadata about tags available and configurations from the

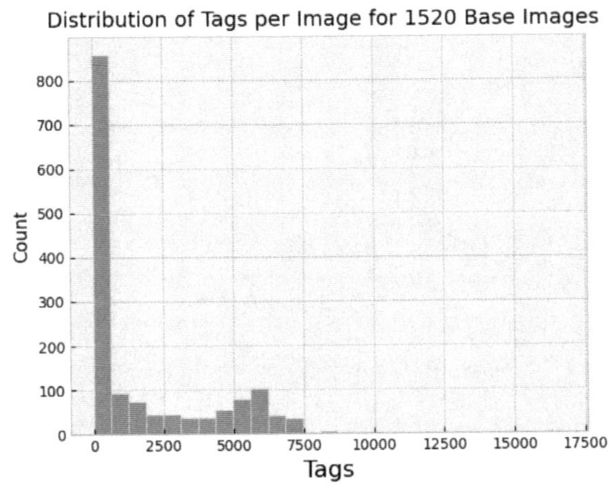

Figure 1. Tags per image with one outlier removed.

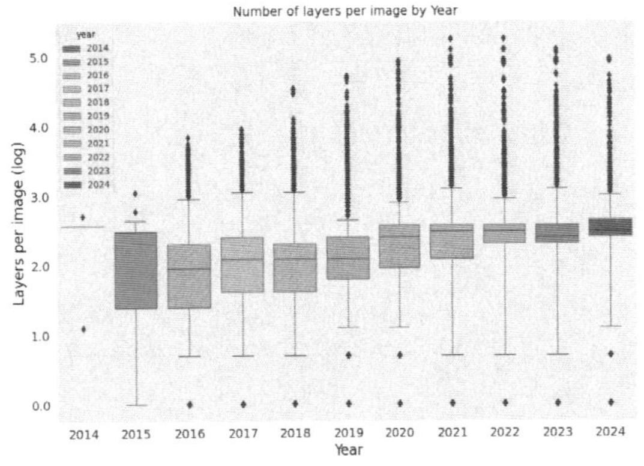

Figure 2. Layers per image by year shows a fairly consistent mean trend with smaller variance and an increase in outliers.

respective registry endpoints. Despite the large number of Dockerfile, the set of unique base images (each with some number of underlying tags, image configurations, and manifests) was much smaller, (2,132) and with huge variance with respect to the number of tags. With one outlier removed (47,428 tags for nix/nixos) (Figure 1), the number of tags ranges from 1 to 16,748, with a mean of 1842 and standard deviation of 2,531 tags.

This tells us that there is quite a bit of variation with respect to release frequency across our set, as each tag is typically indicative of a version or release. We are first interested in the number of layers across images and tags, and how this has changed across time. Seeing that the number of layers has changed over time might reflect a change in build practices. In Figure 2 we see this result for the decade between 2014 and 2024, and while the variation has increased slightly (meaning some images have many more layers) the general means are the same (16.58 +/- 23.66) across time, visually suggesting that people are not building images with significantly more layers. In this exercise, we also found several images from the RedHat registry (8 repositories with a total of 205 tags) with greater than 127 layers. This was an unexpected finding that challenged our "common" knowledge that images could not exceed 127 layers.

We can then use the manifests, which contain layer sizes in bytes, to look at the change in size over this same period (Figure 3). In this figure we see a different pattern – that images are indeed getting larger.

Finally, we might ask how often layers are repeated. This depiction is biased to our dataset, which would more likely have common layers between different tags from the same image. Even still, for a set of 528,449 unique digests (layers) the count of replicated layers drops off quickly, with only 120 instances of a layer being repeated more than 500 times, 52 instances of greater than 1000 times, and only 4 repeated more than 4 times. This data is presented in Table II.

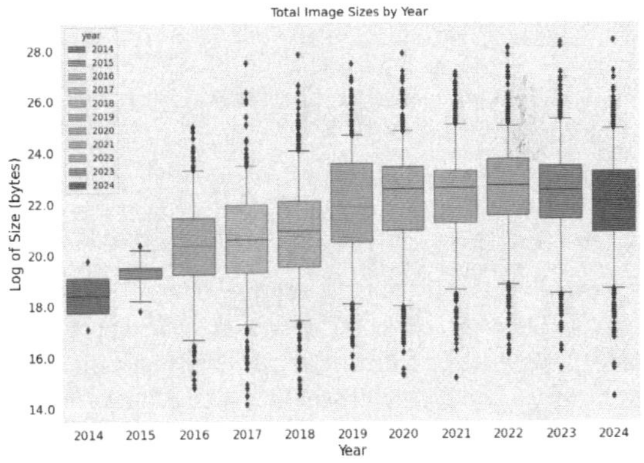

Figure 3. Total image sizes (sum of layers) by year. Outliers with more than 127 layers, the declared maximum, do in fact exist in the RedHat registry.

Interestingly, we discovered an outlier in this set - a layer that appeared to be repeated 67,897 times:

sha256:4f4fb700ef54461cfa02571ae0db9a0dc1e0cdb55
77484a6d75e68dc38e8acc1

Further investigation revealed this was an empty set of 32 bytes that was often associated with a WORKDIR directive in the Dockerfile, but only for cases where the directory already existed. Discussion with OCI maintainers revealed that there is an "empty layer" flag in the image configuration. If the tooling decides not to set the flag, the tool must ship a valid tar+gzip, and that, even without any files being packaged, takes up some space for the tar and gzip headers. This is the empty layer we discovered that when extracted results in the digest that we found. This was implemented before it was realized that /dev/null is an actual valid empty tar file.

TABLE II. REPEATED LAYERS ACROSS DATABASE

Threshold	Count
= 1	312095
>1	216354
>2	136054
>50	9255
>100	3333
>500	120
>1000	52
>3000	4

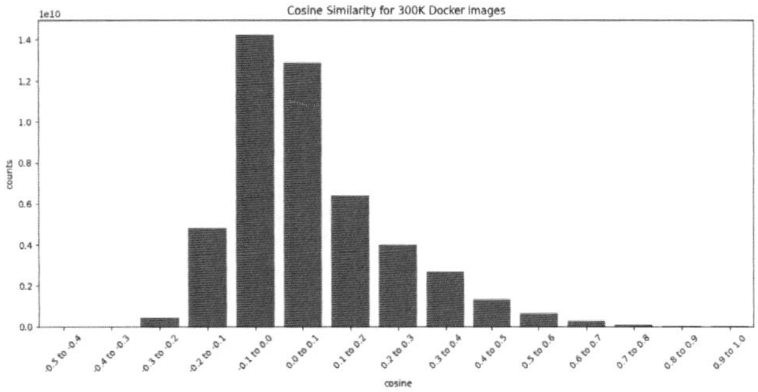

Figure 4. Distribution of image similarities across 300K Docker images, where each is calculated from image build history from the manifest configuration.

C. Content Similarity

We next used the text of the unique layers from the base corpus (N=528,449 layers) to derive both image and layer similarity. We started with 2,132 manifests and treated the layer "history" lines as sentences that make up a document, deriving a set of 309,317 documents. The word2vec embeddings generated from the tokenized documents were then used to calculate pairwise cosine similarity (Figure 4). The cosine matrix generally shows that the bulk of images are not very similar at all, with cosine scores under 0.2.

When we apply the same processing technique to the text from the original scientific Dockerfile (N=77,449) RUN statements we see a similar pattern (Figure 5).

We next want to assess layer similarity. This calculation was more challenging, as we have a total set of 6,535,425 (non-unique) layers across images. We chose a strategy that removes exact duplicates (typically equivalent layers between temporally close tags of the same image), and calculate from the reduced set. Since we are explicitly removing exact duplicates, our goal would not be to say something globally about the ecosystem, but say something about similarity of layers that are not exactly the same. When we tokenize and process and filter down to unique, ensuring that layers from images from the same tag are removed, we have 597,591 layers from base images. When we calculate similarity scores across these layers, we see a similar pattern (Figure 6) where most layers are largely not similar.

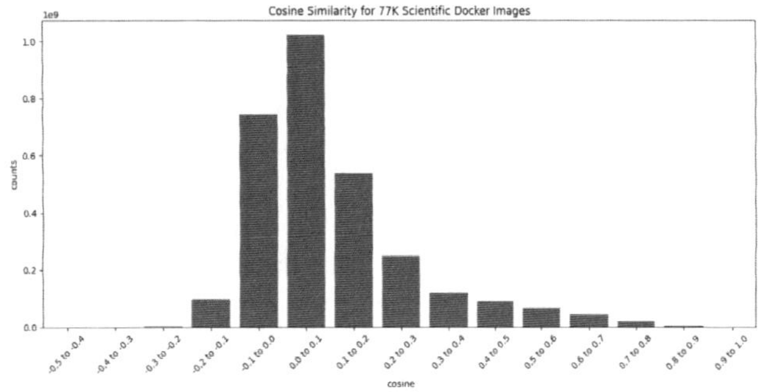

Figure 5. Distribution of image similarities across 77K scientific Dockerfile.

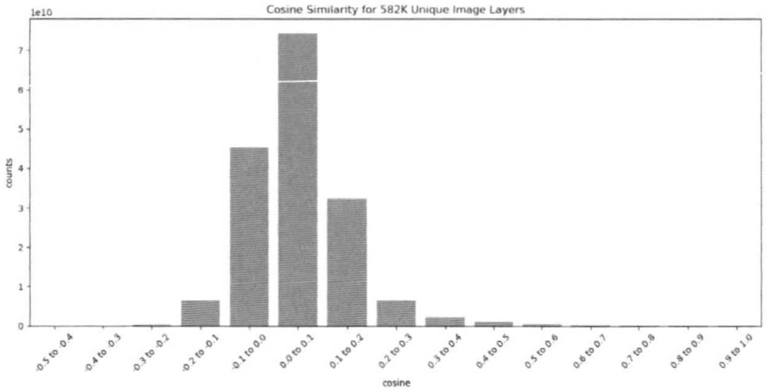

Figure 6. Distribution of layer similarities across 582K unique layers

At a high level, what we can see from this small analysis is that most layers are not re-used across images.

D. Image Bases

When we classify a subset of our images (Table III), removing the version of the image, since we are biased to select for newer images, we find the majority have a debian base, followed by alpine and ubuntu. We also see that values in the similarity score distribution are generally high (Figure 7), indicative of shared paths and thus confidence in the classifications. The minimum score in the above is 0.59, and the maximum is 1. We see that debian is by far the most frequently used, at least for this sample of images we are looking at.

TABLE III. BASE IMAGE CLASSIFICATION

Count	Base Image
debian	393
alpine	95
ubuntu	74
centos	64
fedora	15
rockylinux	11
busybox	4

E. Building Best Practices

In addition to word2vec embeddings generation for similarity calculations, we can use our database of 77K Dockerfile to make observations about image building best practices.

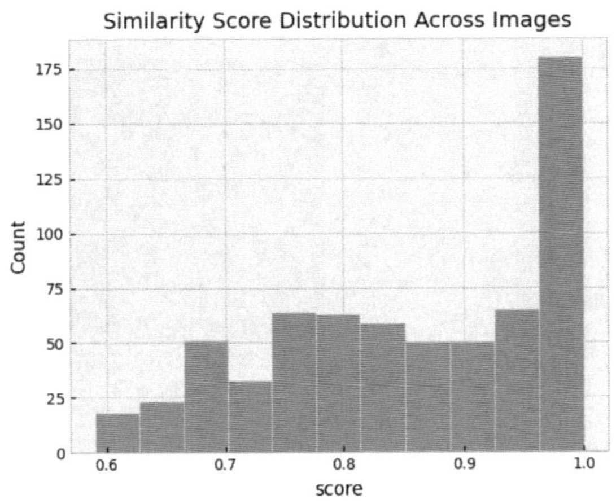

Figure 7. Distribution of image similarity scores used by the "guts" software to derive the base image labels.

1) Limit layers amount

While the maximum number of layers allowed in most registries is 127 and there is no strong guidance on how many layers are good for a single image, we can see from Figure 2 that the layer count has remained relatively stable over time with large variance (16.58 +/- 23.66). We might guess that in practice, people do not explicitly attempt to build images with the fewest layers, but rather build exactly what they need or is easiest.

2) Multi stage builds

Multi-stage builds are useful for separating builds into stages, such as compiling an application and then providing the final binary and libraries in the final image. They are indicated by way of finding more than one FROM statement in the Dockerfile, and considered best practice in that they can reduce the size of the final production image. When we parse our repository of 77K Dockerfile build recipes we can look for greater than 1 FROM statement to indicate such a build. In this set, we find a total of 1984 Dockerfile, which represents 2.56% of image builds.

3) Docker official images

While a Docker "verified" image can come from the docker official images, sponsored open source, or verified publisher, we chose to look explicitly for Docker official images (e.g., ubuntu) as these are provisioned directly by Docker Hub with provided scanning and security checks. We can detect which images are in this set by way of looking at the FROM unique resource identifier. If it has docker.io or library or is missing the registry name (which then will default to the Docker Hub registry) we have found a docker official image. In our database, we found a total of 11,439 images that use a Docker official image, representing 14.77% of the entire set.

4) Latest image

It is conventional wisdom to not use a "latest" tag, the reason being that it is a moving target and can hinder reproducibility. When an image "latest" updates the operating system version, image builds can break as library names or availability can change over time. For our set of 77K Dockerfile, we looked for images that would pull a "latest" tag by way of providing it directly in the unique resource identifier, or leaving out the tag entirely (which defaults to latest). Of the set, we found 4,114 Dockerfile that use a latest image, representing 5.3% of the entire set.

5) Pinned image digest

It is considered better practice to pin an image digest directly, which is more granular than a tag in that it represents an exact build of a base image for a point in time. In our set, we looked for these digests in the FROM statement by searching for the string "sha256," which is the hashing algorithm used for this purpose, and the correct way to specify using a digest. In our set we found only 74 Dockerfile (0.09% of the set) used a pinned digest, reflecting that the practice is not common.

6) Using apt get with apt install in same line

For debian or ubuntu images, it is recommended to use apt get with apt install in the same line to properly use the apt cache. Across our Dockerfile database, for the subset of layers that use apt get (507,695 across Dockerfile images), the large majority (478,742 layers, or 94.3%) take this approach.

7) Using apt get with a clean / autoremove

Since each layer is an isolated unit, and files that are added (and not removed) between layers can lead to bloated layers even if they are cleaned up, it is advisable to remove lists and clean. While debian and ubuntu images automatically run apt-get clean [35], this is arguably still a good practice when applied to other package managers and methods to install software. For our Dockerfile dataset, we find that of the subset that use apt, 67.8% do a clean (clean or autoremove), 0.048% do only an autoremove, and 11.19% do both.

F. Impact of Build Strategy on Digest Similarity

To demonstrate the influence of container building strategy on resulting container layer similarity, we aimed to compare overall layer digest similarity between 10 applications that were built in multiple ways. The spack builds for three containers (low redundancy strategy) were not successful and were not used in the analysis. The Jaccard scores are shown in Figure 8 and summary metrics in Table IV.

Interestingly, the performance study set has a cluster of images that are more similar than the best effort set, likely resulting from having overall a larger number of matching layers between images.

The best effort set of builds (middle panel in Figure 8) that have fewer overall layers would require 33/118 (28%) unique layer pulls. Since we are certain that these containers were built with redundancy of layers in mind, we can state

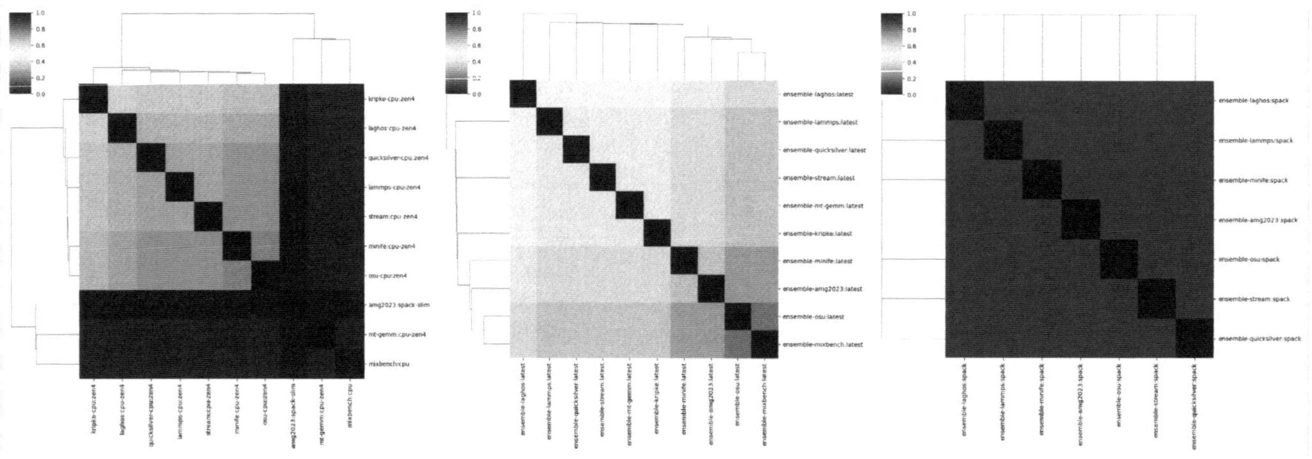

Figure 8. Jacaard scores for three build strategies. A reasonable effort to ensure redundancy (left) that produces a mixture of similar and dissimilar images, a best effort strategy (middle), and a build tool that eliminates the possibility for redundancy (right).

TABLE IV. SIMILARITY OF CONTAINER SETS BASED ON BUILD STRATEGY

Container Set	Total Layers	Unique URIs	Unique Containers	Unique Layer Digests	Jacaard Similarity (mean and s.d)
Performance Study	258	10	10	115	0.40 (0.38)
Best Effort for Redundancy	128	10	10	33	0.66 (0.128)
Low Redundancy Builds (spack)	56	7	7	50	0.2 (0.33)

that this 28% represents the application logic specific to each container. For the performance study where some care was taken for redundancy, 115/258 (45%) of layers would require isolated pulls. Finally, for the spack build strategy that creates a large layer that consists of a custom spack view, 50/56 (89%) of layers would require unique pulls, a strategy that does not allow for large amount of redundancy. We can see this result reflected in the Jaccard similarity cluster maps in Figure 8. The exercise demonstrates that a choice of a build tool can have "trickle down" implications for experiment costs, and often unique application logic makes the task of redundancy a challenging one.

G. Image Pulling Strategy

We assessed the trade-off between number of layers and image size. We found no discernible impact to the number of layers and image pull time (Figure 9). Instead, total image size appeared to be the most important factor to increase pull time. We proceeded with subsequent experiments to only include the median (N=9) number of layers, and a set of 6 larger sizes between the 90th and 100th percentile of the Dockerfile dataset, ranging between 148MB and 19GB.

Pulling from a registry external to the cloud provider (Figure 10) made no difference to pull times as compared to pulling from a registry provided by the cloud (Figure 11)

However, pulling with the presence of LocalSSD (Figure 12) improved times, often by 20-40 seconds (approximately 1.25x), and made pull times more consistent between nodes. This is an advisable strategy as the cost of storage ($0.1046 per GB per month) is relatively inexpensive compared to the

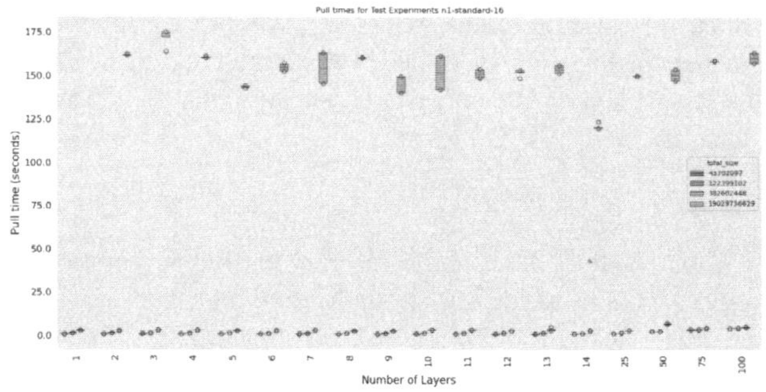

Figure 9. Testing the influence of number of layers across 4 image sizes and 18 different layer counts showed no discernible difference in pull times, but rather, suggested that size was a salient factor.

cost of running experiments.

The most surprising and impressing result was using image streaming, which could reduce pull times down to close to 1 second, assuming to be assisted by a caching strategy [36]. This finding is demonstrated in (Figure 13), where the benefits of image streaming are fully realized after the initial pull of the experiment containers for the size 4 cluster. The caching strategy provided by Google Cloud that makes subsequent cluster pull times almost instantaneous persists across different clusters.

Extending images to a real-world set of applications, the improved pulling times when using image streaming as compared to not using it was still substantial, an approximate 15x improvement (Figure 14).

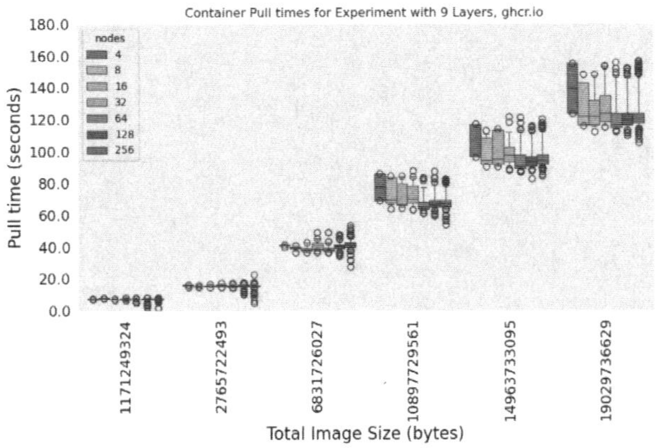

Figure 10. Pull times from a remote registry (GitHub packages) to Google Cloud showed an increase as the size of the container increased.

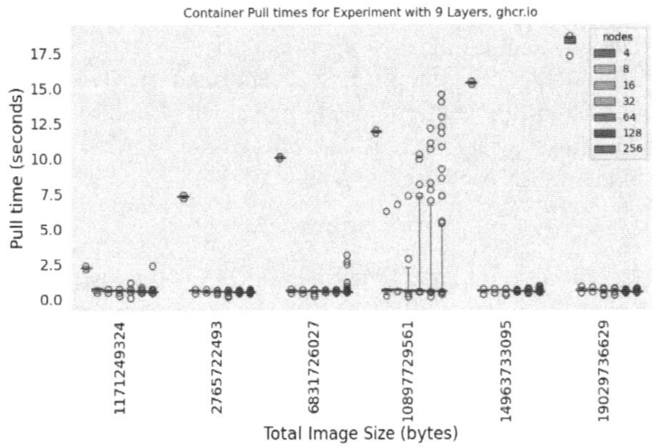

Figure 13. Image streaming pulling times across image sizes. The ability of the container to transition to running was consistently close to 1 second due to caching. Size 4 demonstrates that the first pull of a specific container in Google Cloud benefits from image streaming, but is not instantly available as it is not cached. Larger sizes benefit from a caching strategy [36]

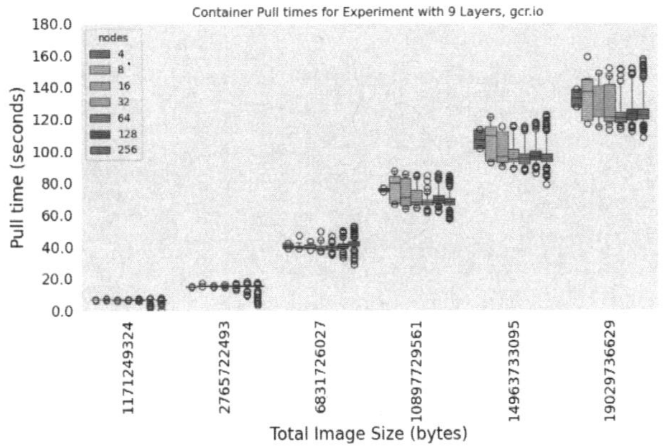

Figure 11. Pull times from a local registry (Google Artifact Registry) to Google Cloud in the same region did not improve pull times.

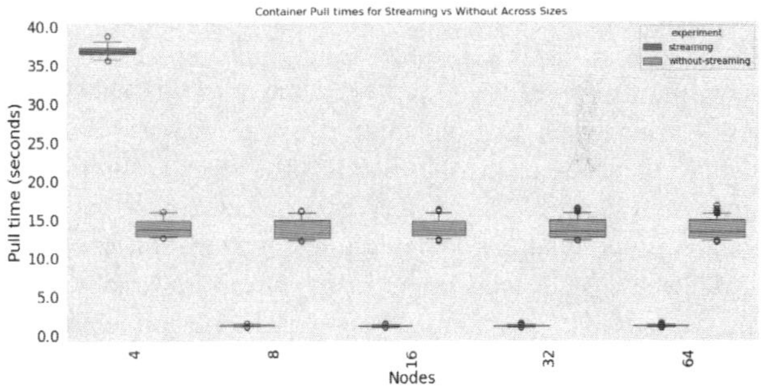

Figure 14. Image streaming pulling times across application images. The reported time for the container to start running was approximately 15x faster for applications LAMMPS, OSU All Reduce, AMG, and Minife. The smallest experiment size did not benefit from Google Cloud caching.

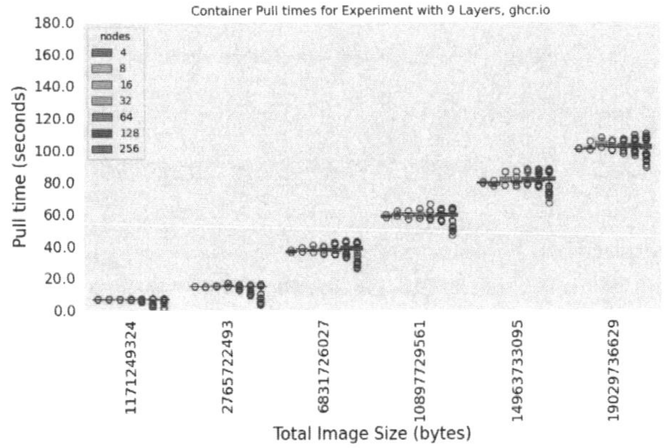

Figure 12. Pull times from a local registry (Google Artifact Registry) with an added local SSD improved pull times between 20-40 seconds and improved consistency of pull times across nodes in the cluster.

H. Node Coordination

Despite pull times not increasing as cluster size increases, the total time to run an experiment increased with number of nodes, resulting in 1383.65, 1392.84, 1408.48, 1426.84, 1535.19, 1940.99, 2884.18 seconds for our initial experiments for sizes 4, 8, 16, 32, 64, 128, and 256, respectively. This suggests that additional time is accumulated elsewhere, and the results of the node coordination tests give a hint to the source of this extra time. Figure 15 shows time differences between events across nodes. This is calculated as, for each container, the earliest timestamp recorded for the event subtracted from the latest across nodes. Doing this calculation across cluster sizes shows us the extent to which an event for a specific container is coordinated. A time of zero indicates that the nodes across a cluster had the event occur at the same time, while a value above that represents a stagger from that. These plots demonstrate that as the size of both containers and clusters increase, so does the variability of events for it between nodes – the largest container (19GB) on the largest cluster size (N=256 nodes) has minimally two nodes that are pulled, created, and started approximately 50 seconds apart. This finding that extra time is accumulated as clusters get larger, a likely result of needing to wait for the slowest node across a large set, is interesting and warrants further exploration for behavior and solutions.

IV. Discussion

In this work, we amass a database of 77K Dockerfile and do a complete assessment of the trends and container ecosystem since 2014, observing that the number of layers has largely not changed, but image sizes are slowly getting larger – a trend we expect to continue with the growing number of machine learning images that are entering the ecosystem. We derive build practices from the data, noting that debian is the most popular base image, redundancy of layers is uncommon, and good practices to pin digests and perform multi-stage builds are uncommon. We finish our study with a set of experiments that first visually show the change in image similarity based on digests for three building strategies, and then performing a comprehensive pulling study that demonstrates using local SSD and a streaming approach can greatly reduce the time between onset of pull and having a running container. It was a surprising result that pull time does not increase with the number of nodes in the cluster, and that other scaling issues must be responsible for longer experimental runs on larger clusters. This finding is interesting and warrants further work.

While Google Cloud offers image streaming easily as an add-on to GKE, no similar easy install method exists for Amazon Web Services Elastic Kubernetes Service (EKS) and so as a supplement to this work we developed a daemonset [16] to automatically install the SOCI snapshotter to a cluster. We anticipate doing further work in the space of snapshotter plugins to further optimize how application assets are loaded with cache pre-fetching and on demand. From these observations, we recommend to the reader to use a streaming image approach when a registry is available that can provide the indexed images, and if not, to fall back to using local SSD for improved pulling times.

A. Docker Layers

The finding that Docker has references that set limits to each of 125 and 128 layers for the overlay fs driver was interesting and worth further exploring. As containerd does not set any maximum, we were able to test building and pushing the image "docker.io/tianon/test:many-layers-256" and it was successful. The limit was originally enforced because there were early issues with mounting layers (length of an argument to a syscall) that led to technical maximums. However, this early issue may not be relevant depending on the host operating system, kernel version, and container runtime being used. Different tools take different approaches to validating this -- containerd and buildkit use a practical approach that does not enforce any checks, but then would propagate the error on mount failure, meaning that the limits are controlled by the kernel. Other tools like Docker hard code manual checks in the

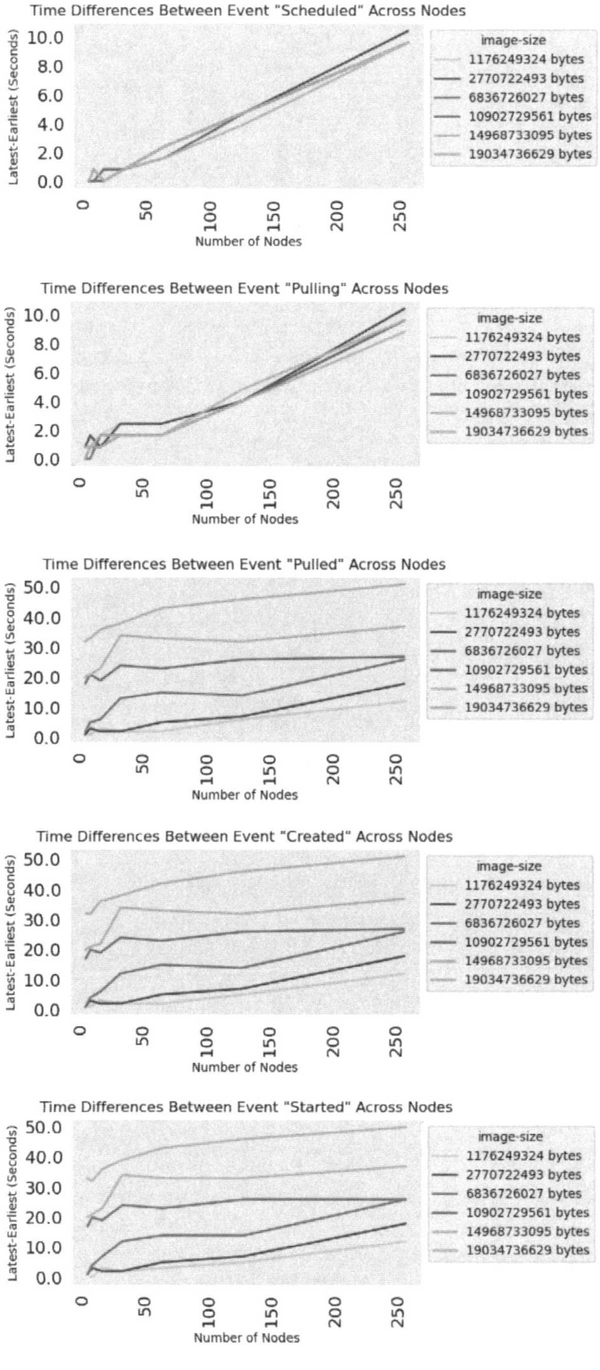

Figure 15. Time differences between events across nodes. This is calculated as the maximum - minimum timestamp across nodes for a cluster sizes, reflecting the extent to which an event for a specific container is coordinated. A time of zero indicates that the nodes across a cluster had the event occur at the same time, while a value above that represents a stagger from that.

code, which might fail earlier, but do not always reflect the true limit enforced by the user's particular kernel. With respect to Docker, the failure often comes after pulling the layers, which arguably is a check that should be done earlier. This was an interesting finding because it represents a cultural practice and established knowledge that is more of a gray area. In practice, many empty or metadata layers are relatively harmless since they are ignored or not relevant to image extraction.

B. Limitations

We recognize that our choice of a software database that would provide scientific images is only a slice of the entire container ecosystem, and this choice was intentional to not include many service-oriented images that might run websites, databases, or other applications not directly related to science.

While using a different compression algorithm can also reduce extraction, we aimed to test solutions that were readily available in the common software being use to build containers, which typically is not containerd [29]. Another viable solution that was not tested here is to preload base images using a daemonset [32], a great idea given containers with a large shared base image. That approach would not have fit our study as our base image was chosen to be minimal and insignificant to the pull time. While we used Google Cloud for this work, the use of the open source project Kubernetes that is available across clouds, and general pattern to use a more performant filesystem can be applied to other cloud environments. A logical next stage of work is to understand how patterns of application data retrieval work with various pulling strategies. For example, requiring download of large data after container startup could have a detrimental effect to application performance. In these cases, optimizing an initial pull to better run in parallel could be an optimal choice.

V. Conclusion

Best practices are often prescribed with little attention to how reasonable they are, or how well they fit into a user workflow or incentive structure. Our work demonstrates that the number of layers is not a salient variable to worry about, but rather total image size. Our takeaways are that a container building strategy optimized for similarity in container layers can increase layer redundancy, decreasing time needed to pull and thus decreasing total time and cost for a study. This improvement becomes more salient when using expensive resources such as GPU, or an auto-scaling strategy that provisions new nodes that do not have images cached. We suggest container streaming as an ideal strategy for quickly starting containers that are large, however caution should be used if large amounts of new data are needed for application execution later in the run. Local SSDs can consistently improve performance without these detrimental effects.

While we cannot say that these benefits extend to other clouds, those using Google Cloud should consider pulling images to a smaller cluster first to take advantage of caching along with image streaming. Layers should (and cannot) go over the registry limit of 10GB, and given this limitation, developers will need to consider strategies for provisioning large models that are intended to be used with containers. As ML images get larger it will be more important to address these issues.

Finally, we suggest to the reader that although the specific strategy chosen for building and pulling might vary based on the experimental resources and application characteristics, it is responsible to have awareness about costs, and strategies for improvement. Given contention for resources such as GPUs, there is an opportunity cost of the extra time used on the resources. Nodes that have excess pulling time are not available for anyone else to use. We encourage the community to think about the costs of their experiments, and to further explore this interesting space of work.

Acknowledgments

Thank you to the AWS EKS team for interesting discussion on the SOCI Snapshotter, and Daniel Milroy for his feedback on the manuscript. Thank you to the OCI Slack for discussion on layers, and to the larger HPC and cloud communities for continuing to make this space of development interesting and gratifying to work in.

This work was performed under the auspices of the U.S. Department of Energy by Lawrence Livermore National Laboratory under contract DE-AC52-07NA27344. Lawrence Livermore National Security, LLC LLNL-CONF-871325

References

[1] D. Moreau, K. Wiebels, and C. Boettiger, "Containers for computational reproducibility," *Nature Reviews Methods Primers*, vol. 3, no. 1, p. 50, 2023.

[2] Honeypot, *Kubernetes: The documentary [PART 1]*, Jan. 2022.

[3] L. W. et al., "Bare-metal vs. hypervisors and containers: Performance evaluation of virtualization technologies for software-defined vehicles," in *2023 IEEE Intelligent Vehicles Symposium (IV)*, IEEE, 2023, pp. 1–8.

[4] J. Baumgartner and L. et al., "Performance losses with virtualization: Comparing bare metal to vms and containers," in *International Conference on High Performance Computing*, Springer, 2023, pp. 107–120.

[5] G. Hu, Y. Zhang, and W. Chen, "Exploring the performance of singularity for high performance computing scenarios," en, in *2019 IEEE 21st International Conference on High Performance Computing and Communications; IEEE 17th International Conference on Smart City; IEEE 5th International Conference on Data Science and Systems (HPCC/SmartCity/DSS)*, IEEE, Aug. 2019, pp. 2587–2593.

[6] S. Buchanan, J. Rangama, and B. et al., "Container registries," *Introducing Azure Kubernetes Service: A Practical Guide to Container Orchestration*, pp. 17–34, 2020.

[7] O. Containers, *Opencontainers/distribution-spec*, en, 2024.

[8] O. Containers, *Opencontainers/image-spec*, en, 2024.

[9] *Dockerfile reference*, en, https://docs.docker.com/reference/dockerfile/, Accessed: 2024-10-2, Sep. 2024.

[10] *Moby/moby github issue*, en, 2024.

[11] T. Harter, B. Salmon, R. Liu, A. C. Arpaci-Dusseau, and R. H. Arpaci-Dusseau, "Slacker: Fast distribution with lazy docker containers," in *14th USENIX Conference on File and Storage Technologies (FAST 16)*, 2016, pp. 181–195.

[12] Honeypot, *Kubernetes: The documentary [PART 1]*, Jan. 2022.

[13] I. Docker, *Multi-stage*, en, https://docs.docker.com/build/building/multi-stage/, Accessed: 2024-10-2, Sep. 2024.

[14] N. Zhao, V. Tarasov, and A. et al., "Large-scale analysis of docker images and performance implications for container storage systems," *IEEE Transactions on Parallel and Distributed Systems*, vol. 32, no. 4, pp. 918–930, 2020.

[15] J. L. Chen, D. Liaqat, M. Gabel, and E. de Lara, "Starlight: Fast container provisioning on the edge and over the WAN," *NSDI*, pp. 35–50, 2022.

[16] V. Sochat, *converged-computing/soci-installer: soci installer release 0.0.0*, version 0.0.0, Oct. 2024. DOI: 10.5281/zenodo.13895822.

[17] V. Sochat, *converged-computing/container-crafter: Container Crafter v0.0.0*, version 0.0.0, Oct. 2024. DOI: 10.5281/zenodo.13871919.

[18] I. Docker, *"best practices"*, en, https://docs.docker.com/build/building/best-practices/, Accessed: 2024-10-2, Sep. 2024.

[19] V. S. et al., "The research software encyclopedia: A community framework to define research software," *Journal of Open Research Software*, vol. 10, no. 1, p. 2, Mar. 2022.

[20] K. W. Church, "Word2vec," *Natural Language Engineering*, vol. 23, no. 1, pp. 155–162, 2017.

[21] I. Docker, *Cache*, en, https://docs.docker.com/build/cache/, Accessed: 2024-10-2, Sep. 2024.

[22] Mikal, *Interpreting whiteout files in docker image layers*, en, https://www.madebymikal.com/interpreting-whiteout-files-in-docker-image-layers/, Accessed: 2024-10-2.

[23] V. Sochat and D. M. et al., *Converged Computing Performance Study Release v0.0.0*, version 0.0.0, Sep. 2024. DOI: 10.5281/zenodo.13738496.

[24] S. Shudler, N. Ferrier, and I. et al., "Spack meets singularity: Creating movable in-situ analysis stacks with ease," in *Proceedings of the Workshop on In Situ Infrastructures for Enabling Extreme-Scale Analysis and Visualization*, 2019, pp. 34–38.

[25] V. Sochat, *converged-computing/ensemble-containers: Ensemble Containers*, version 0.0.0, Oct. 2024. DOI: 10.5281/zenodo.13887339.

[26] V. Sochat, *Singularityhub/guts: Release v0.0.1*, version 0.0.1, Mar. 2023. DOI: 10.5281/zenodo.7703378.

[27] V. Sochat, *singularityhub/shpc-guts: Singularity Registry HPC Guts v0.0.1*, version 0.0.1, Mar. 2023. DOI: 10.5281/zenodo.7703380.

[28] D. Community, *Docker documentation: Number of layers is not documented*, en.

[29] V. Sochat and C. K. et al., *Hpc containers community survey 2024*, May 2024. DOI: 10.5281/zenodo.11206333.

[30] S. Section, *Jobs*, https://kubernetes.io/docs/concepts/workloads/controllers/job/, Accessed: 2023-9-1.

[31] R. Authors, *Kubernetes-event-exporter: Export kubernetes events to multiple destinations with routing and filtering*, en.

[32] T. He and W. Chiang, *Tips and tricks to reduce cold start latency on GKE*, en, https://cloud.google.com/blog/products/containers-kubernetes/tips-and-tricks-to-reduce-cold-start-latency-on-gke, Accessed: 2024-10-2, Jan. 2024.

[33] AWS, *Soci-snapshotter: A containerd snapshotter plugin which enables standard OCI images to be lazily loaded without requiring a build-time conversion step*, en.

[34] K. Tokunaga, *Startup containers in lightning speed with lazy image distribution on containerd*, en, https://medium.com/nttlabs/startup-containers-in-lightning-speed-with-lazy-image-distribution-on-containerd-243d94522361, Accessed: 2024-11-10, Apr. 2020.

[35] D. Community, *Contrib/mkimage/debootstrap at 03e2923e42446dbb830c654d0eec323a0b4ef02a · moby/moby*, en.

[36] G. Cloud, *Use image streaming to pull container images*, en, https://cloud.google.com/kubernetes-engine/docs/how-to/image-streaming, Accessed: 2024-11-10.

Consistent Access to Cloud Services across Regions for Large Enterprises

Pavvan Pradeep
Computer Science and Engineering Department
PES University
Bengaluru, India
e-mail: pavvanpradeep@gmail.com

Aditi Srinivas M
Computer Science and Engineering Department
PES University
Bengaluru, India
e-mail: aditimatti@gmail.com

Prisha Goel
Computer Science and Engineering Department
PES University
Bengaluru, India
e-mail: prishapgoel@gmail.com

Dhruv Sanjaykumar Ratanpara
Computer Science and Engineering Department
PES University
Bengaluru, India
e-mail: dhruv2502@gmail.com

Shilpa S
Computer Science and Engineering Department
PES University
Bengaluru, India
e-mail: shilpas@pes.edu

***Abstract*—In today's world, high availability is critical to meet the needs of uninterrupted operation and customer satisfaction. The expansion of cloud services has permitted substantial progress towards reaching this availability. However, there are issues such as high ownership costs and constant availability across many locations, as not all cloud providers provide comprehensive regional support. This project seeks to demonstrate a strategy for developing platforms for global organizations that are available in multiple regions and provide an improved user experience. Our methodology enables one to seamlessly integrate the Istio service mesh into the existing infrastructure, with a focus on high performance,low latency, multi-region availability across many zones, dispersed deployment for better reliability, and a low total cost of ownership. Our solution uses Istio's features to improve service resilience and distribution, resulting in cost-effective, high-performance multi-region deployments.**

Keywords*—*Istio Service Mesh; Reduced total cost of ownership; Multi-region failover; Availability Zone level failover; Minimized latency.

I. Introduction

High availability, scalability, and scattered deployments are vital in today's technology-driven world, where continuous access to services is essential [1]. Cloud providers such as Amazon Web Services (AWS), Google Cloud Platform (GCP), Microsoft Azure, and Oracle Cloud Infrastructure (OCI) have played significant roles in providing these services with multi-region availability, ensuring that operations continue even when regions fail. AWS is the largest cloud provider, noted for its massive infrastructure, which includes 48 regions and 54 Availability Zones worldwide, with a range of services including processing power, storage, and databases. Cloud providers like AWS use auto-scaling mechanisms to maintain availability during periods of high demand [2]. While each operator provides a variety of global regions and availability zones, achieving seamless worldwide coverage remains a difficulty. Geographic limitations, high ownership costs, and interoperability between providers remain significant difficulties. Most of the industries are moving towards a microservices architecture for their applications to enhance availability. Deploying applications as lightweight portable container enhances scalability and fault-tolerance [3]. However, enterprises frequently struggle to balance high availability needs with cost-effectiveness, particularly when deploying across various geographies [4]. There is also the challenge of managing dispersed applications, data consistency, and compliance requirements, especially when apps cross international borders. Existing cloud-based high-availability solutions face several limitations. Many rely heavily on cloud providers, leading to vendor lock-in and high operational costs. Cloud-based auto-scaling guarantees resource availability, but it falls short in addressing region-level failover. It can be challenging for businesses to maintain a uniform infrastructure around the globe because some cloud services are not accessible everywhere. Given these difficulties, a method that minimizes reliance on the cloud, maximizes latency, and guarantees smooth failover without compromising cost is required.

Our approach involves a one-time infrastructure setup cost, after which it leverages open-source tools like Istio and a custom load balancer to enable seamless failover and minimize latency. Our aim is to integrate the Istio service mesh into large organisations' existing architecture for enhanced traffic routing and service maintenance. This approach aims to improve availability, provide multi-region resilience, and reduce ownership costs. Our technique routes traffic to the nearest region to reduce latency and ensures that users receive responses within an optimal time. When a service in a given availability zone goes down, the zone is tagged as unhealthy, blocking routing of further user requests to it. This feature helps to avoid inter-zone service communication, which might increase latency.

Our approach uses locality-based load balancing to evenly distribute traffic across all healthy zones within a region. Such a balanced distribution ensures stability and prevents services in any zone from being overloaded with user requests thereby increasing total system resilience. Our technique uses the open-source Istio service mesh to manage traffic effectively. By using Istio, we can create a strong architecture with greater stability, availability and scalability while lowering the total cost of ownership.

Our approach focuses on improving the private infrastructure of large-scale industries. It integrates easily with their existing systems to boost availability, reduce latency, and lower costs by reducing reliance on cloud providers. Since cloud services are not available in all regions and don't always work well together, relying on cloud services completely is not a good option for large-scale industries. Moreover migrating applications to the cloud require one to have many procedures in place such as application migration, data migration and dependency checks [5]. Instead large-scale industries can set up their infrastructure in the regions they need and integrate our approach seamlessly to increase the reliability and availability of their services across multiple regions, making their systems more efficient and cost-effective. Hence, our approach is a solution that meets the needs of modern, large-scale industries.

Section 2 presents a literature survey, exploring current strategies aimed at minimizing latency and increasing multi-region availability. The methodology is described in Section 3, along with the technologies utilized, such as the Istio service mesh and Kubernetes in Docker (KinD). This section explains the implementation of our setup, which consists of two clusters and a load balancer to ensure multi-region availability and optimized latency. Results are presented in Section 4, along with our framework's latency measures. The research is finally concluded in Section 5, as part of the future scope the paper suggests use of AI models for fault prediction and resource optimization to enhance system maintenance.

II. Literature Survey

A. Malhotra, A. Elsayed, R. Torres and S. Venkatram [6] explore solutions to achieve near-zero downtime for cloud-native, business-critical applications. Thw authors emphasize on microservices architecture to enhance fault tolerance and scalability. A clustered setup with Kubernetes enables load balancing and seamless failovers within and across regions. Tools like Global Load Balancer (GLB) for geo-based routing, PgBouncer for PostgreSQL optimization, and HAProxy for high availability are integrated. For read-heavy applications, read replicas handle most requests to offload the primary database, while write-heavy setups distribute traffic geographically to optimize latency. Despite its robust approach, the architecture focuses heavily on database resilience, with limited attention to network-level failovers.

A. Anwar's [7] study proposes a high-availability solution leveraging AWS services. Applications are hosted on EC2 instances spread across multiple Availability Zones (AZs) with a load balancer managing traffic distribution. NAT Gateways ensure secure internet connectivity, while auto-scaling groups dynamically adjust resources. Elastic IPs provide stability, maintaining consistent DNS entries during instance restarts. Although this setup withstands zonal outages and high traffic, regional outages remain a challenge. Its reliance on AWS services also leads to high operational costs, which could be optimized by refining auto-scaling policies.

Anna Berenberg and Brad Calder [8] evaluate different deployment models, from zonal to global, highlighting their benefits like increased availability, improved latency, and scalability. By integrating edge computing, it suggests further latency reductions and resource optimization. While the archetypes offer flexibility and future-proofing, managing complex deployment models and addressing global outages pose challenges. Balancing costs with high availability and latency remains an ongoing issue in these strategies.

A. Hajikhani and A. Suominen [9] focus on disaster recovery, this research outlines strategies for applications across Kubernetes clusters using service mesh and serverless workloads. It emphasizes automatic failover mechanisms, resource optimization, and cost reduction in multi-cluster environments. While the paper provides practical insights, it falls short in covering all failure scenarios and complex multi-cluster deployments. Its narrow focus on Kubernetes limits its broader applicability to other cloud setups.

Mohammad Reza Mesbahi, Amir Masoud Rahmani and Mehdi Hosseinzadeh [10] present a roadmap for achieving high availability and reliability in cloud environments. The paper identifies challenges and proposes solutions to align with quality-of-service agreements. While insightful for both providers and consumers, the paper lacks practical validation and oversimplifies complex technical issues. It serves as a theoretical framework rather than a hands-on guide to cloud resilience.

Our proposed architecture aims to address the challenges faced by these previous approaches by removing the dependency on existing cloud providers, and minimizing cost and latency.

III. Methodology

Our methodology is designed to leverage a series of open source technologies, to ensure multi-region availability, efficient load balancing, and reduced latency.

A. *Kubernetes in Docker(KinD)*

KinD (Kubernetes in Docker) is a tool that allows one to easily establish and manage Kubernetes clusters on a local workstation using Docker containers. Kind is intended to simplify Kubernetes development and testing by enabling:

- Experimenting with various Kubernetes versions, configurations, and deployments.
- Simulation of a multi-node Kubernetes setup on a single PC.

B. *Istio Service Mesh*

A service mesh is a software layer that facilitates communication between services in an application. It consists of a network of proxies known as "sidecars" that run alongside each service. A service mesh can help prevent cascade failures, which can cause system-wide downtime. It accomplishes this by including features such as circuit breaking, retries, and timeouts. A service mesh can monitor the status of services, connection, and failures. It can also deliver metrics, logs, and trace data. A service mesh can aid with traffic management, such as load balancing and rate limitation. A service mesh is independent of each service's code, allowing it to function across network boundaries and with various service management systems.

An Istio service mesh is open source and functions as a dedicated infrastructure layer that manages and secures communication between microservices within a distributed application, effectively giving a transparent mechanism to govern traffic flow, security, and observability.
Key elements of the Istio architecture:

- The Data Plane:
  The Data Plane consists of "Envoy" proxy sidecars that handle network traffic, routing, load balancing, and telemetry data collection for each microservice.
- Control Plane (Istio):
  A centralized control system for configuring sidecar proxies, creating traffic routing rules, security policies, and other service mesh operations.

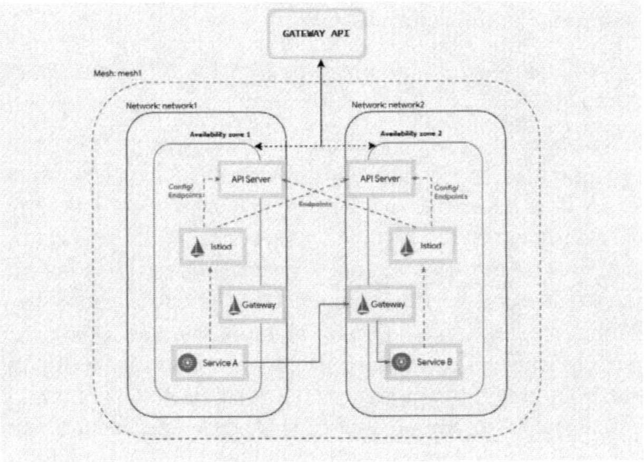

Figure 1. Services running across Availability Zones within a region

C. Multi Primary Istio on Different Networks

The multi-primary Istio configuration across various networks allows two clusters to run with independent control planes, resulting in secure and highly available communication across boundaries. Figure 1 illustrates our multi-primary Istio architecture within a region where there are two clusters on separate networks, each with its own Istio control plane. To support cross-cluster connectivity, both clusters have an Istio east-west gateway in place. This gateway manages east-west traffic for internal and cross-cluster service interactions, allowing ingress and egress traffic to flow smoothly between clusters.

To enable proper service discovery, each cluster's API servers are configured to recognise one another. This is performed by establishing a remote secret key in each cluster, allowing for mutual discovery and secure communication across networks. As a result, cluster 1's API server will be able to access cluster 2's services along with those within its own clusters, and vice versa. This configuration allows the Istio service mesh to effectively distribute traffic across availability zones, providing resilience, fault tolerance, and effective load balancing inside the service mesh.

D. Load Balancer

A Load balancer is used to distribute user requests to the under-loaded services to ensure that no service is overwhelmed with requests. Hence, it is necessary to have a fault-tolerant load balancer to create a highly resilient architecture [11]. If the load is not distributed efficiently across all the available services it degrades the performance and efficiency of computing resources [12]. Our architecture leverages a global load balancer to achieve high availability and optimal performance by routing traffic across two geographically separated regions. The primary goal is to direct users to the nearest healthy instance, thereby minimizing latency and enhancing the user experience. This approach is essential for business-critical applications, as it ensures that users can access the service with minimal delay and without disruption, even in cases of regional failures. To achieve accurate location-based routing, we employ an external API that provides the user's geographical data based on their IP address, which is a reliable method for real-time location determination in distributed systems.

The process begins by constructing a URL with the user's IP address, which is then used to make an HTTP GET request to retrieve the user's location data. From the JSON response body, we parse the latitude and longitude values, which serve as input for calculating the distance to each available instance. Before proceeding with distance calculation, we must first verify the health of each instance to avoid directing traffic to an unavailable or unstable service. For this purpose, we create a health check URL by formatting each server's address and port, which acts as an endpoint to verify its availability. This validation step is crucial, as it prevents unnecessary errors and guarantees that only active and responsive instances are included in the load balancing process. Each server URL is parsed to ensure validity; if it is found invalid, the server is marked as unhealthy, and an error message is logged. To further ensure robust operations, we use a mutex lock, which prevents race conditions by managing concurrent access to shared resources during health checks, a common practice for maintaining consistency in multi-threaded applications.

Once the health of each instance is confirmed, we convert the latitude and longitude coordinates of both the user and each healthy instance into coordinates suitable for distance calculation. To accurately measure the distance between these points, we utilize the Haversine function. This mathematical formula is specifically designed for calculating the shortest distance between two points on a sphere, making it highly effective for geographic distance calculations. The precision of the Haversine function is beneficial for our load balancer,

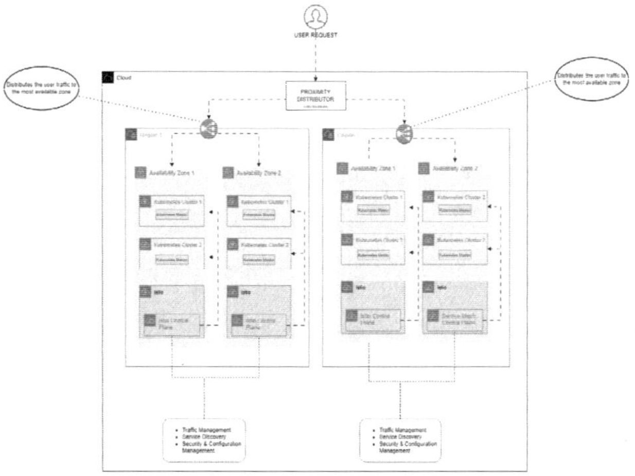

Figure 2. Architecture

as it ensures users are routed to the physically closest instance, which is particularly important in regions with multiple service points.

After calculating the distances, the global load balancer routes traffic to the closest healthy instance, significantly reducing latency and providing users with a faster, more reliable service. In the event that this instance becomes unavailable due to a failure or outage, the load balancer dynamically reroutes traffic to the next closest healthy instance, maintaining continuous availability. This resilient approach to load balancing not only enhances user satisfaction but also aligns with best practices in high-availability architecture by reducing single points of failure and ensuring reliable service continuity across regions. Figure 2 depicts a high level overview of the entire architecture of our setup. By leveraging a multi-cluster Kubernetes setup with Istio, it enhances service discovery and traffic management across all regions. This holistic approach to existing infrastructure of companies guarantees high availability, scalability, and optimal performance for enterprise applications.

E. Our Setup

Our setup is distributed across two regions, each containing two Kubernetes clusters that serve as Availability Zones within those regions. Such an architectural setup ensures high availability and low -latency. These clusters are managed using KinD (Kubernetes in Docker). The regions are labeled as region1 and region2, and the Availability Zones within each region denoted as zone1 and zone2. Figure 3 illustrates our proposed architecture. This setup enables seamless failover and efficient workload distribution across regions. It also helps in mitigating single points of failure by ensuring redundancy at both the regional and availability zone levels. Additionally, traffic routing mechanisms are implemented to direct user requests to the nearest and most responsive cluster, improving overall performance.

Istio is installed in a multi-primary configuration on each cluster. This configuration ensures high availability and functionality by providing each cluster with its own Istio control plane. Each cluster in a multi-primary setup has its own Istio control plane, which allows them to govern traffic, implement rules, and forward requests throughout the mesh. Such a setup ensures system stability and availability. Even if the control plane of one of the clusters fails, the other clusters remain operational and continue to serve the user requests.

The helloworld service is deployed across all clusters, providing redundancy and locality-based access. The service instances are labeled according to their region and zone easier traffic routing:

- The service is labeled as helloworld.region1.zone1 in region1, zone1 and helloworld.region1.zone2 in region1, zone2.
- Similarly, the service is labeled as helloworld.region2.zone1 in region2, zone1 and the service is labeled as helloworld.region2.zone2 in region2, zone2 .
- The helloworld gateway allows access to the services.

To ensure minimal latency and efficient resource utilization, a custom load balancer is deployed on a separate system. This load balancer routes user requests to the nearest region, optimizing performance and reliability.

F. Availability Zone Failover using Istio Locality-Based Routing

For enhanced resilience, Istio's locality-based failover is configured to handle availability zone-specific issues seamlessly. If an issue arises within any zone, marking it unhealthy, Istio's destination rules redirect all traffic to the nearest healthy zones within the same region. This immediate redirection ensures that users experience minimal disruptions, as the system reroutes requests automatically to healthy zones, continuing services which makes the architecture highly available. Highly available systems are designed so that no single failure causes unacceptable service disruption [13]. The destination rule configuration also continuously monitors the health status of each zone. Once the affected zone is restored and services are healthy, it becomes eligible again to receive requests, maintaining balanced and resilient service distribution.

G. Region-Wide Failover for Regional Resilience

In cases of region-level failures, the custom load balancer takes over to prevent routing to any impacted region. It continuously performs health checks across regions to ensure only healthy regions handle requests. If a region fails, the load balancer seamlessly routes traffic to the other available region, ensuring uninterrupted service. As soon as all services in the affected region are confirmed to be operational again, the load balancer resumes routing requests to it.

IV. Results and Discussion

In our observability setup for Cluster 1 in Region 1, Zone 1, we monitored key performance indicators such as latency,

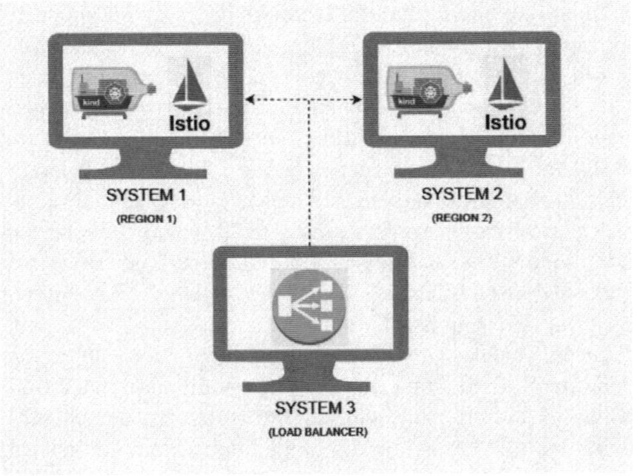

Figure 3. Our setup

success rates, and request volumes. Here are the detailed observations:

A. Traffic Volume and Success Rate:

As seen Figure 4 the incoming traffic volume is 12.2 requests per second, with a recorded success rate of 100%. This indicates that every request was processed successfully, without any loss or errors, reflecting a highly reliable service operation.

Figure 4 shows that both 4xx and 5xx error rates are recorded at 0, showing there were no client-side or server-side errors. The absence of 4xx errors suggests that all client requests were well-formed and valid, while the lack of 5xx errors confirms robust server-side processing and stability.

Figure 4. Observability Metrics

B. Latency Metrics (P50, P90, P99):

Since the helloworld service in Region 2, Zone 2 is also accessible from Region 1, Zone 1, we compared latency across both clusters:

P50 Latency: Figure 4 shows that the median latency, or time within which 50% of requests are processed, is 71.40 ms for Cluster 1 (Region 1, Zone 1) and 73.49 ms for Cluster 2 (Region 1, Zone 2).

P90 Latency: It seen in Figure 4 that the latency within which 90% of requests are completed is 95.49 ms in Zone 1 and 96.14 ms in Zone 2, showing that the majority of requests have relatively low latency.

P99 Latency: Figure 4 shows that for 99% of requests, the latency is 189.57 ms in Zone 1 and 203.00 ms in Zone 2. These values show that even for high-percentile latency, processing times remain well within acceptable ranges.

The slight increase in latency in Zone 2 (Region 1) is attributed to cross-zone access, as requests from Zone 1 accessing services in Zone 2 experience a maximum additional latency of approximately 4 ms.

C. Client and Server Request Volumes and Success Rates:

The client request volume is observed to be 6.4 operations per second (ops/sec), matching the server request volume of 6.4 ops/sec. This consistency indicates that all requests initiated by the client are successfully received and processed by the server, with no data loss or retries.

Both client and server success rates are recorded at 100%, further confirming the absence of failures or unfulfilled requests.

D. Client Request Duration:

From start to finish, client queries typically take around 300 milliseconds. This is the total round-trip time, which includes processing requests, creating responses, and returning them to the client.

E. Gateway Success Rate:

The helloworld gateway's incoming request success rate is 100%, which shows that the gateway setup is operating correctly and consistently, directing traffic without introducing issues.

F. Outgoing Response Rate by Destination Workload:

The destination workload's outbound response rate is measured at 100%, indicating that answers from the destination workload are constantly successful, indicating error-free communication between workloads and optimum processing of outgoing data.

All the metrics point to a robust and highly available system with low latency for both local and cross-zone queries. The multi-region setup can process requests at low latency and ensure that the system is highly responsive. Such a highly available architecture is needed for large enterprises to ensure service uptime and an enhanced user experience. Including observability into the infrastructure using tools like grafana enables enables real-time tracking and timely identification of potential issues.

Such high success rates and low latency values confirms that the setup is configured to withstand traffic spikes and variations without any effect on service quality, thereby emphasizing on its effectiveness in a multi-zone, multi-region architecture.

G. Cost Analysis:

For production-grade servers across regions (e.g., T3.medium or m5.large instances), assuming 10-20 instances per region for redundancy, costs could range from $1,500 to $3,000 per region, totaling $3,000 to $6,000. AWS EKS is priced at $0.10 per hour per cluster along with EC2 costs for worker nodes, could add approximately $1,000 to $2,000 for a multi-region setup. Multiple load balancers and high outbound data transfers may contribute an additional $500 to $2,000, while persistent storage with high availability (e.g., Amazon RDS or S3 for data durability) might cost around $500 to $1,000. Overall, for a mid-to-large-scale deployment, the monthly operational cost might range from $5,000 to $12,000. If large corporations and real-time applications were to implement an existing architecture like this, their costs could increase to anywhere between $20,000 to $50,000 monthly. We aim to target large scale industries who have an existing private infrastructure.By leveraging open-source tools and technologies and avoiding reliance on AWS or any other cloud providers, the total cost of operation for our proposed methodology comes up to $0.

H. Comparison with Cloud-Native Solutions:

Cloud providers such as Google's Anthos and AWS EKS with Istio offer managed service mesh solutions. Our method, leveraging KinD and Istio in a multi-primary setup, eliminates cloud dependency while maintaining low-latency service discovery and failover. Some enterprises, like Cloudflare and AWS CloudFront, deploy edge nodes or use CDNs to reduce latency. Our approach dynamically routes traffic based on region health and network proximity, reducing costs while ensuring resilience. AWS Global Accelerator, GCP Multi-Region Load Balancer, and other providers offer auto-scaling groups, managed load balancers, and cross-region replication. While these services ensure failover and high availability, they introduce vendor lock-in and high operational costs.

V. Conclusion and Future Work

Our solution presents a robust, multi-region architecture in which there are two separate geographical regions which host independent Kubernetes clusters on KinD with Istio installed using the multi-primary approach on different networks. Each cluster is set up with a Hello World service. Each cluster has its own control plane, ensuring independent access across clusters. Such an architecture increases the availability of the service mesh and ensures that failure in one cluster or region does not affect the other clusters, supporting high availability throughout the architecture.

Our setup uses a load balancer that directs traffic based on real-time health monitoring. Every 10 seconds, the load balancer checks the health of each cluster to ensure that traffic only goes to healthy clusters. If a cluster fails, the load balancer identifies the nodes as unhealthy and routes traffic to other healthy nodes in the service mesh. This strategy provides constant uptime and lowers latency, resulting in a smooth user experience even amid infrastructure failures.

Cloud providers like AWS provide ways to design fault-tolerant cloud application using virtualization technologies which emphasize on redundancy and continuous monitoring [14]. However, using such approaches can be very expensive for large-scale industries. Our approach is especially useful for such large-scale businesses who want to optimise their infrastructure and reduce reliance on expensive cloud alternatives. Our setup is a robust, multi-region configuration which leverages open-source solutions like Istio, to deliver multi-regional availability, low latency, and scalability without incurring the significant expenditures associated with cloud services. This design seeks to integrate smoothly with current organisational environments improving resilience and service reliability across many regions. By using open-source solutions, we provide a low-cost way to achieve a distributed, highly available service architecture. This makes our method ideal for large-scale organisations that value service continuity, scalability, and low-latency access for worldwide users.

Integrating powerful AI-powered monitoring capabilities could be one of the ways to improve the infrastructure. By implementing machine learning models, the system can predict faults earlier and optimise resource allocation. Such an approach might provide an additional layer of maintenance by detecting flaws before they impact operations, decreasing downtime and enhancing system reliability, especially during peak demand periods.

Reducing latency across multi-region architectures, particularly during region-wide or availability zone failovers, can improve user experience. Response times could be reduced by using enhanced routing algorithms and advanced load-balancing approaches. By lowering latency, the infrastructure may provide a better user experience while maintaining high availability and performance. This would provide seamless access to services, resulting in a more resilient and efficient system.

References

[1] A. Malhotra, A. Elsayed, R. Torres, and S. Venkatraman, "Evaluate Solutions for Achieving High Availability or Near Zero Downtime for Cloud Native Enterprise Applications," in *IEEE Access*, vol. 11, pp. 85384-85394, 2023, doi: 10.1109/ACCESS.2023.3303430.

[2] A. Johnson and B. Lee, "Auto-Scaling Strategies for High Availability in AWS," in *Proceedings of the International Conference on Cloud Computing*, 2017, pp. 112-125.

[3] H. Lang and C. Li, "Containerization for High Availability in Cloud Environments," in *Proceedings of the International Conference on Cloud Computing and Big Data*, 2019, pp. 201-214.

[4] G. Verma and R. Sushil, *Cloud Computing Implementation: Key Issues and Solutions*, Springer, 2015.

[5] N. Ahmad et al., "Strategy and Procedures for Migration to Cloud Computing," in *Proceedings of the 2018 IEEE 5th International Conference on Engineering Technologies and Applied Sciences (ICETAS)*, 2018, pp. 1-5.

[6] V. Mohammadian et al., "Fault-Tolerant Load Balancing in Cloud Computing: A Systematic Literature Review," in *IEEE Access*, vol. PP, pp. 1-1, 2021.

[7] W. A. Aziz, "High Availability Solution for Cloud Applications," in *International Journal of Simulation: Systems, Science Technology*, vol. 24, 2023.

[8] A. Berenberg and B. Calder, "Deployment Archetypes for Cloud Applications," in *ACM Computing Surveys*, vol. 55, no. 3, Article 61, pp. 1-48, March 2023. doi: 10.1145/3498336.

[9] A. Hajikhani and A. Suominen, "The Interrelation of Sustainable Development Goals in Publications and Patents: A Machine Learning Approach," *Trepo Digital Repository, Tampere University*, 2021.
[10] M. R. Mesbahi, A. M. Rahmani, and M. Hosseinzadeh, "Reliability and High Availability in Cloud Computing Environments: A Reference Roadmap," in *Human-Centric Computing and Information Sciences*, vol. 8, no. 20, 2018. doi: 10.1186/s13673-018-0143-8.
[11] A. Malhotra, A. Elsayed, R. Torres, and S. Venkatraman, "Evaluate Solutions for Achieving High Availability or Near Zero Downtime for Cloud Native Enterprise Applications," in *IEEE Access*, vol. 11, pp. 85384-85394, 2023, doi: 10.1109/ACCESS.2023.3303430.
[12] S. Afzal and G. Kavitha, "Load Balancing in Cloud Computing – A Hierarchical Taxonomical Classification," in *Journal of Cloud Computing*, vol. 8, no. 22, 2019. doi: 10.1186/s13677-019-0146-7.
[13] E. Bauer and R. Adams, "Service Reliability and Service Availability," in *Reliability and Availability of Cloud Computing*, Hoboken, NJ: Wiley-IEEE Press, 2012.
[14] R. Brown and M. Davis, "Designing Fault-Tolerant Cloud Applications: A Virtualization-Based Approach," in *IEEE Transactions on Services Computing*, vol. 18, no. 4, pp. 567-581, 2020.

Combining Flows and Rules in a Low-Code Platform for Smart Water Management

Jens Nicolay*, Bjarno Oeyen*, Samuel Ngugi Ndung'u*, Thierry Renaux*, Maxime Démarest†, Boud Verbeiren†, Wolfgang De Meuter*
*Software Languages Lab, Vrije Universiteit Brussel, Brussels, Belgium
e-mail: {jens.nicolay | bjarno.oeyen | samuel.ngugi | thierry.renaux | wolfgang.de.meuter}@vub.be
†Hydria, Brussels, Belgium
e-mail: {mdemarest | bverbeiren}@bmwb.be

***Abstract*—The paper describes a low-code programming model and environment for automating sensor data processing pipelines for the smart water management domain. We identify visual flow-based programming and rule-based approaches as two promising avenues for building low-code programming models in this domain, but likewise identified a total of five problems faced by these approaches when applied to the domain. We propose a solution that tackles those problems, both as a high-level vision (combining the visual flow-based programming approach with rule-based approach, where each approach is applied for the programming tasks they are best suited for) and as a concrete design of a low-code programming model. We sketch our implementation, and discuss its limitations.**

Keywords-flow-based programming; rule-based programming; visual programming; low-code; sensors; internet of things.

I. Introduction

Low-code programming enables process automation by users that would otherwise not be able to automate their processes. In this paper, we describe a low-code programming model and environment for automating sensor data processing pipelines for the water management domain. Automating the decision making process can save time, but also reduces mistakes in tedious manual tasks [1]. Our goal is to provide the conceptual model and practical tools to enable domain experts (that do not need to be computer programmers) to define, reason about, and maintain software solutions that help them make accurate, timely decisions for managing surface water, sewer, and rainfall drainage infrastructure.

It is generally accepted that the *flow-based* programming paradigm [2] lends itself very well to the task of expressing data processing pipelines, and simultaneously lends itself well to visual programming. Many popular tools exist for visually developing and deploying data processing applications (e.g., Node-RED [3], NoFlo [4], etc.). Despite its advantages, we argue that it falls short at expressing common aspects of those pipelines. Non-trivial logic (e.g., aggregation and correlation) are better expressed as logical deductions in declarative *rule-based* programming paradigm. We found that a straightforward translation of traditional logic rules to a visual flow-based platform does not offer a satisfying solution in our water management scenarios.

The crux of our argument is as follows: if the goal of a visual low-code programming model is to be accessible by domain experts who are non-expert programmers, then the model should enable these domain experts to express the necessary logic with the least amount of friction. In this paper, we show that no single paradigm excels at capturing the concerns that our water domain experts wanted to express. We argue that domain experts need both a flexible system for transforming and filtering data, *and* a capable system for correlating and accumulating different measurements over time. We show that both paradigms can be unified into one uniform model that lends itself to a coherent two-layered low-code data processing platform. In our vision, the parts of a processing pipeline that lend themselves well to being expressed as a pipeline are expressed using a flow-based approach, while the parts that are best expressed as logical deduction are expressed using a block-based low-code programming layer backed by a rule engine.

The remainder of this paper is structured as follows. In Section II, we list two motivating scenarios, which we use to derive a problem statement in Section III. In Section IV, we describe our approach by stating how a visual programming environment combining flows and rules will tackles these problems. In Section V, we provide a bird's eye perspective on the platform, before presenting the conclusion and future work in Section VI.

II. Motivating Scenarios

Our motivation for the design of a uniform low-code programming platform is centred around two driving scenarios from the water management domain.

UC1 *The pre-validation of rainfall measurements.* Raw measurements from the sensor devices are analysed and corrected for known anomalies. Sensors need to be manually calibrated over time. While being calibrated, sensors produce faulty data (e.g., measuring rain when there should not be rain). This use case is concerned with identifying these calibration events, removing the raw measurements, and replacing the missing data with data from the statistically most-correlated, nearby, measurement station(s) that did have actual data.

UC2 *The real-time monitoring of surface water quality.* Specific locations and specific parameters (e.g., temperature, pH, conductivity, etc.) have their own safe ranges and expected behaviours. Both abnormal values (i.e., values that are not in a well-known safe range) and spikes (i.e., measurements that are significantly higher/lower than the previous one) need to be detected. An alert can then be sent out, by the

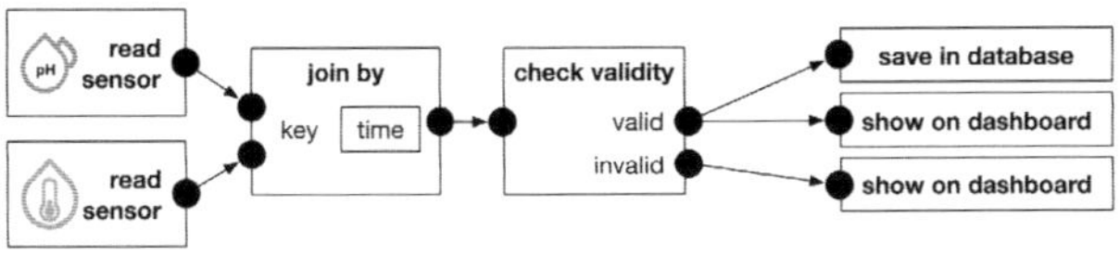

Figure 1: Example of a flow where traditional flow components shine: the shape of the flow intuitively conveys the outcome, the components' behaviours are straightforward to infer.

platform, to investigate the cause of the abnormal readings.

Before the introduction of our low-code platform, necessity dictated that the former scenario was tackled using spreadsheets, commonly recognised as one of the most widely used tools for low-code programming [5]. Unfortunately, this manual process was tedious and error-prone, and was never performed on live data. The latter was only possible in a limited way, and only on raw data as measured and stored into the sensors' data collection platform. I.e., not using any of the validated data as generated by the first use case.

A. Flow-Based Model

Some of the aspects of these use cases fit well in a traditional flow-based programming approach. For example, Figure 1 provides a sketch of a low-code program to validate acidity and temperature readings. By joining the data produced by two sensors, each time step can be validated individually. The general semantics of the program are easy-to-understand from this visualisation: flows consist of components that contain computations, and arrows between them connect the input and outputs of these computations. The flow-based model is, traditionally, well-suited for the development of distributed event-driven systems, such as data processing pipelines, IoT applications, and Cyber-Physical Systems.

B. Rule-Based Model

However, some implementation aspects of the presented use cases are better expressed using a rule-based programming approach. For example, for detecting spikes or applying inter-station correlation the rule-based approach is more favourable.

Rule-based logic or symbolic AI is concerned with expressing and representing human knowledge and logic in a declarative manner, usually based on facts and by specifying "if-then" rules that connect and manipulate attributes of those facts to produce new facts. Foregoing the low-code requirement for a moment, Figure 2 shows a rule-based approach for handling calibrations in UC1. The figure depicts a code-based approach in a variant of Datalog extended with stratified negation [6]. Rules provide fine-grained control over the generation of new facts from existing facts. For example, the `suspiciousRainfall` rule in Figure 2 denotes exactly when a rainfall measurement (of a given quantity `MM`, at a given time `T`, for a specific measurement station `S_ID`) is deemed suspicious: if there is at least 2 mm of rain but no rain at any other measurement station known by the system (i.e. within the same city). In general, rule-based logic is well-suited for capturing complex domain knowledge and for correlating data over time.

```
rainfallAtStationOtherThan(T, S_ID) :=
  rainfall(T, MM, S_ID),
  rainfall(T, MM_OTHER, S_ID_OTHER),
  (S_ID != S_ID_OTHER),
  (MM_OTHER != 0).

suspiciousRainfall(T, MM, S_ID) :=
  rainfall(T, MM, S_ID),
  (MM > 2),
  not rainfallAtStationOtherThan(T, S_ID).

unsuspiciousRainfall(T, MM, S_ID) :=
  rainfall(T, MM, S_ID),
  (MM > 2),
  not suspiciousRainfall(T, MM, S_ID).

unsuspiciousRainfall(T, MM, S_ID) :=
  rainfall(T, MM, S_ID),
  (MM <= 2).
```

Figure 2: Text-based logic programming example for finding suspicious rainfall sensor readings.

III. Problem Statement

The problem statement concerns five sub-problems. Two that emerge from using flow-based programming, and three that emerge from rule-based programming.

A. Obstacles to Process Sensor Data with Flow Operators

We have identified two problems that emerge when flow-based programming is used to build applications like those in the presented use cases.

P1: Poor Visualisation of Correlation in Flows: The main strength of a flow-based environment is its ability to visualise control flow in an easy to grasp manner. However, they fall short in adequately visualising the dependencies in the context of data correlation, especially when that correlation concerns data that arrives over time. To exemplify this problem, we have made three sketches using flow-based abstractions for the identification of temperature spikes. Figure 3a presents a program that utilises custom flow component to correlate facts. These types of components hide the delay needed for time-based correlation in the implementation of the "compare with previous" component. I.e., there is no (visual) indication that the flow delays the processing of temperature readings. Figure 3b and Figure 3c use traditional flow-based components with a "delay" component that delays a reading for one time-step. In the former approach, an "arithmetic transform" component computes the difference between two temperature readings, and an "arithmetic compare" component then identifies the spikes. In the latter approach (based on [7]), individual temperature measurements are delayed and consequently compared to the current temperature reading. Note here that the semantics of the system needs to adequately handle missing values. For example, the "merge" component would need to discard data whenever the "filter" component dropped temperature readings.

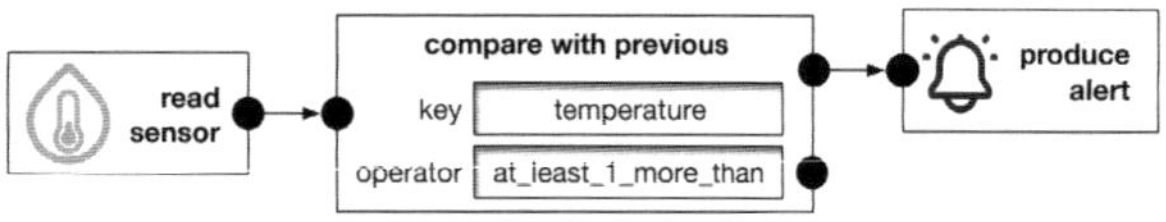

(a) Using custom flow components.

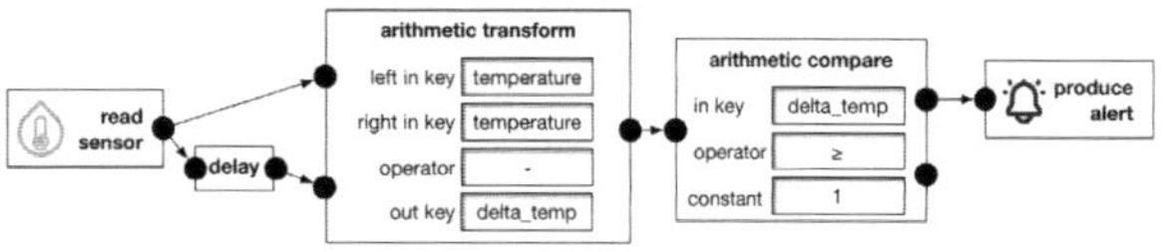

(b) Using an explicit `delay` component and arithmetic components that operate on compound facts.

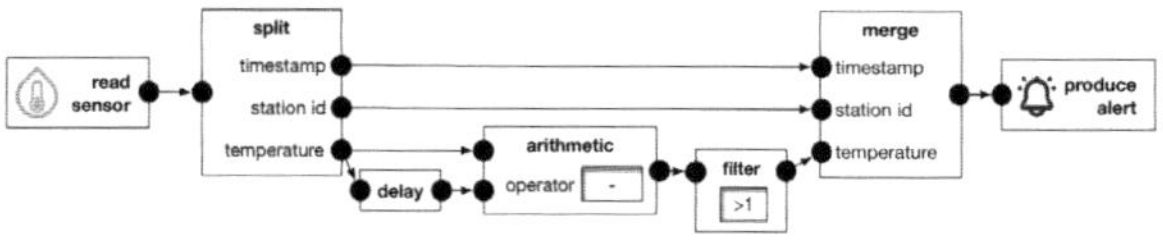

(c) Using an explicit `delay` component applied on an individual field. Comparisons are applied on values, not compound facts.

Figure 3: Three approaches for finding spikes in two consecutive temperature readings.

P2: Poor Abstraction of Sub-tasks in Flows: Many sensor data processing pipelines, such as those in the smart water management domain, mainly reason about compound facts, not individual numbers. In the application domain, typical input values are not merely primitive values like numbers or text, but compound objects or *facts* about the world that consist of multiple properties or *fields*. For instance, a temperature measurement of $25.0\,^{\circ}\mathrm{C}$ is not represented by a raw number "25.0", but by a "Temperature" fact that states that the temperature at some timestamp at some measuring station was "25.0". As a result, the processing pipelines have two layers: one layer dealing with high-level fact routing pipeline, and one layer implementing the multitude of lower-level fact transformation, filtering, and correlation tasks. Traditional flow-based approaches fail to offer low-code tools with which users can abstract over lower-level tasks (and their internal dependencies) in the implementation of the higher-level layer. This is exemplified by Figure 3c, in which individual fields are de-structured. The same visual language for considering whole facts is used on the value level, which makes understanding the flow at a glance more difficult.

B. Obstacles to Process Sensor Data with Rules

We have also identified three problems that emerge from using a rule-based approach in a low-code environment.

P3: Complexity of State Management in Rules: Many rule evaluation engines employ a stateful fixed-point evaluation model: i.e., facts are continuously added and derived throughout the lifetime of an application. While the incremental generation of facts is powerful, a program will eventually run out of memory. As such, there must be a mechanism to discard old facts. Automatic solutions to discard stale data from the knowledge base exist [8][9], though those solutions make assumptions about the facts' data model and about the constraints that the programmer specified in the rules which may not apply in general. This leaves state management a responsibility of the user of the rule engine. In the context of a low-code programming environment, we thus need to minimise the need for state management.

P4: Poor Fit of Rules to Imperative Actions: Rules are a poor fit for expressing imperative actions (e.g., network and file I/O). Imperative actions, like reading sensor data in UC1, do not map well onto the rule-based paradigm.

P5: Poor Modularity of Rules: Many rule-based engines, by default, operate on a single shared fact base for all rules: i.e., all rules are continuously active and operating on the same facts. In code-based approaches to rule-based programming, some advanced scoping mechanisms such as namespaces and modules [10] exist that can be used to prevent that programmers must take into account all combinations of all facts. However, requiring users to make use of such mechanisms as-is is at odds with the simplicity promised by low-code environments.

IV. Approach

We claim that when programming non-trivial applications, the programming model should enable programmers to express both types of logic in the corresponding paradigm. This is especially true in the context of (visual) low-code programming. If the goal of a visual low-code programming model is to be accessible by domain experts, then it is *essential* that both paradigms can be used for expressing programs.

A novel low-code platform that supports the vision outlined in this paper enables experts in the water management domain to express automatic data validation and processing pipelines, and in which the results of those pipelines can be used to make the (alerting) decisions needed to implement the scenarios.

Our solution is composed of a two-layered approach in which flow- and rule-based paradigms are integrated into one coherent low-code platform. The flow-based abstractions provide a clear, general, overview of the behaviour of the application. Complex rule-based abstractions are embedded within the flow and provide powerful abstractions for, e.g., aggregation which are not straightforward to express with pure flow-based abstractions. We now discuss various aspects of this programming environment, and how its design tackles the problems from Section III.

Rule-based Specification of Sub-tasks (P1 and P2): The main paradigm of the system is flow-based. However, complex processing steps can be implemented via rules components whose behaviour integrates well into the visual abstractions of the flow-based system. The system enforces a clear separation of fact types: different fact types are visually distinct in both the flow-based and rules-based programming environments. Edges between components in the visual environment are labelled by the type of facts to easily denote the flow of data, which makes flows easier to understand.

Rules components express application logic using "if-then" clauses. In short, the rule-based components provide users with the tools to abstract over lower-level sub-tasks inside the high-level, flow-based processing pipeline, while using a uniform data language between the high-level (flow-based) abstractions and the low-level (rule-based) abstractions. Dealing with *correlation* of multiple facts is then expressed in this *lower* abstraction. I.e., instead of visualising correlation as a "delay" component (as in Figures 3b and 3c), the rules component as a whole reminds users that the block performs complex aggregation of data. We envision a block-based visualisation for the rule-based layer as those environments compare favourably with respect to flow-based environments [11].

Opt-in Statefulness (P3): Considering that rule-based approaches cannot completely forego state management, we instead let users explicitly choose either a stateful or a non-stateful execution model for each rule-based component. As such, the complexities of state management only need to be considered when users actually require statefulness. In short, we provide a (flow-based) component that contains a fully-fledged rule engine (with fixed-pointing semantics), and another (flow-based) component that applies simple transformations (in which correlations between facts are disallowed). Nonetheless, both use the same block-based visual language to remain accessible to domain experts.

Restricted Imperative Actions (P4): The visual platform uses the flow-based system for all imperative actions like reading data from a file, connecting to a sensor's live feed of measurements, and writing computed facts to a file. As such, these are not a concern in the rule-based programs at all. This simplifies not only the implementation of the rule-based engine, but also helps users to better understand the logic of a program.

Modular Fact Bases for Rules (P5): Each rule-based component reasons about facts from only two origins: the extensional facts that were delivered to the rule-based component along the arrows visualised in the high-level flow program, and the intensional facts that were derived by the rules specified in that specific rule-based component, using only the facts that are local to that specific rule-based component. In both cases the rules of each rule-based component reason only about facts local to that flow component. This design element solves the poor modularity that follows from rules' whole-program scoping in an intuitive manner, linking it back to the way in which data dependencies at the level of facts are visualised in the flow language.

V. Bird's Eye Overview of the Platform

We now present the concrete aspects of the implementation of the platform. I.e., we present how users use this system to define and execute flows. The visual platform is implemented as a web application in which users can define flows and their respective data schemas.

A. Flows, Relations and Datasets

User interaction with flows starts from the main flow tab as shown in Figure 4a. On this tab users can manage flows. They can create a new flow, open the editor for any that have been created previously, as well as start/stop them.

(a) Managing flows

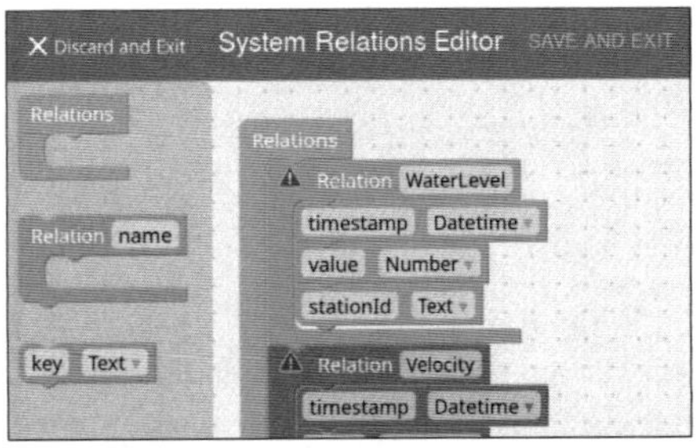

(b) Managing system-wide relations

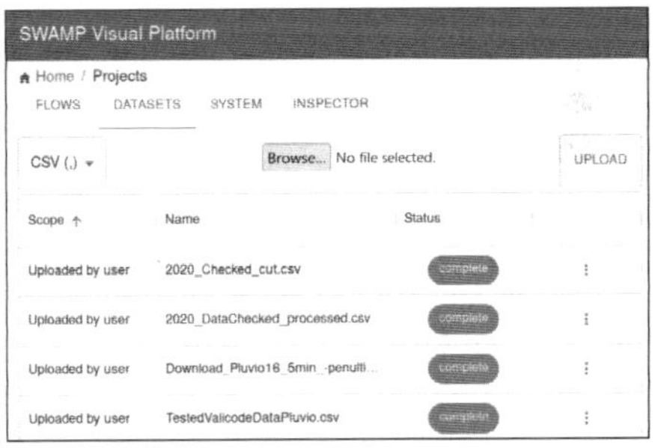

(c) Managing datasets

Figure 4: Screenshots of the visual platform.

To distinguish between different fact types, the system allows for creating so-called "relations". The user can open the relation editor, which is shown in Figure 4b. These show the relations that are available to all flows. The same visual language for building rules is used, which we explain in Section V-C. By default, these relations include fact types relevant to the water management domain: i.e., timestamped measurements. As these are hardcoded by the system, they cannot be modified. However, new ones can be added and also modified from this interface.

Datasets are the platform's abstraction for persisted data. They are, in essence, CSV-files: i.e., an ordered collection of tuples with a certain arity. Datasets can be created by a flow component, or by uploading a CSV-file to the platform via the web interface as shown in Figure 4c. Datasets uploaded as a CSV-file can be loaded via a flow component. Note that datasets do not always correspond with a system-wide relation. As such, configuring a dataset component will automatically generate a relation in the flow where they are being used. To avoid the complexities that arise when multiple flows use the same dataset as input and/or output, only uploaded CSV-files

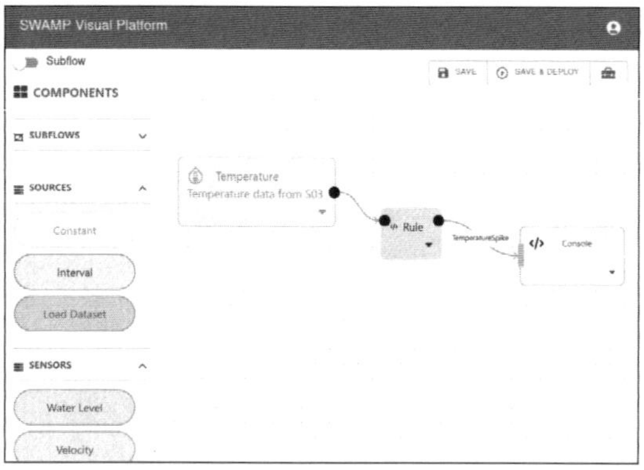

Figure 5: Screenshot of the flow canvas for detecting temperature spikes from a measurement station.

can be used as input in a flow. This design restriction ensures that datasets cannot be used as an inter-flow communication mechanism, which is not supported by the platform.

B. Flow-Based Programming in RuleFlow

The nodes in a flow are components that produce, process, or consume facts. Using the terminology of [2], each component in a flow has zero or more "in ports", and zero or more "out ports". The type of in and out ports that a component has depends on the component's configuration. For instance, if a rule-based component is extended with a new fact pattern of a relation that it did not yet have before, the component will gain an in port for facts of that type.

Users add components to a flow by dragging a representation of one of the existing component kinds from a *component palette* onto the *flow canvas* (see Figure 5). Dependencies among components are established by dragging an arrow from a component's out port to another component's in port. These arrows are labelled with the name of the relation that travels along the arrows, and the arrows are colour-coded. This is similar to, e.g., DiscoPar [12]. Components can be configured by double-clicking on them, which usually opens a modal. Finally, the flow canvas offers the means to edit the global relations, offers buttons to save the state of a flow and to start the flow, and shows a console onto which the results of the flow (or of individual components) can be inspected. The platform is shipped with a number of built-in components, we distinguish between three main types.

1) *Source* components are used to provide input to a flow. There are built-in sources for generating facts with numeric values in a given range, for reading data from an existing dataset, and for connecting to a remote server to fetch (historic or live) data from measuring stations. The configuration of these measuring station components is kept simple: a user only needs to select from a list of measuring stations and the given date–time range for which measurements must be retrieved.
2) *Operator* components apply transformations. There are only two built-in operator nodes: one in which a rule-based program is embedded, and one which only applies simple transformations (as mentioned in Section IV, both use the same visual abstractions). The input and output ports are generated from the embedded rule-based program. For example, if there is a rule that expects "Rainfall" facts, then a "Rainfall" input port will be generated.
3) *Sink* components are the complement to source components. The built-in sink components are used to save facts to a dataset and to send data to the remote sensor platform (i.e., for UC2). There is also a built-in component that is used to send out email alerts (i.e., for UC1).

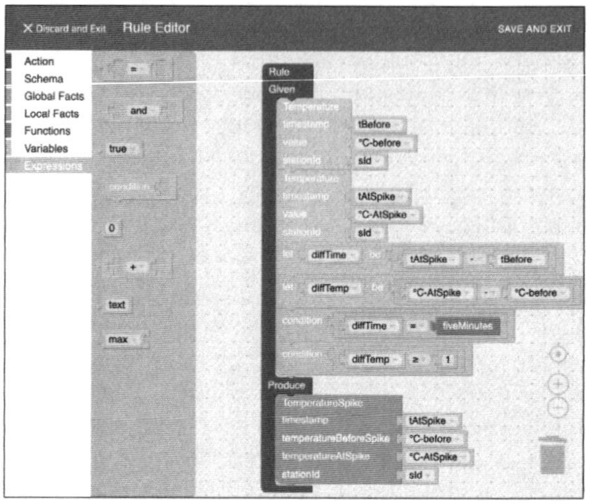

Figure 6: Screenshot of the visual editor for rules to detect temperature spikes.

Besides these built-in components, users of the platform can define their own flows which then become available to other flows as components. Like operator components, *subflow* components can have both input and output ports. While a full overview of the semantics of subflows is not in the scope of this paper, the gist is that flows can be explicitly configured that they can be instantiated by other flows (i.e. top-left of Figure 5): the sources and sink components of these subflows are then parameterised.

C. Rule-Based Programming

Both operator components are configured in a rule-based programming environment, as depicted in Figure 6. Each rule-based subprogram consists of one or more rules, with one or more body fact patterns and one head fact pattern each. The environment is built on top of Blockly [13].

Blocks are provided for managing the data schema of facts (for any relations that are local to the rules component), and for defining rules using fact patterns. The fact patterns in the rules can make use of variable bindings, of an expression language, and of aggregators. In the visual language, the grammar is enforced by the shape of blocks' slots.

The block-based approach makes it possible to use a visual metaphor to denote that the `action` block "accepts" one `head fact`. We found that it was advantageous to use the shapes as blocks as a form of static "type" checking to prevent the construction of structurally wrong programs. On the other hand, we found that disallowing connections due to more complex context-dependent requirements hampered users more than it helped them. Therefore, there are two types of blocks: *(1.)* blocks that deal with facts connect vertically to "notches", and *(2.)* blocks that deal with *fields* of facts connect horizontally to "jigsaw" slots.

When the visual platform detects that the user made a mistake that is not handled by this distinction, the platform allows the user to drop the block in the 'wrong' slot but provides inline feedback on why this connection does not make sense. This design choice serves two purposes: first, it enables the low-code platform to teach its users some of the finer nuances, and second, it allows users to construct programs which are not yet valid, but will become valid when the users finishes adding the blocks they meant to add. This is similar to how textual IDEs allow programmers to temporarily have a program in an invalid state while the programmer is halfway through making an edit.

D. Prototypical Implementation

A prototypical implementation of our approach was built in TypeScript. We leverage ReactFlow [14] for visualising and interacting with flows of components. The rule and expression language Rocks was built on top of Blockly [13]. Access to the platform was given to our research partner who experimented with designing surface water monitoring flows on the platform.

VI. Conclusion and Future Work

We described a low-code programming model and environment for automating sensor data processing pipelines for the surface water management domain. We identified visual flow-based programming and rule-based approaches as two promising avenues for building low-code programming models. Our prototypical platform has been designed specifically for the water management domain. We have shown, throughout the paper, the advantages that our platform provides for two use cases important to the water management domain. However, not all aspects of the problems identified in Section III are wholly resolved, and real-world use of the current design by its users point at avenues for future research.

A. Linking Flow Definition and Use

An important aspect for which our current design does not offer affordances, is the evolution of the low-code programs over time. Because of the way that the flow abstraction mechanism works, the site of use and the site of definition of a subflow are detached. The site of use does not track the site of definition.

B. Hot-swapping of Stateful Components

Evolving long running stateful software systems requires that care is taken to preserve accumulated state across modifications to the software. This holds equally in a flow-based low-code context, where modifying one or more flow components should not invalidate all state in the system. Further complicating the support for hot-swapping [15] is the fact that the state may need to be transformed to be compatible with the modified flow. For instance, if a user decides to merge two consecutive rules components in a flow together into one larger rules component, the system has to provide the means to correctly merge both components' fact bases.

References

[1] M. Hirzel, "Low-code programming models," *Commun. ACM*, vol. 66, no. 10, pp. 76–85, Sep. 2023, ISSN: 0001-0782. DOI: 10.1145/3587691.

[2] J. P. Morrison, "Flow-based programming," in *Proc. 1st International Workshop on Software Engineering for Parallel and Distributed Systems*, CreateSpace, 1994, pp. 25–29.

[3] M. Blackstock and R. Lea, "Toward a distributed data flow platform for the web of things (distributed node-red)," in *Proceedings of the 5th International Workshop on Web of Things, WoT 2014, Cambridge, MA, USA, October 8, 2014*, ACM, 2014, pp. 34–39. DOI: 10.1145/2684432.2684439.

[4] The NoFlo Team, *Noflo: Flow-based programming for javascript*, (accessed: 03.11.2023).

[5] M. Burnett, C. Cook, and G. Rothermel, "End-user software engineering," *Commun. ACM*, vol. 47, no. 9, pp. 53–58, Sep. 2004, ISSN: 0001-0782. DOI: 10.1145/1015864.1015889.

[6] S. Ceri, G. Gottlob, and L. Tanca, "What you always wanted to know about datalog (and never dared to ask)," *IEEE Transactions on Knowledge and Data Engineering*, vol. 1, no. 1, pp. 146–166, 1989. DOI: 10.1109/69.43410.

[7] A. Catalá, P. Pons, J. J. Martínez, J. A. Mocholí, and E. Navarro, "A meta-model for dataflow-based rules in smart environments: Evaluating user comprehension and performance," *Sci. Comput. Program.*, vol. 78, no. 10, pp. 1930–1950, 2013. DOI: 10.1016/J.SCICO.2012.06.010.

[8] T. Renaux, "A distributed logic reactive programming model," English, ISBN 978-9-49307-920-5, Ph.D. dissertation, Vrije Universiteit Brussel, 2019, ISBN: 978-9-49307-920-5.

[9] D. Teodosiu and G. Pollak, "Discarding unused temporal information in a production system," in *Proc. of the ISMM International Conference on Information and Knowledge Management CIKM-92*, Citeseer, Baltimore, MD, 1992, pp. 177–184.

[10] L. Sterling and E. Y. Shapiro, "The art of prolog: Advanced programming techniques," in MIT press, 1994, pp. 243–244.

[11] D. Mason and K. Dave, "Block-based versus flow-based programming for naive programmers," *IEEE Blocks and Beyond Workshop (B&B)*, pp. 25–28, Oct. 2017. DOI: 10 . 1109 / BLOCKS.2017.8120405.

[12] J. Zaman, K. Kambona, and W. De Meuter, "DISCOPAR: A visual reactive programming language for generating cloud-based participatory sensing platforms," in *Proceedings of the 5th ACM SIGPLAN International Workshop on Reactive and Event-Based Languages and Systems*, ser. REBLS 2018, Boston, MA, USA: Association for Computing Machinery, 2018, pp. 31–40, ISBN: 9781450360708. DOI: 10 . 1145 / 3281278.3281285.

[13] E. Pasternak, R. Fenichel, and A. N. Marshall, "Tips for creating a block language with blockly," in *2017 IEEE blocks and beyond workshop (B&B)*, IEEE, 2017, pp. 21–24.

[14] xyflow Team, *React flow - a library for building node-based uis*, https://reactflow.dev/; [retrieved: February, 2025], 2024.

[15] L. Vanbever, J. Reich, T. Benson, N. Foster, and J. Rexford, "Hotswap: Correct and efficient controller upgrades for software-defined networks," in *Proceedings of the Second ACM SIGCOMM Workshop on Hot Topics in Software Defined Networking*, ser. HotSDN '13, Hong Kong, China: Association for Computing Machinery, 2013, pp. 133–138, ISBN: 9781450321785. DOI: 10.1145/2491185.2491194.

Latency-Aware Task Offloading Mechanism for Mobile Edge Computing

Abdulelah Alwabel
Department of Computer Sciences
Prince Sattam Bin Abdulaziz University
AlKharj, Saudi Arabia
e-mail: {a.alwabel}@psau.edu.sa

***Abstract*—Task offloading in Mobile Edge Computing (MEC) is a critical mechanism that enables resource-constrained mobile devices to delegate computational tasks to proximate edge servers for processing. One of the core benefits of task offloading in MEC is the significant reduction in latency. Unlike traditional cloud computing, where data must travel to remote data centers for processing, MEC leverages edge servers positioned at the periphery of the network, close to end users. However, task offloading is not without its challenges. Critical issues, including network reliability, security, data privacy, and effective task scheduling, must be addressed to provide efficient offloading processes. This paper presents a novel latency-aware task offloading mechanism for MEC environments. The proposed mechanism dynamically adapts to latency variations to optimize task placement and migration across edge servers. Unlike traditional approaches, the mechanism operates without prior knowledge of task characteristics, enabling real-time task submission and execution. The mechanism employs a migration policy that minimizes latency by reassigning tasks in the waiting queue based on latency changes caused by mobile device movement, reducing the negative impact of such variations on system performance. To evaluate the effectiveness of the mechanism, a simulation environment was developed to model MEC scenarios. The simulation considered varying task loads and dynamic latency conditions to emulate real-world operations. Results demonstrate that the proposed mechanism achieved an improvement in key performance metrics, including latency, waiting time, and makespan time.**

Keywords-task offloading; dynamic mechanism; latency-aware; MEC.

I. INTRODUCTION

Task offloading in Mobile Edge Computing (MEC) is a critical mechanism that enables resource-constrained mobile devices to delegate computational tasks to proximate edge servers for processing. This approach can bridge the gap between the resource limitations of mobile devices and the increasing computational demands of modern applications, such as Augmented Reality (AR) and video processing [1]. By offloading tasks to edge servers located closer to the end user, MEC reduces latency, enhances energy efficiency, and ensures better utilization of computational resources, thus paving the way for seamless user experiences and efficient system operations.

The proliferation of smart devices and the emergence of data-intensive applications have introduced new challenges in mobile computing. Mobile devices, while portable and versatile, often suffer from limited battery life, computational power, and storage capacity. Task offloading addresses these challenges by transferring computational tasks to edge servers, which are equipped with greater processing power and are located at the network edge, closer to users. This minimizes the delay caused by communication with distant cloud servers and alleviates the burden on mobile devices, thereby extending their operational lifespan and improving their performance [2].

Task offloading in MEC is typically categorized into full offloading and partial offloading [3]. In full offloading, the entire computational task is sent to the edge server, leaving the mobile device to act primarily as an input/output interface. This is especially beneficial for highly complex applications where local execution is infeasible due to resource constraints. Partial offloading, on the other hand, involves splitting the task into smaller components, with some parts processed locally and others offloaded. This approach is ideal for tasks that can be parallelized or for scenarios where network conditions or server availability may not support full offloading.

The process of task offloading in MEC involves several key components, including task partitioning, offloading decision-making, and resource allocation [4]. Task partitioning determines how the task is divided into smaller subtasks, while offloading decisions are made based on parameters such as network bandwidth, device resources, latency requirements, and energy consumption. Resource allocation ensures that edge servers have the capacity to handle offloaded tasks efficiently without overloading the system.

One of the core benefits of task offloading in MEC is the significant reduction in latency. Unlike traditional cloud computing, where data must travel to remote data centers for processing, MEC leverages edge servers positioned at the periphery of the network, close to end users. This proximity reduces the round-trip time for data transmission, enabling real-time processing and low-latency responses [5]. Furthermore, by shifting computational tasks away from mobile devices, task offloading helps conserve battery life, a critical consideration for mobile users.

However, task offloading in MEC is not without its challenges. Critical issues, including network reliability [6], security [7], data privacy [8], and effective task scheduling, must be systematically dealt with to enable seamless and secure offloading processes. Furthermore, dynamic environmental factors, such as fluctuating network conditions and varying server workloads, necessitate the development of adaptive and intelligent offloading strategies. In this study, we propose a novel task offloading mechanism that incorporates awareness of dynamic network conditions to optimize the placement and migration of tasks across edge servers. The proposed approach aims to minimize latency, waiting time, and makespan, thereby enhancing overall system efficiency.

The reminder of this paper is organized as follows. Section II presents related works. Our mechanism is proposed and discussed in Section III. The results of employing our novel mechanism is presented and analyzed in Section IV. The paper concludes with future directions for research in Section V.

II. RELATED WORK

Task offloading in edge computing has been extensively explored, particularly in the context of IoT and its impact on network efficiency. For instance, the study in [9] discusses the significant traffic generated by real-time data management in edge networks with full offloading capacity. The authors propose an algorithm to detect node faults, manage deadlines, and improve data handling efficiency in centralized systems, reducing bandwidth use and scheduling delays.

Edge and cloud server performance comparisons by the authors in [10] highlight the efficiency of edge servers in resource utilization, while cloud servers excel in cost and delay reduction. To handle offloading inefficiencies, they propose an algorithm, which minimizes delays, optimizes resource allocation, and enables parallel task execution, enhancing system responsiveness.

The use of heuristic algorithms is detailed by the researchers in [11], who introduce an approach based greedy policy for resolving task offloading challenges. It integrates MEC to address latency issues in computation-intensive tasks, optimizing task management and resource efficiency while mitigating battery life concerns. However, this work pays little attention to changes of latency during run time.

Decentralized architectures for edge computing are explored in [12], which introduces a hierarchical edge cloud model. This architecture addresses limitations of traditional cloud computing, improving scalability, fault tolerance, and data recovery, particularly for applications requiring high mobility and low latency.

Improved Quality of Service (QoS) in edge computing is a recurring theme. For instance, the authors in [13] advocate for predictive systems using collaborative filtering to prevent delays. The results of this study demonstrate that QoS can be improved using machine learning approaches. In addition, the study in [14] proposes a reliable pooling approach to address task distribution and overhead costs. These approaches enhance system reliability and optimize resource usage.

A novel model for resource-efficient edge computing tailored for smart IoT applications is introduced [15]. A hybrid device-based computation offloading method was developed to optimize resource usage. The primary objective of this research is to enable diverse smart IoT device users to minimize cloud resource consumption while adhering to QoS constraints. A key advantage of the proposed approach lies in its ability to enhance the algorithm's performance, particularly in terms of resource efficiency [16].

The authors in [17] propose a dynamic time-sensitive scheduling algorithm that integrates the First-Come, First-Served (FCFS) policy with priority-aware scheduling. However, the proposed mechanism assumes prior knowledge of tasks to enable prioritization based on their deadline requirements.

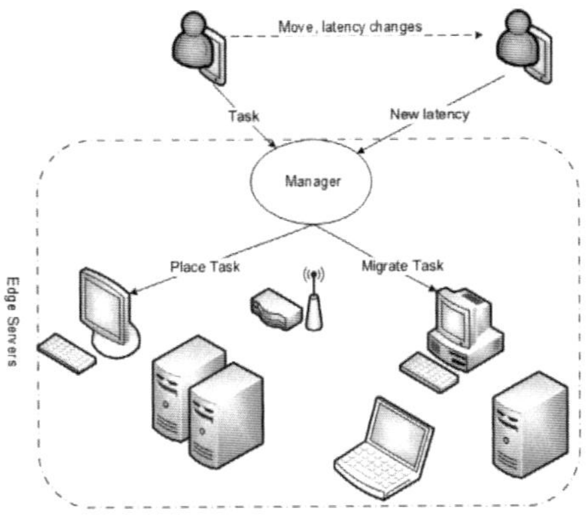

Figure 1. System Model

Overall, the literature highlights the potential in MEC to mitigate latency, optimize task scheduling, and enhance fault tolerance. However, challenges such as dynamic network conditions necessitate further research to refine adaptive and intelligent offloading mechanisms.

Algorithm 1 Initial Placement - DM Mechanism

get $task$, $nodeList$
$mkn_{min} = maximumValue$
foreach $node$ in $nodeList$ **do**
  mkn_{tmp} = Makespan($task$, $node$) //equation 1
  if $mkn_{tmp} < mkn_{min}$ **then**
    mkn_{min} = mkn_{tmp}
    $node_{selected} = node$
  end if
end for
place($node_{selected}$,$task$)
update $nodeList$

III. PROPOSED MECHANISM

This section introduces a Dynamic Mechanism (DM) designed to offload tasks from devices to edge servers within the MEC environment. The proposed mechanism is aware latency variations during runtime that dynamically adapting assigns and migrates tasks without prior knowledge of tasks before their submission with an aim to improve performance. The mechanism allows tasks to be submitted at any point during runtime.

Figure 1 illustrates the system model of a Mobile Device (MD) that offloads a task to a manager module within the MEC environment. The manager finds an edge server, to be called node, to execute this task. This selection plays an important rule to improve the QoS of the system. Algorithm 1 shows an initial placement process to select a suitable node ($node$) to host a recently submitted task ($task$). The process selects a

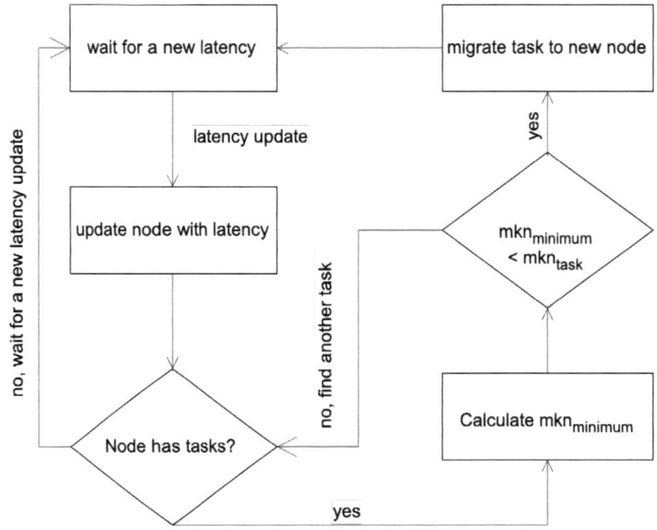

Figure 2. Migrate Process - DM Mechanism

node with a minimum makespan time (mkn). It is calculated as:

$$mkn(task, node) = l + wt(node) + et(task, node) \quad (1)$$

where l denotes the latency of this node which means the time required to send the response from this node to the MD which offloaded. $wt(node)$ refers to the total waiting time for this $task$ before it can be executed, it is calculated as:

$$wt(node) = \frac{\sum_{i=1}^{t}(task_t.length)}{node_{cpu}} \quad (2)$$

where $node_{cpu}$ refers to the processing power of $node$. It is measured in Million Instructions Per Second (MIPS) [18]. $et(task, node)$ denotes the execution time and is given as [19]:

$$et(node) = \frac{task.length}{node_{cpu}} \quad (3)$$

$task.length$ refers to the processing length of a task which is measured in Million Instructions (MI) [20]. In our system, we assume that when an MD moves from one location to another, the latency between the MD and nodes changes (i.e., latency can increase or decrease). This change in latency can significantly impact the overall makespan time of tasks. To address this, the DM mechanism incorporates a migration policy designed to account for latency variations. The migration policy is illustrated in Figure 2. When an MD relocates, the manager module is updated with the MD's new location, and it subsequently updates all nodes with the recent latency changes.

The DM mechanism then calculates the mkn value for each task in the waiting list across all nodes. If a node is identified that can execute a task with a lower mkn than the current assigned node, the manager migrates the task to that node. It is important to note that the DM mechanism applies this migration policy only to tasks that have not yet started execution (i.e., tasks in the waiting list). Tasks already in execution are excluded from this process in order to avoid the impact of migration overhead.

TABLE I. SIMULATION CONFIGURATION

Parameter	Value
Latency:	
Initial value	1-10 ms
Value during runtime	1-100 ms
Update time	1 - 100 ms
Node Specifications:	
RAM	128 MB
CPU	1GB, 1.5GB, 2 GB and 2.5GB
Number of nodes	10
Tasks:	
Processing length	(5, 10, 20, 100) $\times$ 10^3 MIPS
Number of Tasks	1000

IV. EVALUATION

This section presents the results obtained from testing the proposed mechanism in a simulation environment. It begins with a discussion of the simulation settings and concludes with an analysis of the results.

A. Experiment Configurations

We extended the simulation tool DesktopCloudSim [21] to simulate the MEC environment. DesktopCloudSim, which is based on the widely-used cloud simulation framework

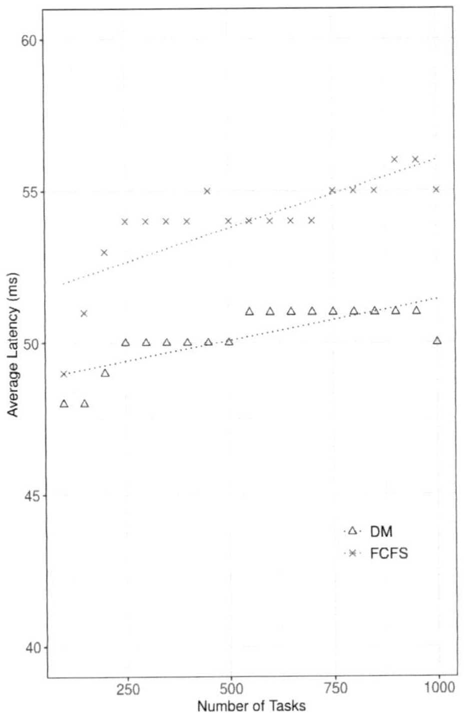

Figure 3. Average Latency

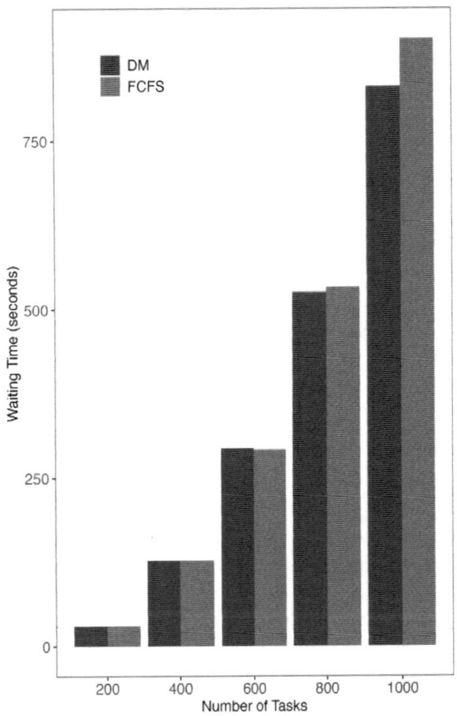

Figure 5. Waiting Time

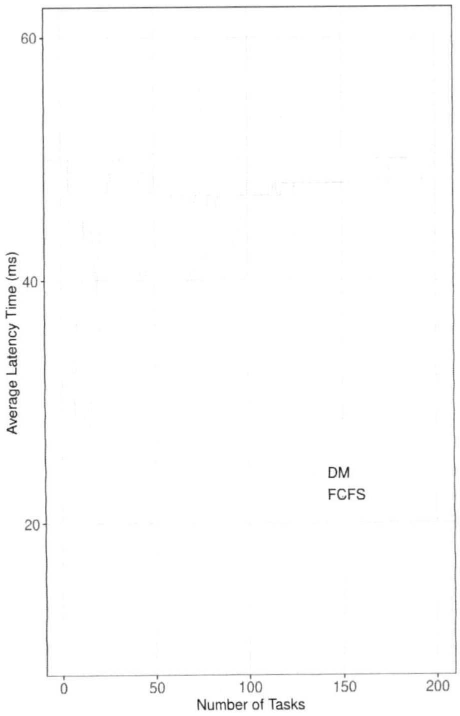

Figure 4. Average Latency (Tasks < 200)

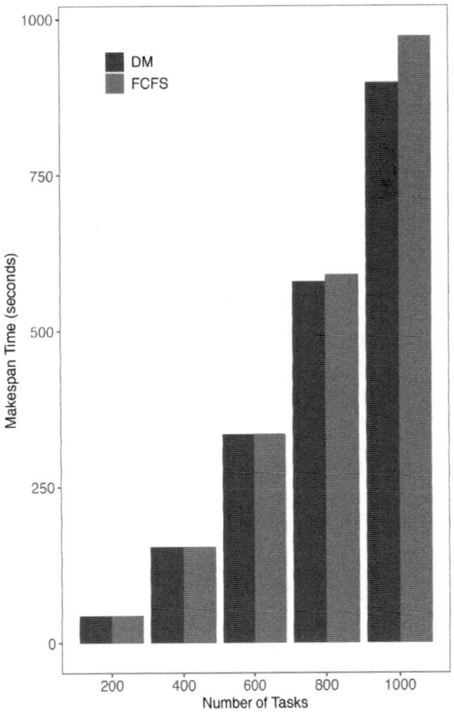

Figure 6. Makespan Time

TABLE II. RESULTS SUMMARY.

Metric	DM Mechanism	FCFS Mechanism
Latency	50 ms	53 ms
Waiting Time	830 ms	938 ms
Makespan Time	898 ms	1010 ms

CloudSim [22], was selected due to its adaptability and extensibility for edge computing scenarios. To evaluate the performance of the proposed mechanism, the simulation was configured with detailed specifications for tasks and edge servers, ensuring an accurate representation of the MEC environment.

Table I presents the configuration of the simulation. It details the initial latency between MDs and nodes, where the latency varies randomly during runtime to simulate the movement of MDs between different locations. The table also specifies the configuration and number of nodes utilized in this study, as well as the total number of tasks submitted to evaluate the DM. The experiment begins with a single task and incrementally increases the number of tasks in each run with one, then two, and continuing up to 1,000 tasks. The length of each task is assigned randomly and is measured in MIPS.

To minimize measurement errors in our simulation tools, we generated tasks randomly, as stated in Table I. These tasks were integrated into the simulation tool in exactly the same way for all evaluated mechanisms. Furthermore, we used a large dataset of 1,000 tasks to further reduce measurement errors in the simulation.

B. Results

Figure 3 demonstrates that the DM mechanism outperformed the FCFS mechanism in terms of average latency as the number of tasks exceeded 200. However, for task counts below 200, the FCFS mechanism performed better than the proposed DM mechanism, as illustrated in Figure 4. This behavior can be attributed to the smaller number of tasks, resulting in fewer tasks in the waiting queue before the MD moves. Since the DM mechanism migrates tasks in the waiting list based on latency changes, any variation in node latency for a task in execution leads to significantly higher latency.

Regarding waiting time, the average waiting time for tasks was approximately 901 ms under the FCFS mechanism, compared to about 829 ms under the DM mechanism. Figure 5 highlights the trend of increasing waiting time as the number of tasks grows.

For makespan time, the DM mechanism achieved an average of 472 ms per task, whereas the FCFS mechanism recorded an average of 487 ms. These results indicate that the DM mechanism reduced the makespan time by approximately 3%. Figure 6 presents a comparison of the makespan results for both mechanisms across the experiment.

Table II presents a summary of the results of this paper, comparing the DM and FCFS mechanisms in terms of latency, waiting time, and makespan time (average values). The results indicate that the DM mechanism consistently outperforms FCFS across all three metrics, demonstrating superior efficiency in task scheduling.

V. CONCLUSION AND FUTURE WORK

Task offloading in MEC presents significant challenges, particularly in managing network reliability and latency variations. To address these issues, this paper proposed a novel task offloading mechanism that dynamically incorporates latency awareness to optimize task placement and migration across edge servers. The experimental results demonstrated that the proposed mechanism effectively reduces latency, waiting time, and makespan compared to the FCFS mechanism, thereby improving overall system performance.

The future directions for this research are twofold. First, the mechanism will be extended to support the migration of tasks that have already commenced execution. This extension will require a comprehensive evaluation of the associated overheads and their impact on system performance. Second, the focus will shift toward exploring additional performance factors, such as load balancing and power consumption of edge servers. These aspects are crucial for enhancing the scalability and energy efficiency of MEC systems.

REFERENCES

[1] B. Zhou, A. V. Dastjerdi, R. N. Calheiros, and R. Buyya, "An Online Algorithm for Task Offloading in Heterogeneous Mobile Clouds," *ACM Transactions on Internet Technology*, vol. 18, no. 2, pp. 1–25, Jan. 2018. DOI: 10.1145/3122981.

[2] P. Mach and Z. Becvar, "Mobile Edge Computing: A Survey on Architecture and Computation Offloading," *IEEE Communications Surveys & Tutorials*, vol. 19, no. 3, pp. 1628–1656, 2017, ISSN: 1553-877X. DOI: 10.1109/COMST.2017.2682318.

[3] F. Saeik *et al.*, "Task offloading in Edge and Cloud Computing: A survey on mathematical, artificial intelligence and control theory solutions," *Computer Networks*, vol. 195, p. 108 177, Aug. 2021. DOI: 10.1016/j.comnet.2021.108177.

[4] W. Tang, S. Li, W. Rafique, W. Dou, and S. Yu, "An Offloading Approach in Fog Computing Environment," in *2018 IEEE SmartWorld, Ubiquitous Intelligence & Computing, Advanced & Trusted Computing, Scalable Computing & Communications, Cloud & Big Data Computing, Internet of People and Smart City Innovation (SmartWorld/SCALCOM/UIC/ATC/CBDCom/IOP/SCI)*, IEEE, Oct. 2018, pp. 857–864. DOI: 10.1109/SmartWorld.2018.00157.

[5] A. Pakmehr, "Task Offloading in Fog Computing with Deep Reinforcement Learning: Future Research Directions Based on Security and Efficiency Enhancements," in *CLOUD COMPUTING 2024 (2024)*, Jul. 2024, p. 34. arXiv: 2407.19121.

[6] K. Peng, Y. Yang, S. Wang, P. Xiao, and V. C. M. Leung, "Reliability-Aware Proactive Offloading in Mobile Edge Computing Using Stackelberg Game Approach," *IEEE Internet of Things Journal*, vol. 11, no. 9, pp. 16 660–16 671, May 2024, ISSN: 2327-4662. DOI: 10.1109/JIOT.2024.3354700.

[7] I. A. Elgendy, W. Zhang, Y.-C. Tian, and K. Li, "Resource allocation and computation offloading with data security for mobile edge computing," *Future Generation Computer Systems*, vol. 100, pp. 531–541, Nov. 2019. DOI: 10.1016/j.future.2019.05.037.

[8] X. He, R. Jin, and H. Dai, "Peace: Privacy-Preserving and Cost-Efficient Task Offloading for Mobile-Edge Computing," *IEEE Transactions on Wireless Communications*, vol. 19, no. 3, pp. 1814–1824, Mar. 2020. DOI: 10.1109/TWC.2019.2958091.

[9] M. Bukhsh, S. Abdullah, and I. S. Bajwa, "A Decentralized Edge Computing Latency-Aware Task Management Method With High Availability for IoT Applications," *IEEE Access*, vol. 9, pp. 138 994–139 008, 2021. DOI: 10.1109/ACCESS.2021.3116717.

[10] L. Liu, H. Zhu, T. Wang, and M. Tang, "A Fast and Efficient Task Offloading Approach in Edge-Cloud Collaboration Environment," *Electronics*, vol. 13, no. 2, p. 313, Jan. 2024. DOI: 10.3390/electronics13020313.

[11] M. Guo *et al.*, "HAGP: A Heuristic Algorithm Based on Greedy Policy for Task Offloading with Reliability of MDs in MEC of the Industrial Internet," *Sensors*, vol. 21, no. 10, p. 3513, May 2021. DOI: 10.3390/s21103513.

[12] S. Meng *et al.*, "A fault-tolerant dynamic scheduling method on hierarchical mobile edge cloud computing," *Computational Intelligence*, vol. 35, no. 3, pp. 577–598, Aug. 2019. DOI: 10.1111/coin.12219.

[13] G. White and S. Clarke, "Short-Term QoS Forecasting at the Edge for Reliable Service Applications," *IEEE Transactions on Services Computing*, vol. 15, no. 2, pp. 1089–1102, Mar. 2022. DOI: 10.1109/TSC.2020.2975799.

[14] T. Dreibholz and S. Mazumdar, "Towards a lightweight task scheduling framework for cloud and edge platform," *Internet of Things*, vol. 21, no. October 2022, p. 100 651, Apr. 2023. DOI: 10.1016/j.iot.2022.100651.

[15] X. Chen, Q. Shi, L. Yang, and J. Xu, "ThriftyEdge: Resource-Efficient Edge Computing for Intelligent IoT Applications," *IEEE Network*, vol. 32, no. 1, pp. 61–65, Jan. 2018. DOI: 10.1109/MNET.2018.1700145.

[16] S. Rahman *et al.*, "Resource Management Across Edge Server in Mobile Edge Computing," *IEEE Access*, vol. 12, pp. 181 579–181 589, 2024, ISSN: 2169-3536. DOI: 10.1109/ACCESS.2024.3503058.

[17] M. Maray, E. Mustafa, J. Shuja, and M. Bilal, "Dependent task offloading with deadline-aware scheduling in mobile edge networks," *Internet of Things*, vol. 23, p. 100 868, Oct. 2023. DOI: 10.1016/j.iot.2023.100868.

[18] Y. Zhang, X. Lan, J. Ren, and L. Cai, "Efficient Computing Resource Sharing for Mobile Edge-Cloud Computing Networks," *IEEE/ACM Transactions on Networking*, vol. 28, no. 3, pp. 1227–1240, Jun. 2020, ISSN: 1063-6692. DOI: 10.1109/TNET.2020.2979807.

[19] R. Mahmud, A. N. Toosi, K. Ramamohanarao, and R. Buyya, "Context-Aware Placement of Industry 4.0 Applications in Fog Computing Environments," *IEEE Transactions on Industrial Informatics*, vol. 16, no. 11, pp. 7004–7013, Nov. 2020. DOI: 10.1109/TII.2019.2952412.

[20] M. Alkhalaileh, R. N. Calheiros, Q. V. Nguyen, and B. Javadi, "Performance Analysis of Mobile, Edge and Cloud Computing Platforms for Distributed Applications," in *Mobile Edge Computing*, Cham: Springer International Publishing, 2021, pp. 21–45. DOI: 10.1007/978-3-030-69893-5_2.

[21] A. Alwabel, R. Walters, and G. B. Wills, "DesktopCloudSim : Simulation of Node Failures in The Cloud," in *The Sixth International Conference on Cloud Computing, GRIDs, and Virtualization CLOUD COMPUTING 2015*, Nice, France: iaria, 2015.

[22] R. N. Calheiros, R. Ranjan, A. Beloglazov, C. A. F. De Rose, and R. Buyya, "CloudSim: A toolkit for modeling and simulation of cloud computing environments and evaluation of resource provisioning algorithms," *Software - Practice and Experience*, vol. 41, no. 1, pp. 23–50, 2011. DOI: 10.1002/spe.995.

Running Kubernetes Workloads on Rootless HPC Systems using Slurm

Jonathan Decker, Sören Metje and Julian Kunkel
Institute for Computer Science, Universität Göttingen,
Goldschmidtstraße 7, 37077 Göttingen, Germany
e-mail: jonathan.decker@uni-goettingen.de | soerenmetje@yahoo.de | julian.kunkel@gwdg.de

Abstract—**Kubernetes has become a widespread orchestrator for cloud workloads but with increasing demand for compute the need arises to also access HPC environments that are operated via batch schedulers such as Slurm. A number of solutions for combining Slurm and Kubernetes are available, which can be categorized further based on the interaction between Slurm and Kubernetes that they provide. In this paper, we consider the use case of utilizing an existing Slurm cluster to run Kubernetes workloads. For this, we introduce a new solution called Kind Slurm Integration (KSI) based on Kind and rootless Podman and compare it based on performance, usability and maintainability to the existing solutions Bridge Operator and High-Performance Kubernetes (HPK). We found that Bridge Operator provides native performance as it effectively submits Slurm jobs through a Kubernetes interface and that HPK provides good performance by creating almost feature complete Kubernetes clusters on top of Apptainer. KSI on the other hand is able to provide fully functional Kubernetes clusters inside Slurm jobs but lacks behind in network performance. Overall, we conclude that more work is needed to run Kubernetes workloads under Slurm without missing out on features or performance.**

Keywords-Kubernetes; HPC; Container; Slurm; Cloud.

I. INTRODUCTION

Kubernetes has established itself as a widespread solution for orchestration of cloud workloads [1][2] and is used for various workloads including service computing, running large amounts of micro services, as well as batch jobs, such as data analytics or machine learning. However, batch jobs would fit better into HPC environments where powerful high-performance compute and networking resources are available. HPC workloads are commonly scheduled using a batch scheduler such as Slurm [3] but Kubernetes itself can also be used for scheduling HPC jobs using a batch scheduler such as Volcano [4] and have already been scaled to large clusters using appropriate workarounds [5]. Nevertheless, while Kubernetes brings a large array of features, its virtualization layers incur a performance overhead compared to bare metal performance [6], which one could achieve with Slurm.

Users might want to bring their Kubernetes workloads into Slurm-based HPC environments to benefit from the reduced overhead compared to a regular Kubernetes cluster or to gain access to additional compute hardware, which could also include specialized hardware only available in HPC environments. Rewriting Kubernetes workloads to be executable in Slurm may require significant effort and expertise with the scheduling systems. However, various approaches and implementations exist for combining Slurm and Kubernetes enabling users to dynamically move workloads between cloud and HPC environments.

As there have been various efforts to combine Kubernetes and Slurm, we consider the definition by Wickberg of Schedmd [7] who defines four categories from the perspective of Slurm for such approaches.

- **Over**: The entire Kubernetes environment exists within a Slurm job and is therefore temporary as it is fully removed once the job completes.
- **Distant**: Compute nodes are part of either a Kubernetes or a Slurm cluster and may be moved between the clusters.
- **Adjacent**: Slurm and Kubernetes utilize some form of plugins or bridging tools to cooperate but can still be used individually.
- **Under**: Kubernetes runs a Slurm cluster within its own environment across one or more pods.

Given the above use case of running Kubernetes jobs in an existing Slurm environment, this fits the **Over** or **Adjacent** model. After investigating existing solutions that implement either of these models we found various approaches that provide the **Adjacent** model but no system for having a Kubernetes cluster running within a Slurm job as described in the **Over** model. Therefore, we present **Kind Slurm Integration (KSI)** [8], an implementation of the **Over** model based on Kubernetes in Docker (Kind) [9]. We systematically evaluate and compare KSI to existing solutions including **Bridge Operator** by IBM [10], **WLM-Operator** by Sylabs [11], **kube-slurm** by Kalen Peterson [12] and **High-Performance Kubernetes (HPK)** [13].

Our evaluation consists of a review of the state of the respective projects with regard to features and maintainability as well as a performance analysis to determine the overhead incurred by the respective approach. For this purpose, we benchmarked the solutions based on workload startup time, CPU compute performance, memory throughput, storage throughput, network latency and network throughput, and compared the results to bare metal. We found that not all of the implementations listed above were able to pass a minimal functionality test. For those that passed, no significant differences in CPU compute performance, memory throughput and storage throughput were found. While our own solution, KSI, is outperformed by the others in terms of startup time and network performance, it still provides the most complete support for Kubernetes features compared to the others.

Overall this paper contributes a systematic evaluation of existing approaches that implement the **Adjacent** or **Over** model to combine Slurm and Kubernetes, the design and implementation of a proof-of-concept for KSI and a final overview of the features and limitations of the evaluated approaches. The work shown in this paper is based on the master's thesis of one of the authors [14].

The remainder of the paper is organized as follows: In Section II the various implementations for integrating Slurm and Kubernetes are discussed. The methods for benchmarking and comparing the solutions as well as the design of KSI are discussed in Section III. The results of the evaluation are given in Section IV. Finally, Section V provides the conclusion and outlook for future work.

II. Related Work

To properly distinguish various approaches for combining Slurm and Kubernetes, we discuss the four models along with notable examples. We also cover related approaches that do not use either Slurm or Kubernetes and then have a more in-depth look at the implementations, which we evaluated in this paper.

A. Models for Integrating Slurm and Kubernetes

The four categories for combining Slurm and Kubernetes defined by Wickberg of Schedmd [7] are **Over**, **Distant**, **Adjacent** and **Under** as defined in Section I.

*a) **Distant** model:* Notable implementations include [15] and [16], which both implement systems for dynamically changing the partitioning of a node pool between a Kubernetes and Slurm cluster.

*b) **Under** model:* Contributions have been made in [17], [18] and [19], in which Slurm is being run as a set of Kubernetes pods. A significant project in this category is Slinky [20] by Schedmd who had created a Slurm Kubernetes bridge implementation as a proof-of-concept before creating Slinky. The proof-of-concept implementation followed the **Adjacent** model, was not functional and has since then been removed from public access.

*c) **Adjacent** model:* Approaches in this category are relatively diverse in their approaches including Bridge Operator [10], WLM-Operator [11] and HPK [13]. Each of these approaches is discussed in more detail in Subsection II-C.

*d) **Over** model:* There are no notable implementations of this model except for KSI [8], which is presented in detail in Subsection III-B.

B. Other Approaches for Integrating HPC and Cloud

While this work focuses on combining Slurm and Kubernetes it should be noted that there are alternative approaches to running HPC workloads through a cloud interface. For example, as mentioned in Section I, Volcano [4] is an extension for the Kubernetes scheduler, which implements features such as batch and gang scheduling. This enables the execution of batch workloads as shown in [21][22].

Another notable approach is **hpc-connector** [23] presented in [16], which enables the submission of jobs through an arbitrary cloud interface to be executed via Slurm. This approach can be considered similar to Bridge Operator but is not bound to Kubernetes but also lacks deeper integration with any specific cloud platform to enable advanced features.

Finally, there is [24] who integrated TORQUE [25] with Kubernetes, enabling scheduling of HPC workloads through Kubernetes to TORQUE similar to the **Adjacent** model.

C. Implementations for **Adjacent** Slurm and Kubernetes

1) WLM-Operator: Sylabs Inc. had developed the WLM-Operator [26] and Singularity-CRI [27] with Singularity-CRI providing a Kubernetes-compatible implementation of the Container Runtime Interface for Singularity [11]. The WLM-Operator implements a Kubernetes operator that is able to interface with Slurm such that Slurm nodes become visible in Kubernetes as virtual nodes.

Moreover, it provides a Custom Resource Definition (CRD) in Kubernetes called *SlurmJob*, which enables the submission of Slurm jobs through Kubernetes. When submitting a SlurmJob, a dummy pod is created in Kubernetes and the actual job is submitted to Slurm to be run in a Singularity container. The results are then collected through another pod via a shared storage before closing the dummy pod once the job completes.

However, on December 30th 2020, both WLM-Operator and Singularity-CRI projects have been archived with no further development planned.

2) Bridge Operator: IBM had developed Bridge Operator [28] in order for a Kubernetes cluster to be able to access external compute resources including Slurm clusters [10]. Bridge Operator implements a Kubernetes operator and provides the *BridgeJob* CRD, which accepts all the details required to launch a Slurm job including the remote URL of a Slurm cluster, what resources to request and a remote storage configuration.

For each BridgeJob, the Bridge Operator starts a monitoring pod and submits the job to Slurm. The monitoring pod regularly updates a Kubernetes ConfigMap with the current status and fetches the job output. The creators of Bridge Operator have also demonstrated how to run Kubeflow workloads through BridgeJobs [29], however, as these jobs are converted to Slurm jobs, the Kubernetes pods are not directly being run in Slurm.

3) HPK: HPK [30] is presented in [13] and [31] as a way to run Kubernetes workloads on Slurm through Apptainer [32]. It is deployed as a single Apptainer container that runs the Kubernetes control plane and a custom implementation of virtual Kubelet [33], which presents an entire Slurm cluster as a single node in the cluster. Whenever a new pod is to be scheduled, it submits a job through Slurm for the pod to be started as a container using Apptainer.

For the container networking to function, it relies on Flanneld service [34] to be installed on the nodes and the Flannel-CNI plugin [35] to be installed for Apptainer. However, only headless services without cluster IPs are supported as the additional layer of load balancing is not possible with the used networking stack. Moreover, the command `kubectl exec`, which is used to execute commands inside Kubernetes pods, is not supported.

4) Kube-Slurm: The kube-slurm project [12] provides a tool for controlling Kubernetes resources using Slurm jobs. When deploying, Slurm and Kubernetes must both be installed on the same set of nodes with kubectl available on all nodes. Once deployed, users can submit Slurm jobs, which get scheduled by the tool as Kubernetes pods onto the nodes selected by the Slurm scheduler.

The deployment can also be completed with the **Under** model by having Slurm run within Kubernetes but still using Slurm to schedule the pods. Nevertheless, due to the way the access is provided to the Slurm scheduler, all users receive the same access to the Kubernetes cluster making this approach unfit for multi-user setups with potentially malicious users.

III. METHODOLOGY

This work focuses on approaches for combining Kubernetes and Slurm that allow running workloads on an existing Slurm cluster following the **Over** or **Adjacent** model and investigates the suitability of the existing solutions. For that purpose we define the following research questions:

RQ1 Can workloads be submitted using Kubernetes tooling, e.g., `kubectl`?
RQ2 Can workloads be scheduled and executed on machines managed by an existing Slurm cluster without root access?
RQ3 Can workloads be executed across multiple machines in parallel?
RQ4 What is the performance overhead imposed by the tool?
RQ5 Is the tool easy to operate for the end user?
RQ6 Is the tool well maintained?

RQ1, **RQ2** and **RQ3** define the functional requirements. For a solution to be a valid approach for utilizing a Slurm cluster through Kubernetes, it should answer yes to at least **RQ1** and **RQ2** with a yes to **RQ3** being desirable but not strictly required. Notably, these requirements do not include whether a solution must be able to run Kubernetes workloads or if it may run Slurm workloads through a Kubernetes interface. For example, Bridge Operator accepts Slurm workloads submitted through Kubernetes while HPK takes Kubernetes workloads submitted through a Kubernetes interface, with both executing the workloads on a Slurm cluster. Moreover, the distinction between the **Over** and **Adjacent** model breaks down to whether the deployment requires an existing component, such as a Kubernetes cluster, to be running before the Slurm job that will handle the target workload is submitted.

RQ4 is concerned with the performance cost of a given solution. Depending on the architecture and optimization a given implementation may cost additional compute power or delay the start of workloads, which should be minimal for an application to fully harvest the power of HPC machines.

RQ5 and **RQ6** cover the usability and maintainability of a given software providing an indication for the viability in productive use.

While **RQ1**, **RQ2** and **RQ3** can be answered as yes or no questions, **RQ4**, **RQ5** and **RQ6** require a graded answer. We use a three point scoring from + (positive) over o (average) to − (negative) to be able to quickly compare the results for multiple implementations. + is the best score, which is given if the implementation fulfills the requirements without any significant drawbacks. o is the middle score, which indicates that some limitations apply and − is the lowest score, which applies if significant shortcomings exist.

A. Selection of Implementations to Evaluate

In Section II-C we had introduced the WLM-Operator, Bridge Operator, HPK and Kube-Slurm. Before starting our evaluation we performed a minimal functionality test and found that the latest version of WLM-Operator is no longer functional on recent operating systems. Despite our best efforts and reaching out to Sylabs, we were unable to reproduce the minimal examples in the repository. Therefore, WLM-Operator can be considered retired and we will not further consider it.

Kube-Slurm requires the installation of a Kubernetes cluster on all nodes as part of its deployment, which violates **RQ2** that it must be able to operate without root access. Therefore, we will not further consider Kube-Slurm.

This only leaves HPK and Bridge Operator as viable targets for further evaluation along with KSI, which is introduced in the next section. However, when testing Bridge Operator we ran into a number of issues, which we reported on Github and created a pull request [36] with our code adjustments.

B. Kind Slurm Integration (KSI) Design

Our main objectives of designing another approach for combining Slurm and Kubernetes were that it should follow the **Over** model and support all Kubernetes features. Following the **Over** model, KSI can be run strictly inside Slurm jobs without relying on external components. This was important to us, as our use case involved a multi-user HPC system in which the users of KSI would not be able to deploy a control plane outside of Slurm jobs as it is required by HPK. Moreover, as we could not find any existing projects employing the **Over** model, we consider this a research gap.

We utilized rootless Kind [9] via its experimental Podman support to create a script that receives a Kubernetes workload, initializes a cluster inside a Slurm job, executes the workload and then closes the cluster as the Slurm job ends. Before settling on rootless Kind, we also considered Minikube [37], K3D [38] and Usernetes [39] but found rootless Kind to be the most suitable.

Kind [40] was developed with local development and automatic testing of Kubernetes in mind. It can deploy a fully functional Kubernetes cluster on a single node by deploying a "node" image, which internally runs another container runtime from which all containers belonging to the cluster are run. From the perspective of the host system, only a single container is running for the control plane node of the cluster. Moreover, by deploying multiple "node" images on the same host, Kind can simulate a multi-node cluster.

For operating KSI inside of Slurm jobs without access to root permissions, which are required for regular container operation, we employ rootless Kind [9]. Rootless Kind relies on a container runtime, in our case Podman, which uses Cgroups v2 features to run rootless containers. Besides Cgroups v2, Podman also relies on the shadow-utils package, which provides subuids and subgids for user namespaces.

However, Kind itself is not designed for multi-node clusters across multiple physical machines or VMs, so in order to achieve **RQ3**, we would require a tool such as Kilo [41] or Liqo [42]. With these it is possible to aggregate multiple Kubernetes cluster into a single cluster by representing each cluster as a virtual Kubelet in the main cluster. With this KSI could be deployed across a number of nodes in a multi-node Slurm job and all the worker nodes would use Kilo or Liqo to register with the cluster on the main node, which in turn would be able to schedule work across all nodes. When using this approach, each node has to run KSI and initialize its own Kubernetes cluster, which includes running all control plane components, before joining together via Kilo or Liqo to form a single cluster. We have not implemented this feature for the version of KSI under evaluation in this paper, but expect that the same overhead, in terms of CPU and memory consumption by the control plane components that applies to a single node running KSI, would then also apply to each individual node in such a multi-node setup.

In order to deploy KSI, the nodes must provide a recent Linux operating system with support for Cgroups v2, rootless Podman must be set up, as well as slirp4netns [43], to provide networking for rootless Podman. Since the experiments for this work have concluded, Podman 5.0 [44] was released, which uses pasta [45] as its default rootless network driver instead of slirp4netns. Workloads can be configured and embedded via `run-workload.sh`, which sets up the Kubernetes cluster when submitted via Slurm. `srun -N1 /bin/bash run-workload.sh example-workload.sh` would set up a single node cluster and then run the workload described in `example-workload.sh`. The workload script should internally use kubectl to create the required Kubernetes resources and then wait for the workload to finish. Upon completion of the workload script, the cluster is stopped and removed such that the Slurm job is also closed.

The produced KSI code, documentation and workload examples are released under the GPL-3.0 license on Github [8].

C. Performance Evaluation

To assess the performance overhead to answer **RQ4** we have broken down our benchmarking into the following factors:

- Startup time: Measured with a dummy workload
- CPU compute performance: Measured with Sysbench [46]
- Memory throughput: Measured with Stream [47]
- Storage throughput: Measured with Fio [48]
- Network latency: Measured with Netperf [49]
- Network bandwidth: Measured with iPerf3 [50]

We consider these as representative factors for user workloads that might be run through any of the tools under study.

As the bare metal baseline we run the benchmarks through Slurm without Kubernetes. All benchmarks were run on two machines with hardware specifications as shown in Table I. On the nodes we used software versions as shown in II. The Kubernetes version v1.27.3 is the most recent version at the time of the experiments and was used for the external cluster for the Bridge Operator as well as by KSI. HPK, however, is pinned to v1.25.0 in its code base. Furthermore, we disabled SELinux, swap and write caching to more clearly measure the respective factors.

TABLE I. HARDWARE SPECIFICATIONS OF THE BENCHMARK MACHINES.

CPU	Intel(R) Xeon(R) CPU E5-2695 v3
CPU Sockets	2
Cores per socket	14
Threads per core	2
Total threads	56
RAM	24 DIMMs DDR4 16 GB 1866 MHz
Total RAM	384.00 GB
Storage	1 Verbatim Vi550 S3 SATA Revision 3.2 SSD
Total storage	128.00 GB
Network interface	QLogic BRCM 10G/GbE 2+2P 57800-t rNDC

TABLE II. SOFTWARE VERSIONS OF THE BENCHMARK MACHINES.

Linux OS	CentOS Stream 9
Slurm	23.02.5
Podman	4.6.1
slirp4netns	1.2.2-1
Kind	0.20.0
Kubectl	v1.28.2
Kubernetes	v1.27.3
HPK Kubernetes	v1.25.0
shadow-utils	2:4.9-8

D. Project State Evaluation

Evaluating the maintainability and usability of software has been studied extensively [51][52] with many tools and methods having been proposed. For this work, in order to answer **RQ5** and **RQ6**, we have to consider what methods to employ.

In order to grade usability we consider the state of the available documentation as well as the difficulty of setting up and operating the respective tools for an assumed non-expert user based on our own experience of working with the tools during this study. For grading maintainability we reviewed the state of the code bases based on its complexity, whether it has been kept up-to-date and how well issues are being addresses. Moreover, we consider that a code base that does a comparatively simple job while relying on more well maintained dependencies is itself more maintainable than a larger code that has more moving parts that may require maintenance.

We acknowledge that more sophisticated methods are available but consider our approach sufficient to compare three projects on a three point grading schema.

IV. RESULTS

The commit hashes of the implementation versions used in our tests are as follows:

- Bridge Operator: `56334fa57caf2de28df6ff76df8a6e6232021421`
- HPK: `a902acbf2436e8a85a4620fddfa5745523f443d4`
- KSI: `780ef3a0562ad4bb12611f9ef43fa743fe0277d0`

A. Functional Requirements

For all Bridge Operator, HPK and KSI, the answer to **RQ1**, **RQ2** and **RQ3** is yes with the exception that KSI requires an additional integration with Kilo, Liqo or a similar tool to support multi-node execution, which has not been implemented yet.

B. Project State

a) Bridge Operator: When submitting a workload through Bridge Operator, it requires the user to create an instance of the CRD BridgeJob. With that no understanding of Slurm by the user is required. However, the available documentation for Bridge Operator is limited with some examples not working such that a patch was required to make it work [36]. While the project itself depends only on the Slurm REST API giving it a stable foundation, the project itself seems abandoned with no activity after late 2022. Due to this, we rate it ○ in both usability and maintainability. We would have rated + for usability if the examples were all functional and for maintainability if the project was actively being maintained.

b) HPK: Similar to Bridge Operator, HPK can be controlled directly through `kubectl` without additional understanding of Slurm by the user. Nevertheless, while its documentation is also limited, after we had completed our experiments [30] was released along with `v0.1.2` of HPK containing a number of bug fixes. This shows that the project is being actively developed, moreover, when we ran into issues, we quickly received community support from the maintainers. With this we rate the maintainability as + and the usability as ○ because in addition to the points mentioned above, HPK does not support certain Kubernetes features, most notably `kubectl exec` and services, such that users need to work around these limitations.

c) KSI: Unlike the other two tools, KSI is started via Slurm as it has no active component outside of the Slurm job. Its usage is documented with several examples and it depends on Podman and Kind, which are both well maintained projects. The project delivers a feature complete Kubernetes cluster via a set of scripts making it both usable and maintainable so we rate KSI + for both factors. However, as KSI is our own creation, we cannot claim that this evaluation is unbiased and should be regarded as such.

C. Performance

The benchmarking scripts, as well as the raw test data, are available online [53]. Each benchmark was repeated 10 times to minimize random error with the standard deviation shown in the graphs.

TABLE III. WORKLOAD STARTUP TIME, LOWER IS BETTER.

Integration Approach	Startup Time [s]
bare metal	0.141
Bridge Operator	2.725
HPK	2.497
KSI	53.921

1) Startup Time: The startup delays given in Table III have negligible standard deviation and show that Bridge Operator and HPK start a workload in 2 to 3 seconds while KSI requires almost one minute. This result is as expected since Bridge Operator and HPK already have an active Kubernetes cluster running before they submit their Slurm job while KSI has to set up a Kubernetes cluster from scratch. Considering that HPC workloads often run for multiple hours, one minute extra start up time is not great but acceptable. Due to this we rate Bridge Operator and HPK with + and KSI with ○.

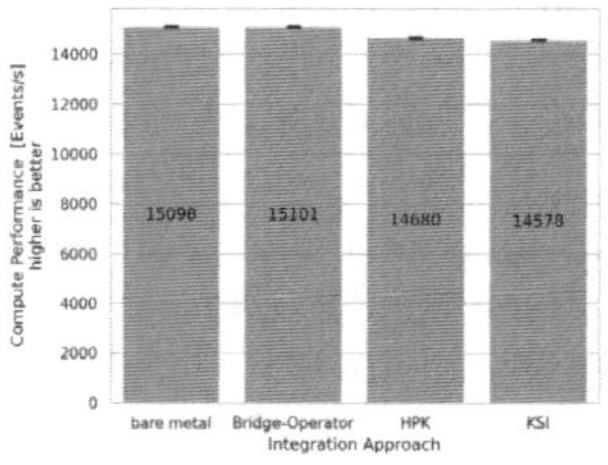

Figure 1. CPU compute performance results using Sysbench.

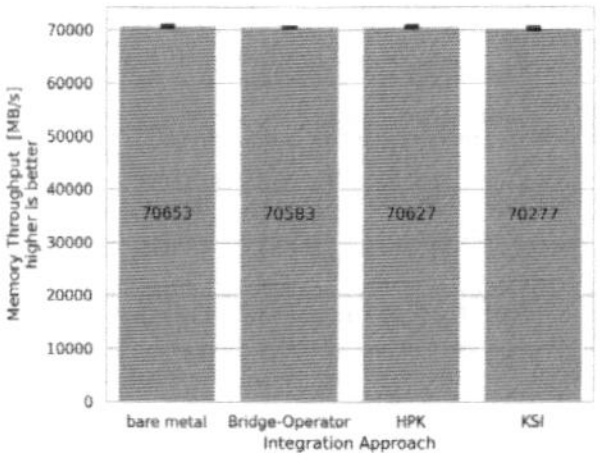

Figure 2. Memory throughput results using Stream.

2) Compute Performance: Figure 1 shows that Bridge Operator and bare metal are effectively on the same performance level while HPK and KSI are slightly lower than bare metal (2.7% and 3.4%, respectively). The difference arises due to the virtualization overhead and additional active components running for HPK and KSI but is overall negligible such that we rate all approaches with +.

3) Memory Performance: Figure 2 shows similar to Figure 1 only minor differences for HPK and KSI due to the additional active components and virtualization such that we also rate all with + here.

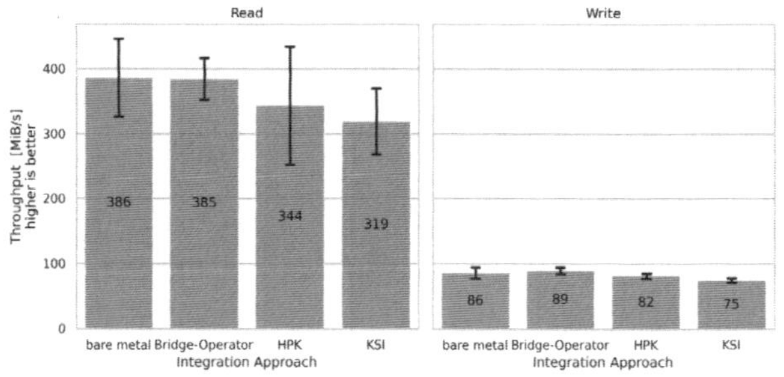

Figure 3. Storage throughput results using Fio and sequential operations.

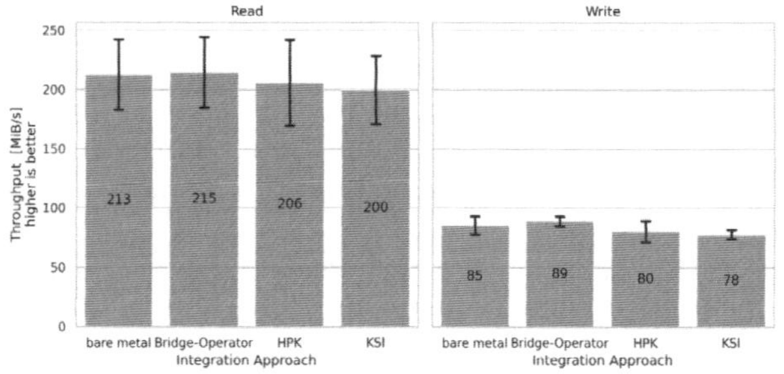

Figure 4. Storage throughput results using Fio and randomized operations.

4) Storage Performance: The sequential read and write shown in Figure 3 shows a similar pattern as the random read and write shown in Figure 4 with Bridge Operator being on the same level as bare metal and HPK and KSI lacking behind. More specifically HPK is about 11% slower in sequential and 5% slower in random reading and KSI is overall 17% slower in reading and 13% slower in writing than bare metal. These differences can also be attributed to the additional virtualization and overall resource consumption. While 17% slower reading is not good we rate it still as acceptable so HPK and KSI are rated as ○ and Bridge Operator as +.

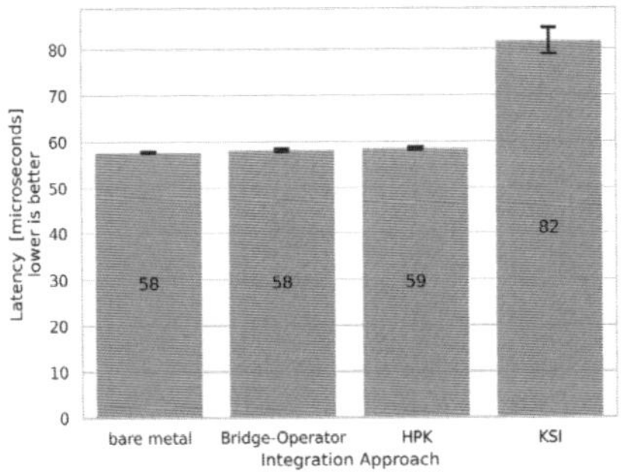

Figure 5. Network latency results using Netperf.

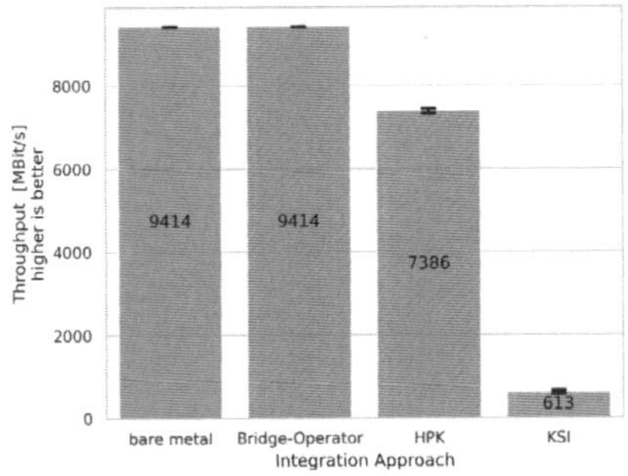

Figure 6. Network bandwidth results using iPerf3.

5) Network Performance: For these benchmarks, the respective tool executed a workload containing a test client that executed the network benchmark against a server running on the other of the two nodes in our test setup. What is shown as the bare metal latency and throughput are therefore the latency and peak throughput between the two nodes. Figure 5 shows network latency with all solutions on the same level except for KSI, which is 42% slower than bare metal. In Figure 6 the network throughput is even worse for KSI with HPK already being 21% slower than bare metal, KSI is 93.5% slower. As KSI operates via rootlesss Podman, it uses slirp4netns as its driver, which according to the Podman documentation [54] results in degraded performance compared to rootful Podman networking. Since our experiments concluded, pasta had replaced slirp4netns as the default network driver for rootless Podman, which promises better performance but initial tests could not show a significant overall improvement [55]. Our ratings are + for Bridge Operator, ○ for HPK and - for KSI.

D. Evaluation

TABLE IV. PROJECT ASSESSMENT REGARDING QUALITY REQUIREMENTS. * SELF-EVALUATION OF KSI IS NOT UNBIASED.

Project	RQ4 Startup	RQ4 Comp.	RQ4 Storage	RQ4 Net.	RQ5 Usab.	RQ6 Maintainab.
B-O	+	+	+	+	○	○
HPK	+	+	○	○	○	+
KSI	○	+	○	-	+*	+*

Table IV summarizes the ratings we have assigned throughout this section with Startup, Compute, Storage and Network performance all aiming at **RQ4** and Usability and Maintainability aiming at **RQ5** and **RQ6**, respectively.

Bridge Operator has shown performance close or identical to bare metal, which is as expected since it effectively submits a Slurm job through Kubernetes and does not start additional software in that Slurm job. This brings some limitations as it is not actually running a given workload using Kubernetes. Nevertheless, it has presented itself as a valid approach for extending a Kubernetes cluster via access to a Slurm cluster.

HPK provides a good middle ground for running Kubernetes jobs on Slurm with some performance deficiencies compared to bare metal. If WLM-Operator would be functional, we would have probably seen similar performance to HPK as WLM-Operator is based on Singularity and HPK is based on Apptainer and both projects still share the majority of their implementation. While HPK does not support all Kubernetes features, e.g., services and `kubectl exec` are not supported, it provides a solid choice for natively running Kubernetes workloads through Slurm.

KSI is functionally the most complete Kubernetes environment within a Slurm job and requires no external parts to be started and kept running outside of it. This comes with performance costs, as KSI shows the weakest performance in all benchmarks, especially in startup time and networking. The slow startup time is understandable as KSI has to bootstrap the Kubernetes control plane and cannot rely on an existing Kubernetes cluster. For network performance, KSI relies on slirp4netns, which is known for causing performance degradation [54]. While other network drivers are available they are necessarily a silver bullet to resolve this issue [55].

All the projects suffer from being either only proof-of-concept implementations, not having being maintained or not being properly documented such that none of them provide a production ready solution for running Kubernetes inside of Slurm jobs.

V. CONCLUSION AND FUTURE WORK

In this paper, we analyzed the state of solutions for combining Slurm and Kubernetes with the goal to enable dynamic computation between either environment. We focused on a subset of the available solutions to support our use case of running Kubernetes workloads on an existing Slurm cluster.

For this purpose, we introduced our own solution KSI, which is based on Kind and rootless Podman and is able to deploy a fully functional Kubernetes cluster inside a Slurm job. From the available solutions we took a closer look at Bridge Operator, HPK and KSI and found that they fulfill our functional requirements, except for KSI, for which multi-node support has not been implemented yet. We further evaluated their performance and reviewed the state of their respective implementations.

We found that Bridge Operator delivers effectively bare metal performance equal to directly running a job through Slurm as this is effectively what Bridge Operator does. HPK established itself as a middle ground solution, providing an almost fully functional Kubernetes cluster inside a Slurm job with minor performance overhead. On the other hand, our solution KSI showed slightly higher overhead compared to HPK and significantly less network throughput. With this KSI provides the most feature complete Kubernetes clusters but should not be considered for workloads that significantly rely on network throughput compared to other factors. Still, if a user's workload relies on Kubernetes networking features such as services, from the evaluated solutions, only KSI can support this.

We conclude that the problem of running Kubernetes inside Slurm workloads is not fully solved as it either comes at the cost of performance or reduced feature sets with only unmaintained or proof-of-concept solutions available.

The next steps for KSI include evaluating different network drivers to mitigate its biggest short coming and to extend it to support multi-node workloads while exploring alternative approaches based on Minikube, K3D or Usersnetes.

REFERENCES

[1] "CNCF Annual Survey 2023", CNCF, Apr. 9, 2024, [Online]. Available: https://www.cncf.io/reports/cncf-annual-survey-2023/ (visited on 2024.12.30).

[2] "9 Insights on Real-World Container Use | Datadog", [Online]. Available: https://web.archive.org/web/20230318234844/https://www.datadoghq.com/container-report/ (visited on 2024.12.30).

[3] A. B. Yoo, M. A. Jette, and M. Grondona, "SLURM: Simple Linux Utility for Resource Management", in *Job Scheduling Strategies for Parallel Processing*, D. Feitelson, L. Rudolph, and U. Schwiegelshohn, Eds., Berlin, Heidelberg: Springer, 2003, pp. 44–60, ISBN: 978-3-540-39727-4. DOI: 10.1007/10968987_3.

[4] "Volcano-sh/volcano", Volcano, Dec. 30, 2024, [Online]. Available: https://github.com/volcano-sh/volcano (visited on 2024.12.30).

[5] "Scaling Kubernetes to 7,500 Nodes", Jan. 2021, [Online]. Available: https://openai.com/blog/scaling-kubernetes-to-7500-nodes/ (visited on 2021.02.12).

[6] A. M. Beltre, P. Saha, M. Govindaraju, A. Younge, and R. E. Grant, "Enabling hpc workloads on cloud infrastructure using kubernetes container orchestration mechanisms", in *2019 IEEE/ACM International Workshop on Containers and New Orchestration Paradigms for Isolated Environments in HPC (CANOPIE-HPC)*, Nov. 2019, pp. 11–20. DOI: 10.1109/CANOPIE-HPC49598.2019.00007.

[7] T. Wickberg, "Slurm and/or/vs Kubernetes", Dec. 30, 2024, [Online]. Available: https://slurm.schedmd.com/SC23/Slurm-and-or-vs-Kubernetes.pdf (visited on 2024.12.30).

[8] S. Metje, "Kubernetes Slurm Integration based on Kind", 2023, [Online]. Available: https://github.com/soerenmetje/kind-slurm-integration.

[9] "Kind – Rootless", [Online]. Available: https://kind.sigs.k8s.io/docs/user/rootless/ (visited on 2024.12.30).

[10] B. Lublinsky, E. Jennings, and V. Spišaková, "A kubernetes 'bridge' operator between cloud and external resources", in *2023 8th International Conference on Cloud Computing and Big Data Analytics (ICCCBDA)*, 2023, pp. 263–269. DOI: 10.1109/ICCCBDA56900.2023.10154770.

[11] Staff, "Introducing HPC Affinities to the Enterprise: A New Open Source Project Integrates Singularity and Slurm via Kubernetes", Sylabs, May 7, 2019, [Online]. Available: https://sylabs.io/2019/05/introducing-hpc-affinities-to-the-enterprise-a-new-open-source-project-integrates-singularity-and-slurm-via-kubernetes/ (visited on 2024.12.30).

[12] K. Peterson, "Kalenpeterson/kube-slurm", Aug. 17, 2024, [Online]. Available: https://github.com/kalenpeterson/kube-slurm (visited on 2024.12.30).

[13] A. Chazapis, F. Nikolaidis, M. Marazakis, and A. Bilas, "Running kubernetes workloads on HPC", in *High Performance Computing*, A. Bienz, M. Weiland, M. Baboulin, and C. Kruse, Eds., ser. Lecture Notes in Computer Science, Cham: Springer Nature Switzerland, 2023, pp. 181–192, ISBN: 978-3-031-40843-4. DOI: 10.1007/978-3-031-40843-4_14.

[14] S. Metje, *Running Kubernetes Workloads on Rootless HPC Systems using Slurm*, GRO.data, Jan. 9, 2024. DOI: 10.25625/GDFCFP.

[15] F. Liu, K. Keahey, P. Riteau, and J. Weissman, "Dynamically negotiating capacity between on-demand and batch clusters", in *Proceedings of the International Conference for High Performance Computing, Networking, Storage, and Analysis*, ser. SC '18, Dallas, Texas: IEEE Press, Nov. 11, 2018, pp. 1–11.

[16] B. Wu, M. Hu, S. Qin, and J. Jiang, "Research on fusion scheduling based on Slurm and Kubernetes", in *International Conference on Algorithms, High Performance Computing, and Artificial Intelligence (AHPCAI 2024)*, vol. 13403, SPIE, Nov. 18, 2024, pp. 476–485. DOI: 10.1117/12.3051639.

[17] G. Zervas, A. Chazapis, Y. Sfakianakis, C. Kozanitis, and A. Bilas, "Virtual clusters: Isolated, containerized HPC environments in kubernetes", in *High Performance Computing. ISC High Performance 2022 International Workshops*, H. Anzt, A. Bienz, P. Luszczek, and M. Baboulin, Eds., ser. Lecture Notes in Computer Science, Cham: Springer International Publishing, 2022, pp. 347–357, ISBN: 978-3-031-23220-6. DOI: 10.1007/978-3-031-23220-6_24.

[18] T. Menouer, N. Greneche, C. Cérin, and P. Darmon, "Towards an Optimized Containerization of HPC Job Schedulers Based on Namespaces", in *Network and Parallel Computing*, C. Cérin, D. Qian, J.-L. Gaudiot, G. Tan, and S. Zuckerman, Eds., Cham: Springer International Publishing, 2022, pp. 144–156, ISBN: 978-3-030-93571-9. DOI: 10.1007/978-3-030-93571-9_12.

[19] C. Cérin, N. Greneche, and T. Menouer, "Towards Pervasive Containerization of HPC Job Schedulers", in *2020 IEEE 32nd International Symposium on Computer Architecture and High Performance Computing (SBAC-PAD)*, Sep. 2020, pp. 281–288. DOI: 10.1109/SBAC-PAD49847.2020.00046.

[20] "SlinkyProject/slurm-operator", SlinkyProject, Dec. 26, 2024, [Online]. Available: https://github.com/SlinkyProject/slurm-operator (visited on 2024.12.30).

[21] P. Liu and J. Guitart, *Fine-grained scheduling for containerized HPC workloads in kubernetes clusters*, Nov. 21, 2022. DOI: 10.48550/arXiv.2211.11487. arXiv: 2211.11487[cs].

[22] D. Medeiros, J. Wahlgren, G. Schieffer, and I. Peng, "Kub: Enabling elastic HPC workloads on containerized environments", in *2023 IEEE 35th International Symposium on Computer Architecture and High Performance Computing (SBAC-PAD)*,

ISSN: 2643-3001, Oct. 2023, pp. 219–229. DOI: 10.1109/SBAC-PAD59825.2023.00031.

[23] "PRIMAGE / hpc-connector · GitLab", GitLab, Feb. 22, 2023, [Online]. Available: https://gitlab.com/primageproject/hpc-connector (visited on 2025.01.02).

[24] N. Zhou *et al.*, "Container orchestration on HPC systems through Kubernetes", *Journal of Cloud Computing*, vol. 10, no. 1, p. 16, Feb. 22, 2021, ISSN: 2192-113X. DOI: 10.1186/s13677-021-00231-z.

[25] G. Staples, "TORQUE resource manager", in *Proceedings of the 2006 ACM/IEEE Conference on Supercomputing*, ser. SC '06, New York, NY, USA: Association for Computing Machinery, Nov. 11, 2006, 8–es, ISBN: 978-0-7695-2700-0. DOI: 10.1145/1188455.1188464.

[26] "Sylabs/wlm-operator", Sylabs Inc., Nov. 5, 2024, [Online]. Available: https://github.com/sylabs/wlm-operator (visited on 2025.01.02).

[27] "Sylabs/singularity-cri", Sylabs Inc., Mar. 1, 2024, [Online]. Available: https://github.com/sylabs/singularity-cri (visited on 2025.01.02).

[28] B. Lublinsky, E. Jennings, and V. Spišaková, "A Kubernetes 'Bridge' operator between cloud and external resources", Jul. 6, 2022, arXiv: 2207.02531 [cs], [Online]. Available: http://arxiv.org/abs/2207.02531 (visited on 2025.01.02), pre-published.

[29] "Bridge-Operator/kubeflow at main · IBM/Bridge-Operator", [Online]. Available: https://github.com/IBM/Bridge-Operator/tree/main/kubeflow (visited on 2025.01.02).

[30] "CARV-ICS-FORTH/HPK", Computer Architecture and VLSI Systems (CARV) Laboratory, Dec. 26, 2024, [Online]. Available: https://github.com/CARV-ICS-FORTH/HPK (visited on 2025.01.02).

[31] A. Chazapis, E. Maliaroudakis, F. Nikolaidis, M. Marazakis, and A. Bilas, "Running Cloud-native Workloads on HPC with High-Performance Kubernetes", Sep. 25, 2024, arXiv: 2409.16919 [cs], [Online]. Available: http://arxiv.org/abs/2409.16919 (visited on 2025.01.02), pre-published.

[32] "Apptainer/apptainer", The Apptainer Container Project, Dec. 30, 2024, [Online]. Available: https://github.com/apptainer/apptainer (visited on 2025.01.02).

[33] "Virtual-kubelet/virtual-kubelet", virtual kubelet, Feb. 24, 2025, [Online]. Available: https://github.com/virtual-kubelet/virtual-kubelet (visited on 2025.02.24).

[34] "Flannel-io/flannel", flannel-io, Feb. 25, 2025, [Online]. Available: https://github.com/flannel-io/flannel (visited on 2025.02.25).

[35] "Flannel-io/cni-plugin", flannel-io, Jan. 31, 2025, [Online]. Available: https://github.com/flannel-io/cni-plugin (visited on 2025.02.25).

[36] "Fix #2 #3 #6 by soerenmetje · Pull Request #4 · IBM/Bridge-Operator", [Online]. Available: https://github.com/IBM/Bridge-Operator/pull/4 (visited on 2025.01.02).

[37] "Kubernetes/minikube", Kubernetes, Jan. 2, 2025, [Online]. Available: https://github.com/kubernetes/minikube (visited on 2025.01.02).

[38] "K3d-io/k3d", k3d, Jan. 2, 2025, [Online]. Available: https://github.com/k3d-io/k3d (visited on 2025.01.02).

[39] "Rootless-containers/usernetes", rootless-containers, Dec. 30, 2024, [Online]. Available: https://github.com/rootless-containers/usernetes (visited on 2025.01.02).

[40] "Kind", [Online]. Available: https://kind.sigs.k8s.io/ (visited on 2025.02.21).

[41] L. S. Marín, "Squat/kilo", Dec. 24, 2024, [Online]. Available: https://github.com/squat/kilo (visited on 2025.01.02).

[42] "Liqotech/liqo", LiqoTech, Dec. 27, 2024, [Online]. Available: https://github.com/liqotech/liqo (visited on 2025.01.02).

[43] "Rootless-containers/slirp4netns", rootless-containers, Feb. 23, 2025, [Online]. Available: https://github.com/rootless-containers/slirp4netns (visited on 2025.02.25).

[44] "Releases · containers/podman", GitHub, [Online]. Available: https://github.com/containers/podman/releases (visited on 2025.02.25).

[45] "Passt - Plug A Simple Socket Transport", [Online]. Available: https://passt.top/passt/about/ (visited on 2025.02.25).

[46] A. Kopytov, "Akopytov/sysbench", Jan. 2, 2025, [Online]. Available: https://github.com/akopytov/sysbench (visited on 2025.01.02).

[47] J. Hammond, "Jeffhammond/STREAM", Dec. 24, 2024, [Online]. Available: https://github.com/jeffhammond/STREAM (visited on 2025.01.02).

[48] J. Axboe, "Flexible I/O Tester", 2022, [Online]. Available: https://github.com/axboe/fio (visited on 2025.01.02).

[49] "HewlettPackard/netperf", Hewlett Packard Enterprise, Dec. 10, 2024, [Online]. Available: https://github.com/HewlettPackard/netperf (visited on 2025.01.02).

[50] "Esnet/iperf", ESnet: Energy Sciences Network, Jan. 2, 2025, [Online]. Available: https://github.com/esnet/iperf (visited on 2025.01.02).

[51] L. Ardito, R. Coppola, L. Barbato, and D. Verga, "A Tool-Based Perspective on Software Code Maintainability Metrics: A Systematic Literature Review", *Scientific Programming*, vol. 2020, no. 1, p. 8 840 389, 2020, ISSN: 1875-919X. DOI: 10.1155/2020/8840389.

[52] K. A. Dawood *et al.*, "Towards a unified criteria model for usability evaluation in the context of open source software based on a fuzzy Delphi method", *Information and Software Technology*, vol. 130, p. 106 453, Feb. 1, 2021, ISSN: 0950-5849. DOI: 10.1016/j.infsof.2020.106453.

[53] S. Metje, "Soerenmetje/kubernetes-slurm-evaluation", Jun. 28, 2024, [Online]. Available: https://github.com/soerenmetje/kubernetes-slurm-evaluation (visited on 2025.01.02).

[54] "Podman/docs/tutorials/performance.md at main · containers/podman", GitHub, [Online]. Available: https://github.com/containers/podman/blob/main/docs/tutorials/performance.md (visited on 2025.01.03).

[55] "Rootless network performance (pasta vs slirp4netns) · containers/podman · Discussion #22559", GitHub, [Online]. Available: https://github.com/containers/podman/discussions/22559 (visited on 2025.01.03).

Configuring Edge Devices That Are Not Accessible Via The Internet

Sebastien Andreo
SI CTO EAAS
Siemens AG
Erlangen, Germany
Email: Sebastien.Andreo@siemens.com

Uwe Hohenstein
FT RPD SSP
Siemens AG
Munich, Germany
Email: Uwe.Hohenstein@siemens.com

Abstract—**In the context of Industrial Internet of Things and Edge Computing, there are often computing devices that run software on the edge device. In real industrial settings, these computing devices are not accessible from the Internet. This raises a problem if software components on the device require configuration changes, such as adjusting some parameters to customize software, restarting one or several applications that behave badly on the device, or rotating passwords to name a few. This paper presents a novel approach to configure software on such computing devices. The details of the cloud-based approach are presented and how the approach has successfully been applied in an industrial project.**

Keywords-internet of things; IoT; cloud computing; industrial use case; configuration.

I. INTRODUCTION)

The Internet of Things (IoT) [9] is a rapidly emerging Internet-based information service architecture where many devices are interconnected [3][36]. Devices are equipped with communication, sensing, computing and actuating capabilities to collect and exchange data with their surroundings to enable analysis, optimization and control. Devices also perform a task in the physical world like opening or closing a valve. Recent technological achievements support the vision of a connected world [22]. In fact, different IoT use cases have successfully been implemented [31].

Many traditional IoT approaches use the Cloud for analyzing devices' data, i.e., devices forward data to the Cloud where intelligent analysis is performed because of the Cloud's high reliability, availability, unlimited scalability and resources. However, a lot of incarnations of IoT have increasingly challenged this approach [1] because transmitting large amounts of data to the Cloud burdens the network traffic. Recent approaches, such as edge [27], fog [6][38] and osmotic computing [33], thus target at processing and putting more data intelligence and decision making processes [16][18][37] at the edge of the network, i.e., near the devices [28][30]. Filtering and pre-processing data occurs before submission to the Cloud, thus decreasing the volume of data and reducing the network traffic [25].

In these cases, computing devices run some installed software on the hardware. However, in real industrial settings, devices are deployed in remote and hard-to-reach environments. As a consequence, devices do not allow any access from the Internet due to strong security requirements.

This raises a problem. Usually, software requires some configuration, which might change from time to time. For example, software is mostly designed in a generic manner to satisfy several customers or deployments. Thus, running the generic software needs some configuration during startup to customize software accordingly. Only then a customer-specific implementation can be avoided.

Changes of the configuration will also occur during operation. For example, transferring data to the Cloud in the context of edge devices requires credentials to access Cloud services, e.g., a Cloud storage, such as AWS S3 storage. This does not seem to be a problem at a first glance. But security policies in industrial contexts require an expiration and periodic password rotation. That is, renewed passwords must then be passed to the device at runtime in order to avoid downtime.

In general, further parameters for the software have often to be adjusted, e.g., thresholds, according to changing system behavior or environment. Similarly, if a software component behaves badly, restarting it might become necessary from the outside, maybe after changing some parameters to remedy a component. And finally, there are often scheduled jobs that require a modifiable Cron specification for periodic tasks.

Hence, a configuration of devices and their components is indispensable. But any kind of such configuration is a problem if the device and components running on that device are not accessible via the internet – as in the case of industrial settings.

One possible solution is to securely log into the computing device and to configure locally and directly. This requires advanced access from outside, e.g., by the Common Remote Service Platform [8] – if possible at all. Without a remote login, configuration must be done directly at the device's location, i.e., usually at the plant's site.

The main contribution of this paper is to tackle these configuration issues. Hence, Section II presents a novel approach to control and configure software on edge devices that are not accessible by the Internet. Details about the organization of software are presented in Section III, before Section IV applies and evaluates the approach in a real industrial context with corresponding use cases. In Section V, we compare the presented approach with other work done in the literature. Finally, Section VI summarizes the works and gives an outlook about future work.

II. APPROACH

In the context of Industrial Internet of Things and Edge Computing, there are computing devices that run some installed software on the hardware. This paper targets at allowing for externally provided configurations. In the following, we use the following terms:

- *Computing Device (CD)*: Can be any device, such as a computer, an industrial PC, industrial boxes, such as Siemens X300 box, or a RaspberryPi. A CD might also be part of embedded hardware.
- *Device Component (DC)*: A piece of software that runs in a computing device to fulfill a certain task within the computing device. In modern IoT architectures, these DCs typically run in virtualization, especially Docker containers.
- *Configuration*: Some data required by a device component DC to adjust its behavior, for instance, to set some thresholds, credentials, and time intervals, or to trigger actions, such as enforcing a restart.

The proposed solution to allow for an external configuration is as follows.

There is a new component *ConfigurationManager-Backend* (*CMB*) running on a separate computer (maybe hosted in the Cloud). The CMB keeps configurations and possesses a publicly available but secured service. Dedicated users can send configuration data to the CMB service for a Device Component on a CD by means of an API; the CMB persists the configuration data internally. Furthermore, CMB can also be asked for configurations. Thus, CMB is a REST service that offers a GET operation to retrieve configuration data and a POST and PUT to store and update configurations. The CMB is responsible for several CDs.

Another component *ConfigurationHandler* (*CH*) is installed on the DC to periodically pull configuration data from the CMB by using a GET request. The GET request works in such a way that each request from CH to CMB returns NOT MODIFIED (e.g., code 304 for HTTP/REST) whenever a configuration has not been changed at the CMB (this can be determined by using the ETAG mechanism and the lastModified timestamp); otherwise, a package with all configurations for the CD is returned. There is a CH for each CD. Each CH obtains credentials to access the CMB REST API to get only its configurations. The credentials are changed periodically and passed to CH using the mechanism explained below.

The configuration itself is stored as a zipped file `package.zip` and organized as follows:

- There is a directory for each device component named like the DC. It is assumed that each DC possesses a unique name or identifier.
- Several files can be put in such a component's directory; the format can be json or XML.

The following is a sample `package.zip`:

```
|- bulk-transfer
    |- x.json
    |- y.json
|- db-inserter
    |- z.json
```

The first level of the hierarchy determines the components, here `bulk-transfer` and `db-inserter`. And files `x.json` and `y.json` contain configurations for the DC bulk-transfer. Further configuration files can be added at any time.

As already explained, CH calls the CMB service periodically, particularly initially after a restart of CH. Whenever a successful response is received, the packaged data is analyzed by CH and internally distributed to all device components DC running on the computing device CD. The communication between CH and components is done by means of a message queue, e.g., supporting MQTT. That is, having received a configuration change, CH splits the configuration `package.zip` into parts according to the returned package structure so that individual configuration files for each DC are extracted. The contents of all the files belonging to the same DC are merged to one file.

CH keeps the latest configuration state for each DC in an internal storage. If something has changed for a component compared to the last state (determined by using a hash key or similar), CH puts a message into the message queue with a topic `/configuration/<DC>` that identifies the DC being supposed to receive it. Otherwise, the configuration will not be pushed since nothing has changed for the respective component.

Each device component listens to incoming configuration changes in the message queue concerning itself (identified by its topic `/configuration/<DC>`). It takes the message payload, i.e., its configuration part. Afterwards, the DC can react according to the new configuration, for instance, adjusting some parameters or performing a certain action. Figure 1 illustrates the approach for such a periodic configuration update.

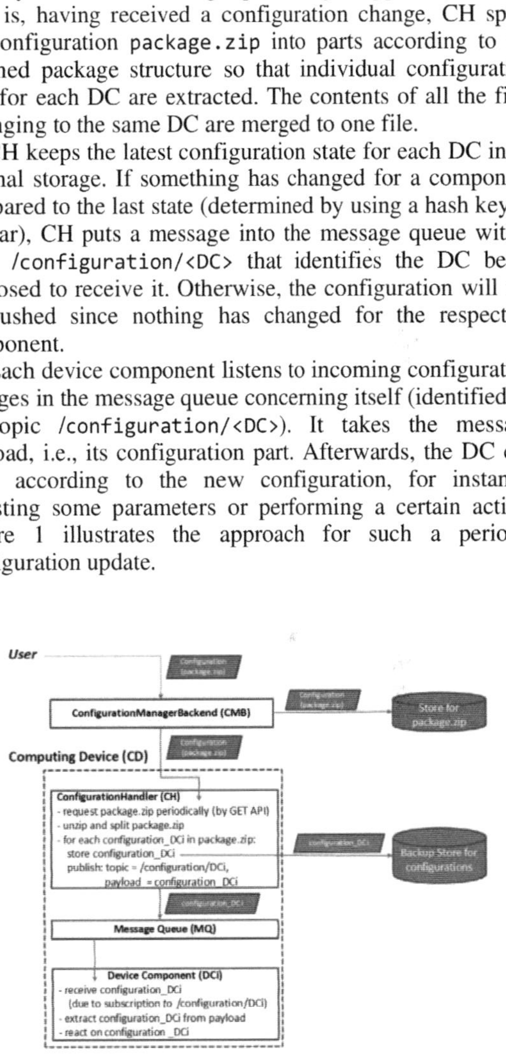

Figure 1. Periodic configuration update.

This is the typical scenario of notifying DCs about configuration changes. Another scenario is important for restarting components. After a restart of a device component DC, the DC might have missed some configuration changes that occurred during downtime. Hence, DC is enabled to ask for its latest configuration explicitly. Therefore, the DC can publish a corresponding message to the message queue with a topic `/request/<DC>`. CH listens to topic `/request/#`, i.e., all those topics (due to "#") starting with `/request`, and reacts by issuing a request to the CMB service and behaving as described before. Figure 2 illustrates the procedure.

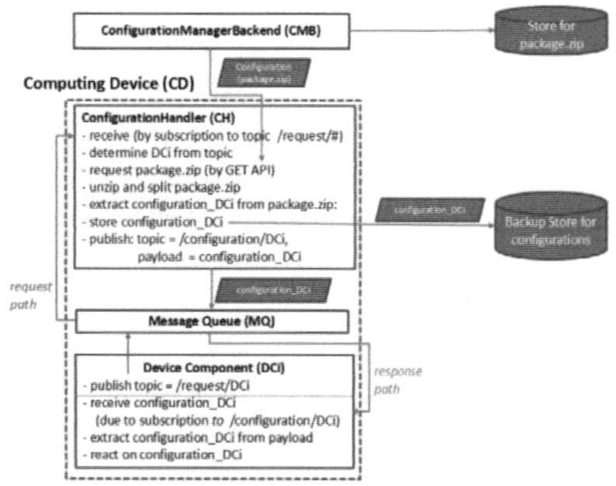

Figure 2. Explicit configuration update.

In case the CMB service is unreachable by CH (e.g., due to network problems), the latest version of a configuration as stored in CH is issued if explicitly asked for a configuration by a DC. Once CMB is reachable again, the usual mechanism works as described before.

Indeed, there is some monitoring of the overall system to detect any issues as early as possible and sending alerts to responsible persons.

Using a message queue has the advantage that all the components do not need to be known in advance or have been registered somewhere. In other terms, new components can be added by using the mechanism immediately. If a component mentioned in the package does not exist, a message is published to the message queue but nothing else happens due to the lack of a consuming DC.

The Cloud is beneficial for CMB due to global accessibility and high reliability, but not mandatory for this approach.

Compared to other approaches mentioned in Section V, advantages are:

- A computing device can be secured by not being accessible from the Internet while still obtaining configuration changes.
- Moreover, the configuration can be done at any time and outside of the computing device CD, independent of its location.

III. ORGANIZATION OF SOFTWARE

The common parts for letting a DC request a configuration at startup and listening to request changes can be placed in a common piece of code so that all the DCs can share the logic (e.g., by inheritance).

The following are some code snippets in python, however, omitting some details, such as proper exception handling.

There is a superclass (indicated in python by `ABC`) with the common code to be shared with every component:

```
class Component(ABC):
  def __init__(self, broker_url:str, broker_port:int):
    initialize message queue mqtt;
    set component_name and topic;
    on_message = lambda msg: self.on_msg(msg)
    subscribe to message queue with topic and on_message
      as callback;
  def on_msg(self, msg):
     payload = json.loads(msg.payload.decode('UTF-8'))
  def start_listening(self):
    self.mqtt_client.broker_client.loop_start()
  def stop_listening(self):
    self.mqtt_client.broker_client.loop_stop()
  @abstractmethod
  def update_configuration(self):
    pass #  to be implemented by every derived class
  def request_configuration(self):
    data = { "component": self.component_name }
    self.mqtt_client.publish(message=json.dumps(data),
                        topic='/request' + self.component_name)
```

on_message is a callback function that is used to subscribe to the message queue with a particular topic. Functions start_listening and stop_listening start and stop listening to a specific topic in the message queue, resp. update_configuration is an abstract function that must be implemented in a component to react on received configuration changes.

Every component has to be derived from this superclass as follows.

```
class SpecificComponent(Component):
  def main(): # will run in a docker container
    super().__init__(broker_url, broker_port)
    self.start_listening()
    self.request_configuration() # get first configuration for
                                 # start-up
  def update_configuration(self,payload):
    if 'config_a' in payload:
      react on payload['config_a']
    if 'config_b' in payload:
      react on payload['config_b']
```

Here, SpecificComponent runs in a docker container, which executes the main function. Invoking start_listening starts listening on configuration changes. During start-up of the component, a configuration is requested by request_configuration. Any configuration change will automatically invoke update_configuration, where component-specific behavior is implemented how to react.

IV. Evaluation in an Industrial Context

This section discusses the evaluation of the approach in an industrial context by using a concrete application.

A. *Industrial Context*

Indeed, there are many different industrial IoT projects within our company. However, it turned out that many of them have similar requirements and follow the same behavioral scheme. As one important characteristic, there is no internet access to the devices. Moreover, there is a strong need to deploy project-specific applications at the edge.

This leads to one common architecture to be set up several times in industrial projects. The overall generic approach follows the Lambda [23] architecture and is based upon container technology. Indeed, IoT applications are increasingly deployed using containers [24].

The common use case is to gather data from IoT devices. Data is processed and used twofold.

First, there are several calculations of key performance indicators (KPIs) that are resource-consuming and run on a daily schedule producing some kind of daily analysis and summary. For these applications, a component like a batch layer [23] is sufficient. That is, data is regularly pushed into the Cloud, and analysis and calculating KPIs is then performed in the Cloud using the submitted data. Calculated KPIs and any detected anomalies are visualized in dashboards. Further applications in this context are predictive maintenance etc. since they also have higher needs on compute power.

Second, other use cases behave in the sense of a speed layer [23] and require data in real-time to immediately react on events in the data, e.g., to control a device. Those applications typically run at the edge in the sense of edge computing.

The overall common architecture consists of several components running in Docker containers. Each component has a dedicated task to fulfil.

At first, a *Connector* abstracts from various industrial protocols, such as OPCUA, MODBUS, or BACNET to get sensor data from devices. Hence, this is a central component to handle all the various protocols and their heterogeneity for receiving data from devices. The Web-of-Things [34], particularly the concept of thing description, is the basis for this component; it keeps the information about the device and its protocol and handles data access.

The Connector sends data to a *Forwarder* component immediately by means of an efficient protocol like web sockets. The Forwarder then puts the received data into a message queue with a particular topic.

Using a message queue has the reason to let other application-specific components immediately consume events from the message queue, similar to the speed layer in the Lambda architecture [23].

An *Inserter* listens to the message queue by subscribing to the topics used by the Forwarder. It stores the received data in a timeseries database, such as InfluxDB. Again, other application-specific components are enabled to read data from the database.

The *BulkTransfer* component transfers a bulk of sensors' data from the timeseries database to the Cloud regularly in a configurable interval, e.g., every hour. This means the data for, e.g., the last hour is then transported. This scheduled job is reasonable for Cloud-based analysis and algorithms that do not require streamed data [23].

The rationale behind this architecture, especially using a message queue and a timeseries database, is to allow for project-specific components to be plugged in. Depending on a particular project, further application-specific components can be deployed to consume and process data directly and immediately from the message queue or timeseries database. Those applications can also store data there to be processed by others or being transferred to the Cloud. Application-specific components are especially used for controlling devices.

This is quite a generic and flexible approach. Various configurations are possible in this architecture for dedicated scenarios due to keeping components exchangeable.

B. *Application*

We applied the configuration approach successfully to achieve several configurations being explained below.

As mentioned previously, the *Inserter* listens to the message queue and stores the received data in a timeseries database. From a performance point of view, it is not reasonable to store record by record. Hence, a bulk approach gathers data until a certain number of records have been received or a certain time threshold has been passed; it then stores the bulk of records. The time threshold is reasonable in order to avoid that records are not stored for a longer period of time because of incomplete bulks. Both the bulk size and the time threshold are configurable for the *Inserter* to adjust to specific loads using our approach.

Next, the *BulkTransfer* runs periodically as some kind of Cron job to move bulks of data from the timeseries database to the Cloud. Here, the schedule is configurable. Intervals can be configured according to how often data is processed in the Cloud by means of a Cron schedule. Moreover, the *BulkTransfer* requires S3 credentials to access the Cloud storage. Due to key rotation, the credentials are periodically changed in the Cloud. New secrets can now be updated so that *BulkTransfer* becomes able to submit data to the Cloud storage.

There are also some more general applications of configurations. Having several components and containers in a device, the communication between them, for instance IP addresses and ports, are timeseries database at startup. Similarly, several configurations for the timeseries database and message queue are configurable. Also, the logging level can be changed at runtime. This turned out to be very important since the logging level can be increased for debugging purposes and reset after having detected issues.

In the architecture, a thing description (TD) plays an important role, particularly to describe the sensors. Whenever new sensors are delivered by a device, via OPCUA or MODBUS connectors, the software components become aware of new sensors by receiving the enhanced TD with new sensors by means of configuration. Hence, data from new sensors can be processed immediately.

It could happen that a container behaves badly. A configuration parameter is used to enforce a restart, maybe with changing parameters.

Further configurations are used for bypassing components. For instance, the *Inserter* can be configured to directly forward data to the Cloud, then skipping the *BulkTransfer* and allowing for data processing in a streamed manner in the Cloud. However, due to our experiences, this is only useful for smaller amounts of data due to higher costs for the IoT solutions of Cloud vendors.

V. RELATED WORK

There are many reference architectures for IoT, edge, and fog computing [2][4][5][11][13][14][17][19][25][35] in the literature. They provide generic taxonomies for the components of IoT platforms and differentiate several functional components, such as device, sensor, actuator, and gateway. Reference architectures then pose components in three [39] or more layers [12]. They all have in common to pay no attention on how to configure components properly.

State-of-the-art reviews, such as [32] – despite discussing so far unsolved challenges in the field of edge applications – also do not mention configuration problems, especially in case of unreachable devices as a challenge.

Several approaches could benefit from such an approach despite not mentioning configuration issues. For example, Stankovski et al. [26] proposed a distributed self-adaptive architecture for container-based technologies to ensure the QoS for time-critical applications. Monitoring data is used to allocate required resources for each container; end-users, application developers and/or administrators can define operational strategies to handle resources in a better manner. Indeed, these strategies are a form of configuration.

CloudScale is a monitoring system proposed by [21]. The system analyses the performance of distributed applications at runtime, thereby adopting user-specified scaling policies for provisioning and de-provisioning of virtual resources. Policies are again another type of configuration.

Olorunnife et al [24] evaluate various approaches for failure recovery for IoT applications. Monitoring the output of IoT applications. Their approach automatically diagnoses faults with IoT devices and gateways; and effectively manages and re-configures container-based IoT software to achieve a minimal downtime upon the detection of software failures. This technique can particularly be applied to scenarios where IoT software is deployed in embedded or hard to reach scenarios, i.e., with difficult or no physical access. But this approach merely focuses on automatic recovery without any interaction from the outside.

VI. CONCLUSIONS

In this paper, we discuss the problem of configuring devices that are unreachable from the Internet in the context of Internet-of-Things (IoT).

We motivate the need for configurations by presenting typical examples such as Cron schedules for running periodical jobs, parameters or thresholds for components, changing credentials because of password rotation to name a few. Especially the latter one is required in industrial settings due to high security requirements where passwords must be renewed regularly. These kinds of configurations are usually indispensable for an effective operation in industrial contexts. However, if devices are unreachable by the Internet, operators have to perform configurations at the device site causing efforts and costs.

The approach that is pursued to solve this issue is discussed in detail. There is mainly a central service running in the Cloud to keep configurations. New configurations can be submitted to that service. Each IoT device is equipped with a component that polls the central service periodically about configuration changes and distribute configurations to the components running in that device

We evaluate the approach in a real industrial application where several types of configurations are required.

Our future work will evaluate even more complex scenarios, such as enabling or disabling components in the architecture at runtime. We also want to investigate the impact of the approach on the overall system performance. Moreover, we want to tackle further industrial issues for IoT devices, such as enhancing fault tolerance by self-healing and monitoring.

REFERENCES

[1] A. Al-Fuqaha, M. Guizani, M. Mohammadi, M. Aled-hari, and M. Ayyash, "Internet of Things: A Survey on Enabling Technologies Protocols and Applications", IEEE Communications Surveys Tutorials, Vol. 17 (4), pp. 2347-2376, June 2015, ISSN 1553-877X.

[2] M. Aazam, I. Khan, A. Alsaffar, and E. Huh, "Cloud of Things: Integrating Internet of Things and Cloud Computing and the Issues Involved", Int. Bhurban Conf on applied sciences and technology.

[3] L. Atzori, A. Iera, and G. Morabito, "The Internet of Things: A Survey", Computer Networks 2010, Vol. 54 (15), pp. 2787–2805.

[4] M. Bauer, M. Boussard, N. Bui, J. C. De Loof, C. Magerkurth, S. Meissner, A. Nettsträter, J. Stefa, M. Thoma, and J. W. Walewski, "IoT Reference Architecture. In: Enabling Things to Talk: Designing IoT solutions with the IoT Architectural Reference Model", Springer Berlin Heidelberg 2013.

[5] S. Biswas and S. Misra, "Designing of a Prototype of e-Health Monitoring System", IEEE Int. Conf on Research in Computational Intelligence and Communication Networks (ICRCICN) 2015, pp. 267–272.

[6] F. Bonomi, R. Milito, P. Natarajan, and J. Zhu, "Fog Computing: A Platform for Internet of Things and Analytics", Big Data and Internet of Things: A roadmap for smart environments, pp. 169–186. Springer.

[7] B. Costa, J. Bachiega, R. Carvalho, M. Rosa, and A. Araujo, "Monitoring Fog Computing: A Review, Taxonomy, and Open Challenges", Computer Networks Vol. 215, Elsevier 2022, pp. 1–30.

[8] "Remote Services – For the High-Performance Operation of Your Plant", https://www.siemens.com/global/en/products/services /digital-enterprise-services/field-maintenance-services/remote-services.html) [retrieved: March, 2025].

[9] B. Dorsemaine, J.-P. Gaulier, J.-P. Wary, N. Kheir, and P. Urien, "Internet of Things: a Definition & Taxonomy", 9th Int. Conf on Next Generation Mobile Applications, Services and Technologies, ISBN 978-1-4799-8660-6/15, 2015.

[10] K. Fatema, V. Emeakaroha, P. Healy, J. Morrison, and T. Lynn, "A Survey of Cloud Monitoring Tools: Taxonomy, Capabilities and Objectives", Journal of Parallel and Distributed Computing 2014, Vol. 74 (10), pp. 2918–2933.

[11] J. Guth, U. Breitenbucher, M. Falkenthal, F. Leymann, and L. Reinfurt, "Comparison of IoT Platform Architectures: A Field Study Based on a Reference Architecture", Cloudification of the Internet of Things (CIoT) 2016, pp. 1–6.

[12] J. Guth, U. Breitenbücher, M. Falkenthal , P. Fremantle, O. Kopp, F. Leymann, and L. Reinfurt , "A Detailed Analysis of IoT Platform Architectures: Concepts, Similarities, and Differences", Internet of Everything: Algorithms, Methodologies, Technologies and Perspectives, Springer 2018, pp. 81-101.

[13] J. Gubbi, R. Buyya, and S. M. P. Marusic, "Internet of Things (IoT): A Vision, Architectural Elements, and Future Directions", Future Generation Computer Systems 2013, Vol. 29 (7), pp. 1645–1660.

[14] S. A. S. Haller, M. Bauer, and F. Carrez, "A Domain Model for the Internet of Things", Proc. of IEEE Int. Conf on Green Computing and Communications and IEEE Internet of Things and IEEE Cyber Physical and Social Computing. IEEE (2013).

[15] B. Hazarika and T. J. Singh, "Survey paper on Cloud Computing & Cloud Monitoring: Basics", SSRG Int. Journal on Comput. Science Engineering 2015, Vol. 2 (1), pp. 10-15, ISSN:2348–8387.

[16] J. Kua, G. Armitage, P. Branch, and J. But, "Adaptive Chunklets and AQM for Higher-Performance Content Streaming", ACM Transactions on Multimedia Computing, Communications, and Applications (TOMM) 2019, Vol. 15, pp. 1–24

[17] J. Kim, J. Lee, J. Kim, and J. Yun, "M2M Service Platforms: Survey, Issues, and Enabling Technologies", IEEE Communications Surveys & Tutorials 2014, Vol. 16 (1), pp. 61–76.

[18] J. Kua, S. H. Nguyen, G. Armitage, and P. Branch, "Using Active Queue Management to Assist IoT Application Flows in Home Broadband Networks", IEEE Internet of Things Journal 2017, Vol 4 (5), pp. 1399–1407.

[19] S. Krco, B. Pokric, and F. Carrez, "Designing IoT and Architecture(s)", In: Proc. of the IEEE World Forum on Internet of Things (WF-IoT). IEEE (2014).

[20] S. Karumuri, F. Solleza, S. Zdonik, and N. Tatbul, "Towards Observability Data Management at Scale", ACM SIGMOD Record, Vol. 49, pp. 18–23.

[21] P. Leitner, C. Inzinger, W. Hummer, B. Satzger, and S. Dustdar, "Application-level Performance Monitoring of Cloud Services Based on the Complex Event Processing Paradigm", Proc. of 5th IEEE Int. Conf. on Service-Oriented Computing and Applications (SOCA'12). IEEE, Taipei, Taiwan, pp. 1–8.

[22] I. Lee and K. Lee, "The Internet of Things (IoT): Applications, Investments, and Challenges for Enterprises", Business Horizons 2015, Vol. 58 (4), pp. 431–440.

[23] N. Marz: "How to Beat the CAP Theorem", 13 October 2011. http://nathanmarz.com/blog/how-to-beat-the-cap-theorem.html [retrieved: March, 2025].

[24] K. Olorunnife, K. Lee, and J. Kua, "Automatic Failure Recovery for Container-Based IoT Edge Applications", Electronics 2021, Vol. 10.

[25] V. Prasad, M. Bhavsar, and S. Tanwar, "Influence of Montoring: Fog and Edge Computing", Scalable Computing: Practice and Experience 2019, Vol. 20 (2), pp. 365-376.

[26] V. Stankovski, J. Trnkoczy, S. Taherizadeh, and M. Cigale, "Implementing Time-Critical Functionalities with a Distributed Adaptive Container Architecture", Proc. of 18th Int. Conf. on Information Integration and Web-based Applications and Services (iiWAS2016). ACM, Singapore, pp. 455–459.

[27] W. Shi and S. Dustdar, "The promise of Edge Computing", Computer, Vol. 49 (5), pp. 78–81, May 2016.

[28] K. Saharan and A. Kumar, "Fog in Comparison to Cloud: A Survey", Int. Journal of Computer Applications, Vol. 122 (3), 2015.

[29] E. Solaiman, R. Ranjan, P. P. Jayaraman, and K. Mitra, "Monitoring Internet of Things Application Ecosystems for Failure", IT Professional 2016, Vol. 18 (5), pp. 8–11.

[30] M. Satyanarayanan, P. Simoens, Y. Xiao et al., "Edge Analytics in the Internet of Things", IEEE Pervasive Computing 2015, Vol. 14 (2), pp. 24–31.

[31] A. Srinivasa and D. Siddaraju, "A Comprehensive Study of Architecture, Protocols and Enabling Applications in Internet of Things (IoT)", Int. Journal of Science & Technology Research 2019, Vol. 8, Issue 11.

[32] S. Taherizadeh, A. Jones, I. Taylor, Z. Zhao, and V. Stankowski, "Monitoring Self-Adaptive Applications within Edge Computing Frameworks: A State-of-the-Art Review", Journal of Systems and Software 2018, Vol 136, pp. 19-38.

[33] M. Villari, M. Fazio, S. Dustdar, O. Rana, and R. Ranjan, "Osmotic Computing: a New Paradigm for Edge/Cloud Integration", IEEE Cloud 2016.

[34] Web of Things in a Nutshell. https://www.w3.org/WoT/documentation [retrieved: March, 2025]

[35] L. D. Xu, W. He, and S. Li, "Internet of things in industries: A survey", IEEE Transactions on Industrial Informatics Vol. 10 (4).

[36] F. Xia, L. T. Yang, L. Wang, and A. Vinel, "Internet of Things", Int. Journal of Communication Systems 2012, Vol. 25 (9), pp. 1101–1102.

[37] W. Yu, F. Liang, X. He, W. G. Hatcher, C. Lu, J. Lin, and X. Yang, "A Survey on the Edge Computing for the Internet of Things", IEEE Access 2018, Vol 6, pp. 6900–6919.

[38] S. Yi, C. Li, and Q. Li, "A Survey of Fog Computing: Concepts, Applications and Issues", Proc. of Workshop on Mobile Big Data. (Mobidata 2015), pp. 37–42.

[39] L. Zheng, H. Zhang, W. Han, X. Zhou, J. He, Z. Zhang, Y. Gu, and J. Wang, "Technologies, Applications, and Governance in the Internet of Things", Internet of Things – Global Technological and Societal Trends. River Publishers (2009).

LLM-based Distributed Code Generation and Cost-Efficient Execution in the Cloud

Kunal Rao, Giuseppe Coviello, Gennaro Mellone, Ciro Giuseppe De Vita and Srimat Chakradhar
NEC Laboratories America, Inc., Princeton, NJ
email: {kunal, giuseppe.coviello, gmellone, cdevita, chak}@nec-labs.com

***Abstract*—The advancement of Generative Artificial Intelligence (AI), particularly Large Language Models (LLMs), is reshaping the software industry by automating code generation. Many LLM-driven distributed processing systems rely on serial code generation constrained by predefined libraries, limiting flexibility and adaptability. While some approaches enhance performance through parallel execution or optimize edge-cloud distributed processing for specific domains, they often overlook the cost implications of deployment, restricting scalability and economic feasibility across diverse cloud environments. This paper presents *DiCE-C*, a system that eliminates these constraints by starting directly from a natural language query. *DiCE-C* dynamically identifies available tools at runtime, programmatically refines LLM prompts, and employs a stepwise approach—first generating serial code and then transforming it into distributed code. This adaptive methodology enables efficient distributed execution without dependence on specific libraries. By leveraging high-level parallelism at the Application Programming Interface (API) level and managing API execution as services within a Kubernetes-based runtime, *DiCE-C* reduces idle GPU time and facilitates the use of smaller, cost-effective GPU instances. Experiments with a vision-based insurance application demonstrate that *DiCE-C* reduces cloud operational costs by up to 72% when using smaller GPUs (A6000 and A4000 GPU machines vs. A100 GPU machine) and by 32% when using identical GPUs (A100 GPU machines). This flexible and cost-efficient approach makes *DiCE-C* a scalable solution for deploying LLM-generated vision applications in cloud environments.**

Keywords-Cloud Computing; Large Language Models (LLMs); Distributed systems; Code generation; Cost reduction.

I. INTRODUCTION

Advancements in Generative AI, particularly LLMs, are reshaping how vision applications are developed and deployed. Tools like ViperGPT [1] demonstrate how LLMs can generate application-specific vision code directly from natural language queries. For instance, users can issue queries, such as "detect traffic accidents" or "identify unattended objects", and ViperGPT automatically generates the required vision program. Figure 1 illustrates a scenario where an operator dynamically deploys such vision applications in real-time. While this represents a significant leap in automation and flexibility, deploying these applications in cloud environments often incurs substantial cost inefficiencies.

DiCE [2] and DiCE-M [3] are existing systems that take ViperGPT-generated serial code as their starting point and transform it into distributed code for parallel execution. While DiCE focuses on improving performance by exploiting API-level parallelism for faster execution of vision applications, DiCE-M targets marine applications using an edge and cloud approach to balance processing across distributed resources. However, neither system addresses the cost implications of

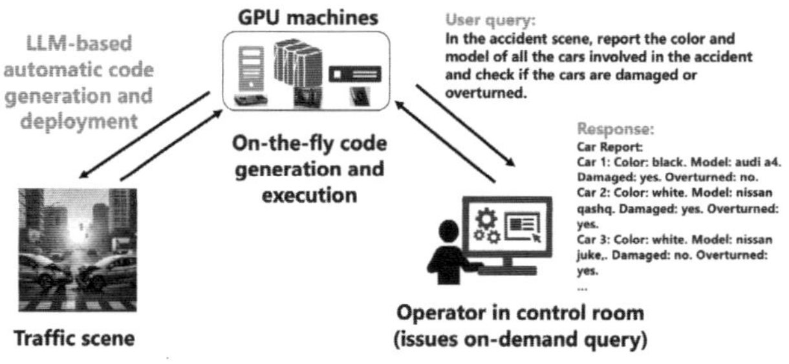

Figure 1: Use case scenario.

deploying these applications, particularly in cloud settings. Additionally, both systems rely on the use of `image_patch` library, which exposes only a handful APIs. This limits the applicability to a very narrow set of applications. If additional functions are required for an application, then it cannot be built since `image_patch` does not have the necessary APIs.

In this paper, we introduce *DiCE-C*, a system that removes the dependency on ViperGPT and the `image_patch` library. Unlike DiCE, *DiCE-C* starts with the original natural language query and dynamically discovers available tools through runtime APIs. It programmatically constructs prompts to guide an LLM to first generate serial code and then transform it into distributed code, leveraging a step-by-step approach that improves performance and accuracy. This flexibility enables *DiCE-C* to adapt to diverse workflows while focusing specifically on cost optimization in cloud environments.

After generating serial code, similar to DiCE, *DiCE-C* identifies high-level parallelism at the API level and transforms serial code into distributed code for efficient execution. By leveraging a Kubernetes-based runtime, *DiCE-C* dynamically manages API calls as services, allocating GPU resources only for the duration of individual service calls. This approach minimizes GPU idle time, allows the use of smaller, cost-efficient GPUs, and significantly lowers operational costs in cloud environments.

Our key contributions in this paper are:

- We identify the cost inefficiencies of deploying LLM-generated monolithic code in cloud environments, including GPU over-provisioning and under-utilization, and propose solutions to optimize resource allocation and execution to address these challenges.
- We introduce *DiCE-C*, which programmatically updates LLM prompts based on runtime API documentation to generate both serial and distributed code. This approach enhances flexibility, adaptability, and cost efficiency by leveraging dynamic tool discovery and resource optimiza-

tion.

- We demonstrate, using a real-world vision-based insurance application, that *DiCE-C* lowers cloud operational costs by up to 72% with smaller GPUs such as A6000 and A4000 GPU machines and by 32% with identical A100 GPU machines, both evaluated in the Hyperstack cloud.

The rest of the paper is organized as follows. Section 2 discusses related work. In Section 3, we examine the cost inefficiencies associated with deploying monolithic/serial code in cloud environments. Section 4 details the design and implementation of *DiCE-C*, focusing on how it generates serial code, transforms serial code into distributed code and then manages execution through a Kubernetes-based runtime. Section 5 reports experimental results highlighting the cost savings achieved by *DiCE-C* and showcases a prototype system. Finally, Section 6 concludes the paper.

II. Related Work

Optimizing cloud computing costs for AI-driven applications has garnered significant attention due to the increasing adoption of resource-intensive models in production environments. Systems like CloudScale [4], SpotDNN [5], SpotLake [6], Wang et. al [7], DEARS [8], ELASTIC [9], Saxena et. al [10], Ahmad et. al. [11], Alelyani et. al. [12] explore different strategies for efficient application execution in cloud computing environment. These works focus on leveraging spot instances, predictive scaling, and scheduling optimizations which can minimize operational expenses. However, they primarily target general-purpose workloads, whereas *DiCE-C* is specifically designed for LLM-generated vision applications, emphasizing API-level parallelism and distributed execution.

Kubernetes-based systems, such as Knative [13] and Kubeflow [14], provide platforms for scalable and efficient resource management. These frameworks offer primitives for deploying containerized workloads but lack the ability to dynamically adapt to the inherent parallelism of LLM-generated code. *DiCE-C* bridges this gap by integrating a runtime that transforms serial code into distributed code, dynamically managing API-level services, and optimizing GPU utilization, thereby reducing costs without requiring changes to the underlying Kubernetes infrastructure.

Recent advances in LLMs have contributed to code generation and parallelization. Tools like DSPy [15], AutoParLLM [16] and HPC-Coder [17] showcase the ability of LLMs to generate efficient pipelines and parallel programs. Systems like DiCE [2] leverage LLMs for transformation of serial code to distributed code for faster execution. DiCE-M [3] leverages LLMs to generate distributed code which can be executed in an edge + cloud infrastructure for marine applications. While these systems focus on improving performance or enabling edge + cloud execution, *DiCE-C* extends this paradigm to address cost optimization by integrating runtime-discovered tools and adapting workloads to varying cloud configurations.

Traditional compiler-based solutions like TVM [18] and Polyhedral [19] optimize program execution through low-level techniques such as memory layout transformations and loop optimizations. Although highly effective for individual tasks, these approaches are less applicable to the distributed, API-driven workloads targeted by *DiCE-C*. By focusing on high-level parallelism and runtime adaptability, *DiCE-C* complements such optimizations to address the unique challenges of cloud-based vision applications.

To the best of our knowledge, *DiCE-C* is the first system to integrate dynamic LLM-driven code generation with runtime cost optimization for vision applications, addressing the inefficiencies of monolithic code deployment and enabling scalable, cost-efficient execution in distributed cloud environments.

III. Motivation

Recent advancements in visual question answering benchmarks, such as RefCOCO, RefCOCO+ [20], GQA [21], OK-VQA [22], and NeXT-QA [23], have enabled tools like ViperGPT to synthesize visual programs directly from natural language queries using libraries such as `image_patch`. These tools showcase the capability of addressing real-world queries beyond benchmark datasets. Building on these advancements, *DiCE-C* eliminates the dependency on predefined libraries and dynamically generates serial code from user queries, enabling a wide range of applications, including the automation of complex, labor-intensive tasks like traffic accident reporting for insurance claim processing. For example, consider the query:

Query: In the accident scene, report the color and model of all the cars involved in the accident and check if the cars are damaged or overturned.

Rather than relying on monolithic code generated by ViperGPT, *DiCE-C* dynamically constructs prompts based on documentation retrieved from the runtime API. These prompts guide an LLM to generate serial code, which is shown in Figure 2. The code utilizes AI models, such as `glip` [24], `blip` [25], and `xvlm` [26] to detect cars, extract their attributes, and evaluate their condition through API calls. Since these AI models require GPUs for execution, sequentially running the code on a single large GPU instance leads to inefficiencies, including extended idle times during CPU-bound operations and under-utilization of GPU resources for lightweight tasks.

This approach has substantial cost implications in cloud computing environments. Large GPU instances must often be provisioned to handle multiple AI models, even if a query only uses a subset of these models. Such instances are expensive to rent and may be unavailable during periods of high demand. Additionally, idle GPU time during CPU processing further inflates operational costs.

The code inherently offers opportunities for parallelism. After the initial `glip` API call to detect cars, subsequent API calls to query their properties (`blip` and `xvlm`) are independent and can be executed concurrently. This parallelism enables the use of smaller, more cost-effective GPU instances instead of relying on a single large GPU. Refactoring the code into a distributed format, where API calls are managed as independent services, allows for dynamic resource allocation,

```
import asyncio
import hermod
from PIL import Image

async def execute_query(image_filename):
    image = Image.open(image_filename)

    # Detecting cars in the image
    cars = await hermod.call("glip", image=image, object_name="car")

    if not cars:
        print("No cars detected in the image.")
        return

    for i, car in enumerate(cars):
        # Crop the image to the bounding box of each detected car
        car_patch = image.crop((car["x"], car["y"],
                                car["x"] + car["width"],
                                car["y"] + car["height"]))

        # Query for the color of the car
        car_color = await hermod.call("blip", image=car_patch, question="What is the color of the car?")
        # Query for the model of the car
        car_model = await hermod.call("blip", image=car_patch, question="What is the model of the car?")
        # Check if the car is damaged
        car_damaged = await hermod.call("xvlm", image=car_patch, object_name="car", property="damaged")
        # Check if the car is overturned
        car_overturned = await hermod.call("xvlm", image=car_patch, object_name="car", property="overturned")

        # Compile the information
        car_info = f"Car {i+1}: Color - {car_color.get('answer', 'Unknown')}, " \
                   f"Model - {car_model.get('answer', 'Unknown')}, " \
                   f"Damaged - {car_damaged.get('result', False)}, " \
                   f"Overturned - {car_overturned.get('result', False)}"

        print(car_info)

image_filename = "accident_scene.jpg"
asyncio.run(execute_query(image_filename))
```

Figure 2: Serial code generated by *DiCE-C* for an accident scene query.

reduces GPU idle time, and significantly lowers operational costs.

IV. Design and Implementation

Unlike existing systems such as DiCE [2] and DiCE-M [3], which rely on ViperGPT-generated monolithic code and are constrained by libraries like `image_patch`, *DiCE-C* removes these limitations. By leveraging runtime APIs to dynamically discover available tools and programmatically con-

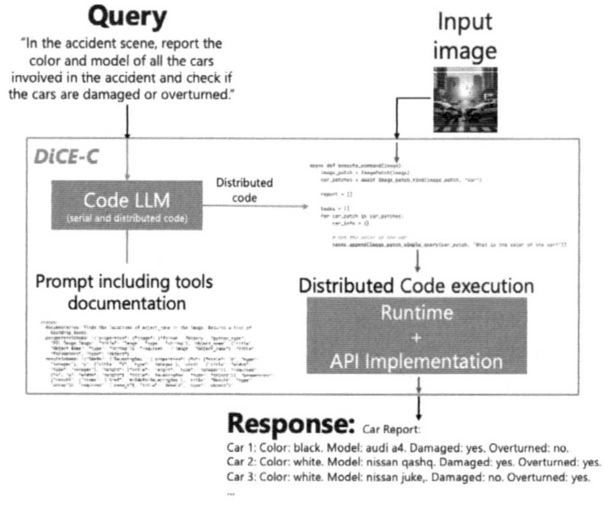

Figure 3: *DiCE-C* overview.

struct LLM prompts, *DiCE-C* enables flexible, cost-efficient deployments tailored to diverse workflows.

As shown in Figure 3, *DiCE-C* consists of two key components:

1) **Code Generation**: This includes the generation of serial code directly from natural language queries and its subsequent transformation into distributed code for parallel execution.
2) **Runtime**: A Kubernetes-based runtime that ensures cost-optimized deployment of distributed code by dynamically managing resources and minimizing GPU idle time.

A. Serial Code Generation

The first phase of *DiCE-C* involves generating functional serial code from a user-provided natural language query. This process begins by querying the runtime API to retrieve metadata about the available tools. Commands such as `kubectl get functions` and `kubectl get functions <function-name> -o yaml` provide detailed documentation, including the tool's functionality, input parameters, and output schemas. An example runtime API output for the `glip` function is shown in Figure 4.

This information is embedded into the LLM prompt alongside the natural language query. The prompt guides the LLM to generate serial code (in Python programming language) tailored to the tools available in the runtime. Figure 2 shows an example of serial code generated by *DiCE-C*. While functional, this sequential code may suffer from inefficiencies such as GPU idle time during CPU-bound operations and underutilization when lightweight tasks run on large GPUs, motivating the need for distributed code generation.

B. Distributed Code Generation

The second phase of *DiCE-C* transforms the serial code into distributed code by exploiting API-level parallelism. Figure 5 illustrates this process. Updated prompts are constructed using

```
$ kubectl get functions glip -o yaml
apiVersion: hermod.nec-labs.com/v1
kind: Function
metadata:
    ...
status:
  documentation: Finds the locations of object_name in the image. Returns a list of
    bounding boxes.
  parametersSchema: '{"properties": {"image": {"format": "binary", "python_type":
    "PIL.Image.Image", "title": "Image", "type": "string"}, "object_name": {"title":
    "Object Name", "type": "string"}}, "required": ["image", "object_name"], "title":
    "Parameters", "type": "object"}'
  resultSchema: '{"$defs": {"BoundingBox": {"properties": {"x": {"title": "X", "type":
    "integer"}, "y": {"title": "Y", "type": "integer"}, "width": {"title": "Width",
    "type": "integer"}, "height": {"title": "Height", "type": "integer"}}, "required":
    ["x", "y", "width", "height"], "title": "BoundingBox", "type": "object"}}, "properties":
    {"result": {"items": {"$ref": "#/$defs/BoundingBox"}, "title": "Result", "type":
    "array"}}, "required": ["result"], "title": "Result", "type": "object"}'
```

Figure 4: GLIP function details obtained from runtime API.

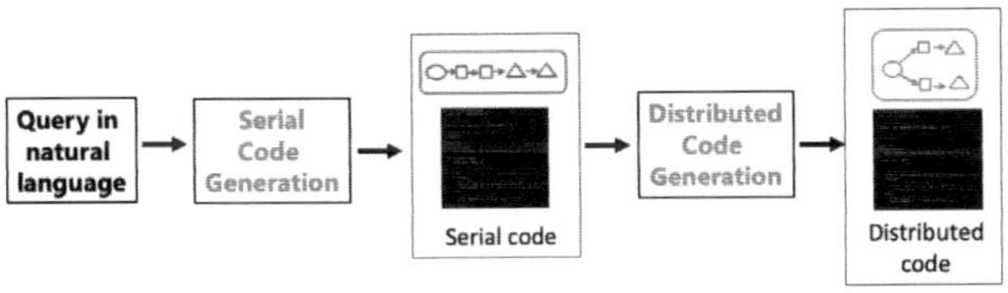

Figure 5: Distributed code generation overview.

information from the runtime API, which enables the LLM to identify independent API calls in the serial code and refactor them for concurrent execution. Additionally, *DiCE-C* incorporates elements from the prompt structure used in DiCE [2], adapting them to dynamically include runtime-discovered tools. This ensures that *DiCE-C* generates distributed code tailored to the specific environment.

Figure 6 shows the distributed code generated by *DiCE-C* using Python's *asyncio* library. By enabling concurrent execution of independent API calls, the distributed code utilizes multiple smaller GPU instances instead of relying on a single large GPU. This reduces idle GPU time, improves resource utilization, and lowers operational costs.

C. Runtime for Distributed Code Execution

The distributed code generated by *DiCE-C* is executed within a Kubernetes-based runtime (Figure 7). Each API call is treated as an independent service, allowing dynamic allocation of GPU resources. By reserving GPUs only for the duration of individual service calls, the runtime minimizes idle time and enables cost-efficient execution.

The runtime architecture, shown in Figure 8, processes requests through service queues, where each API call is transparently mapped to a GPU running the associated AI model. This design facilitates efficient resource sharing across multiple workloads, further reducing the cost of cloud-based deployments. By handling workloads dynamically, the runtime ensures scalable and adaptable execution of vision applications.

D. Cost-Optimized Execution in DiCE-C

Figure 9 illustrates the contrast between the baseline monolithic execution and *DiCE-C*'s distributed execution. In the baseline, all AI models are loaded onto a single large GPU, which remains reserved for the entire job duration. Conversely, *DiCE-C* transforms the code into a distributed version, enabling API calls to run as independent services on smaller GPUs. This minimizes idle GPU time and allows for dynamic scaling based on workload demands, resulting in substantial cost savings.

By combining serial and distributed code generation with a runtime, *DiCE-C* ensures scalable and cost-efficient deployment of vision applications in cloud environments.

V. Experimental Setup and Results

In this section, we evaluate the cost savings achieved by *DiCE-C* compared to the baseline execution of monolithic code in cloud computing environments. The experiments are based on the real-world insurance application use case described in Section III, where the task is to generate detailed accident reports from images. We validate the correctness of the distributed code generated by *DiCE-C* by manually comparing its output with that of the serial code generated by ViperGPT, and both outputs matched.

Figure 6 shows the distributed code generated by *DiCE-C* for the insurance application use case. The code introduces concurrency using Python's *asyncio* library, enabling independent API calls (e.g., querying color, model, damage status, and overturned status) to execute in parallel. This distributed execution reduces GPU idle time and allows dynamic resource allocation for servicing the API calls, thereby achieving substantial cost savings.

A. Experimental Setup

To evaluate cost efficiency, we created a batch of 1000 vision programs (tasks) by replicating the distributed code shown in Figure 6. Thirty different accident scene images were generated using OpenAI's "GPT-4o" model, and these images

```python
import asyncio
import hermod
from PIL import Image

async def get_car_details(car_patch, index):
    try:
        tasks = [
            hermod.call("blip", image=car_patch, question="What is the color of the car?"),
            hermod.call("blip", image=car_patch, question="What is the model of the car?"),
            hermod.call("xvlm", image=car_patch, object_name="car", property="damaged"),
            hermod.call("xvlm", image=car_patch, object_name="car", property="overturned")
        ]

        # Execute all tasks for the car patch in parallel
        car_color, car_model, car_damaged, car_overturned = await asyncio.gather(*tasks)

        # Compile the information
        car_info = f"Car {index + 1}: Color - {car_color.get('answer', 'Unknown')}, " \
                   f"Model - {car_model.get('answer', 'Unknown')}, " \
                   f"Damaged - {car_damaged.get('result', False)}, " \
                   f"Overturned - {car_overturned.get('result', False)}"

        return car_info
    except Exception as e:
        return f"Car {index + 1}: Error occurred - {str(e)}"

async def execute_query(image_filename):
    try:
        image = Image.open(image_filename)

        # Detecting cars in the image
        cars = await hermod.call("glip", image=image, object_name="car")

        if not cars:
            print("No cars detected in the image.")
            return

        car_tasks = []
        for i, car in enumerate(cars):
            # Crop the image to the bounding box of each detected car
            car_patch = image.crop((car["x"], car["y"],
                                    car["x"] + car["width"],
                                    car["y"] + car["height"]))

            # Collect car detail tasks
            car_tasks.append(get_car_details(car_patch, i))

        # Run all car detail tasks in parallel
        car_info_list = await asyncio.gather(*car_tasks)

        for car_info in car_info_list:
            print(car_info)
    except Exception as e:
        print(f"Failed to execute query on the image: {str(e)}")

image_filename = "accident_scene.jpg"
asyncio.run(execute_query(image_filename))
```

Figure 6: Distributed code generated by *DiCE-C*.

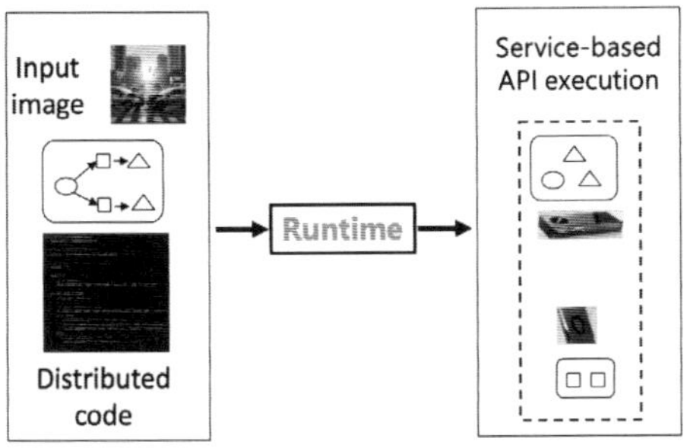

Figure 7: Runtime overview.

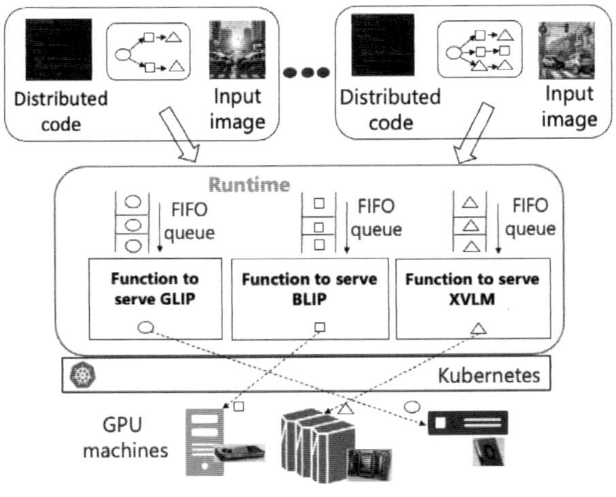

Figure 8: Runtime architecture.

were randomly assigned across the 1000 tasks. Figure 12 shows three sample images used in the experiments.

The experiments were conducted using machines in the Hyperstack [27] cloud under two configurations:

- **Identical hardware:** Both the baseline and *DiCE-C* used A100 GPU nodes (\$2.2/hour).
- **Different hardware:** The baseline used A100 GPUs, while *DiCE-C* utilized a combination of A6000 and A4000 GPUs (\$1.3/hour combined).

Figures 10 and 11 illustrate the execution patterns of the

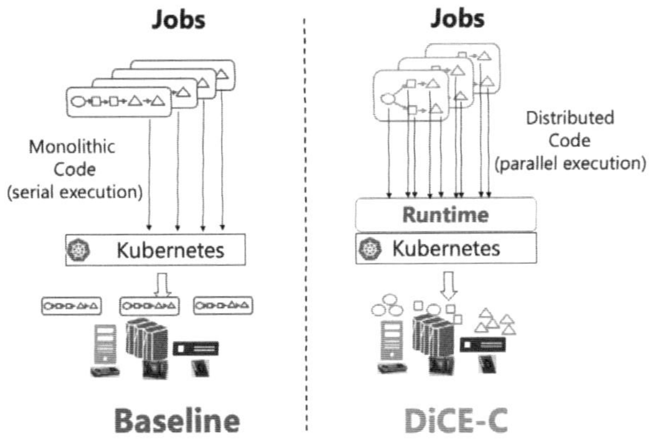

Figure 9: Execution in baseline vs *DiCE-C*.

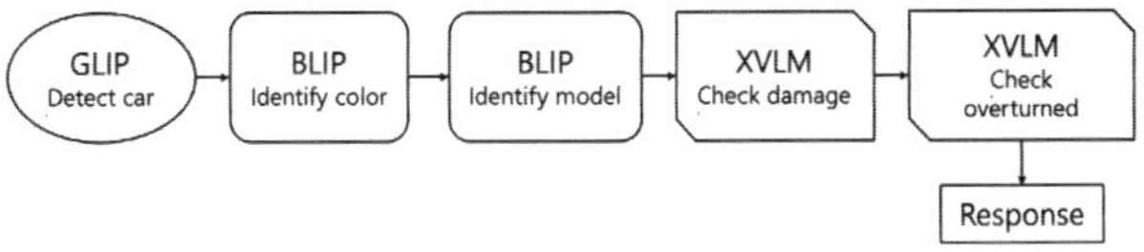

Figure 10: Execution of AI models in baseline.

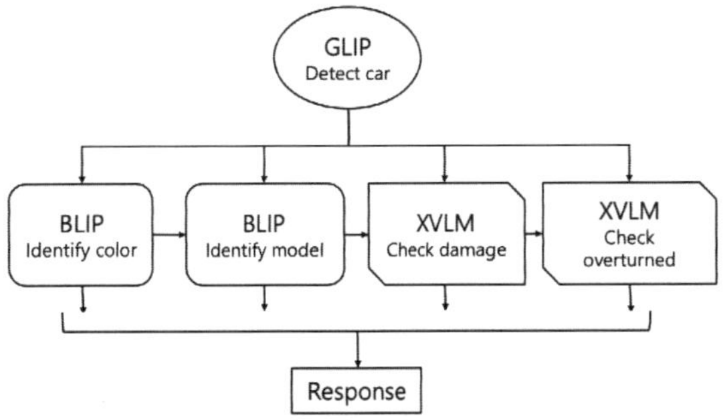

Figure 11: Parallel execution of AI models in *DiCE-C*.

baseline and *DiCE-C*, respectively. In the baseline, API calls are executed sequentially, whereas in *DiCE-C*, after the initial API call to detect cars (using `glip`), the remaining API calls (`blip`, `xvlm`) are executed concurrently. This parallel execution allows *DiCE-C* to minimize GPU idle time and optimize cloud resource usage.

B. Using Identical Hardware

We perform experiments using configurations of 1, 2, 4, 6, and 8 identical nodes. In the case of baseline, only 1 task runs on a machine at a time, whereas in the case of *DiCE-C*, we allow 16 tasks to run simultaneously. Table I shows the total execution time in each case and the corresponding

(a) Scene 1. **(b)** Scene 2. **(c)** Scene 3.

Figure 12: Sample accident scenes.

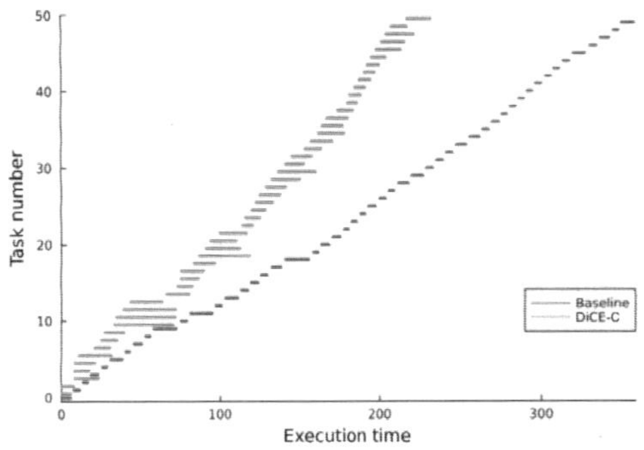

Figure 13: Execution pattern of first 50 tasks.

TABLE I: COST REDUCTION (USING IDENTICAL HARDWARE).

Nodes	**Cost per minute (USD)**		**Total Execution Time (minutes)**		**Total Cost (USD)**		**Cost Reduction (%)**
	Baseline	*DiCE-C*	Baseline	*DiCE-C*	Baseline	*DiCE-C*	
1	\$ 0.037	\$ 0.037	141	79	\$ 5.17	\$ 2.90	44.0 %
2	\$ 0.073	\$ 0.073	75	54	\$ 5.50	\$ 3.96	28.0 %
4	\$ 0.147	\$ 0.147	36	25	\$ 5.28	\$ 3.67	30.6 %
6	\$ 0.220	\$ 0.220	26	18	\$ 5.72	\$ 3.96	30.8 %
8	\$ 0.293	\$ 0.293	17	12	\$ 4.99	\$ 3.52	29.4 %

TABLE II: COST REDUCTION (USING DIFFERENT HARDWARE).

Nodes	**Cost per minute (USD)**		**Total Execution Time (minutes)**		**Total Cost (USD)**		**Cost Reduction (%)**
	Baseline	*DiCE-C*	Baseline	*DiCE-C*	Baseline	*DiCE-C*	
1	\$ 0.037	\$ 0.022	141	68	\$ 5.17	\$ 1.47	71.5 %
2	\$ 0.073	\$ 0.043	75	35	\$ 5.50	\$ 1.52	72.4 %
4	\$ 0.147	\$ 0.087	36	17	\$ 5.28	\$ 1.47	72.1 %
8	\$ 0.293	\$ 0.173	17	8	\$ 4.99	\$ 1.39	72.2 %

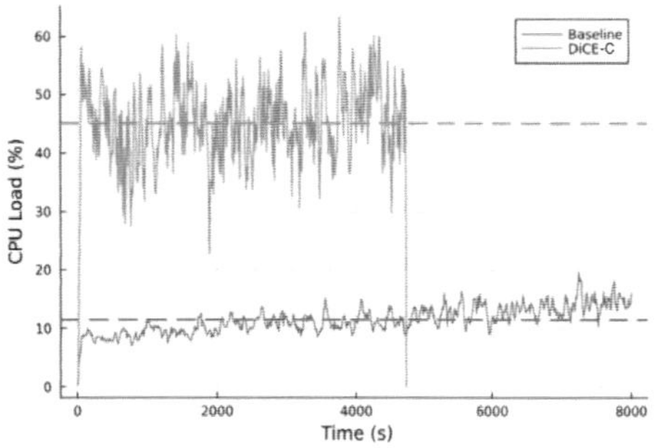

Figure 14: CPU Load.

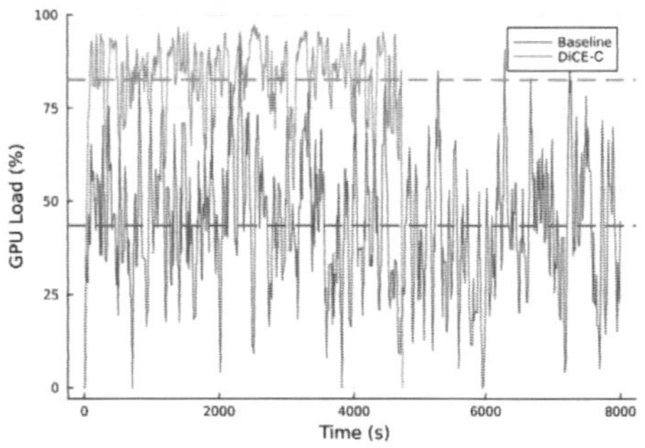

Figure 15: GPU Load.

cost incurred to complete the execution of a batch of 1000 tasks. We observe that on average *DiCE-C* saves up to 32 % operating cost.

We further dive deeper to understand how the execution goes in each case. Figure 13 shows the execution pattern for the first 50 tasks when running on a single node. We observe that in the case of baseline, the tasks start one after the other, as expected, since only 1 job runs at a time and the latency for execution (shown by horizontal line length) varies depending on the image that is used. In case of *DiCE-C*, we clearly see the overlap in execution across different tasks and note that there is a slight increase in latency for each task due to the contention of resources on the same hardware.

Overall, the execution for the batch of tasks goes faster using *DiCE-C* compared to the baseline (higher throughput), and this directly results in cost savings, since the machines in the cloud are used for less time. Figures 14 and 15 show the CPU and GPU load, respectively, when the batch of 1000 tasks is run on a single node. We observe that due to increased utilization, the load is higher in the case of *DiCE-C*, leading to faster completion of tasks.

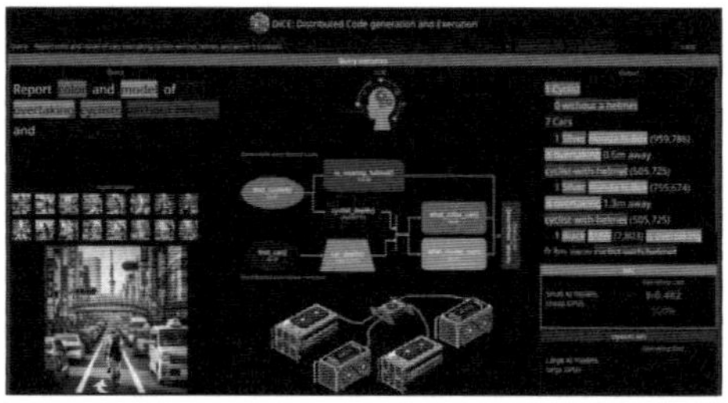

Figure 16: Prototype system for *DiCE-C*.

C. Using Different Hardware

Table II shows the total execution time and cost reduction when using cheaper and smaller GPUs in *DiCE-C*. We observe that *DiCE-C* achieves an average 72 % reduction in operating cost by using smaller and cheaper GPUs. This highlights *DiCE-C*'s adaptability and efficiency in cloud computing environments.

D. Prototype system

Figure 16 shows a prototype system for *DiCE-C*. In this system, the user can write a query in natural language and behind the scenes, *DiCE-C* initially generates the serial code and then transforms this code into a distributed code version, which is then executed on a Kubernetes-based distributed cluster. In the user interface, we show the different AI models that are being used and the execution flow in the baseline vs *DiCE-C* case. In addition, we also show the cost savings achieved by using *DiCE-C*.

VI. CONCLUSION AND FUTURE WORK

In this paper, we introduced *DiCE-C*, a cost-efficient system for deploying vision applications in cloud environments. Unlike prior approaches that rely on monolithic code generated by tools like ViperGPT, *DiCE-C* programmatically generates distributed code by leveraging runtime-exposed tool documentation. By dynamically managing API calls as independent services on Kubernetes, *DiCE-C* reduces GPU idle time and supports the use of smaller, cost-efficient GPUs, significantly lowering operational expenses while preserving the correctness and functionality of the original application.

Experimental evaluations on a real-world insurance application demonstrated that *DiCE-C* achieves an average cost reduction of 32% on identical GPU hardware and up to 72% when using smaller GPUs. Although this work focuses on vision applications, our future work involves incorporating additional functions and tools support in the runtime, so that a wide range of applications and workloads can be supported and enabled by *DiCE-C*.

REFERENCES

[1] D. Surís, S. Menon, and C. Vondrick, "ViperGPT: Visual inference via python execution for reasoning," in *2023 IEEE/CVF International Conference on Computer Vision (ICCV)*, 2023, pp. 11 854–11 864. DOI: 10.1109/ICCV51070.2023.01092.

[2] K. Rao, G. Coviello, and S. Chakradhar, "DiCE: Distributed Code Generation and Execution," in *2024 IEEE Conference on Pervasive and Intelligent Computing (PICom)*, 2024, pp. 8–15. DOI: 10.1109/PICom64201.2024.00008.

[3] G. Coviello, K. Rao, G. Mellone, C. G. De Vita, and S. Chakradhar, "DiCE-M: Distributed Code Generation and Execution for Marine Applications - An Edge-Cloud Approach," in *2024 IEEE/ACM Symposium on Edge Computing (SEC)*, 2024, pp. 468–475. DOI: 10.1109/SEC62691.2024.00054.

[4] Z. Shen, S. Subbiah, X. Gu, and J. Wilkes, "CloudScale: Elastic resource scaling for multi-tenant cloud systems," in *Proceedings of the 2nd ACM Symposium on Cloud Computing*, ser. SOCC '11, Cascais, Portugal: Association for Computing Machinery, 2011, ISBN: 9781450309769. DOI: 10 . 1145 / 2038916.2038921.

[5] R. Shang *et al.*, "SpotDNN: Provisioning Spot Instances for Predictable Distributed DNN Training in the Cloud," in *2023 IEEE/ACM 31st International Symposium on Quality of Service (IWQoS)*, 2023, pp. 1–10. DOI: 10.1109/IWQoS57198. 2023.10188717.

[6] S. Lee, J. Hwang, and K. Lee, *SpotLake: Diverse Spot Instance Dataset Archive Service*, 2022. arXiv: 2202.02973 [cs.DC].

[7] C. Wang, B. Urgaonkar, A. Gupta, G. Kesidis, and Q. Liang, "Exploiting Spot and Burstable Instances for Improving the Cost-efficacy of In-Memory Caches on the Public Cloud," in *Proceedings of the Twelfth European Conference on Computer Systems*, ser. EuroSys '17, Belgrade, Serbia: Association for Computing Machinery, 2017, pp. 620–634, ISBN: 9781450349383. DOI: 10.1145/3064176.3064220.

[8] M. Hassan, H. Chen, and Y. Liu, "DEARS: A deep learning based elastic and automatic resource scheduling framework for cloud applications," in *2018 IEEE Intl Conf on Parallel and Distributed Processing with Applications, Ubiquitous Computing and Communications, Big Data and Cloud Computing, Social Computing and Networking, Sustainable Computing and Communications (ISPA/IUCC/BDCloud/SocialCom/SustainCom)*, 2018, pp. 541–548. DOI: 10.1109/BDCloud.2018. 00086.

[9] Y. Li *et al.*, "ELASTIC: Edge workload forecasting based on collaborative cloud-edge deep learning," in *Proceedings of the ACM Web Conference 2023*, ser. WWW '23, Austin, TX, USA: Association for Computing Machinery, 2023, pp. 3056–3066, ISBN: 9781450394161. DOI: 10.1145/3543507.3583436.

[10] D. Saxena and A. K. Singh, *Workload forecasting and resource management models based on machine learning for cloud computing environments*, 2021. arXiv: 2106.15112 [cs.DC].

[11] S. G. Ahmad, T. Iqbal, E. U. Munir, and N. Ramzan, "Cost optimization in cloud environment based on task deadline," *J. Cloud Comput.*, vol. 12, no. 1, Jan. 2023, ISSN: 2192-113X. DOI: 10.1186/s13677-022-00370-x.

[12] A. Alelyani, A. Datta, and G. M. Hassan, "Optimizing Cloud Performance: A Microservice Scheduling Strategy for Enhanced Fault-Tolerance, Reduced Network Traffic, and Lower Latency," *IEEE Access*, vol. 12, pp. 35 135–35 153, 2024. DOI: 10.1109/ACCESS.2024.3373316.

[13] Knative Community, *Knative: Kubernetes-based platform to deploy and manage modern serverless workloads*, https : // knative.dev/, Accessed 2025-03-04, 2024.

[14] Kubeflow Community, *Kubeflow: The machine learning toolkit for kubernetes*, https://www.kubeflow.org/, Accessed 2025-03-04, 2025.

[15] O. Khattab *et al.*, "DSPy: Compiling declarative language model calls into self-improving pipelines," *arXiv preprint arXiv:2310.03714*, 2023.

[16] Q. I. Mahmud, A. TehraniJamsaz, H. D. Phan, N. K. Ahmed, and A. Jannesari, *Autoparllm: Gnn-guided automatic code parallelization using large language models*, 2023. arXiv: 2310.04047 [cs.LG].

[17] D. Nichols, A. Marathe, H. Menon, T. Gamblin, and A. Bhatele, "HPC-Coder: Modeling parallel programs using large language models," in *ISC High Performance 2024 Research Paper Proceedings (39th International Conference)*, 2024, pp. 1–12. DOI: 10.23919/ISC.2024.10528929.

[18] T. Chen *et al.*, *Tvm: An automated end-to-end optimizing compiler for deep learning*, 2018. arXiv: 1802.04799 [cs.LG].

[19] U. Bondhugula, A. Hartono, J. Ramanujam, and P. Sadayappan, "A practical automatic polyhedral parallelizer and locality optimizer," in *Proceedings of the 29th ACM SIGPLAN Conference on Programming Language Design and Implementation*, ser. PLDI '08, Tucson, AZ, USA: Association for Computing Machinery, 2008, pp. 101–113, ISBN: 9781595938602. DOI: 10.1145/1375581.1375595.

[20] L. Yu, P. Poirson, S. Yang, A. C. Berg, and T. L. Berg, *Modeling context in referring expressions*, 2016. arXiv: 1608. 00272 [cs.CV].

[21] D. A. Hudson and C. D. Manning, *Gqa: A new dataset for real-world visual reasoning and compositional question answering*, 2019. arXiv: 1902.09506 [cs.CL].

[22] K. Marino, M. Rastegari, A. Farhadi, and R. Mottaghi, *Ok-vqa: A visual question answering benchmark requiring external knowledge*, 2019. arXiv: 1906.00067 [cs.CV].

[23] J. Xiao, X. Shang, A. Yao, and T.-S. Chua, *Next-qa:next phase of question-answering to explaining temporal actions*, 2021. arXiv: 2105.08276 [cs.CV].

[24] L. H. Li *et al.*, *Grounded language-image pre-training*, 2022. arXiv: 2112.03857 [cs.CV].

[25] J. Li, D. Li, S. Savarese, and S. Hoi, *Blip-2: Bootstrapping language-image pre-training with frozen image encoders and large language models*, 2023. arXiv: 2301.12597 [cs.CV].

[26] Y. Zeng *et al.*, "$X^2$2-vlm: All-in-one pre-trained model for vision-language tasks," *IEEE Transactions on Pattern Analysis amp; Machine Intelligence*, vol. 46, no. 05, pp. 3156–3168, May 2024, ISSN: 1939-3539. DOI: 10.1109/TPAMI.2023. 3339661.

[27] Hyperstack, *Hyperstack*, https : // www . hyperstack . cloud/, Accessed 2025-03-04.

Proactive Optimization of Virtual Machine Placement Using Predictive Models Based on Time Series

Naby Doumbouya
EPROAD, UR 4669
Université de Picardie Jules Verne
Amiens, France
e-mail: ndoumbouya@u-picardie.fr

Mhand Hifi
EPROAD,UR 4669
Université de Picardie Jules Verne
Amiens, France
e-mail: mhifi@u-picardie.fr

***Abstract*—To overcome the limitations of traditional reactive VM placement strategies, which often struggle with dynamic workload variations, this paper introduces an innovative proactive approach based on predictive time series analysis. By evaluating the ARIMA, LSTM, and Prophet models, we assess their effectiveness in accurately forecasting VM workload fluctuations, thereby minimizing unnecessary migrations, reducing energy consumption, and lowering operational costs. These predictions are then integrated into an advanced optimization algorithm to determine optimal VM placement in anticipation of workload spikes, leading to significant improvements in system performance, stability, and quality of service across distributed data centers.**

Keywords-Cloud computing; virtual machine placement; time sequences; ARIMA; LSTM; Prophet; cloudsim; Time series forecasting; Proactive optimization.

I. Introduction

The proactive optimization of virtual machine (VM) placement is crucial for enhancing resource efficiency in cloud environments, where dynamic resource management is essential to ensure optimal performance. Cloud systems often face fluctuating demands, making predictive methods imperative for effective resource allocation.

Time series forecasting models such as ARIMA, Prophet, and LSTM offer various approaches to anticipate future resource needs. ARIMA is well suited for stationary datasets, while Prophet excels in handling seasonal data. LSTM provides flexibility for modeling complex patterns in dynamic contexts [1].

Cloud resource management relies on reactive and proactive approaches. The reactive approach adjusts resources based on current demand, while the proactive approach leverages historical data to predict future needs and optimize resource utilization. Proactive resource allocation has become a major research topic in cloud computing, aiming to optimize resource management and utilization [2].

Our approach combines ARIMA, LSTM, and Prophet to generate accurate workload forecasts. These forecasts are used in an optimization algorithm that minimizes energy consumption and reduces VM migrations while respecting server capacity constraints. By anticipating future workloads, our method enables more efficient resource allocation and improves system performance. The remainder of this paper is organized as follows. Section II reviews the state of the art in VM placement and predictive optimization. Section III formulates the problem as a multi-objective optimization model incorporating energy consumption and migration cost. Section IV describes the proposed methodology, combining time series forecasting with hybrid prediction weighting and linear programming. Section V presents the experimental setup and results obtained on the CloudSim dataset. Section VI highlights our main contributions in terms of prediction accuracy and optimization efficiency. Finally, Section VII concludes the paper and outlines future research directions.

II. Background

Classical approaches to VM placement optimization, such as First Fit, Best Fit, and genetic algorithms, do not account for workload forecasting. Time series models (ARIMA, LSTM, Prophet) enable proactive decision making but struggle with sudden workload fluctuations [3].

Advanced optimization algorithms like Harris Hawk Optimization (HHO) outperform traditional methods, achieving a 27% reduction in energy consumption and a 17% increase in resource utilization [4]. Hybrid approaches combining optimization algorithms and machine learning are essential for efficient cloud resource allocation.

ARIMA excels with stationary series, and Prophet performs well with seasonal data, but both are limited in handling nonlinear variations and unexpected spikes [5]. LSTM captures long-term dependencies but requires significant computational resources [5]. Hybrid models like TempoScale enhance forecast accuracy and system stability [3].

Traditional optimization approaches face challenges related to resource heterogeneity and workload variability [6]. Hybrid solutions combining classical methods with artificial intelligence are promising for optimizing VM placement and ensuring proactive resource management [7].

This evolution highlights the need for integrated strategies to maximize cloud infrastructure efficiency. Future research should further explore hybrid approaches and assess their practical implementation for responsive and sustainable resource allocation.

III. Problem Modeling

We model the VM placement problem as a **multi-objective optimization problem** with the following objectives:

A. Minimize Energy Consumption

The total energy consumption is calculated as the sum of the energy consumed by each server, weighted by the CPU usage of the VMs placed on it [8]:

$$E_{total} = \sum_{i=1}^{m} \sum_{j=1}^{n} x_{ij} \cdot E(M_i) \tag{1}$$

where x_{ij} is a binary variable indicating whether VM j is placed on server i, and $E(M_i)$ is the energy consumption of server i.

B. Minimize VM Migrations

When VMs change their host between time steps $t-1$ and t, it incurs a cost. We define $x_{ij}^{(t)}$ and $x_{ij}^{(t-1)}$ as binary variables indicating placement at time t and $t-1$, respectively.

The migration cost function is given by:

$$C_{mig} = \sum_{i=1}^{m} \sum_{j=1}^{n} \left| x_{ij}^{(t)} - x_{ij}^{(t-1)} \right| \cdot D_{mig}(V_j) \tag{2}$$

where $D_{mig}(V_j)$ denotes the migration cost (e.g., based on memory size or state size) of VM V_j [9], [10]. This penalty discourages unnecessary movement and ensures SLA stability.

Constraints The total resource usage of VMs on each server must not exceed the server's capacity:

$$\sum_{j=1}^{n} x_{ij} \cdot R(V_j) \leq C(M_i), \quad \forall i \tag{3}$$

where $R(V_j)$ is the resource requirement of VM j, and $C(M_i)$ is the capacity of server i. In addition, a VM must be placed on exactly one server:

$$\sum_{i=1}^{m} x_{ij} = 1, \quad \forall j \tag{4}$$

IV. PROPOSED METHODOLOGY

Our methodology involves three steps: **data preprocessing**, **workload prediction**, and **VM placement optimization**.

A. Data preprocessing and Workload prediction

We use time series data from cloudsim, aggregated at 5 minutes intervals, and train predictive models (ARIMA, LSTM, Prophet) using a sliding window approach.

B. VM Placement Optimization

The predicted workloads are used as input to a **linear programming (LP)** optimization problem. The objectives are two fold: (1) minimize energy consumption and (2) minimize the cost of VM migrations, while respecting server capacity constraints.

Predictive-Aware Placement Strategy: The predicted workload for each VM is generated using a weighted combination of ARIMA, LSTM, and Prophet forecasts:

$$\hat{L}_j = \sum_{m \in \{\text{ARIMA, LSTM, Prophet}\}} w_m \cdot \hat{L}_{j,m} \tag{5}$$

with weights w_m based on the inverse of each model's error (RMSE + MAE), normalized:

$$w_m = \frac{1}{\text{RMSE}_m + \text{MAE}_m + \epsilon} \Big/ \sum_{m'} \frac{1}{\text{RMSE}_{m'} + \text{MAE}_{m'} + \epsilon} \tag{6}$$

These predicted loads are injected into the optimization model to guide placement before overloads occur.

Solver: The combined multi-objective function is minimized using a weighted-sum scalarization:

$$\min \left(\alpha \cdot E_{total} + \beta \cdot C_{mig} \right) \tag{7}$$

where α and β are tunable coefficients reflecting the trade-off between energy efficiency and migration stability, as recommended in [11], [12].

This LP model is implemented with `PuLP` in Python. The forecast-driven optimization allows proactive VM placement while balancing operational cost and performance constraints.

C. General scheme

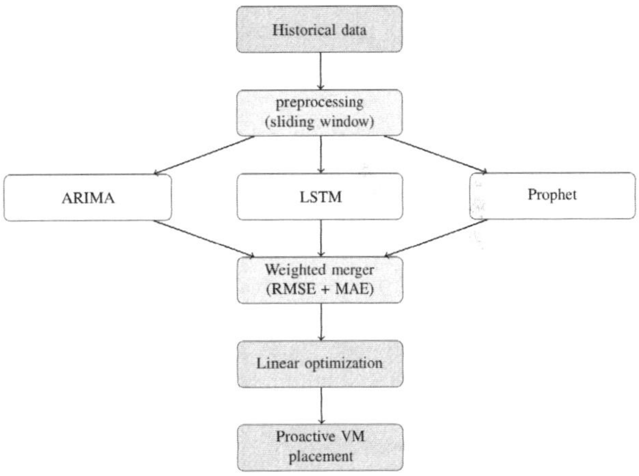

Figure 1. Overview of the proposed method

V. EXPERIMENTS AND RESULTS

We evaluate our approach on the **CloudSim Dataset**. Key findings include:

- **Energy Efficiency**: Energy consumption is reduced by 15%, with an additional 5% improvement from the RMSE + MAE weighting.
- **VM Migrations**: Migrations are reduced by 20%, with a further 10% reduction due to the RMSE + MAE weighting.
- **Robustness**: The RMSE + MAE weighting improves stability under workload variations.

VI. Our Contribution

Our work makes the following key contributions:

- **Hybrid Prediction Model**: We propose a novel approach that combines the strengths of three predictive models ARIMA, LSTM, and Prophet using a weighted average based on both **RMSE** and **MAE**. This hybrid approach improves prediction accuracy and robustness compared to using individual models.
- **Proactive Optimization Framework**: Unlike traditional reactive methods, our framework uses predicted workloads to proactively optimize VM placement, reducing energy consumption and unnecessary migrations.
- **RMSE + MAE Weighting Scheme**: We introduce a weighting scheme that balances the impact of large errors (RMSE) and average errors (MAE), leading to more stable and reliable predictions. This scheme significantly improves the robustness of the optimization process.
- **Energy and Migration Efficiency**: Our approach demonstrates a **15% reduction in energy consumption** and a **20% reduction in VM migrations** compared to traditional methods, with further improvements achieved through the RMSE + MAE weighting.

VII. Conclusion and Perspectives

Our proactive VM placement strategy, which integrates hybrid time series forecasting with a weighted integer linear optimization model, has proven effective in reducing energy consumption and eliminating unnecessary migrations. The weighted combination of ARIMA, LSTM, and Prophet based on RMSE and MAE metrics significantly enhances forecasting robustness.

The results obtained demonstrate that our method offers a reliable and efficient trade-off between resource optimization and service stability. The approach remains scalable, and the low computation time allows real-time or near-real-time decision-making.

As future work, we plan to:

Extend the optimization model to a distributed and federated cloud environment, where coordination among data centers is required;

Incorporate network-related constraints such as bandwidth, latency, and routing cost;

Integrate adaptive dynamic weights based on SLA policies and QoS priorities;

Experiment on real-world traces such as the **Google Cloud Cluster Trace Dataset** to evaluate the model at scale.

References

[1] J. Chen, Y. Wang, and T. Liu, "A proactive resource allocation method based on adaptive prediction of resource requests in cloud computing", *EURASIP Journal on Wireless Communications and Networking*, vol. 2021, p. 24, 2021. DOI: 10.1186/s13638-021-01912-8.

[2] T. Kamble, S. Deokar, V. S. Wadne, D. P. Gadekar, and H. B. Vanjari, "Predictive resource allocation strategies for cloud computing environments using machine learning", *Journal of Electrical Systems*, vol. 19, no. 2, pp. 68–77, 2023.

[3] L. Wen, M. Xu, A. N. Toosi, and K. Ye, "Temposcale: A cloud workloads prediction approach integrating short-term and long-term information", in *2024 IEEE 17th International Conference on Cloud Computing (CLOUD)*, 2024.

[4] H. S. Madhusudhan, T. S. Kumar, P. Gupta, and G. McArdle, "A harris hawk optimisation system for energy and resource efficient virtual machine placement in cloud data centers", *PLOS ONE*, vol. 18, no. 8, e0289156, 2023. DOI: 10.1371/journal.pone.0289156.

[5] S. Yadav, "A comparative study of arima, prophet and lstm for time series prediction", *Journal of Artificial Intelligence, Machine Learning and Data Science*, vol. 1, no. 1, pp. 1813–1816, 2022. DOI: 10.51219/JAIMLD/sandeep-yadav/402.

[6] A. Abdelaziz, M. Anastasiadou, and M. Castelli, "A parallel particle swarm optimisation for selecting optimal virtual machine on cloud environment", *Applied Sciences*, vol. 10, p. 6538, 2020. DOI: 10.3390/app10186538.

[7] A. Poghosyan *et al.*, "An enterprise time series forecasting system for cloud applications using transfer learning", *Sensors*, vol. 21, p. 1590, 2021. DOI: 10.3390/s21051590.

[8] X. Li, Z. Qian, S. Lua, and J. Wu, "Energy efficient virtual machine placement algorithm with balanced and improved resource utilization in a data center", *Mathematical and Computer Modelling*, vol. 58, pp. 1222–1235, 2013. DOI: 10.1016/j.mcm.2013.02.003.

[9] M. Masdari and H. Khezri, "Efficient vm migrations using forecasting techniques in cloud computing: A comprehensive review", *Cluster Computing*, vol. 23, pp. 2629–2658, Jan. 2020. DOI: 10.1007/s10586-019-03032-x.

[10] M. T. et al, "Borg: The next generation", in *Fifteenth European Conference on Computer Systems (EuroSys '20)*, 2020, pp. 1–14. DOI: 10.1145/3342195.3387517.

[11] C. Vijaya and P. Srinivasan, "Multi-objective meta-heuristic technique for energy efficient virtual machine placement in cloud computing data centers", *Informatica*, vol. 48, pp. 1–18, Jun. 2024. DOI: 10.31449/inf.v48i6.5263.

[12] R. Keshri and D. P. Vidyarthi, "Energy-efficient communication-aware vm placement in cloud datacenter using hybrid aco–gwo", *Cluster Computing*, vol. 27, pp. 13 047–13 074, 2024. DOI: 10.1007/s10586-024-04623-z.